The Political Economy of the Middle East

Series Editor
Ashraf Mishrif, Centre for Middle East & Mediterranean Studies, King's College London, London, UK

This series explores the nature of Middle Eastern political regimes and their approaches to economic development. In light of the region's distinctive political, social and economic structures and the dramatic changes that took place in the wake of the Arab spring, this series puts forward a critical body of high-quality, research-based scholarship that reflects current political and economic transitions across the Middle East. It offers original research and new insights on the causes and consequences of the Arab uprisings; economic reforms and liberalization; political institutions and governance; regional and sub-regional integration arrangements; foreign trade and investment; political economy of energy, water and food security; finance and Islamic finance; and the politics of welfare, labor market and human development. Other themes of interest include the role of the private sector in economic development, economic diversification, entrepreneurship and innovation; state-business relationships; and the capacity of regimes and public institutions to lead the development process.

More information about this series at
https://link.springer.com/bookseries/14415

Emre Özçelik · Yonca Özdemir
Editors

# Political Economy of Development in Turkey

1838 – Present

palgrave
macmillan

*Editors*
Emre Özçelik
Economics Program
Middle East Technical University
Northern Cyprus Campus
99738 Kalkanlı
Güzelyurt, Mersin 10
Turkey

Yonca Özdemir
Political Science and International Relations Program
Middle East Technical University
Northern Cyprus Campus
99738 Kalkanlı
Güzelyurt, Mersin 10
Turkey

ISSN 2522-8854 ISSN 2522-8862 (electronic)
The Political Economy of the Middle East
ISBN 978-981-16-7317-7 ISBN 978-981-16-7318-4 (eBook)
https://doi.org/10.1007/978-981-16-7318-4



This Palgrave Macmillan imprint is published by the registered company Springer Nature Singapore Pte Ltd.
The registered company address is: 152 Beach Road, #21-01/04 Gateway East, Singapore 189721, Singapore

# Foreword

It is the mother of all debates in economic development: Are developing nations' paths shaped largely by external or internal factors? Do countries remain poor and under-developed because of the inappropriate policies imposed on them by great powers and by their inescapable position in the global division of labor? Or do they shape their fortunes themselves, with underdevelopment the result of their governing elites' reliance on the wrong ideas and the wrong strategies?

When I ask my own students this question at the start of my class on economic development, I find broad support for both positions. Many students, particularly from low-income African countries, see their countries' development blocked by both a disadvantageous history and an inhospitable present. On the one hand, there is the legacy of colonialism, imperialism, and (for many countries) the slave trade, which has left these countries with arbitrary borders, lopsided social structures, and weak institutions. On the other, there is the undeniable facts of global power, denying the global poor of voice in international rules and governance.

Others lay the blame on their own elites and political classes. Many students from Asia and Latin America have seen their countries go through extended periods of rapid economic development, which points to the possibility of doing well no matter how constraining history or external conditions may be. They have also seen how some of these development experiences have met with failure ultimately, not because of decisions made elsewhere but because of the proclivity of home governments to over-borrow, print too much money, or decimate entrepreneurship through bad policy. When the IMF is called in to impose austerity as a last resort, these students understand that the fault lies not with Washington but with decisions taken earlier in Jakarta, Buenos Aires, or indeed Ankara.

Thinking about development policy requires hopefulness, or what Albert O. Hirschman called 'possibilism.' You have to believe that conditions can improve, and that people in developing countries have the agency to make the decisions that will make a difference in their lives. You do not have to deny the roles that history, power politics, or global economic constraints play in shaping present-day outcomes. You simply have to believe that domestic conditions and choices play a big part as well.

And how could you not? Consider the wide variation in experience among developing countries since the end of the Second World War and de-colonization. Some (such as those in East and Southeast Asia) have done extremely well, others (many in Sub-Saharan Africa) have done generally poorly, and most have experienced periods of rapid growth as well as crises or periods of slow growth. Whatever role history or external conditions may have played, they cannot account for the full variation across countries. If colonialism was decisive, for example, how could we explain the fact that there is as much variation in incomes per capita among countries that were colonialized as there is among countries that were never colonialized? If it was a matter of informal control by great powers, how can we explain the phenomenal success of Japan and (in recent decades) China, despite the great powers' success at imposing on these nations free trade and economic concessions during the nineteenth century? If Bretton Woods institutions or contemporary trade rules have produced stifling effects on development, why is it that so many countries, even in Africa (e.g., Mauritius and Botswana), have managed to escape those constraints?

Turkey was never colonized, but the Ottoman Empire found itself under increasing pressure from the great powers during the nineteenth century as it declined militarily. It had to grant foreign merchants special privileges and submitted to a trade treaty that restricted its autonomy. Resorting to foreign borrowing in order finance its military campaigns, the Ottomans eventually found themselves bankrupt, unable to service the debt, and ended up under foreign receivership. Was the Ottoman Empire's (and subsequently the nascent Turkish Republic's) economic weakness a direct result of these external circumstances? Perhaps. But not too dissimilar foreign pressures exerted on Japan resulted in a remarkably different path. Under the Meiji restoration, the Japanese elites crafted a remarkable economic strategy that produced the first successful industrialization outside of Europe and North America—and this despite their hands being tied on foreign trade policies due to an earlier trade treaty with the USA. It is not entirely clear that such a path would have been foreclosed to the late Ottomans.

Or to take later examples: Was Turkey's adoption of a developmental strategy delayed by World Bank and US pressure in the early post-war years? (Perhaps, but what about a counterfactual such as South Korea, a country that was even more dependent on US aid?) Was the collapse of Turkish import-substituting industrialization during the late 1970s inevitable? (I would say no. The crisis was the result of irresponsible macroeconomic policies by the coalition governments of the time.) Was the unbalanced opening to foreign capital after the late 1980s the result of external pressure? (Not really. It was Turgut Özal's own decision to extend his liberalization to the financial sphere.) Wasn't Recep Tayyip Erdogan's curious mix of neoliberalism and populism substantially home-grown? (Clearly yes.)

The great virtue of the chapters in this volume is that they balance discussions of the dependency versus national autonomy models of development with clear, nuanced accounts of the Turkish specificities. The reader gets not only a panoramic view of the political economy of Turkey's development in a chronological presentation, she is also given the material to refine or make up her own mind on these larger developmental debates. The editors are to be congratulated for having successfully coaxed the authors of the individual chapters—distinguished scholars themselves—to stay on theme and on message. As a result, this is a rare collection where the whole is greater than the sum of the parts.

As the individual chapters make clear, Turkish governments and elites had to make their choices against the backdrop of the ideas and interests of powerful foreign actors. Domestic policy is never made from scratch and in a vacuum. As the constellation of external ideas and interests changed over time, they exerted distinct pressures on Turkish policies. But there were margins for maneuver. Ideas and interests of domestic origin were to play a key part as well.

The world economy is at a crossroads as I write these words (in June 2021). The neoliberal consensus has lost its intellectual appeal, hyper-globalization is under retreat, and the rise of China has substantially altered the geopolitical landscape. When democracy returns to Turkey, the country's leaders will have to chart a new course that is perhaps less constrained by global ideological orthodoxy than at anytime in recent memory. One hopes that they will have the vision and self-confidence to articulate a model that not only serves Turkey better but also provides an example for other countries.

June 2021

Dani Rodrik
Harvard University
Cambridge, MA, USA

# Contents

# Notes on Contributors

**Seven Ağır** holds a Ph.D. degree in Near Eastern Studies from Princeton University, USA; and M.Sc. and B.Sc. degrees in Economics from the Middle East Technical University (METU), Ankara, Turkey. She completed her post-doctoral research in the Economic History Program at Yale University, USA, and joined faculty at the Economics Department of METU, Ankara, in 2012. Her main research field is the historical development of economic institutions in the Middle East, with a special focus on the late Ottoman Empire and early Turkish Republic. In 2012, she was awarded a Marie Curie Grant that enabled her to conduct a four-year research project on the evolution of business organizations in Turkey by constructing and analyzing a database of Ottoman and Turkish enterprises. Based on the analysis of this novel data-set, the project shed light on the hitherto unexamined areas of Ottoman economic and business history and contributed to the debates on the reasons underlying economic backwardness of the Middle East. In 2018, she was awarded a Fulbright academic grant to pursue a research project entitled 'Entrepreneurship and Legal Institutions in Turkey: A Business History Perspective' at Cornell University, USA. She also participated in several international research teams focusing on comparative research on business history—one based in Japan, funded by Shibusawa Foundation, and the other based in Murcia, Spain, funded by the Spanish Ministry of Education. She published several articles in top field journals, such as *Economic*

*History Review* and *Journal of Economic History*, along with several chapters in books by internationally acclaimed publishers, such as Routledge, Palgrave Macmillan, Classiques Garnier, and Berghahn Books.

**Ümit Akçay** is Associate Professor of Economics. He has been a Visiting Scholar at Berlin School of Economics and Law, Germany, since 2017. He previously held academic positions in Turkey at İstanbul Bilgi University; Atılım University; Middle East Technical University, Ankara Campus; TOBB Economy and Technology University; and Ordu University. He was a research scholar at New York University, USA, in the Department of Politics and the Department Middle Eastern and Islamic Studies between 2011 and 2015. He has Ph.D. and M.A. degrees in Development Economics and Economic Growth from Marmara University, Turkey; and a B.A. degree in Public Administration from İstanbul University, Turkey. He is the co-author of *Financialization, Debt Crisis, and Collapse: The Future of Global Capitalism* (in Turkish, Ankara: Notabene Press, 2016); and the author of *Money, Bank, State: The Political Economy of the Central Bank Independence* (in Turkish, İstanbul: SAV Press, 2009) and *Planning of Capitalism: Transformation of Planning and the State Planning Organization in Turkey* (in Turkish, İstanbul: SAV Press, 2007). His research focuses on comparative development studies, international political economy, and financialization in emerging market economies. He writes a weekly column at *Gazete Duvar*, an internet newspaper, on various aspects of international political economy and political economy in Turkey, and also a monthly column in the online journal '*1+1 Forum*' in Turkish and English. His other works are available at: https://hwr-berlin.academia.edu/UmitAkcay.

**Korkut Boratav** is Professor Emeritus of Economics, retired from the Faculty of Political Science, Ankara University, Turkey. He is a graduate of the Faculty of Law (1959) of the same university, where he also obtained his PhD degree in economics (1964). He was a post-doctoral Visiting Scholar in the University of Cambridge, UK (1964–1966, funded by the Rockefeller Foundation). He was promoted to Associate Professorship in 1972 and served as a faculty member in the Department of Economics, Ankara University between 1972 and 1982. He worked as a Consultant at the Division of Social Affairs, United Nations, Geneva, Switzerland (1974). He was promoted to Professorship in 1980 by the Senate of the Ankara University. He was relieved of his post in 1983 by the military regime in Turkey. He worked as a faculty member in the Zimbabwe

University (1984–1986) and then continued his studies as an independent researcher (1987–1988). By the decision of the Council of State in 1989, he was re-appointed as full Professor of Economic Development and International Economics at the Ankara University, where he served until his retirement (2002). He worked as a Consultant at UNCTAD, Geneva, Switzerland (1997, 1999–2003). He was awarded the 'Superior Service Prizes' by the Turkish Academy of Sciences in 1997 and by the Middle East Technical University in 2016. He has been one of the founding members of the Society for Independent Social Scientists since 2000. He also served as the Chairperson of the Turkish Social Sciences Association (2004–2006). Throughout his academic life, Dr. Boratav published 30 books (in Turkish, English and German), four of which are co-authored. He has also numerous articles and chapters published in academic journals and books (in French as well as in the aforementioned three languages), along with many conference papers and research projects. His main research fields include a diversity of areas such as development issues, political economy, Marxist economics, class analysis, and the Turkish economy. He is the Author of a now-classic monograph (in Turkish) on Turkish economy—*Türkiye İktisat Tarihi, 1908–2015* (İmge Publishing) [*Economic History of Turkey, 1908–2015*, which has passed through 24 editions since its first publication in 1987].

**Yakup Kepenek** is Professor Emeritus of Economics, retired from the Middle East Technical University (METU), Ankara, Turkey. After graduating from the Faculty of Law, Ankara University, Turkey; he was awarded a government scholarship through a nationwide examination and studied economics at the Graduate School of Social Sciences in New York University, USA, where he obtained his Ph.D. degree in economics in 1970. He joined the Department of Economics at METU, Ankara, as a faculty member in 1971. Main courses he taught were: 'Turkish Economy' at both undergraduate and graduate levels; 'History of Economic Analysis' and 'Mathematical Economics' at undergraduate level. He chaired the Department for two years. He was also elected by the faculty members in 1978 to become a two-year member of the University Council, which was the highest governing body of the university. During the 1980–1981 academic year, he carried out research on the Turkish economy in the US archives in Washington, DC, with a Fulbright scholarship. Professor Kepenek founded 'Science and Technology Policy Studies' Program (TEKPOL)—an academic unit granting master's and doctorate degrees—at METU, Ankara, in 1997, and chaired TEKPOL until 2001. He entered politics from the Republican People's Party (CHP) and served as a member of the Turkish Parliament during the 2002–2007 period. He returned to the university after 2007 and taught at the Economics Program of METU, Northern Cyprus Campus. From 2011 onwards, he has been a part-time professor of economics at Başkent University, Ankara, Turkey. His research has focused mainly on the history and dynamics of the Turkish economy, on which he published many academic articles and 10 books, along with numerous regular columns in daily Turkish newspapers *Cumhuriyet* and *Birgün*. He is the Author of a now-classic monograph, entitled *Türkiye Ekonomisi* (*The Turkish Economy*, Remzi Publishing, İstanbul), which has passed through 31 editions since its first publication in 1983. In 2011, he also published a book (in English) on the Turkish economy: *Development and Structure of the Turkish Economy* (METU Press, Ankara). His latest book was published in 2019 (YKKED, İzmir), entitled *Cumhuriyet Çağdaşlaşmasından Günümüze Türkiye'nin Değişimi* (*Turkey's Change From the Republican Modernization to the Present*).

**Ziya Öniş** is Professor of International Political Economy at Koç University, İstanbul, Turkey. He obtained his B.Sc. and M.Sc. degrees in economics from the London School of Economics (LSE), UK, in 1978 and 1979, respectively. His Ph.D. degree in Development Economics was awarded by the University of Manchester, UK, in 1984. He is the former Director of both the Center for Research on Globalization, Peace and Democratic Governance (GLODEM) (2010–2013) and the Graduate School of Social Sciences and Humanities (2006–2009) at Koç University. Prior to his appointment at Koç University, he was a faculty member in the Economics Department at Boğaziçi University, İstanbul, Turkey. He was elected Fellow of the Turkish Academy of Sciences (TÜBA) and received the prestigious TÜBİTAK Science Award in Social Sciences in 2012. He also received the Outstanding Faculty Award of Koç University in 2012. He has published many books as author/editor, along with numerous articles in academic journals such as *Journal of Development Economics*, *Third World Quarterly*, *Development and Change*, *Review of International Political Economy*, *New Perspectives on Turkey*, *Political Science Quarterly*, *Comparative Politics*, *Journal of International Affairs*, *New Political Economy*, among others. His recent research focuses on the challenges posed by the emerging post-liberal international order and its implications for future patterns of globalization, southern and northern varieties of capitalism, democratization dilemmas in emerging powers, global political economy of right-wing populism, the rise of illiberal politics in the European Periphery, the political economy of Turkey, new directions in Turkish foreign policy, and domestic politics-foreign policy interactions. He is also the co-editor of *Turkey and the Global Economy: The New Phase of Neo-Liberal Restructuring and Integration in the Post-Crisis Era* (Routledge, 2009).

**Özgür Orhangazi** is Professor of Economics and Chair of the Department of Economics at Kadir Has University, İstanbul, Turkey. He received his BSc degree in economics from the Middle East Technical University, Ankara, Turkey, and M.A. and Ph.D. degrees in economics from the University of Massachusetts, Amherst, USA, in 1999, 2002, and 2006, respectively. He taught economics at the University of Massachusetts, Amherst, USA; Roosevelt University, Chicago, USA; Boğaziçi University, İstanbul, Turkey; City University of New York, USA; and University of Seoul, South Korea. He also served as graduate faculty at the University of Missouri-Kansas City, USA. He held visiting positions at the Central Bank of Venezuela; Political Economy Research Institute, University of Massachusetts, Amherst, USA; and University Paris 13, France. He is the Author of *Financialization and the US Economy* (Edward Elgar, 2008) and *The Structure of the Turkish Economy* (İmge, 2020—in Turkish). He contributed to books such as *Heterodox Macroeconomics—A Keynes-Marx Synthesis for Understanding the Contradictions of Globalization* (Routledge, 2009); *The Demise of Finance-Dominated Capitalism: Explaining the Financial and Economic Crises* (Edward Elgar, 2015); *The Great Global Meltdown of 2008: Systemic, Conjunctural or Policy-created?* (Edward Elgar, 2016); *Financialization and the Financial and Economic Crises—Country Studies* (Edward Elgar, 2016); and *Routledge Handbook of Heterodox Economics: Theorizing, Analyzing and Transforming Capitalism* (Routledge, 2018). He also published many journal articles on issues ranging from financialization and its impact on capital accumulation processes, the causes and consequences of financial and economic crises, alternative economic policies, and various aspects of the Turkish economy in academic journals such as *Cambridge Journal of Economics*, *Review of Keynesian Economics*, *Review of Radical Political Economics*, and *Review of Political Economy*. His current research focuses on 'concentration' and 'monopolization' in the US economy, and financial fragility and crises in Turkey and other developing economies.

**Emre Özçelik** is currently Associate Professor of Economics at the Middle East Technical University (METU), Northern Cyprus Campus (NCC). He obtained his B.Sc., M.Sc., and Ph.D. degrees in Economics at METU, Ankara Campus, Turkey, in 1998, 2000, and 2006, respectively. He participated in a two-week workshop entitled 'Cambridge Advanced Programme on Rethinking Development Economics' (CAPORDE, funded by the Ford Foundation) in July 2002. He was a post-doctoral Visiting Scholar at the Development Studies Committee of the University of Cambridge, UK (funded by the Scientific and Technological Research Council of Turkey, TÜBİTAK) from September 2007 to August 2008. He has been a full-time faculty member since 2010 and served as the Coordinator of Economics Program from September 2012 to April 2021 at METU-NCC, where he has taught International Economics, Development Economics, Structure of the Turkish Economy, Economic History, and History of Economic Thought. He is the English-to-Turkish translator of *Reclaiming Development: An Alternative Economic Policy Manual* (by Ha-Joon Chang & Ilene J. Grabel, Zed Books). He published articles in such academic journals as *Research Policy*, *Journal of Economic Issues*, and *Development and Change*, along with several book chapters. He co-edited three books (in Turkish)—one on the contemporary relevance of John Maynard Keynes, and the other two on the Turkish economy. Political economy of development and the Turkish economy are two of his main research interests.

**Yonca Özdemir** obtained her B.Sc. degree in Business Administration at the Middle East Technical University, Ankara Campus, Turkey. She holds an M.A. degree in Political Science and International Relations from the University of Delaware, USA. She received her Ph.D. in Public and International Affairs (with concentrations in 'International Political Economy' and 'Development Policy') from the University of Pittsburgh, USA. In 2007, she joined faculty at the Political Science and International Relations Program of the Middle East Technical University, Northern Cyprus Campus (METU-NCC), where she is still employed as a full-time faculty member, teaching both undergraduate and graduate courses. Before she joined METU-NCC, she taught courses in several other institutions, including Instituto Tecnológico y de Estudios Superiores de Monterrey, Mexico; Carnegie Mellon University, USA; and University of Pittsburgh, USA. She received her 'Associate Professor' title from the Council of Higher Education of Turkey in 2017. She specializes mainly in international political economy and comparative political economy. Her research examines the politics of economic reform, development theory and policy, foreign aid, neoliberalism, economic globalization, financial liberalization, and economic crises. She recently focuses on the links between neoliberalism and the rise of populism. Her work includes cross-country studies along with single-country and comparative case studies of Turkey, Cyprus, and some Latin American countries like Argentina and Brazil. She published several articles in journals such as *Middle Eastern Studies*, *Revista Brasileira de Política Internacional*, and *Contemporary Politics*. She has also contributed to some edited books and participated in numerous prestigious international conferences.

**M. Erdem Özgür** received his Ph.D. degree in economics from George Mason University, USA, and his M.Sc. and B.Sc. degrees in economics from the Middle East Technical University, Ankara, Turkey, in 2005, 1998, and 1995, respectively. He is currently Professor of Economics at Dokuz Eylül University, İzmir, Turkey. He is the Chair of the Economics Department at the Faculty of Business, and the Head of the Division of Economic History. Prior to joining the Faculty of Business at Dokuz Eylül University, he was employed by Bülent Ecevit University, Zonguldak, Turkey, where he served as the Vice Director of the Maritime Business School. His research interests include economic history and history of economic thought with a specific focus on the nineteenth century and the early twentieth century. He published articles and book chapters, as well as co-edited books on the economic history of and economic thought in the Ottoman Empire, Turkey, Europe, and the USA. *History of Economic Thought & Policy*, *Historia Agraria*, *Archivum Ottomanicum*, *Scottish Journal of Political Economy*, *Panoeconomicus*, *Middle Eastern Studies*, and *History of Economic Ideas* are among the academic journals he published in. He has served on the editorial board of several peer-reviewed journals. The courses he taught include History of Economic Thought, Institutional Economics, Economic History, and Principles of Economics. He is currently interested in the ideas and projects of economic and political unions beginning from the early nineteenth century.

**Eyüp Özveren** is currently an Independent Scholar and Retired Full Professor from the Middle East Technical University (METU), Ankara,

Turkey. He received his Ph.D. in Sociology from State University of New York at Binghamton, USA, in 1990, where he took part in various activities of the Fernand Braudel Center for the Study of Economies, Historical Systems, and Civilizations. He joined METU in 1991, where he also served as Dean of the Faculty of Economic and Administrative Sciences (2009–2015). He taught primarily institutional political economy, history of economic thought, and economic history on a regular basis, and widely published in these subfields. He participated in international research projects and networks and taught as visiting professor in Turkey as well as in France, Germany, and the USA. He retired in August 2018. His current interdisciplinary research interests concentrate in Mediterranean and Black Sea studies. He published articles in journals such as *Cambridge Journal of Economics*, *European Journal of the History of Economic Thought*, *History of Economic Ideas*, *Journal of Economic Issues*, *Journal of Evolutionary Economics*, *Journal of Mediterranean Studies*, *Mediterranean Studies*, *New Perspectives on Turkey*, *Panoecomicus*, *Review—A Journal of the Fernand Braudel Center*, *Review of Political Economy*, and *European Legacy*. He co-edited (with Thomas Faist) *Transnational Social Spaces: Agents, Networks and Institutions* (Routledge, 2004), and contributed to numerous edited volumes by recognized publishing houses including Routledge. One of his most recent publications is: 'James Steuart versus Adam Smith: Tempest in a Teapot?' in José Manuel Menudo (ed.), *The Economic Thought of James Steuart—First Economist of the Scottish Enlightenment* (Routledge, 2019).

**Fikret Şenses** is Professor Emeritus of Economics, retired from the Middle East Technical University (METU), Ankara, Turkey. He obtained his B.A., M.A., and Ph.D. degrees in economics in the UK—University of Warwick (1970), University of Lancaster (1971), and London School of Economics and Political Science (1979), respectively. He worked as a full-time faculty member at the Department of Economics, METU, Ankara, from 1980 until his retirement in 2014. Since then, he has continued to research and teach graduate-level courses on development issues and the Turkish economy, as a part-time professor in the same department. He was a Visiting Scholar in Harvard University, USA (1987–1988), University of Sussex, UK (September 1989), Institute of Developing Economies, Tokyo, Japan (July–October 1990), and a Visiting Fulbright Scholar in Columbia University, USA (March–August 1997). He served as Editor-in-Chief of *METU Studies in Development* (1983–1987), Chairperson of the Department of Economics at METU (1991–1992), Elected Member of the Higher Education Council of Turkey (2005–2009), and Elected Member of METU Senate (2010–2014). He was granted many academic awards and honors, such as the Educator of the Year Awards, High Achievement and Excellence in Education Award at METU, and awards for international publications by Turkish Academy of Sciences and METU. As author/editor, he contributed to 16 books and monographs, along with more than 70 articles and chapters published in academic journals and books (in English and Turkish). His main research fields include development issues, international political economy, and the Turkish economy. *The Developing Economies*, *METU Studies in Development*, *Journal of Development Economics*, *New Perspectives on Turkey*, and *Development and Change* are among the journals he published in. He is also the co-editor of *Turkey and the Global Economy: The New Phase of Neo-Liberal Restructuring and Integration in the Post-Crisis Era* (Routledge, 2009).

**Erol Taymaz** is Professor of Economics at the Middle East Technical University (METU), Ankara, Turkey. He graduated from the Department of Mechanical Engineering (METU) in 1982. He received his M.Sc. degree in Economics at METU (1985) and Ph.D. degree in Economics at Case Western Reserve University, USA (1989). He worked as a Research Engineer at ASELSAN Electronics Industries (Ankara, Turkey, 1982–1985), Research Assistant at CWRU (Cleveland, USA, 1985–1989), and Research Fellow at Industrial Research Institute (IUI, Stockholm, Sweden, 1989–1992). He has been a faculty member at the Department of Economics of METU, Ankara since 1992. He served as the Vice President at the Northern Cyprus Campus of METU (2010–2014). He was an Advisor to the Turkish Statistical Institute (1999–2000), the Scientific and Technological Research Council of Turkey (TÜBİTAK, 2001–2004), and the Central Bank of the Republic of Turkey (2005–2006). He visited Université Panthéon–Assas (Paris, France), Université Montesquieu Bordeaux IV (Bordeaux, France), Universidad de Deusto (San Sebastián, Spain), and Royal Institute of Technology (Stockholm, Sweden) as a visiting professor. He participated in various research projects supported by TUBİTAK, TTGV, FEMISE, ERF, KDI, IDRC, Eurofund, ILO, UNDP, the World Bank, and the EU. His current research interests include economics of technology and innovation;

industrial, technology, and innovation policies; industrial dynamics; firm demography; small business economics; economics of labor markets; micro-simulation modeling and data science. He published numerous articles in academic books and journals on these fields, as well as on the Turkish economy. *Labour Economics*, *British Journal of Industrial Relations*, *Research Policy*, *Small Business Economics*, *Journal of Productivity Analysis*, *Regional Studies*, *Journal of Evolutionary Economics*, *Review of Industrial Organization*, *Structural Change and Economic Dynamics*, *World Development*, and *New Perspectives on Turkey* are among the academic journals he published in. His webpage is available at http://users.metu.edu.tr/etaymaz.

**Zafer Toprak** is a Historian, Writer, and Academician. He graduated from the Faculty of Political Science, Ankara University, Turkey, and obtained his master's degree from the London University, UK, and his doctorate degree in İstanbul University, Turkey. He joined faculty in Boğaziçi University, İstanbul, Turkey, in 1977, where he founded the History Department in 1981 and directed Atatürk Graduate School for Modern Turkish History for 20 years. He is currently teaching in İstanbul at Koç and Boğaziçi universities, and a member of the Science Academy in Turkey. He has served as the curator of several museums in Turkey, such as the Financial Musem (İş Bank), İstanbul; Economic Independence Museum, Ankara; and Borusan Industrial Museum, İstanbul. He authored/edited institutional-history books for prominent organizations/companies in Turkey (such as İstanbul Stock Exchange, Sümerbank, Şişe Cam, Akbank, Yapı Kredi Bank, Milli Reasürans, Anadolu Sigorta, Borusan, Darüşşüfaka, and Sabancı Group). He also served as the General Coordinator of two major encyclopedias in Turkish (Yurt Encyclopedia, 11 volumes; and İstanbul Encyclopedia, 8 volumes). He has been a member of Economic and Social History Foundation of Turkey. He managed projects and organized many symposiums in the European Science Foundation. He was awarded prestigious prizes, such as Prof. Dr. Aptullah Kuran Superior Service Prize (Boğaziçi University), The Prize for History of Banking and Finance (Osmanlı Bank-Garanti Bank), and Sedat Simavi Prize for Social Sciences (Society of Turkish Journalists). His academic research has focused on Turkey in the nineteenth and twentieth centuries. He published 30 books and about 250 articles mainly in Turkish, and also in English, French, German, and Italian. Some of his published academic books are: *Türkiye'de*

*Milli İktisat, 1908–1918* [*National Economics in Turkey, 1908–1918*, Yurt Publishing, Doğan Publishing, İş Bank Publishing]; Türkiye'de Ekonomi ve Toplum—Milli İktisat—Milli Burjuvazi [*Economy and Society in Turkey—National Economics—National Bourgeoisie*, Tarih Vakfi Yurt Publishing]; *From Imperial Debt to Global Offerings—The Rise of the Istanbul Stock Exchange*(İstanbul Stock Exchange Publishing; also in French and Japan); *İttihat-Terakki ve Cihan Harbi: Savaş Ekonomisi ve Türkiye'de Devletçilik, 1914–1918* [*Union-Progress and World War: War Economy and Statism in Turkey, 1914–1918*, Homer Publishing, Kaynak Publishing]; *Türkiye'de Popülizm 1908–1923* [*Populism in Turkey, 1908–1923*, Doğan Publishing]; *Türkiye'de Kadın Özgürlüğü ve Feminizm, 1908–1935* [*Woman Freedom and Feminism in Turkey, 1908–1935*, Tarih Vakfi Yurt Publishing]; *Türkiye'de İşçi Sınıfı, 1908–1946* [*Working Class in Turkey, 1908–1946*, Tarih Vakfi Yurt Publishing]; and *Türkiye'de Yeni Hayat—İnkılap ve Travma, 1908–1928* [*New Life in Turkey—Revolution and Trauma, 1908–1928*, Doğan Publishing].

**Oktar Türel** graduated from the İstanbul Technical University, Turkey, in 1960 with a B.Sc. degree in Civil Engineering, and received his M.Sc. and Ph.D. degrees in economics from the University of Southampton, UK (1969) and the University of Ankara, Turkey (1977), respectively. His career as an Economist was essentially linked to two institutions in Turkey; namely, the State Planning Organisation (SPO, 1965–1975 and 1978–1979) and the Middle East Technical University (METU, Ankara, 1975–1977 and 1980–2004). He joined the Department of Economics at METU in 1975 as an instructor; later, he was promoted to assistant professorship in 1977, to associate professorship in 1986, and finally to professorship in 1996. On leave from METU in academic years 1993–1994 and 1994–1995, he served as a visiting lecturer at the Department of Economics, School of Oriental and African Studies (SOAS), UK, under the Modern Turkish Studies Programme. He also assumed some administrative responsibilities at SPO and METU: At SPO, he was the Chairman of the Department of Economic Planning from February 1978 to December 1979. At METU, he served as Chairperson of the Department of Economics (September 1996–November 1997) and as Dean of the Faculty of Economic and Administrative Sciences (April 2000–March 2003). He retired in August 2004, but continued teaching in various Turkish universities as part-time lecturer (University of Ankara, 2006–2007 and 2007–2008; İstanbul Bilgi University,

2008–2009 and 2009–2010; METU, 2010–2011 and 2011–2012). He has been a member of Turkish Social Science Association since 1990, Turkish Economic Association since 1995, and the Group of Independent Social Scientists since 2001. His major areas of interest in economics have been macroeconomics, the economics of industrial development and technological change, international political economy, as well as the political economy of Turkey. He published 4 books, 30 book chapters, and 34 journal articles in Turkish and English. His research articles were published in such academic journals as *New Perspectives on Turkey*, *Yapı-Kredi Economic Review*, *METU Studies in Development*, *World Development*, and *Review of International Political Economy*.

**Ebru Voyvoda** is Professor of Economics at the Middle East Technical University (METU), Ankara, Turkey. She received her B.Sc. degree in Industrial Engineering, and M.A. and Ph.D. degrees in Economics from Bilkent University, Ankara, Turkey in 1996, 1998, and 2003, respectively. She was a visiting researcher at the Department of Economics, University of Utah, USA, in 2003–2004, and at the Department of Environmental and Resource Economics, Environmental Management at the Center for European Economic Research (ZEW), Germany in 2011–2012. She was on leave from METU in 2015–2016 to serve as Economic Affairs Officer at the United Nations Conference on Trade and Development (UNCTAD), Division of Globalization and Development Strategies (GDS), Geneva, Switzerland. Her research interests include applied general equilibrium modeling for policy analysis, quantitative methods in macroeconomic models, and economic growth. She has widely published on the Turkish economy as chapters in books by such international publishers as Routledge, Edward Elgar, and Springer, along with research articles published in academic journals such as *Economic Modeling*, *New Perspectives on Turkey*, *Journal of Policy Modeling*, and *Canadian Journal of Development Studies*, among others. She has also co-authored *Macroeconomics of Climate Change in a Dualistic Economy: A Regional General Equilibrium Analysis* (Elsevier—Academic Press, 2018), where the interaction between regional dualities of a developing economy and policies toward sustainability are analyzed, using Turkey as the primary example.

**A. Erinç Yeldan** is Professor and Dean of the Faculty of Economics, Administrative and Social Sciences, and Acting Chair of the Department of International Relations at Bilkent University, Ankara, Turkey. He is the funding director of the Energy Policies Research Center at Bilkent University, and serves as one of the thirty members of the International Resource Panel of the UN Environment Programme. He is also one of the executive directors of the International Development Economics Associates (IDEAs), New Delhi, India. He received his B.A. degree in economics from Boğaziçi University, İstanbul, Turkey in 1982, and his Ph.D. degree in economics from University of Minnesota, USA, in 1988. He joined the Department of Economics at Bilkent University in 1988. During the 1994–1995 academic year, he was a Visiting Scholar at the University of Minnesota, USA, where he taught applied general equilibrium analysis. In 2007–2008, he was a Fulbright scholar at the University of Massachusetts, Amherst, USA, and at Amherst College, USA. Along his academic career as an educator, he directed more than 20 master's theses and supervised 6 doctoral dissertations. His recent research focuses on development macroeconomics, vulnerability and fragmentation of labor markets, deindustrialization, economics of climate change, empirical dynamic general equilibrium models, as well as the Turkish economy. On these areas, he has contributed over 50 refereed articles and authored/edited 13 books and participated in numerous project reports and briefings. *Structural Change and Economic Dynamics*, *New Perspectives on Turkey*, *Economic Modeling*, *Canadian Journal of Development Studies*, *Journal of Policy Modeling*, *Review of Radical Political Economics*, *Review of International Political Economy*, *Development Policy Review*, *World Development*, *Development and Change*, and *Journal of Development Economics* are some of the academic journals he published in. He also published many chapters in books by such international publishers as Elsevier (Academic Press), Palgrave Macmillan, Springer, Edward Elgar, Oxford University Press, and Routledge.

# List of Figures

# List of Tables

CHAPTER 1

# Political Economy of Global Capitalism: A Framework for Turkey's Dependent Development, 1838–2020

*Yonca Özdemir and Emre Özçelik*

Turkey is a developing country which has always encountered various dilemmas during its struggle for economic growth and democracy. Since the establishment of the Republic of Turkey in 1923, one of the main concerns of its policymakers and intellectuals has been "development." As a latecomer in industrialization, from the beginning of the twentieth century, Turkey has tried to catch up with the advanced countries through

Y. Özdemir (✉)
Political Science and International Relations Program, Middle East Technical University, Northern Cyprus Campus, 99738 Kalkanlı, Güzelyurt, Mersin 10, Turkey
e-mail: yoncita@metu.edu.tr

E. Özçelik
Economics Program, Middle East Technical University, Northern Cyprus Campus, 99738 Kalkanlı, Güzelyurt, Mersin 10, Turkey
e-mail: ozemre@metu.edu.tr



E. Özçelik and Y. Özdemir (eds.), *Political Economy of Development in Turkey*, The Political Economy of the Middle East,
https://doi.org/10.1007/978-981-16-7318-4_1

modernization reforms from above. For that purpose, Turkey has tried different economic models throughout its history (e.g., economic liberalism, statism, import-substituting industrialization, export-led growth, neoliberalism); but no matter how Turkey strived for becoming a modern nation with a modern economy, it has only succeeded partially. Hence, Turkey has developed to a certain degree, but it has failed to become an advanced country.

From the late Ottoman period onward, Turkey has generally experienced "dependent development" to varying degrees, with perhaps the exception of the episode of the 1930s. Despite the historical nonoccurrence of explicit and formal colonization by Western powers, Turkey has not been able to escape the dependency relations exerted through global capitalism. Dependency patterns and dependent development of Turkey have their historical roots that can be traced back to the nineteenth-century Ottoman Empire. Although the Empire was a significant player in world politics, it missed the first industrial revolution; and by the nineteenth century, it lagged significantly behind the major Western powers in economic, technological, and institutional terms. In fact, industrialization in Europe and the consequent political-economic rivalry among the European powers in the nineteenth century led to the "peripheralization" of the Ottoman Empire without conventional colonization, similar to the case of China (Keyder, 1987: 36). Although there were some favorable instances when Turkey could implement relatively more independent policies, the political-economic history of Turkey is mostly a story of dependent development.

Another feature of modern Turkey was that, at the beginning, it had a more-or-less "egalitarian" socioeconomic structure inhabited dominantly by small- and medium-size farmers, with no prominent landed aristocracy and national bourgeoisie. Such an initial socioeconomic condition could be an important advantage for fast-track development, but instead, Turkey gradually evolved into an unequal semi-industrialized nation. It is quite puzzling that Turkey today resembles Latin American countries like Mexico, Argentina, and Brazil, rather than the Southern European or East Asian countries. Although it cannot be claimed that Turkey's development experience was a complete failure, it nonetheless seems that Turkey could not utilize its developmental potential as effectively as certain success stories, such as South Korea and Taiwan that were poorer than Turkey up until the 1960s. Therefore, Turkey is categorized as an upper-middle-income country today, having failed to jump to the high-income status despite century-long efforts to achieve sustained development in the economic and democratic spheres.

All in all, Turkey did succeed in building up some important industries, as compared to its highly backward economy in the 1920s. However, due mainly to its peripheral position in the world system, its economy has generally been vulnerable to crises, and thus, has never shifted to a stable and sustained growth path. Even when it experienced some impressive "growth spurts," eventually it has not been able to escape the recurrent crises pertaining to a less-developed economy within global capitalism. However, this diagnosis is not to argue that Turkey has been *completely* shaped by the world system. Indeed, what Turkey has achieved has been influenced and limited by its position in the world system despite its unique domestic features. Its domestic class structure, along with its developmental orientation, has also evolved in an uneven manner over time, creating its own internal constraints and contradictions and leading to serious economic crises up until today.

Yet another historical puzzle that Turkey displays is its political trajectory. Turkey's political development has been even more disillusioning than its economic development. The Ottoman Empire was one of the biggest empires in the world between the fifteenth and nineteenth centuries. From its ruins emerged the Republic of Turkey in 1923. Turkey started as a one-party authoritarian state in 1923, but then rather peacefully transitioned into a multi-party democracy along the 1946–1950 period. However, since then, there have been frequent political disorders with periods of relative democracy followed by military coups and interventions. Eventually, today, Turkey is back to quite an authoritarian rule under the heavy dominance of Recep Tayyip Erdoğan, the President of the Republic, and his Justice and Development Party (*AKP*). Hence, Turkey launched one of the most important modernization revolutions of the twentieth century only to find itself back to a rather conservative and autocratic regime with prominent Islamic/Islamist connotations, toward the centennial commemoration of the Republic.

Why is Turkey an important case to analyze? First of all, it is one of the biggest developing countries in the world. With over 84 million people, Turkey is ranked the 17th in the world in terms of population and the 20th in terms of GDP. However, it is ranked the 73rd when it comes to GDP per capita.[1] It is quite a typical developing country in many respects. It does not have a significant amount of natural resources and mineral reserves; hence, it is a net importer of energy. In every epoch, the governments in Turkey have usually followed the dominant political-economic trends within global capitalism. Like other developing countries, Turkey was affected by such global trends and adopted similar strategies. Thus, the political-economic history of Turkey is characterized by the same broader shifts between "economic liberalism" and "state interventionism," corresponding to the prevalent tendencies in the world through successive phases of capitalist development.

As mentioned, Turkey had started from a point of no significant industries and national bourgeoisie. However, economic development at its early stages in the less-developed countries requires industrialization, which, in turn, necessitates the formation of a productive national bourgeoisie, alongside a capable and active state. The history of less-developed countries reveals that building industrial bourgeoisie from scratch or building one out of commercial bourgeoisie is a very formidable challenge (Rapley, 2007: 169). It has been a particularly difficult task for the less-developed countries of the twentieth century, because even when domestic conditions for development were favorable, the global economic system and international division of labor have constrained the developmental options and prospects of these countries. Turkey's development story, by and large, also attests to the historical and instrumental roles played by external constraints as such.

## Theoretical Framework

There is no scholarly consensus on the sources of underdevelopment and the possibility of narrowing the gap between the less-developed countries (the Global South) and the advanced ones (the Global North). One major scholarly attempt to explain this developmental duality was the "modernization theory," which saw "modern values and institutions" as the historical keys to the North's development. So proponents of this theory advised the South to hastily adopt "Northern" social, political, and economic institutions for successful development. Indeed, most of the "Southern" societies were still backward in terms of the dominance of their religious, rural, and traditional institutions. In the broad and quite heterogeneous context of the modernization theory, even a kind of "universal" blueprint was outlined in terms of linear stages that would pave the way for rapid economic growth and development (Rostow, 1960).[2] Despite its lack of a coherent and homogeneous set of arguments, the modernization theory can be understood broadly as an influential perspective that has considered political-economic backwardness as an initial state from which the South had to start and then proceed along linear stages through industrialization, which could have been effectively supported by financial aid and technology transfers from the North.

Modernization theory envisaged what may be called an "ethnocentric" view of development as it glorified Western societies, attributing superiority to their sociocultural values and political-economic institutions. Nevertheless, critics tended to argue that the values and institutions in the South were not easy to change, and even if they changed, the consequent development trajectory might not have resembled the earlier stages of the North. Indeed, most societies in the South could only achieve partial modernity. More importantly, attempts for modernization without attaining significant levels of industrialization remained superficial at most. Industrialization in the twentieth century turned out to be all the more difficult because of the increasing complexity of impediments imposed on the latecomers through the international economic system. Hence, less-developed countries' peripheral position in the world system and their economic and technological dependence on the advanced countries have provided the North with more political leverage to maintain an international system of "unequal exchange" (Emmanuel, 1972), which accompanied the persistence of "development of underdevelopment" (Frank, 1966) at the level of the world economy. Such radically critical arguments were put forward by the "dependency theory" that started to attack the pro-capitalist optimism of the modernization theory from the 1960s onward.

According to the dependency theory, the international context faced by the less-developed countries in the twentieth century was significantly different from the context within which the advanced countries began their industrialization in the second half of the eighteenth century and the nineteenth century. The first industrializers faced much less competition and impediments for their development. They also had the advantage of colonizing other parts of the world and thus controlling important markets and resources. In the aftermath of the Second World War, the less-developed countries faced the competitive products of the North and the already established unequal trade links with it. Therefore, the post-war international system has not been conducive to the development of the South. Indeed, the international division of labor between the North and the South has been detrimental to the development possibilities of the latter, as it has served as a mechanism of surplus transfer from the periphery to the core of the world economy. For dependency theorists, the international capitalist system is exploitative and creates inequality at global level. Capitalists exploit labor at home and abroad, and the advanced (core) countries exploit the less-developed countries (periphery). Thus, capitalism generates uneven development patterns at both national and international levels. Peripheral countries might achieve partial industrialization, along with low wages and low living standards, usually with no indigenous technological innovations, while the core countries have benefitted from the underdevelopment of the peripheral countries (Valenzuela & Valenzuela, 1978). Thus, the main premise of the dependency theory is that there has been an ongoing dependency relationship between the center and peripheral states of the world economy, which benefits the former and harms the latter in a historical and persistent manner (Amin, 1980; Frank, 1967; Wallerstein, 1979). Therefore, the far-famed "mutual-benefit claim" on the part of both orthodox economics and modernization theory was definitely rejected by the dependency theory.[3]

At the background of the dependency theory was Latin American structuralism, especially the ideas of Raul Prebisch, who was appointed the director of UN Economic Commission for Latin America (ECLA) in 1950. Structuralists focused on the structural impediments to the development of less-developed countries. Under the rubric of "Prebisch-Singer thesis," they argued that less-developed countries were disadvantaged in the international division of labor due to a tendency for "declining terms of trade," as they could export only relatively cheaper primary and agricultural goods, rather than manufactured and industrial products, which was leading them to have chronic trade deficits and external indebtedness. Thus, they advised the less-developed countries to change the structure of their economies through industrialization (Martinussen, 1997; Prebisch, 1950; Singer, 1950). Such structural change could not happen through free trade and laissez-faire policies; it required protectionism and state interventionism. According to the structuralists, the less-developed countries had to create their own industries and decrease their import-dependence on the advanced countries. Also, they should have increased trade among themselves. Their suggestions were initially for Latin America but then they spread to most of the developing world (Rapley, 2007). That is how import-substituting industrialization (ISI) became a popular strategy among the less-developed countries.

At first, the difference between structuralists and modernization theorists was not very pronounced, as both favored foreign investment as a source of development. Yet as the second-generation structuralists elaborated their approach, in juxtaposition to the newly emerging dependency theory, more radical voices were raised to repudiate the modernization theory. It was Amin (1974, 1976) and Emmanuel (1972), the two well-known dependency theorists, who developed the concept of "unequal exchange" as an anti-systemic extension of the Prebisch-Singer thesis. The dependency theorists were much more pessimistic than the structuralists in terms of the prospects of development in the international capitalist system. They argued that the capitalist world system, along with its core countries, was responsible for limiting, indeed, precluding development in the underdeveloped world. Besides, class relations linked internal and external forces and "compradors" in the South acted as intermediaries between the international capitalist system and less-developed economies, reinforcing the exploitative dependency relations between the North and the South. Therefore, the dependency theorists pushed for anti-capitalist revolutions and cutting economic relations with the North, that is, "delinking" from the capitalist world economy (Amin, 1983).

Despite the fact that dependency theorists took class relations into account, they were criticized by more classical or orthodox Marxists.[4] Another criticism against them was, since they explained underdevelopment through external factors (international system and its core countries), the natural conclusion was that no matter what the developing countries did for their development, they would never become developed.[5] However, there were important differences among the dependency theorists themselves, when it came to the factors they emphasized. While Frank (1967) accentuated the external constraints on development and argued that the core benefitted from the underdevelopment of the periphery, Cardoso and Faletto (1979) put more emphasis on the local and international variations in dependency relations and also on the relatively independent effect of internal structures in addition to external conditioning. Cardoso and Faletto (1979) were also more optimistic insofar as they saw industrialization as a possibility in some peripheral countries. They argued that economic progress might occur in a peripheral setting if a beneficial alliance among foreign capital, domestic capital, and the state could be established so as to enable the country to take advantage of the process of capital accumulation to result in a certain degree of industrialization. Nevertheless, such progress would still be a dependent type of development. Similarly, Evans (1979) examined the relationships among multinational corporations (MNCs), local entrepreneurs, and the state and demonstrated how their divergent interests, power relations, and capabilities have produced a certain degree of industrialization, benefitting only the rich few and excluding the larger segments of society.

This possibility of industrialization in some developing countries and their "dependent development" could explain the case of some semi-industrialized countries like Argentina, Brazil, and Turkey, as well as the rise of Asian Tigers. Such countries were later categorized under the rubric of "semi-periphery" by the world-systems analysts, and they were considered to be the more advanced exemplars of dependent development rather than models of genuine economic success (Evans, 1979). World-systems analysts considered the international division of labor among the core, semi-periphery, and periphery as a permanent feature of the capitalist world economy (Chase-Dunn & Grimes, 1995; Wallerstein, 1979). However, the world-systems perspective tended to consider states as significant actors insofar as the role they played in the economic sphere of the capitalist world system. They have been criticized for overly emphasizing the institutions and relations of exchange at the expense of forces of production and also for preoccupying with global structures as determinants of national structures rather than examining the two-sided interactions between the two (Pieterse, 1988; Skocpol, 1977). One may, thus, argue that the world-systems analysis is presumably less explanatory when it comes to country-level case studies of development, even though it provides a broader and useful perspective for elaborating capitalism as a historical world system.

All in all, the dependence of the developing countries on the advanced ones through trade, investment and finance, along with their subordinate position in the international capitalist system, tends to constrain their prospects of development and lead frequently to financial imbalances and political-economic distortions. Yet there is a significant diversity among these countries in terms of their histories and institutions, political and economic structures, and development priorities and orientations. In conjunction with such diversity, some have been trapped in poverty and misery, some others have failed to catch up with the high-income countries despite decent rates of economic growth over the long term, while some like the Asian Tigers have displayed much more impressive economic achievements. Given this mixed and complicated configuration of the developing world, external constraints alone may not *completely* and *adequately* explain the developmental obstacles. We need to pay attention *also* to the national histories, domestic institutional structures, and internal political-economic dynamics of these countries, in juxtaposition to their modes of integration with global capitalism. Such a balanced approach, encompassing both the external and internal constraints to development, can be all the more appropriate and instrumental in analyzing dependent-development cases, like Turkey, within a realistic and still critical framework. Besides, the outright declaration of the impossibility of "genuine development" within global capitalism should not forestall a thematic focus on the essentially "dependent" nature of capitalist development in the case of less-developed countries. Such a focus on "dependency" can help us better identify and understand the historical and current "limits of the possible" associated with development under capitalism. Indeed, the above-discussed studies by Cardoso and Faletto (1979) and Evans (1979) can be regarded as two examples in this line of dependency analysis.

Although dependency theory has been largely marginalized in the mainstream discussions of development due to such factors as the success of the East Asian Tigers, the collapse of the Soviet Union, and the rise of neoliberalism, many contemporary scholars argue that it is still relevant and can offer significant insights into development issues (Fischer, 2015; Kvangraven, 2021; Slater, 2004; Tausch, 2010). Yet as emphasized above, it is difficult to talk about a single and coherent version of dependency theory. Therefore, the dependency theory should be seen more as a research program than a theory. The dependency approach is deeply historical and global in terms of its research orientation. It theorizes the polarizing effects of capitalist development, focuses on structures of production, and emphasizes particular impediments to development in the periphery of the global economic system. It is essentially an interdisciplinary approach. While it is systematic, it also pays attention to the particularities of the peripheral economies. It is these characteristics which make the "dependency framework" a holistic and comprehensive approach to development (Kvangraven, 2021). Even though we are not overtly adopting the "dependency approach" or any a specific version of it in this book; we emphasize, in a rather broad and pluralist framework, Turkey's "dependent" position in the world economic system and how dependency has come to constrain what countries like Turkey could accomplish in terms of development.

Within the "dependency" tradition, especially the contribution of Cardoso and Faletto (1979) is noteworthy as they focus on how less-developed economies are integrated into the global economic system by examining the combination of domestic class forces, the capacity of the state, and contingent choices by political actors in order to explain divergent development experiences. Some of the specific constraints that peripheral countries face in the global capitalist system, as identified by the classical dependency scholars, are technological dependence, unequal exchange, and falling terms of trade. However, for countries like Turkey, financial constraints have also been very crucial. Financial bottlenecks and the constraints imposed by recurrent balance-of-payments problems have tended to generate low-growth episodes as well as economic crises in the periphery. It has also been a major problem that peripheral countries are unable to borrow in their own currencies, and they have also been constrained in the implementation of monetary policies (Chandrasekhar & Ghosh, 2018; Stiglitz, 2017; Tavares, 1985; Vernengo, 2006; Wade & Veneroso, 1998).

Poverty and underdevelopment in the South can still be attributed to the peripheral or semi-peripheral positions of the less-developed countries in the capitalist world system (Tausch, 2010). Traditional and new forms of dependency continue to persist today, creating deeper economic asymmetries in the world. The economies of the South are still conditioned by and dependent on the economies of the North. Benefits of globalization have been distributed quite unequally and the North–South divide still persists.

The dependency relationships between the core and periphery have been quite dynamic, along with transformations taking place in the capitalist system through distinct stages. Periodic crises are an inherent characteristic of capitalism, and global capitalism advances through recurrent boom and bust cycles (Aydın, 2005). Each crisis triggers a readjustment of the political-economic relationship between the core and periphery, ensuring the ceaseless continuation of the process of capital accumulation globally. "In other words, different phases of capitalist development are characterized by different modes of capital accumulation which necessitate different forms of relationship between the core and periphery" (Aydın, 2005: 6). However, although the external conditions imposed by the global capitalist system are similar for all peripheral countries, how these conditions are reproduced and manifested by the domestic institutional context of individual countries and their abilities to handle them can differ significantly. That is the reason why some versions of dependent-development studies also take the domestic context into consideration seriously.

Despite contrary appraisals, dependency theory does not only focus on the external constraints, but it also expounds the relationship between the internal and external factors and makes in-depth analysis of historical and even country-specific factors. Its key premise is that we should analyze the dynamics of developing countries in relation to the dynamics of the center countries, because processes of global capitalist system condition peripheral countries in similar ways despite their diversity (Fischer, 2015). In fact, the strongest versions of the dependency theory are the ones that have been combining economic explanations with historical, political, and institutional analyses in particular contexts of dependence (Kvangraven, 2021). However, some versions of the dependency theory have focused more on the global structures (e.g., Frank, 1978; Sunkel, 1973; Wallerstein, 1974), while others have focused more on the local structures (e.g., Cardoso & Faletto, 1979; Furtado, 1970). Cardoso and Faletto (1979) claim that, under specific conditions, states can become agents of rapid development even when they are under extensive dependency. For them, in the periphery, the state has become an arbitrator for the class struggle and was used as an apparatus for redistribution both within the capitalist classes and to the masses (Cardoso & Faletto, 1979).

Development strategies are contingent on various factors, such as historical background, institutional setting, global economic conditions, resources availability, and so on. The family of what may be called the "dependent-development studies" recognize such contingencies and help us account for both the similarities and differences among the development experiences of the less-developed countries. Versions of such heterodox studies, to varying degrees, point out the continuation of uneven development, focus on the specific limitations that less-developed countries face, stress the structures of production, and employ a global historical approach. Thus, they help us study important problems related to development, globally and domestically.[6] Therefore, this family of development studies is a relevant, useful, and pluralist framework for analyzing the political economy of Turkey's dependent development. And, in order to analyze Turkey's development with consideration of its dependency, we first need to take a look at the origins and evolution of the capitalist world system and then attempt to explain its reflections in Turkey by paying attention to Turkey's specific history and political-economic structures.

In this regard, it should be emphasized that "dependence" is essentially an ***asymmetrical*** relationship, in contradistinction to the concept of "interdependence" that accentuates mutually beneficial political-economic relations. "Whereas interdependence involves a high level of mutual economic interaction and mutual sensitivity, dependence denotes highly unequal economic interaction and highly unequal sensitivity" (Spero, 1977: 14). Dependence arises in different forms within the inter-related segments of the capitalist world economy: trade, investment, finance, aid, technology, and so on. Many developing countries earn a large portion of their national incomes through exports of goods and services to the North. Many of them are dependent on imports from the North, not only in consumption goods but also in investment goods and intermediate inputs. Most technological improvements, accompanied by both product and process innovations, are still carried out predominantly in the advanced countries, perpetuating the general technological dependence of the developing world. Large amounts of financial and physical investments in developing countries are owned by investors from the North. Multinational corporations control important sectors in the South, such as raw material and export industries. Many developing countries also suffer from chronic balance-of-payments difficulties and rely heavily on foreign capital inflows. Many of them are prone to financial and economic crises and apply for IMF assistance when the need arises, which then exerts significant influence over the economic policies of these countries. Foreign aid is also important in shaping dependency patterns since it not only serves the political-economic interests of the North, but also paves the way for manipulation, management, and decision-making from outside. Dependence also means that peripheral countries have lacked clout on international economic organizations like the WTO, World Bank, and IMF up until today. The agricultural, industrial, monetary, fiscal, and trade policies of the North directly affect the development prospects of the developing countries. Such dependency-oriented political-economic structure of the world system implies that global capitalism is run without due consideration of the developing countries' interests, desires, and goals. In this way, the system continually perpetuates the South's dependent position. Well, how did we get there?

Addressing this question requires a concise history of global capitalism from at least the Industrial Revolution onward.

## History of Global Capitalism

Turkey's history of development cannot be considered apart from the world system. That is why it is essential to examine and discuss the history of world capitalism first. Historians generally consider the Treaty of Westphalia, which ended the Thirty Years' War in 1648, as the origin of the "modern inter-state system" because, with this treaty, earlier forms of a new *political* unit, nation-state, emerged as the main actor in the international system (Pearson & Payaslian, 1999). As far as the economic sphere at the level of the world is concerned, the Industrial Revolution is generally deemed to be the most important turning point for the world capitalist system. Ever since the Industrial Revolution began, a persistent feature of the world economy has been its unevenness, as capitalism tends to develop unevenly by creating inequalities between and within nation-states (Firebaugh, 2000). Hence, countries have been competing with each other on very unequal terms based on prominent disparities in their technological, institutional, and economic capacities.

From the geographical discoveries of the second half of the fifteenth century to the mid-eighteenth century approximately, mercantilism shaped the economic policies of the major states, especially in Europe. In the mercantilist period, governments controlled and regulated economic activities at both the national and international levels, along with establishing overseas colonies. With the onset of the Industrial Revolution and the resultant economic growth at unprecedented rates, Britain started to gradually put an end to the mercantile era. The Industrial Revolution was, indeed, a gradual yet robust process, commencing in the second half of the eighteenth century and extending through the long nineteenth century. It transformed the nature of economic activity from commercial capitalism to modern industrial capitalism. Britain was certainly the first country to industrialize, and as the first industrialized nation, it reaped huge economic advantages which raised it to the hegemonic status in the nineteenth century. Although substantial international economic relations did exist before, it was in the nineteenth century when industrialization spread from Britain to continental Europe and North America, creating a much more global economy with growing interdependence among the nations (Lairson & Skidmore, 2003: 44). It is against this momentous global backdrop that this volume starts telling the political-economic and developmental story of Turkey from the nineteenth century.

### *World Under the British Hegemony*

The century preceding the First World War had the highest rates of economic growth and interdependence in the world, as compared to the previous eras. Not only Britain but also many European states abandoned their protectionist policies and adopted a liberal free trade policy during the nineteenth century (Kindleberger, 1975). World trade grew and overseas investments increased at an unprecedented level. At the end of this hundred-year period, also huge developmental disparities emerged at global level as only a few Western nations and Japan were able to shift to the path of industrialization, leaving the rest behind. The nineteenth century was also a period of "imperialism" as the clashing political-economic interests of great powers aggravated expansionist and overseas rivalries over the control and exploitation of underdeveloped regions and countries, through political-military interventions as well as by means of technological and economic superiority reflected dominantly in commercial and financial relations. Under Britain's global leadership, accompanied by great-power rivalry, backward countries were forced to keep their markets open to industrial products, leading to the dissolution of their existing, newly emerging or potential industrial production and leaving them as producers and exporters of merely the primary goods and raw materials (Lairson & Skidmore, 2003: 57).

In the nineteenth century, the international system was dominated by the British hegemony. As Britain had turned out to be the first industrializing country, it also had the most competitive and productive economy. Especially after 1815, other Western nations started to be wary of strong British competition, so some forms and degrees of trade protectionism lingered in foreign economic relations (Kindleberger, 1975). The golden age of free trade started in 1860 with the Cobden-Chevalier Treaty signed between Britain and France, which triggered a series of other bilateral free trade agreements in Europe. This movement toward free trade was somewhat reversed in the late 1870s due to the effects of the Long Depression which started with the Panic of 1873,[7] but Britain maintained its free trade policy (Krasner, 1976). Also, the declining costs of trade due to technological innovations (especially in transportation) and the adoption of the Gold Standard system[8] facilitated high rates of international trade and substantial levels of economic integration (Lairson & Skidmore, 2003: 51).[9] Overall world trade and international financial flows grew at a rapid and unprecedented rate during the nineteenth century (Estevadeordal et al., 2003).

In the national context of the European countries, free trade debate was the outcome of a cleavage between the landed classes, who wanted protectionism, and the rising bourgeoisie, who supported free trade (Spero, 1977). The political roots of free trade can be practically traced back to the period when Napoleon imposed an economic embargo on Britain (1806–1814), pushing a transformation of the British economy from trading with Europe to trading overseas. Even after the embargo was over, Britain continued in the same path. Between 1815 and 1845, Britain lost its capacity to feed its own population and its exports began to stagnate. Its agricultural sector was protected through the Corn Laws. Yet the actors in the manufacturing and financial sectors began to promote the idea of free trade as a solution to Britain's economic problems. Finally, in the 1840s, not only the Corn Laws, but also the Navigation Acts that restricted transport to British ships were repealed. Although the idea of free trade was circulating widely in Britain well before the 1840s (since at least Adam Smith's publication of *The Wealth of Nations* in 1776), only after the alliance of domestic political forces in favor of free trade got stronger and defeated the protectionist agricultural forces could Britain adopt free trade as its main foreign economic policy (Lairson & Skidmore, 2003: 47).

After these internal changes, Britain began to construct a much more systematic free trade system at international level. It exported its manufactured goods all through the world, imported raw materials from less-developed regions, and increased its overseas investments. In fact, the period from 1820 to 1879 can be considered as the backdrop of gradually increasing liberalization in international trade and capital movements under the rising hegemony of Britain. Britain made many treaties with the European countries, expanding the system to the continent. By using its military power, Britain also forced other parts of the world to open up to world trade (Krasner, 1976). Alongside commercial expansion, international trading of stocks and bonds also turned out to be widespread, and there were almost no restrictions on such flows of financial capital. Primarily it was British investors who were lending to other governments through bonds. The Gold Standard system, managed by Britain, stabilized the currencies, and facilitated not only such financial flows, but also international trade. Huge amounts of money flowed from Britain toward the US, Canada, Latin America, and the colonies of the British Empire, making London the world's financial center (Spero, 1977). Thus, a complex division of labor, based on geography and industrialization level, emerged in the world economy.

The British hegemony peaked around the 1870s, and thereafter its competitiveness and share in world production and trade started to decline. Although Britain remained as the financial and commercial center of the world economy, the US started to surpass Britain in technological innovations by the 1870s. As the British hegemony started to decline and power differentials (especially among Britain, the US, and Germany) narrowed toward the end of the nineteenth century, new versions of nationalism gained momentum and the international system assumed a much more rivalrous character. Thus, the "liberal" world system was accompanied by the imperialist endeavors of the great powers. The drive for new investment opportunities and markets led to territorial partition of the peripheral areas of the world according to colonial interests. The great powers internationally dominated investment, trade, finance, and production; exploited labor in the overseas colonies; and thus, integrated the peripheral areas to the international economy for their own benefit, creating structures of economic dependency. Yet from 1873 to 1914, also the first efforts of industrialization started to emerge in some peripheral areas like India and China, but most notably in Japan.

The rise of new imperialism also reflected domestic political developments. It coincided with the rising power of the military and capitalist classes in the advanced countries (Spero, 1977). Moreover, the technological and industrial developments generated new economic opportunities for also working classes, but labor increasingly became dependent on the bourgeoisie for its livelihood. These new conditions expanded and deepened exploitation of labor, particularly the immigrants and women. As a result, organized labor unions started to proliferate in the last decades of the nineteenth century. Along with the unions, pro-labor and socialist political parties also began to emerge. In juxtaposition to labor movements and mass participation in the industrialized countries, imperialist discourses and practices also served to the domestic political-economic purposes by contributing to the legitimatization of the national governments in power (Hobsbawm, 1987).

### *The Greatest Crisis of Capitalism*

By the beginning of the twentieth century, the world economy was already global. At the same time, the world was becoming more and more divided between the rich and poor nations. Yet the First World War disrupted the world economy, decreased trade and financial flows, and eventually redistributed international economic power. Much of the international economic integration established during the first globalization era disappeared.

It can be argued that the First World War caused a shift of industrial production away from Europe to other parts of the world (especially the US and Japan) and created a huge international debt burden. The classical Gold Standard was also abandoned. Hence, the governments carried out monetary expansion to finance war spending, causing high inflation, loss of international competitiveness, and large trade deficits in especially Europe. This situation continued even after the war, rendering the overall world economy quite unstable (Lairson & Skidmore, 2003: 59–60). At the end of the war, the US emerged as the world's largest power in terms of industrial production and finance, but it was reluctant to assume an international leadership role (Kindleberger, 1973). In the absence of a global hegemon, political-economic instabilities and tensions escalated from the end of the First World War until the Second World War, and major powers failed to reconfigure the capitalist world system effectively.

First of all, the economic consequences of the First World War were not handled well. Britain and France claimed gigantic reparations from Germany, while the US as the major creditor country demanded repayment of all war debts. Economic recovery in Europe turned out to be all the more difficult under such debt obligations. At the same time, the US started to increase its tariff rates, deteriorating the current account balance of the European states further. As the US lending and imports declined, adverse pressures on the world economy increased, leading eventually to a major systemic collapse, the "Great Depression" (Lairson & Skidmore, 2003).

A complex set of factors led to the outbreak of the Great Depression, including high interest rates, falling investment in new production capabilities, sudden decline in public confidence, economic populism and mercantilism, shortage of gold in the world economy, the lack of international financial institutions, and the absence of a hegemonic country to maintain stability in the financial markets (Pearson & Payaslian,

1999). As the US Federal Bank moved to restrict credit in 1928, the foreign lending of the US decreased, the US production declined, world commodity prices fell, and eventually the stock market crashed in October 1929. With the start of the Great Depression in 1929 and the resultant economic downturn, the world retreated into autarchy and protectionism as numerous nations tried to defend their domestic economies through nationalistic impulses (Lake, 2000). There was no effective international mechanism to keep the system stable. According to Kindleberger (1973), Britain's incapability and the US's reluctance to assume responsibilities of a hegemon was the most fundamental reason which made the Great Depression so wide, so deep, and so long.

The US passed the Smooth-Hawley Tariff in 1930, which significantly limited US imports and triggered a retaliatory cycle of trade protectionism in the world. The spiral of falling trade and investment, rising bankruptcy and unemployment, declining prices, and increasing defaults and bank failures continued between 1930 and 1932. In countries like Japan, Germany, and Italy economic crisis led to the increased power of military, which sought to resolve domestic problems through territorial expansionism. In 1931, Japan invaded Manchuria in China to secure markets and resources. In the same year, the German economy collapsed and Germany stopped paying war reparations in 1932. As Adolf Hitler rose to power in 1933, Germany started an aggressive scheme of national economic planning, deficit spending, conscription, and arms production to spark economic recovery. On the other hand, following the disintegration of the classical Gold Standard at the First World War, a new international monetary system, the Gold-Exchange Standard, had gradually evolved during the 1920s. However, along with the economic and financial difficulties arising from the Great Depression, Britain and the US withdrew from the inter-war monetary system in 1931 and 1933, respectively. In 1933, the US devalued the US dollar and concentrated its efforts on domestic economic recovery (Lairson & Skidmore, 2003). In 1934, Britain and France defaulted on their war debts. Eventually, the catastrophic worldwide economic depression was followed by another catastrophic world war.

The Great Depression was a turning point not only for the advanced capitalist economies, but also for the less-developed countries, yet in a more positive way. As the advanced countries' economies collapsed, so did their demand for imports from the less-developed world, resulting in sharp decreases in the prices of primary products and raw materials, the traditional export items from the periphery. Hence, the export revenues of the less-developed countries fell drastically, leading to economic populism, extremism, and political instability in some of them. In Latin American countries, such dynamics generated military coups ousting democratic governments.[10] However, the collapse of international trade markets also led to the first industrialization attempts by the underdeveloped countries. Especially the Latin American countries, and also Turkey, began establishing big state-owned factories. Some of them encouraged private enterprises to produce the imported goods at home. In this way, they started an earlier version of "import-substituting industrialization" (ISI), which would turn out to be a common and systematic development strategy a few decades later. By the end of the First World War, the dissolution of the European empires had already started, while anti-imperialist national liberation movements in peripheral regions gained new momentum to demand independence from colonial rules during the inter-war period. However, the process of putting a definitive end to the old European colonial system could only be started after the Second World War.

Another positive effect of the Great Depression was the rise of "welfare state." The depression created a demand among the populace for government intervention in the economy (Spero, 1977). In juxtaposition to the New Deal in the US, which relied on a greater economic role to be played the state; the influential British economist John Maynard Keynes, whose "macroeconomic revolution" was becoming increasingly popular at the time, also demonstrated the need for governmental intervention in the economy through aggregate-demand management, and especially by means of fiscal policy. In such a political-economic milieu, many governments started to intervene in and regulate their economies at both the macroeconomic and sectoral levels. National goals could be prioritized in the absence of both a global hegemon and effective international economic organizations during the inter-war period, resulting in relatively "independent" political-economic relations at international level. However, as many countries resorted to "beggar-thy-neighbor" policies, such as high retaliatory tariffs and excessively competitive devaluations, economic and political instabilities escalated immensely, leading eventually to the Second World War.

### *World Under the US Hegemony*

The Second World War devastated all major economies in Europe, along with the Japanese economy, whereas the immense industrial base of the US remained intact and undamaged. With such economic might and unprecedented military strength, the US finally assumed the hegemonic leadership role and directed the post-war reconstruction and redesign of the international system. The economic experiences before the war (the Great Depression) and the ideological orientations after the war (the Cold War) shaped the hegemonic efforts of the US in the post-war period.

With the lessons learned from the inter-war period, the major states settled for cooperation in order to reconfigure and regulate the international system to ensure economic stability and international peace. Before the Second World War ended, delegates from 44 countries met at the Bretton Woods Conference in the US in July 1944. Despite the participation of many developed and less-developed countries, the Conference was held predominantly as an Anglo-American event. Britain and the US decided to establish the General Agreement on Tariffs and Trade (GATT), the International Bank for Reconstruction and Development (IBRD, the origin of the World Bank), and the International Monetary Fund (IMF). These institutions, which were established largely through US political initiatives, created and imposed a set of rules and procedures, known as the Bretton Woods System (BWS), in order to regulate international economic relations. The BWS was effective in limiting economic tensions and achieving stability until at least the early 1970s.

In the context of the BWS, economic and political power was concentrated in a few countries in Northern America and Western Europe, led by the US, and they were able to make and impose the global decisions, with a shared belief in capitalism and liberalism. The goal was to maintain convertible currencies, low trade barriers, a system of fixed exchange rates, and a well-functioning multilateral system of trade and payments. The international monetary regime under the BWS involved a new gold-exchange standard, based on "adjustable" fixed exchange rates and managed by the US, as the value of US dollar was fixed to gold at 35 dollars per ounce while other countries anchored their currencies to the US dollar. The IMF's main tasks were to provide short-term financial assistance to the countries with balance-of-payments difficulties and help maintain the fixed value of currencies against the US dollar. The World Bank initially focused on the post-war recovery of Europe, and from the 1950s onward it became a major provider of medium- and long-term loans for the development projects undertaken by the less-developed countries. The GATT turned out to be quite instrumental in the reduction of trade barriers, most notably import tariffs.

The BWS and the domestic economic policymaking of the major economies of the time were highly influenced by Keynesian ideas, which also reverberated in the state-led development policies of the less-developed countries. Thus the post-war economic system has often been referred to as the "Keynesian golden age," implying the rise of "managed capitalism" against "laissez-faire capitalism" that was discredited by the Great Depression. This version of capitalism also corresponded to "embedded liberalism" (Ruggie, 1982), as many social-democratic parties which came to power in Europe committed themselves to a more equitable socioeconomic order. Therefore, in the post-war period, for about three decades, capitalism was managed along with a redistributive orientation (Rapley, 2007: 18).

After the Second World War, also the United Nations (UN) was established. Throughout the post-war decolonization process, many nations gained their political independence and were granted the right to self-determination and to become a full member in the UN. In comparison with the era of British hegemony, the US hegemony considerably restricted the rights and powers of sovereign states by imposing certain principles, norms, and rules through international institutions.[11]

The strength of the US economy, the lessons of the inter-war period, and the Cold War made the US leadership necessary and acceptable not only within the US, but also for the European states and Japan. The Europeans and the Japanese needed the US assistance to rebuild their economies. Economic cooperation was necessary also for security reasons. With the perceived communist threat, there was a greater willingness among these countries to compromise and share the economic burden. As a result, the post-war decades generated unprecedented prosperity, booming world trade, and an extraordinary expansion of international economic cooperation. Growth in international trade was a main factor behind fast economic growth rates. World trade grew even faster than world production between 1950 and 1970 due mainly to declining tariff rates and stable exchange rates. The average tariff rates decreased from 40% in 1940 to 13% in 1970.[12] The recovery in Europe and Japan was a substantial driving force as well (Lairson & Skidmore, 2003). Europe and Japan recovered rapidly and strongly thanks to the US aid, surge in investment, and political stability accompanied by a favorable security environment.

In the 1940s and the 1950s, the US had the largest productive resources and the highest productivity in the world. There was also a huge balance-of-payments imbalance between the US and the other countries due to the large current surplus of the US. Between 1945 and 1949, the US supplied $28 billion to finance the balance-of-payments deficits of the rest of the world. In 1950 and 1951, Marshall Aid served to the same purpose and also the US continued to provide at least military aid to its allies. As a result of these, the US dollar became the main world currency in international transactions (Lairson & Skidmore, 2003: 78). The US dominated world production, pushed for major trade initiatives, and acted like the world's central banker.

The international management of the post-war capitalism relied on the economic and political hegemony of the US. However, the post-war period also saw the emergence and escalation of the Cold War, that is, an essentially ideological rivalry between capitalist and communist camps, led by the two superpowers, the US and the Soviet Union. The US was dominant over Western Europe, Japan, and the non-communist segments of the less-developed world, while the Soviet Union had satellites mainly in Eastern Europe and allies in Africa and Asia, along with Mao's communist China. In this Cold War context, the US pushed Europe for economic and political unity and eventually six European states (France, West Germany, Belgium, Luxembourg, Italy, and the Netherlands) established the European Economic Community (EEC) by signing the Treaty of Rome in 1957.

With the increased rivalry posed by the Soviet Union, the Cold War got more militarized and the US military spending rose significantly. By the late 1950s, Europe largely completed its recovery process and US payments deficits with Europe started to emerge. With an internationally weakened dollar and worsening balance of trade, the US economy began to give signs of trouble in the 1960s. These problems ultimately led to the collapse of the gold-exchange standard of the BWS during the period 1971–1973, as the US in 1971 ran its first trade deficit since 1893. With the pressure on dollar increasing, President Nixon suspended the US commitment to exchange gold for dollars, imposed domestic wage and income controls, devalued dollar, and introduced a 10-percent tariff on US imports, which were against the principles of the BWS. As monetary component of the BWS completely ended in March 1973, a system of floating exchange rates was gradually adopted. Thus, although the US was still the largest and most influential economy in the world and the guarantor of Western security, its hegemonic position in the world system weakened considerably by the early 1970s.

Along with the collapse of the monetary regime of the BWS, the management of the broader international economic system was also seriously threatened. Hence, the capitalist world economy entered a period of disorder. As the international monetary system collapsed, states began to turn more protectionist, while the OPEC crisis resulted in two major oil shocks in 1973 and 1979, causing stagflation in the developed countries and triggering a serious debt crisis in the less-developed ones. In the dust and heat of the 1970s, a group of less-developed countries, via the United Nations Conference on Trade and Development (UNCTAD), demanded a "new international economic order" that would serve better to their economic interests; however, it turned out to be a vain attempt. Alongside these developments, the Keynesian "embedded liberalism" fast approached its end, paving the way for the rise of "neoliberalism" in the late 1970s and early 1980s.

By the 1980s the US position in the world economy further declined. The US dollar was still the dominant currency, but new competing centers of economic power from within the capitalist camp, such as Germany, Japan, and the EU, started to challenge the US's position in world trade and investment. Thus, from that point on, the US role has become more of "prominence" than "dominance" (Pearson & Payaslian, 1999: 100). However, the US influence in the world persisted significantly. As neoliberalism became the new political-economic paradigm, the US did not fail to disseminate the neoliberal ideology and policies throughout the world. Consequently, the 1980s and 1990s witnessed further economic integration in the world and the emergence of the "second globalization era."

## The History of Less-Developed Countries Under Global Capitalism

While the history of global capitalism was mostly shaped by the advanced nations, developing countries have also been part of that process. In fact, advanced countries' economic objectives and progress were generally at the expense of the less-developed countries (Baran, 1962). Thus, a North–South divide has prevailed in the world when it comes to development. Since Turkey is also part of the South, it is essential to explain and discuss the history of less-developed countries separately.

By the early twentieth century, the world economy was globally integrated to a significant extent under the weakening British hegemony. Most of the world was under political control of the European imperial powers and they were able to hold on to their colonial possessions until the decolonization process that started after the Second World War. A key element in the US post-war political goals was dismantling the formal colonial system established by the European powers. Therefore, the world witnessed a period of decolonization approximately from the late 1940s to the 1970s. During the Cold War, the Soviet Union tried to take advantage of this process and sought to expand its sphere of influence through these newly independent territories. In response, the US increased its financial and military aid to these countries and carried out even military interventions when it deemed necessary in order to maintain and strengthen its position. Fidel Castro's victory in Cuba and his shift toward the Soviet Union intensified this trend. As a result, both the US and the Soviet Union carried their rivalry to the South, giving out vast amounts of economic and military aid to their strategic allies in the context of the Cold War (Pearson & Payaslian, 1999; Spero, 1977; Taffet, 2007).

The decolonization movement, especially in the 1960s, transformed the North–South relations. Many African and Asian countries gained their political independence and joined the UN. They also started to strive for economic independence. Politically speaking, the "Non-Alignment Movement" had started in 1955 and most of those countries tried to stay neutral during the Cold War.[13] The post-war international economic system established under the US hegemony was based largely on principles of free trade liberalism, which, however, was considered to be an unrealistic model for the less-developed countries as they were trying to achieve rapid economic development and state- and nation-building. To many of these "peripheral" countries, economic liberalism looked like an indirect neo-colonial strategy that aimed to maintain their exploitation by the "core" countries of the capitalist world system. Therefore, many of them tried to implement an economic third way between capitalism and socialism. While few of them opted for socialism (e.g., China, Cuba, and Tanzania), most of them chose the ISI strategy that could be followed by remaining within the capitalist system (Rapley, 2007).

For the policymakers in the South, there was an urgent need to catch up with the North. In the 1950s and the 1960s, ISI was hailed as the cure to the South's underdevelopment, not only by structuralists but also by many modernization theorists. As argued by Gerschenkron (1962), late industrializing nations faced specific advantages, but also disadvantages, as compared to early industrializers. They encountered much more developed competitors that had complex technologies, higher education levels, and well-established institutions. In order to compensate for their weaknesses and to develop, latecomers had to rely on their governments to finance and even establish enterprises, especially in the much needed industries such as coal and steel. The state usually should have also created the social infrastructure needed for a modern society. If these were done, the advantage of the late developers would be that they could grow more rapidly than the advanced countries and initiate a significant spurt in industrialization. However, at the same time, such industrialization might also lead to the emergence of social forces hostile to liberal capitalism and democracy. Gerschenkron (1943, 1962) recognized that an effort to catch up with advanced countries implied exploitation and a huge downward pressure on consumption, which would create resentment and resistance. Thus, "catching up" was unlikely to be achieved under democracy. This approach was also in line with the thesis of Barrington Moore's famous book, *Social Origins of Dictatorship and Democracy*, which argued that economic latecomers to industrialization would achieve development through a non-democratic path due to the weakness of their bourgeois class (Moore, 1967). Indeed, historically speaking, almost none of the less-developed countries could achieve to become stable democracies. As O'Donnell (1978) suggested through his "bureaucratic authoritarian model," despite their political instabilities, the countries which implemented ISI could be democratic during their ISI phases, because ISI offered significant benefits to the masses, such as creation of new jobs. However, democracy tended to stumble when ISI reached to its limits and the industries had to start exporting to correct the balance-of-payments disequilibria.

In the post-war period, the South as a whole still made some considerable progress. Nevertheless, this initial period of rapid and widespread industrialization in the South was also described at times as the period of "neo-colonialism." Such arguments indicated that the formal political independence of these former colonial territories had not changed the relations of domination and exploitation by the North over the South.

However, despite the fact that "imperialism" implied exploitation and inequality, it also provided conditions for capitalist development in the South (Warren, 1973). The formal independence had at least given the less-developed countries a degree of maneuver, initiative, and ability to control and regulate their economies to a certain extent, which was eventually conducive to economic development. With establishment of central banks, export–import controls, and taxation and spending systems, capitalist social relations of production grew substantially throughout the South (Warren, 1973). Independence has facilitated industrial advancement by ending the monopoly of the colonialist powers and creating conditions through which peripheral countries could develop by utilizing inter-imperialist and East–West rivalries and MNCs. Politically speaking, industrialization also stimulated nationalism and popular pressures for higher living standards.

Many less-developed countries with large domestic markets implemented ISI in order to achieve development and diversification of their productive activities. However, as the global economic boom ended and the world economy started to slow down by the end of the 1960s and the 1970s, the flaws of the ISI started to become more evident (Rapley, 2007: 47–52). The ISI strategy, along with the "infant industries" established through ISI, mostly failed to create efficient and competitive economies in the South. They were still struggling to catch up within the international capitalist system dominated by the industrialized countries. They observed that their relations with the advanced countries were shaped by power asymmetries, and they tried to counterbalance the systemic advantages of the advanced countries in vain. Less-developed countries were still in need of technology and capital goods from the North and their exports were not enough to finance them; in other words, they were still heavily dependent on the North.

Confronting political-economic disadvantages and enduring dependency patterns, developing countries started to work together through the UN and established some collaborative mechanisms, such as the Group of 77 (G-77), to demand pro-South reforms in the North–South relations. In 1964, the G-77 organized the first UN Conference on Trade and Development (UNCTAD), which then became a permanent organ of the UN. UNCTAD has openly supported the developing countries' interests since then, but advanced countries refused it to become the main platform for trade negotiations.

By the 1970s, less-developed countries were increasingly dissatisfied with the international system, which shaped their economies effectively but excluded them from its decision-making processes and gave them an unequal share of its benefits. The countries of the North generally tried to deny them any access. Inspired by OPEC's success in hiking oil prices in 1973, the countries of the South attempted to negotiate a "new international economic order" (NIEO). NIEO called for changes in the rules of the international economic system, such as higher and stable the commodity prices, lower advanced country barriers to less-developed countries' manufactured exports, more aid from the North to South, greater voting power for the South in international economic institutions, effective global rules for regulating the activities of the MNCs, debt relief, and wider access to North's technology. Despite OPEC's endorsement of these demands and the negotiations between the developing countries and G-7 on these issues, this push toward change proved inadequate, indeed futile, by the 1980s. The North was already reluctant to admit a real change, as such a change was seen to be contrary to the North's benefit, but the biggest blow was the outburst of the Third World debt crisis in 1982, which seriously hampered the bargaining power of the less-developed countries against the advanced ones and the international financial institutions. In fact, many of the less-developed countries, which were implementing the ISI strategy, were struggling with balance-of-payments difficulties and high debt problems in the late 1970s. With the debt crisis, in a sense, they fell directly into the arms of IMF, which was ready to change their inward-oriented developmentalist economic strategies rather than changing the international economic system (Ould-Mey, 1994; Spero & Hart, 2003).

The origin of the 1982 debt crisis lies in the dependence of less-developed countries on foreign capital due to the insufficiency of their internal savings to finance their economic growth. During the 1950s and 1960s, most of the capital flows to the South was in the form of foreign aid and foreign direct investment (FDI). From the late 1960s onward, the loans extended by commercial banks in the North started to become a more significant source of foreign capital. The demanding and strict terms of commercial bank lending paved the way for the Third World debt crisis of the 1980s. The oil price hikes in the 1970s led to huge increases in the export revenues of the OPEC, which, in turn, were deposited in Western banks. Eurodollars and petrodollars in the Western banks found their way to the South, while the developed countries slipped into stagflation. Less-developed countries needed foreign exchange to pay for their imports of oil and capital goods which they needed for their newly built factories under ISI, especially in Latin America, as well as in Turkey. As the stagflationary pressures in the North deepened, exports of the South declined, creating foreign exchange bottlenecks and aggravating balance-of-payments difficulties. Yet these countries had to continue to borrow to maintain debt repayments and economic growth, but this was an unsustainable process, which officially ended in August 1982 as Mexico defaulted on its foreign debt and agreed to follow an IMF stabilization plan.

As more developing countries underwent balance-of-payments problems, like Mexico, and sought new loans and renegotiation of the existing ones, the IMF quickly resumed a much more central role. IMF saw it as a problem of economic mismanagement and expected the debtor countries to implement corrective austerity policies, the so-called bitter medicine. The IMF typically prescribed "neoliberal policies" for the troubled less-developed countries, forcing them to dismantle ISI policies and replace them with free market ones. The first step was to correct trade imbalances by currency devaluations, accompanied by dampening domestic demand through tight fiscal and monetary policies. With these quite standard IMF programs, the era of Washington Consensus started for the South.

The Washington Consensus involved the implementation of neoliberal prescriptions for growth and development, mostly through "stabilization packages" and "structural adjustment programs" (SAPs), imposed by the IMF and the World Bank. According to the neoliberal view, by ignoring comparative advantages in trade, ISI had done more harm than good in the South. ISI was seen as an inefficient and unproductive strategy, and the neoliberal alternative was "export-led growth" along with the minimization of the economic role and weight of the state. This new orientation also signaled the end of "economic planning" in the South. The stabilization packages and the SAPs included neoclassical prescriptions to economic problems, such as fiscal austerity, monetary discipline, privatization of state-owned economic enterprises, trade liberalization, financial openness, and general deregulation of the economy. Major goal was "to remove perceived structural blockages to the efficient operation of the markets" (Rapley, 2007: 79). Numerous countries implemented such neoliberal policies in the 1980s and 1990s, yet the desired outcomes could not be achieved in general. These policies not only failed to bring about higher rates of growth and development, but also aggravated problems of inequality and poverty (Stiglitz, 2017).

Neoliberalism also had important *political* implications. In the context of the export-led growth model, competitiveness in export markets required higher productivity and lower labor costs. Thus, with the start of the neoliberal era in the South, employment decreased, the wages were pushed down, and social security spending was cut. These anti-labor practices generated unfavorable socioeconomic conditions for large segments of society. Therefore, neoliberal transformation was, in fact, not an easy task in a democracy. In many cases, indeed, the economic reforms and policies were carried out through military or other type of authoritarian regimes. Therefore, it is not surprising that some ISI countries were stricken with political instability and coups in the 1980s (e.g., Bolivia, Turkey, and Bangladesh). Yet having an authoritarian government was no guarantee for economic success either.

In the meanwhile, some countries in East Asia, called the "Asian Tigers" (Hong Kong, Taiwan, South Korea, and Singapore), were recording high growth rates since the 1960s. Their development model began to be referred as "export-oriented industrialization." In the 1950s, they had also started their industrialization through ISI, but they used limited and temporary protectionism for their "infant industries" to prepare them for international competition. Due to the Cold War concerns, they received extensive financial and technological aid from the US. Since these countries had relatively smaller domestic markets, they had to target international markets, and thus they had to have competitive products. Relying on their cheap labor force and authoritarian regimes, they achieved rapid industrialization and became important exporters of manufactured goods. When ISI countries were struggling with foreign debt and crisis in the 1980s, the Asian Tigers were able to grow relying on their domestic savings and maintaining their economic stability (Lairson & Skidmore, 2003: Chap. 9; Stiglitz, 1996).

Since the 1980s, many developing countries have moved toward neoliberalism as they reduced state intervention in the economy, relied more on free markets, and liberalized their trade and foreign investment (Biersteker, 1992). Especially in the 1990s, not only the ex-communist countries, but also the South at large was going through deep institutional changes, leaving their state-led development models and adopting neoliberal policies (Sachs, 1999). Globalization of finance and production accelerated. MNCs expanded in terms of their size, number, and economic influence, and became the principal agents of globalization. The rising role of the MNCs was mainly an outcome of the general trend in capital-account liberalization. Global FDI annually grew at 13% on average between 1980 and 1997 (Lairson & Skidmore, 2003: 347). As the less-developed countries dismantled domestic regulations that impeded or discouraged FDI, the MNCs began to shift their production to the South to take advantage of lower labor costs. FDI was redirected especially to East and Southeast Asia, but Latin America turned out to be another popular destination. However, major industries that entail dynamic innovation and high-technology, know-how, and a high-skilled labor force remained generally in the North. Depending on the domestic context, the struggle between neoliberal-minded policymakers and their more nationalist adversaries varied in terms of intensity and pace. Joint ventures and other partnerships between the local companies and the MNCs also became common. During the neoliberal era, many MNCs have continued to make handsome profits in their operations in the South, which are essential for them to remain globally competitive. On the other hand, certain developing countries (such as South Korea, China, and Brazil) fostered their own globally competitive MNCs which have grown in number and size.

As capital-account liberalization became a common policy, portfolio investments began to replace bank loans as the primary source of foreign finance for many developing countries in the 1990s (Lairson & Skidmore, 2003). Most of these funds are provided on a short-term basis and relatively liquid forms of investment. Therefore, they are far from meeting the financing needs for long-term development. They have also created serious financial instabilities for these countries. In fact, in the 1990s, a series of financial crises occurred in the South. The first crisis was the Turkish crisis in April 1994. However, a more significant one was the "Mexican Tequila Crisis" in the same year. Mexico was praised as a model of neoliberal transformation as it implemented a radical trade liberalization program in the first half of the 1990s, along with its membership in NAFTA in January 1994. Many investors got attracted to Mexico due to its free market reforms and financed the rising Mexican imports; however, a financial bubble was created. With the reversal of financial flows, a huge financial crisis started in December 1994. Mexico had to go through a tough stabilization program to overcome the crisis.

In the meanwhile, another financial bubble was developing in East Asia. The 1997 Asian crisis, which mostly affected Thailand, South Korea,

Malaysia, and Indonesia, occurred shortly after the rapid liberalization of their financial systems and capital accounts. The crisis proceeded through plunges in exchange rates, stock markets, and real estate prices as the global investors lost confidence in these economies. This crisis also represented a huge blow to the successful "Asian model" of development and fired up a serious criticism of IMF policies and neoliberalism in general.

Between 1997 and 1999, the Asian crisis deepened and expanded to the global level. Russia in 1998 and Brazil in 1999 underwent their own crises. Argentina and Turkey followed in 2001. All these crises had devastating effects on the respective countries, which also prompted important domestic political changes. In the aftermath of the crises, Vladimir Putin rose to power in Russia, Luiz Inácio Lula da Silva's Workers' Party took power in Brazil, the "pink tide" started in Argentina through Kirchner governments, and Recep Tayyip Erdoğan's AKP came to power in Turkey.

With these continuous outbreaks of financial crises in the South, many observers started to question the neoliberal model and financial globalization. Not only the crises, but also the persistence of poverty and increasing inequality discredited neoliberalism and its main promoters (IMF and World Bank) in the 1990s. As a result, especially the World Bank started to shift its approach toward "institutionalism" and recognized the importance of the state's regulatory and institutional roles in development through "good governance." Another shift was its greater emphasis on social policies through social safety net and poverty alleviation programs. As such elements were incorporated into the development agenda imposed on the developing countries by international economic organizations, an "augmented" and "regulatory" version of neoliberalism, "Post-Washington Consensus," commenced (Marangos, 2009; Öniş & Şenses, 2005; Rodrik, 2006).

In sum, from the end of the Second World War until today, the developing countries have tried to expand their development possibilities and break away from their dependency on the advanced countries. While dependency has remained as a constant condition, some of the developing countries have become more successful and achieved some significant industrialization. During the second globalization era, especially in the 1980s and the 1990s, the gap between the North and the South widened, with the exception of a number of "emerging economies." In fact, the gap among the developing countries has also increased. Except a few East and Southeastern countries, developing countries have generally been frustrated in their efforts to promote their economic development and exert influence in the international economic system (Bourguignon, 2016; Hickel, 2017). Despite its industrialization to some extent, Turkey has also been one of these frustrated countries that have never been able to shift upward to the high-income status.

## Explaining Turkey's Development

Turkey can be considered a typical semi-peripheral country in many respects. It has achieved an apparent degree of industrialization and social progress during the twentieth century, and it has been considered an important "emerging market" in more recent decades. Yet Turkey's development was neither a rapid nor a smooth process. Rather, the history of modern Turkey is full of political crises and coups in addition to economic crises. Having started from a quite equal society of small- and medium-sized farmers a hundred years ago, it has evolved into an unequal semi-industrialized society today. Despite accomplishing one of the most impressive modernization revolutions in the South during the 1920s and the 1930s, it could never become a robust democracy, attesting to the argument by Gerschenkron (1943, 1962) and O'Donnell (1978) that democracy is a difficult endeavor for the late-comers to industrialization. Periods of relative democratization have always been intertwined with periods of political-economic crisis and authoritarianism in Turkey. More recently, Turkey has been under the pressure of a particular version of "authoritarian populism" with Islamist connotations. Therefore, Turkey can be regarded as a typical and unique case at the same time. Such combination of conventionality and singularity is presumably the reason why Turkey has become a hot subject of debate in the political-economy literature.

### *Explanations of Turkey's Development*

Politically speaking, one of the major purposes of this edited volume is to consider the controversial rise and evolution of Erdoğan's AKP regime during the first two decades of the twenty-first century, connecting it essentially with the broader context of Turkey's historical background encompassing the nineteenth and the twentieth centuries. Many political scientists have tried to explain AKP's rise and popularity so far. Some have emphasized the divided nature of Turkish society, that is to say, the clash between the more socio-culturally liberal, secular, elitist, and urbanized people who supposedly dominated Turkish politics until AKP *versus* the more religious, conservative, and sub-urban or provincial people who have been supposedly empowered since AKP came to power. Such views are generally based on Şerif Mardin's (1973) "center-periphery" perspective, which argues that Turkish society is divided into two; as the secularized and westernized elites (the center) *versus* the religious, traditional, and provincial people (the periphery). Although he refers to this division to explicate the late Ottoman era and the one-party period in Turkey (1923–1946), some contemporary scholars have used it to draw attention to the still divided nature of Turkish society (Demiralp, 2012; Gülalp, 2001; Kalaycıoğlu, 2012). There are several weaknesses in this kind of a "center-periphery" approach. It tends to disregard the economic factors which have led to the rise of AKP. Besides, a merely cultural definition of the periphery and center is reductionist. As a critical political-economy approach is adopted in this volume, we do not think that the above-mentioned "center-periphery" framework is proper for analyzing Turkey's development experience. In contradistinction, the center-periphery perspective implicated in this volume pertains to the higher and broader level of global capitalism. The "dependent-development" framework of this volume involves an effort to situate Turkey in the world capitalist system dominated by the core countries. Chapters in this volume attempt to emphasize the political limits and economic constraints Turkey has faced due to its position as a semi-peripheral country in the world system. They analyze how Turkey's political-economic relations with the capitalist core, along with its integration to the global markets, have been reflected on its developmental orientations at the domestic level.

There are also important studies when it comes to the analysis of Turkey's economic history. Two prominent examples are: Korkut Boratav's *Türkiye İktisat Tarihi, 1908–2015* (Economic History of Turkey, 1908–2015) and Yakup Kepenek's *Türkiye Ekonomisi* (The Turkish Economy) (Boratav, 2003; Kepenek, 2016). As these books are in Turkish, they have reached only to the Turkish audience. As a source in English, *The Political Economy of Turkey* by Zülküf Aydın (2005) analyzes the political and socioeconomic problems encountered by Turkey as the country integrated more and more with the global economy. While offering a broader critique of globalization, Aydın (2005) explicates how Turkey, like many other developing countries, has become dependent on foreign capital and international financial institutions. In that sense, it is in the same line with our book, but it does not go back as far as the late Ottoman era and does not contain the AKP period, which has become a major puzzle in modern Turkish history.

A more recent study on Turkey's economic history is *Uneven Centuries* by Şevket Pamuk (2018). Pamuk emphasizes two sets of factors in explaining Turkey's long-term development: its historical roots, that is, the roots of its formal and informal social, political, and economic institutions; and its relative factor endowments, their respective returns, and technology. He develops a framework to reflect mainly on institutions and institutional changes in order to explain Turkey's growth and development experience through important historical details. This book is similar to our volume in terms of its historical span and orientation, but it does not explicitly consider the dependency patterns pertaining to the capitalist world system.

Adopting a critical political-economy approach, chapters in this volume attempt to pay due attention to the "dependent" nature of Turkey's developmental history. Through a pluralist and balanced perspective in the line of what may be called "dependent-development studies," this volume situates Turkey in the capitalist world system, explains how its "semi-peripheral" position has conditioned its development path and shaped its political-economic prospects, and how external constraints have been instrumental in configuring domestic-policy orientations. In that sense, Çağlar Keyder's *State and Class in Turkey* (1987) can be perhaps considered *somewhat* similar to this volume, but our time frame is broader as we extend the analysis until 2020. Keyder explains how the dependency of Turkey has defined the context in which domestic actors operate. He argues that the secular and cyclical tendencies in the world capitalist system have transformed the structure of Turkey's dependency over time, creating domestic sociopolitical tensions through the emergence of certain classes or divisions within classes. Unlike Keyder's book, this volume does not particularly put class analysis at the center stage. What mainly unifies the chapters of this volume is their relatively common attitude toward Turkey's essentially *dependent* development within global capitalism from the nineteenth century to 2020.

Expectedly, the nine main chapters that follow this one emphasize the role of external and internal factors at varying degrees due mainly to the specific political-economic characteristics of the periods under consideration. However, all the main chapters (Chapters 2–10) have a similar structure in the sense that both the limitations imposed and incentives provided by external conditions and how they have shaped internal dynamics are examined and discussed. Although Turkey occasionally tried to overcome its dependency on the core of the capitalist world system, its regular external deficits since the late 1940s and thus its dependence on foreign capital, foreign technology and imports have allowed only a dependent type of development. As this kind of economic development has not produced strong pro-democracy alliances, Turkey's political development has been even less successful than its economic development.

### *Purpose and Outline of the Book*

A large portion of political-economy literature centers on the political and economic development of a single nation-state, and this book is also a case study of Turkey's development experience. Yet national economies cannot be properly studied as self-contained units of analysis. Specific national instances of different development models (be it economic liberalism, statism, import-substituting industrialization, export-led growth, or neoliberalism) are influenced predominantly by the dynamics of global capitalism. Thus, we need to elaborate on Turkey's development experience by linking it to the world economy in order to understand and explain the phases it has gone through in a long-term historical perspective. Therefore, Turkey's "semi-peripheral" position in the world economy is scrutinized in this book so as to link domestic political-economic transformations to the shifting power structures and development agendas within the broader context of global capitalism.

Broadly speaking, in "peripheral" and "semi-peripheral" economies, each phase of capitalist development stems usually from specific connections with the world economy and generates particular class relations domestically. At the center of each new developmental phase are global shifts. Each phase is also facilitated by new political-economic alliances. Eventually, each phase of capitalist development in a dependent economy tends to come to a deadlock, culminating in an economic crisis that threatens the regularity and continuity of the capital-accumulation process. Therefore, economic crises can create a push for a different pattern of accumulation. They can also trigger political crises that dismantle old political alliances and create new ones. One common way to resolve political crises is through changes in the political regime, which, in turn, aim to resolve the economic deadlock by attempting to initiate a new phase of capitalist development. Thus, power blocs and the domain of politics are reshaped, along with the reconfiguration of development agendas. Like many developing countries, Turkey has also followed such a trajectory, more or less. The purpose of this book is to analyze that trajectory within a critical and historical political-economy perspective, paying due attention to the changing nature of state-economy and economy-society relations.

All in all, this book is an original collection of articles that focus on Turkey's economic-development experience since the nineteenth century. It provides a systematic and chronological examination of Turkey's major historical dynamics in the economic and sociopolitical spheres. The chapters are organized according to the consecutive phases of Turkey's political-economic development. Each chapter not only reflects on the country-specific aspects of those development phases, but also considers the dependence of domestic-policy orientations on the dynamics of the world economy. The principal aim of the book is to provide a historically-conscious, political-economic account of Turkey's dependent-development experience. More broadly, in light of Turkey's historical dependent-development patterns, one can also argue that sustained economic and institutional development is a much more formidable task than the mainstream approaches have conceived.

The starting point of this book is the Treaty of Balta Liman (1838), a major Anglo-Ottoman free trade agreement, which was followed immediately by the "Imperial Edict of Reorganization" (*Tanzimat Fermanı*) of 1839, paving the way for certain Western-oriented political, administrative, and military reforms that aimed at modernization. The endpoint is Turkey in 2020, characterized by an autocratic political regime facing severe economic and developmental problems, along with quite tense relations with the Western world and worrisome circumstances in the Middle East and Eastern Mediterranean. With a time span of approximately two hundred years, the chapters in this book examine Turkey's political-economic transformations and developmental shifts in conjunction with the dynamics of the capitalist world system. They reveal modern Turkey's historical dependence on the world economy and international politics. Each historical phase is examined and discussed in a separate chapter by different contributing authors. The division of labor among the authors was determined according mainly to their scholarly expertise in the historical periods under consideration. On the whole, an absorbing story emerges as to how modern Turkey's integration to the capitalist world system has affected its developmental possibilities, resulting eventually in the electoral victories of the AKP and the subsequent autocratic regime associated with the "Erdoğan era" of the last two decades. Indeed, another rationale behind this book is the idea that nearly two-decade-old Erdoğan era in Turkey can be better understood through a systematic analysis of the political-economic dependency patterns that pertain to the nineteenth and twentieth centuries.

The chapters are organized according to the more-or-less conventional periods of Turkish history. In Chapter 2, Seven Ağır examines the late Ottoman period (1838–1908), during which the Ottoman Empire began to integrate into the world economy as a "peripheral" country while the world was experiencing its "first globalization era." Zafer Toprak analyzes the modernization efforts of the 1908–1929 period in Chapter 3, at a time when Turkish nationalism was on the rise, along with efforts to create a "national bourgeoisie" under formidable political-economic circumstances. In Chapter 4, M. Erdem Özgür and Eyüp Özveren focus on the "Statist Era" (1929–1947), during which Turkey, like some other underdeveloped countries, found a temporary opportunity to pursue a relatively "independent" path through a protectionist trade regime along with a state-led industrialization strategy. In Chapter 5, Yakup Kepenek elaborates how Turkey, between 1947 and 1960, started retreating from the state-led and relatively independent economic model under strong American influence and guidance, accompanied by populist pressures coming from the rural and the emerging bourgeois segments of society. Ümit Akçay and Oktar Türel, in Chapter 6, evaluate Turkey's ISI experience (1960–1980), which significantly facilitated the growth of national-industrial bourgeoisie, along with the strengthening of industrial labor under relatively more democratic conditions, but later paved the way for a severe political and economic crisis once the global conditions deteriorated. Chapter 7 by Ziya Öniş and Fikret Şenses concentrates on the initiation of the "first-generation" neoliberal reforms in the 1980s, implemented initially under military rule and then under Turgut Özal's governments, culminating in the capital-account liberalization of 1989. Erinç Yeldan, in Chapter 8, explains and discusses how financial openness under the coalition governments of the 1990s, along with the IMF's exchange-rate-based disinflation program, eventually resulted in the biggest crisis in the history of the Turkish economy in 2001. In Chapter 9, covering the 2001–2009 period, Erol Taymaz and Ebru Voyvoda illuminate how the devastating 2001 crisis created the circumstances for the implementation of "second-generation" neoliberal reforms, while at the same time preparing the political ground for AKP's rise to power under favorable global economic conditions, which were prominently instrumental in AKP's political-economic success in its first decade. Korkut Boratav and Özgür Orhangazi, in Chapter 10, analyze the 2009–2020 period when Turkey gradually shifted from neoliberal populism to authoritarian crony capitalism, accompanied by increasing dependence on capital inflows within the problematic context of construction-centered and jobless growth, in conjunction with worsening global political-economic conditions. Eventually, such vulnerabilities led to a serious economic downturn in Turkey, manifested in the 2018 currency crisis and exacerbated by the COVID-19 pandemic, eroding the political support base of AKP. In the concluding Chapter 11, we provide an overall evaluation of the analyses and arguments presented in the preceding chapters and conclude that no matter how Turkey has tried to develop its national capitalism, all it achieved has amounted to a case of uneven and unstable "dependent development."

## Notes

1. The data are taken from IMF's *World Economic Outlook Database* (October 2020) at: https://www.imf.org/en/Publications/WEO/weo-database/2020/October/.
2. Actually, modernization theory refers to a heterogeneous body of theoretical framework that became popular in the 1950s and 1960s, that is, at the peak of the Cold War, concerning the problems of economic, social, and political development and suggesting the poor, newly independent nations to adopt modern values and institutions of the West to help their development. Its antecedents include nineteenth-century sociologists such as Maine, Tonnies, Durkheim, and Weber (Valenzuela & Valenzuela, 1978). Although the modernization theory does not have a homogeneous set of arguments, a principal common claim is that economic development, cultural change, and political change go together in coherent, and to some extent, predictable patterns (Inglehart, 1997). Some proponents of modernization theory were prominent political scientists, such as Gabriel Almond, Bingham Powell, James Coleman, Samuel Huntington, David Apter, and Martin

Lipset, who argued that traditionalism is an expression and cause of underdevelopment, so underdeveloped nations should acquire modern values and institutions in order to make a transition to modernization and development (Handelman, 2005: 12–13). On the other hand, some early development economists are considered as pioneers of economic modernization theory, assuming linear stages of growth. Prior to Rostow (1960), Paul Rosenstein-Rodan (1943), Ragnar Nurkse (1952), and Kurt Mandelbaum (1945) adopted what may be called a modernization-oriented approach. Industrialization was vital, but it could be restricted by domestic institutions and social attitudes (illiteracy, agrarian structure, traditionalism, low division of labor, lack of infrastructure, etc.), which impeded savings rate and investments. They argued that a "big push," that is, heavy investment in infrastructure and state planning, was necessary for igniting and stimulating industrialization. They were mainly influenced by the Harrod-Domar growth model, which emphasized the savings rate and capital intensity for economic growth (Domar, 1946; Harrod, 1939). The "big push" model also created a case for foreign aid to less-developed countries from the advanced ones (mainly the US), in case they lacked domestic savings needed for the "big push" (Millikan & Rostow, 1957). Another influential economist in this line of research was Arthur Lewis (1955), who came up with his dual-sector model, which explained the potential dynamics through which the abundant and cheap labor in the traditional agriculture sector could be utilized to build up a modern industrial sector.

3. See Hirschman (1981) for an apt appraisal of the evolution of development economics until the late 1970s. His classification of development theories is especially noteworthy in this regard, which is based on the assertion/rejection of the mutual-benefit claim and monoeconomics claim. According to this categorization, the neo-Marxist theories, including the dependency theory, are identified as opponents of both of these claims (Hirschman, 1981: 3–5).
4. There are several examples of Marxist criticism against the dependency theory. To mention a few, Johnson (1981) criticized the dependency theory's emphasis on exchange relations rather than production relations, and Edelstein (1981) found fault with the dependency framework for its neglect of the labor processes. On

the other hand, Angotti (1981) disapproved dependency theory for diverting attention from the socialist revolution and reducing the class antagonisms to a struggle among nations. In a similar vein, Brenner (1977) attacked the dependency theory for deviating from classical Marxist analysis.

5. Ray (1973) and Smith (1979) are examples to the "liberal" criticism of the dependency approach.
6. As demonstrated in Table 1 in Kvangraven (2021: 87), various heterodox theories of development have actually used the method ("global historical analysis") and/or some of the core assumptions of the "Dependency Research Programme."
7. The Panic of 1873 is considered as the first truly international economic crisis. The crisis led to a depression that lasted from 1873 to 1879, which coincided with declining international commodity prices and caused many agricultural and industrial producers to suffer losses and face bankruptcies (Lairson & Skidmore, 2003).
8. The Gold Standard system developed in the 1870s when Britain and some other major states fixed the value of their currencies in terms of a specified amount of gold. Then, their currencies were freely convertible at home or abroad into a fixed amount of gold per unit of currency. As a result, an international monetary system, which was built around British management and protection of Britain's own position, evolved.
9. Due to the unprecedented levels of trade and financial interdependence among the world's economies, this era (1870–1913) is usually considered the "first globalization era."
10. The effects of Great Depression triggered a series of coups in Latin America in 1930; first in Bolivia; and then in Peru, Argentina, and Brazil.
11. Yet according to Arrighi (1990), the expansion of the "free enterprise system" at the level of the world economy, that is, freeing the multinational corporations (MNCs) from all previous "vassalage" to state power, had been the most distinctive outcome of the US hegemony, typifying its limit at the same time. Accordingly, the rise of the MNCs has marked the beginning of the end of the Westphalian system of sovereignty, and the beginning along with start of the withering away of the traditional interstate system (Arrighi, 1990: 403).
12. By 1990, the average tariff rate was around 5%.

13. The Non-Alignment Movement started in 1955 at the Bandung Conference when the newly independent countries of Asia and Africa called for abstaining from allying with either of the two superpowers and instead joining together in support of national self-determination against all forms of colonialism and imperialism. The Movement was officially founded and held its first conference in Belgrade in 1961 under the leadership of Josip Broz Tito of Yugoslavia, Gamal Abdel Nasser of Egypt, Jawaharlal Nehru of India, Kwame Nkrumah of Ghana, and Sukarno of Indonesia.

## References

Amin, S. (1974). *Accumulation on a world scale: A critique of the theory of underdevelopment* (B. Pearce, Trans.). Monthly Review Press.

Amin, S. (1976). *Unequal development: An essay on the social formations of peripheral communities*. Monthly Review Press.

Amin, S. (1980). The class structure of the contemporary imperialist system. *Monthly Review, 31*(8), 9–26.

Amin, S. (1983). Expansion or crisis of capitalism? *Third World Quarterly, 5*(2), 361–385.

Angotti, T. (1981). The political implications of dependency theory. *Latin American Perspectives, 8*(3–4), 124–137.

Arrighi, G. (1990). The three hegemonies of historical capitalism. *Review (Fernand Braudel Center), 13*(3), 365–408.

Aydın, Z. (2005). *The political economy of Turkey*. Pluto Press.

Baran, P. (1962). *The political economy of growth*. Monthly Review Press.

Biersteker, T. J. (1992). The 'triumph' of neoclassical economics in the developing world: Policy convergence and bases of governance in the international economic order. In J. Rosenau & E. O. Czempiel (Eds.), *Governance without government: Order and change in world politics* (pp. 102–131). Cambridge University Press.

Boratav, B. (2003). *Türkiye İktisat Tarihi, 1908–2015* (Economic history of Turkey, 1908–2015). İmge Kitabevi.

Bourguignon, F. (2016). Inequality and globalization. *Foreign Affairs, 95*(1), 11–15.

Brenner, R. (1977). The origins of capitalist development: A critique of neo-Smithian Marxism. *New Left Review, 104*, 25.

Cardoso, H. F., & Faletto, E. (1979). *Dependency and development in Latin America* (M. Mattingly Urquidi, Trans.). University of California.

Chandrasekhar, C. P., & Ghosh, J. (2018). A decade of speculation. *The Economic and Labor Relations Review, 29*(4), 410–427.
Chase-Dunn, C., & Grimes, P. (1995). World-systems analysis. *Annual Review of Sociology, 21*, 387–417.
Demiralp, S. (2012). White Turks, black Turks? Faultlines beyond Islamism versus secularism. *Third World Quarterly, 33*(3), 511–524.
Domar, E. (1946). Capital expansion, rate of growth, and employment. *Econometrica, 14*(2), 137–147.
Edelstein, J. C. (1981). Dependency: A special theory within Marxian analysis. *Latin American Perspectives, 8*(3–4), 103–107.
Emmanuel, A. (1972). *Unequal exchange: A study of the imperialism of trade*. Monthly Review Press.
Estevadeordal, A., Frantz, B., & Taylor, A. M. (2003). The rise and fall of world trade, 1870–1939. *The Quarterly Journal of Economics, 118*(2), 359–407.
Evans, P. (1979). *Dependent development: The alliance of multinational. State, and local capital in Brazil*. Princeton University Press.
Firebaugh, G. (2000). The trend in between-nation income inequality. *Annual Review of Sociology, 26*(1), 323–339.
Fischer, A. M. (2015). The end of peripheries? On the enduring relevance of structuralism for understanding contemporary global development. *Development and Change, 46*(4), 700–732.
Frank, A. G. (1966). The development of underdevelopment. *Monthly Review, 18*(4), 17–31.
Frank, A. G. (1967). *Capitalism and underdevelopment in Latin America*. NYU Press.
Frank, A. G. (1978). *World accumulation 1492–1789*. Macmillan.
Furtado, C. (1970). *Economic development of Latin America: A survey from colonial times to the Cuban revolution*. Cambridge University Press.
Gerschenkron, A. (1943). *Bread and democracy in Germany*. University of California Press.
Gerschenkron, A. (1962). *Economic backwardness in historical perspective*. Harvard University Press.
Gülalp, H. (2001). Globalization and political Islam: The social bases of Turkey's Welfare Party. *International Journal of Middle East Studies, 33*(3), 433–448.
Handelman, H. (2005). *The challenge of third world development* (4th ed.). Pearson.
Harrod, R. F. (1939). An essay in dynamic theory. *The Economic Journal, 49*(193), 14–33.
Hickel, J. (2017). Is global inequality getting better or worse? A critique of the World Bank's convergence narrative. *Third World Quarterly, 38*(10), 2208–2222.

Hirschman, A. O. (1981). The rise and decline of development economics. In A. O. Hirschman, *Essays in trespassing—Economics to politics and beyond* (pp. 1–24). Cambridge University Press.

Hobsbawm, E. J. (1987). *The age of empire, 1875–1914*. Vintage Books.

Inglehart, R. (1997). *Modernization and postmodernization: Cultural, economic, and political change in 43 societies*. Princeton University Press.

Johnson, D. L. (1981). Economism and determinism in dependency theory. *Latin American Perspectives, 8*(3–4), 108–117.

Kalaycıoğlu, E. (2012). Kulturkampf in Turkey: The constitutional referendum of 12 September 2010. *South European Society and Politics, 17*(1), 1–22.

Kepenek, Y. (2016). *Türkiye Ekonomisi* (The Turkish economy). Remzi Kitabevi.

Keyder, Ç. (1987). *State and class in Turkey. A study in capitalist development*. Verso.

Kindleberger, C. P. (1973). *The world in depression, 1929–1939*. University of California Press.

Kindleberger, C. P. (1975). The rise of free trade in Western Europe, 1820–1875. *Journal of Economic History, 35*(1), 20–55.

Krasner, S. D. (1976). State power and the structure of international trade. *World Politics: A Quarterly Journal of International Relations, 28*(3), 317–347.

Kvangraven, I. H. (2021). Beyond the stereotype: Restating the relevance of the dependency research programme. *Development and Change, 52*(1), 76–112.

Lairson, T. D., & Skidmore, D. (2003). *International political economy: The struggle for power and wealth*. Thomson/Wadsworth.

Lake, D.A. (2000). British and American hegemony compared: Lessons for the current era of decline. In J. A. Frieden & D. A. Lake (Eds.), *International political economy: Perspectives on global power and wealth* (pp. 127–139). Wadsworth/Thompson Learning.

Lewis, W. A. (1955). *The theory of economic growth*. Allen & Unwin.

Mandelbaum, K. (1945). *The industrialisation of backward areas*. Basil Blackwell.

Marangos, J. (2009). What happened to the Washington Consensus? The evolution of international development policy. *The Journal of Socio-Economics, 38*(1), 197–208.

Mardin, Ş. (1973). Center-periphery relations: A key to Turkish politics? *Daedalus, 102*(1), 169–190.

Martinussen, J. (1997). *Society, state and market: A guide to competing theories of development*. Zed Books.

Millikan, M. F., & Rostow W. W., with the collaboration of Rosenstein-Rodan, P. N. and others at the Center for International Studies, MIT. (1957). *A proposal. Key to an effective foreign policy*. Harper and Brothers

Moore, B. (1967). *Social origins of dictatorship and democracy: Lord and peasant in the making of the modern world*. Penguin.

Nurkse, R. (1952). Some international aspects of the problem of economic development. *The American Economic Review, 42*(2), 571–583.
O'Donnell, G. (1978). Reflections on the patterns of change in the bureaucratic-authoritarian state. *Latin American Research Review, 13*(1), 3–38.
Ould-Mey, M. (1994). Global adjustment: Implications for peripheral states. *Third World Quarterly, 15*(2), 319–336.
Öniş, Z., & Şenses, F. (2005). Rethinking the emerging post-Washington consensus. *Development and Change, 36*(2), 263–290.
Pamuk, Ş. (2018). *Uneven centuries: Turkey's economic development since 1820.* Princeton University Press.
Pearson, F. S., & Payaslian, S. (1999). *International political economy: Conflict and cooperation in the global system.* McGraw-Hill.
Pieterse, J. N. (1988). A critique of world system theory. *International Sociology, 3*(3), 251–266.
Prebisch, R. (1950). *The economic development of Latin America and its principal problems.* United Nations.
Rapley, J. (2007). *Understanding development: Theory and practice in the third world.* Lynne Rienner.
Ray, D. (1973). The dependency model of Latin American underdevelopment: Three basic fallacies. *Journal of Interamerican Studies and World Affairs, 15*(1), 4–20.
Rodrik, D. (2006). Goodbye Washington consensus, hello Washington confusion? A review of the World Bank's economic growth in the 1990s: Learning from a decade of reform. *Journal of Economic Literature, 44*(4), 973–987.
Rosenstein-Rodan, P. N. (1943). Problems of industrialisation of eastern and south-eastern Europe. *The Economic Journal, 53*(210/211), 202–211.
Rostow, W. W. (1960). *The stages of economic growth: A non-communist manifesto.* Cambridge University Press.
Ruggie, J. G. (1982). International regimes, transactions, and change: Embedded liberalism in the postwar economic order. *International Organization, 36*(2), 379–415.
Sachs, J. D. (1999). Twentieth-century political economy: A brief history of global capitalism. *Oxford Review of Economic Policy, 15*(4), 90–101.
Singer, H. (1950). The distribution of gains between investing and borrowing countries. *American Economic Review, 40*(2), 473–485.
Skocpol, T. (1977). Wallerstein's world capitalist system: A theoretical and historical critique. *American Journal of Sociology, 82*(5), 1075–1090.
Slater, D. (2004). *Geopolitics and the post-colonial: Rethinking North-South relations.* Blackwell.
Smith, T. (1979). The underdevelopment of development literature: The case of dependency theory. *World Politics: A Quarterly Journal of International Relations, 31*(2), 247–288.

Spero, J. E. (1977). *The politics of international economic relations*. St. Martin's Press.

Spero, J. E., & Hart, J. A. (2003). *The politics of international economic relations* (6th ed.). Thomson/Wadsworth.

Stiglitz, J. E. (1996). Some lessons from the East Asian miracle. *The World Bank Research Observer, 11*(2), 151–177.

Stiglitz, J. E. (2017). *Globalization and its discontents—Revisited*. W. W. Norton.

Sunkel, O. (1973). Transnational capitalism and national disintegration in Latin America. *Social and Economic Studies, 22*(1), 132–171.

Tausch, A. (2010). Globalisation and development: The relevance of classical "dependency" theory for the world today. *International Social Science Journal, 61*(202), 467–488.

Taffet, J. F. (2007). *Foreign aid as foreign policy*. Routledge.

Tavares, M. (1985). A retomada da hegemonia Americana [The resumption of American hegemony]. *Revista de Economia Política, 5*(2), 5–16.

Valenzuela, J. S., & Valenzuela, A. (1978). Modernization and dependency: Alternative perspectives in the study of Latin American underdevelopment. *Comparative Politics, 10*(4), 535–557.

Vernengo, M. (2006). Technology, finance, and dependency: Latin American radical political economy in retrospect. *Review of Radical Political Economics, 38*(4), 551–568.

Wade, R. H., & Veneroso, F. (1998). The Asian crisis: The high debt model versus the Wall Street-Treasury-IMF complex. *New Left Review, 1*(228), 3–23.

Wallerstein, I. (1974). The rise and future demise of the world capitalist system: Concepts for comparative analysis. *Comparative Studies in Society and History, 16*(4), 387–415.

Wallerstein, I. (1979). *The capitalist world-economy*. Cambridge University Press.

Warren, B. (1973). Imperialism and capitalist industrialization. *New Left Review, 81*(1), 344.

CHAPTER 2

# Peripheralization of the Ottoman Economy, 1838–1908

*Seven Ağır*

## Introduction

The study of the late Ottoman era provides key insights into the various mechanisms through which the region was integrated into the world economy and sheds light on the legacy of that integration for modern Turkey's economic development path. It was during the long nineteenth century that the region first experienced the strong pull of the European markets and eventually turned into a periphery through the formation of commercial, financial, and political linkages with the core of the world economy.[1] This peripheralization happened in ways similar to those experienced by most countries in Latin America and Asia as they were shaped by the changes in the modes of production and capital accumulation at the level of global capitalism.

S. Ağır (✉)
Department of Economics, Middle East Technical University, Ankara, Turkey
e-mail: sevenag@metu.edu.tr



E. Özçelik and Y. Özdemir (eds.), *Political Economy of Development in Turkey*, The Political Economy of the Middle East,
https://doi.org/10.1007/978-981-16-7318-4_2

The pace and nature of the Ottoman/Turkish dependent development, however, were shaped by the unique conditions of the region and the heritage of Ottoman political economy. First, unlike most peripheral regions, Ottoman Empire was not subject to direct colonial rule. The constraints on political sovereignty were imposed covertly through diplomatic pressures against the background of military weaknesses and fiscal fragilities of the Empire. Yet, there was ample room for negotiation at least up until the second half of the nineteenth century. As such, the inner dynamics of Ottoman society are relevant for understanding how and to what extent the Ottoman polity was accommodating the demands of the core regions. Secondly, Ottoman political elite was willing to embrace "modern" institutions and introduced legal and political reforms in an attempt to catch up with the Western powers, albeit in a selective way, throughout the nineteenth century. These reforms against the background of political power asymmetries, embedded in a context of dependent development, led to legal and institutional outcomes that diverged significantly from those of the core regions and had further (and sometimes unintended) consequences for economic development. Thirdly, given its multiethnic demographic structure, economic integration had uneven implications for the Muslim and non-Muslim communities, creating divergences exacerbated by the rise of nationalism and nation building during the later period. This political-economic legacy would also shape the ethnonationalistic tone of the developmental agenda in the early twentieth century.

While Turkey's formal economic institutions and policies underwent a great deal of change during the last century, the late Ottoman era had a long-lasting impact on the latter period. The next section of this chapter focuses on the historical background, with particular attention to major economic actors and institutions prior to the nineteenth century and how they changed throughout the eighteenth century paving the way for the Ottoman incorporation into the European economy. Then, the direct impact of the industrial transformation in the core regions is elaborated, along with a discussion of how the capitalist world economy led to the peripheralization of Ottoman economy. The peripheralization is analyzed in two subsequent periods. In the following section, the period of 1800–1860 is covered to explain Ottoman integration into the world economy through a liberal trade policy adopted in accordance with the convergence of domestic fiscal/military needs and foreign interests. The rise in external terms of trade (the ratio of the price of exports to the price of imports) along with supply-side factors in Ottoman agriculture led to a strong trend of deindustrialization during this period.[2] While the deindustrialization was uneven across regions, it undermined potential backward and forward linkages that foreign direct investment (FDI) could have provided in the latter period. The next section focuses on the period of 1860–1908, when further integration through foreign borrowing and FDI resulted in financial dependency that curtailed political sovereignty in the economic realm and undermined the later attempts of development. Paradoxically, the fall in external terms of trade slowed down and even reversed the deindustrialization trend during this period. Yet, as the core countries moved to the production and export of technologically more complex goods, the temporary industrialization was not sufficient to create a major rupture within the course of dependent development. Rather, both the foreign control of financial resources and the asymmetric legal framework undermined the power of domestic actors whose interests accorded with an alternative course of development. The concluding section presents the broader impact of the Ottoman peripheralization on political-economic power dynamics at societal level and its long-term implications for the nature of dependent development in modern Turkey.

## Historical Background

Pioneering in Britain, the industrial revolution started a new era in the global history of capitalism. The ever increasing output of British manufactured goods, in particular cotton textiles, led to an export boom that created a new division of labor in the world economy. Broadly speaking, the era can be divided into two parts. During the first half of the nineteenth century (or more specifically, the period from the 1820s to 1860s), the British exports grew at an unprecedented rate. The search for new markets for British manufactured goods was justified with liberal ideas that were embraced by the majority of politicians and intellectuals who advocated that the right recipe for economic growth and development was free trade, both at home and abroad. While the British search for raw materials and markets for manufactured goods led to the colonization of many regions in Asia, Latin America, and Africa, the British diplomats pushed for free trade in other regions, leading to a series of free trade treaties to cut down import tariffs and internal customs duties. In the second part of the era (1860s–1900s), industrialization took off in other core countries, such as France, Germany, Austria, and the United States.

The political-economic rivalry among the core countries was intensified by the spread of modern technologies in transportation, in particular railways and steamships, which were introduced to the less-developed regions mostly through FDI. As the industrial transformation in core regions were diversified to include chemicals, electricity, and communication technologies, FDI was channeled also to support domestic industries in the periphery, forging new forms of dependency in the spheres of finance and politics.

How was the Ottoman economy affected by these global trends? To answer this question, we first need to briefly present the social and economic conditions in the Ottoman Empire prior to the opening up of trade in the nineteenth century. Such a retrospective synopsis will help us show that the pace and nature of the Ottoman incorporation into the world economy was not unilaterally determined by external forces, and that the domestic political and economic institutions were also instrumental in shaping the ways through which the Ottoman economy was integrated into global capitalism. Secondly, it will also help us understand how the distribution of economic and political power in Ottoman society was reconfigured by European trade expansion at its initial stages. In this way, we will be able to explore what these changes implied for the positioning of different social groups with respect to their attitudes toward and roles in dependent development.

### *Decline of the Guilds and Janissaries*[3]

In order to understand how the Ottoman economy was integrated into the world economy in the nineteenth century, we need to take a look at the major actors, and the institutions within which they operated. As the empire spanned three continents, it is difficult to talk about homogenous characteristics and generalizable patterns. Yet, there were some distinguishing elements of Ottoman political economy, which were relevant from a comparative perspective. First, in terms of the degree and nature of foreign trade, the Ottoman economy was not yet substantially integrated into the European economy by the end of the eighteenth century.[4] During the eighteenth century, the volume of Ottoman foreign trade, especially with the French, was on the rise. Increasing foreign trade not only led to the growth of the major port cities, but also raised the number of foreign merchants residing in these ports, who had connections with local merchants and familiarity with the Ottoman administrative practices. More importantly, this trade expansion brought dramatic changes for the "intermediate group consisting of non-Muslim traders and financiers" (Eldem, 1999: 12). But, the eighteenth-century Ottoman-European trade was a small fraction of the total volume of Ottoman trade, while its composition was diverse and its impact was localized. As such, the expansion of foreign trade did not result in a division of labor that could be depicted as a "center-periphery" relationship whereby the center produces and exports high value-added manufactured goods while the periphery specializes in low value-added raw materials and primary products. Nevertheless, the trade expansion led to agricultural commercialization and changes in modes of production along with a rise in merchant capital in certain parts of the Ottoman Empire. These changes were relevant for understanding the ways through which the Ottoman economy was integrated into the world economy and are explained in detail in the next section.

During the sixteenth, seventeenth, and eighteenth centuries, the state intervened to regulate the circulation of goods within the Empire through various means such as internal duties, preemptive purchasing licenses, price controls, and export bans in line with the objective of provisioning the needs of the urban centers. Manufacturing activity was mostly organized around craftsmen organizations known as guilds. Barriers to entry were central to the functioning of the guild system: In order to open a shop or operate an itinerant business in any sector, one needed to become a member of the relevant guild. Membership was restricted through various means, such as the requirement of formal apprenticeship, the imposition of an entry fee, and the existence of a *numerus fixus* (a fixed membership size). In the Ottoman Empire, the most straightforward tool for restricting entry was a legal code that limited the number of individuals or stalls that were allowed to operate in a certain branch of business and in a certain district. This legal code, known as *inhisar-ı bey ü şira* (or *inhisar*), was in effect in all sectors until the last decade of the eighteenth century and prevented people outside the guilds from legally pursuing any trade or craft in urban areas. In retail sectors, *inhisar* served to regulate demand for inputs and supply of outputs, thus enabling control over prices and profits. Taking an active role in the allocation of factors of production and intermediate goods, guild administration had both monopsonistic and monopolistic power, by way of which it was authorized to set the price of final commodities at just levels, ensuring both the livelihood of the guild members and the well-being of the consumers.

Of course, it is questionable whether the guilds were ever able to regulate handicraft production and retail shop-keeping as effectively in practice as the legal regulations called for. There was considerable variation as to the extent of autonomy and profit-making capacities of the individual members. The archival evidence indicates that there were many practices challenging and circumventing the regulations, including the increasing volume of contraband trade in the eighteenth century. There is, however, no doubt that these regulations constituted barriers to entry that rendered production and trade in certain sectors more costly for potential entrants. Otherwise, urban craftsmen and tradesmen in guilds would not have rigorously organized and claimed the right of exclusive dealing in their sector prior to the nineteenth century. In the Ottoman Empire, guild members' efforts to prevent entry are documented to have surged especially in times of economic contraction, as was the case in the seventeenth and eighteenth centuries. During this period, organized craftsmen and tradesmen solicited charters limiting the number of legitimate businesses in their respective sectors, prohibiting potential entrants within a certain geographical area.

The power of guild regulations was embedded in the peculiar dynamics of the Ottoman urban life. The Janissaries, originally an elite section of the infantry corps, started to integrate into urban commercial life during the seventeenth century. The fact that guild members were able to acquire Janissary status, while the Janissaries were able to acquire licenses issued for practicing crafts and trades (*gediks*), resulted in the coalescence of these two groups. While there were many complaints about Janissary involvement in the urban economy, it was difficult to distinguish between Janissary and non-Janissary factions in most guilds by the late eighteenth century. Furthermore, due to fiscal decentralization, and in particular the practice of tax farming, administrative positions in most guilds and the offices of market supervision came to be held by those with military titles. On many occasions Janissaries employed coercive methods to circumvent existing rules and regulations in commercial life for their own advantage. In other words, the corps had become "an institutional base by which various urban elements tried to protect their privileges and interests against the ruling elite" (Sunar, 2006: 1). This integration of the Janissaries with urban elements enabled the guilds to enjoy more autonomy, limiting the efforts of the central administration to reorganize the economy. In fact, guild members played a significant role in the popular riots of the eighteenth century, including the one that led to the dethronement and death of Sultan Selim III, who attempted to abolish the Janissary corps and remove entry barriers during his tumultuous reign.

This guild-Janissary coalition started to weaken in the early decades of the nineteenth century; yet it was not primarily the market forces that seem to have played a role in the decline of guilds, unlike in the case of Northwestern Europe. As long-distance trade expanded and market-supporting institutions emerged in Europe, medieval guilds had lost prominence. In the Ottoman Empire, proto-industrialization that might have undermined guild-imposed regulations was confined to rural regions in the Balkans. It is true that the trade expansion of the eighteenth century, in particular the rising demand for agricultural commodities, led to the rise of large agricultural estates and the growing scale of commercialization in the western parts of the Empire (Frangakis-Syrett, 1988; Kasaba, 1988; Stoianovich, 1960). In line with the rise of these wealthy notables and merchant networks, as well as in response to the pressures on the traditional redistributive mechanisms (Ağır, 2013), the Ottoman political elite developed a more tolerant attitude toward removing controls over internal trade and recognizing private property on land. The Ottoman government had also its own reasons to undermine the autonomy of the guilds. Nineteenth century witnessed the intensification of Ottoman rulers' efforts to centralize and modernize the fiscal and economic realms. Such efforts were at odds with the restrictions associated with the traditional prerogatives of the guilds. In particular, Mahmud II's reforms, the centralization of previously tax-farmed offices concerning marketplace regulations, reduced the guild-Janissary coalition's control over the urban economy. Increasing foreign competition during the early nineteenth century also undermined guilds' restrictions on access to both input and output markets. In fact, guild members, including the armed Janissaries, attacked foreigners' shops and quarters in Istanbul on several occasions. In 1826, the Janissary corps were abolished, which led to the elimination, albeit temporarily, of such a resistance against foreign competition.

### *Rise of Legal Extraterritoriality*[5]

Foreign merchants in the Ottoman Empire had long enjoyed extraterritorial privileges thanks to the capitulations signed with European powers. These privileges allowed foreign merchants to use consular jurisdiction (rather than Ottoman sharia courts) in both civil and commercial disputes involving issues such as enforcing contracts and collecting debts. Such disputes were addressed not in Ottoman sharia courts but in consular courts in line with the privileges granted in capitulations. During the eighteenth and nineteenth centuries, increasing trade with the West made appeals to this extraterritorial jurisdiction much more common. As new commercial laws were enacted in their home countries, European merchants and bureaucrats justified these extraterritorial exemptions by claiming that local legal institutions were "backward" in the Ottoman Empire (Kayaoğlu, 2010: 18). The ensuing consular interference in Ottoman legal affairs and the circumvention of local courts, even in cases involving Ottoman subjects, led to serious political concern by the late eighteenth century.[6] In this context, like in other semi-colonial cases, legal reform was seen as the key for ending extraterritoriality and achieving full legal sovereignty (Hussin, 2016; Singh, 2019). The legal reforms of the *Tanzimat* era (1839–1876) were also part and parcel of a swing toward secularization during the nineteenth century (Toprak, 2020). Ağır and Artunç (2021) show, however, that the legal reforms in the second half of the nineteenth century, including the outright borrowing from the French Commercial Code in 1850, were not able to prevent foreign merchants' claims to consular jurisdiction.

What made these extraterritorial privileges especially concerning for the Ottoman government was non-Muslim Ottoman subjects' access to them. European ambassadors extended these privileges to local non-Muslims by selling "letters of protection" called *berats*.[7] The *berats* placed their holders out of Islamic courts' reach and granted access to European jurisdictions. In this way, the extraterritorial privileges became available to non-Muslims as the sale of the protegee status turned out to be common during the eighteenth century. The extraterritoriality enabled wealthy non-Muslims, who owned and managed the older and more experienced businesses in the region, to "exit" Ottoman law through their access to European consular courts (Ağır & Artunç, 2021). Their legal privileges associated with the capitulations, such as access to foreign jurisdiction and exemption from customs duties, had constituted one (although not necessarily the most important) reason behind non-Muslim communities' domination of large-scale commercial and financial activities. By the late eighteenth century, non-Muslim Ottomans, especially Greeks, with the aid of European extraterritorial protection, set up firms with partners in London, France, Italy, and the Black Sea so as to emerge as the central group in the Ottoman-European trade (Artunç, 2015; de

Beaujour, 1800: 288; Ubicini, 1856: 350–351). Their widening connections with European trade networks and increasing access to European courts familiarized them with European law. Some even set up joint-stock companies for carrying out textile trade (Stoianovich, 1960: 257). By the early 1800s, the French law had become the customary law for non-Muslim Ottoman merchants, who benefitted from the Napoleonic commercial code both at home and abroad (Pepelasis, 1959: 178). This difference between Muslims and non-Muslims, in terms of both their participation in trade networks and familiarity with the foreign institutions, had long-term consequences, which we will discuss in the last section.

## Peripheralization: Deindustrialization, Fast and Slow

As explained above, the increasing volume and the changing structure of Ottoman foreign trade did not result in the peripheralization of the Ottoman economy prior to the nineteenth century. However, the nineteenth century brought about a different story in this respect. During the Napoleonic Wars in the early nineteenth century, the share of French trade had decreased. Subsequently, Britain emerged as the major trading partner of the Ottoman Empire, contributing to the rise in the volume of Ottoman foreign trade. What enabled this trade expansion was the industrial transformation that led to huge productivity rises in Manchester's cotton textiles, which later spread to other regions and sectors. As industrialization enabled Britain to produce much higher levels of manufactured goods at lower prices, the British exports started to grow at historically unexampled rates. There were, however, two types of barriers constraining this trade expansion: foreign governments' regulations preventing free trade and high transportation costs. In the 1830s, the British government pursued an aggressive foreign policy, including both diplomatic endeavors and military threats, to overcome the first barrier. In the 1860s, the spread of modern technologies in transportation to less-developed regions, mostly through FDI, relieved the second constraint.

During the first period (1800–1860), the British power, although challenged by the first set of latecomers such as the French and the German, was still in a hegemonic position. Also, during this period, global terms of trade were in favor of manufactured goods, undermining the traditional industries[8] and leading to a fast wave of deindustrialization in less-developed regions around the world. The latter period (1860–1914) brought about two changes in the capitalist world economy: First, global terms of trade shifted in favor of agricultural goods as the manufacturing wages rose in the industrialized core and thus led to the weakening and sometimes even reversal of deindustrialization pressures in the periphery. Secondly, economic, financial, and political competition among core regions intensified as industrial manufacturing spread to other European countries. This competition created more channels through which the periphery came to be integrated into the world economy, providing both new constraints and opportunities for latecomers in terms of their ability to maneuver vis-à-vis their dependent position. This was also the period during which British liberalism lost its ideological dominance and protectionist ideas took a hold in the peripheral regions, leading to the rise of a new discourse of "developmentalism." In line with this broad periodization, this section focuses mainly on the strong pattern of deindustrialization.

## A Period of Strong Deindustrialization: 1800–1860

During this period, like in many other regions in Asia and Latin America, the Middle East opened up as a market for the ever increasing output of British manufactured goods. In the early nineteenth century, the declining power of the guilds in the Ottoman Empire had already made it easier for foreign merchants to compete for domestic markets and resources. The domestic trade restrictions, in particular preemptive purchasing rights of the state agents (*yed-I vahid*), however, still stood on the way of the sale of Ottoman raw materials to foreign merchants and had become an issue for them. The British government had already begun to play a more active role to support British merchants' interests through its consular representatives, who were previously paid by the Levant Company (Owen, 2009: 89). In the 1830s, domestic social problems, such as the rise of Chartism against the rise in urban unemployment, contributed to the British determination to "export abroad the same self-regulating system which was transforming British society" (Cain & Hopkins, 1986: 523).[9] Lord Palmerston, the Foreign Secretary, was among those who were well aware of "the presence of European and American competition and of the urgent need for new markets for industry and commerce in the underdeveloped world" (Cain & Hopkins, 1986: 523). Utilizing Ottoman dependence on British military and political support, Palmerston was able convince the Ottoman government to sign the Balta Limanı Treaty of 1838, which firmly abolished all monopolies in domestic trade, exempted British merchants from internal customs duty, and reduced the autonomy of Ottoman government in imposing unilateral import tariffs.

In the Ottoman-Turkish economic history, the Balta Limanı Treaty is usually considered to be a watershed event as it stood as an obvious indicator of the Ottoman surrender to British economic liberalism. In fact, as the above-discussed legal extraterritoriality indicates, foreign consular intervention in commercial matters had already been prevalent in the Ottoman Empire. Furthermore, the previous administrative and fiscal reforms had already undermined institutions supporting the internal barriers to trade.[10] In fact, this treaty was not even the first free trade treaty signed by the Ottomans (Kasaba, 1993: 220). The 1829 Treaty of Adrianople had already granted the Russian merchants freedom of commerce and navigation in Ottoman lands and seas, while the 1830 treaty signed with the United States had similar stipulations and contributed to the expansion of American trade in Ottoman opium. As such, the Balta Limanı Treaty did not represent a drastic rupture in terms of the Ottoman attitudes toward foreign trade (Pamuk, 1987: 20). Rather, it marks a change in terms of the priorities of British foreign policy as Britain took a firm stand against the expansionist ambitions of France and Russia through a commitment to maintaining the territorial integrity of the Ottoman Empire (Kasaba, 1993: 221).

In fact, foreign trade with Britain had already increased dramatically before 1838: "British exports to the empire had doubled in value during the late 1820s and doubled again before 1837" (Quataert, 1994: 825). But, the timing and the content of the treaty reveal how and to what extent Ottoman integration with the world economy matched up with the global patterns of nineteenth-century peripheralization. In many ways, the Balta Limanı Treaty was similar to the Nanking Treaty of 1842, signed between Britain and China at the end of the first Opium War. Both treaties reflected the British desire to spread free trade across the globe. This desire was intensified with the social problems in England in the 1830s. Yet, the negotiations and the outcomes were shaped by the interaction of domestic conditions. The Balta Limanı Treaty was more comprehensive than the Nanking Treaty, albeit the latter was signed after an armed conflict with the British and seemed harsher as it contained some punitive clauses (Kasaba, 1993: 217):

> The Balta Limani Treaty declared the foreign merchants and their agents equal to their Ottoman counterparts in all respects. It prohibited all government monopolies, outlawed locally imposed surcharges, and specified the rate and manner of collection of import, export, transit, and local duties. All these provisions were to be valid in all the possessions of the empire and were to cover all its subjects. (Kasaba, 1993: 218)

The Ottomans were more accommodating toward the British, as compared to the Chinese, because of the economic and political developments of the eighteenth century, in particular the expansion of the Ottoman-European trade, which created a political and social environment in favor of liberal ideas. In the eighteenth century, the growing export market for agricultural commodities had already contributed to the rise of wealthy notables and merchant networks in the western parts of the Empire. Rather than resisting these changes, by the early nineteenth century, the Ottoman central administration was inclined to cooperate and coordinate with these groups in order to contain social change. Accordingly, it took a series of steps that favored markets and free trade, including "partial deregulation of grain prices, relaxation of the central bureaucracy's monopsonistic privileges over some food stuffs and raw materials, and the growing, though de facto, recognition of both private property in land and the legitimacy of accumulated wealth" (Kasaba, 1993: 219). These rather liberal attitudes were also consistent with a multitude of political concerns that the Ottoman state had, regarding how to solve provisioning problems and encourage agricultural production (Ağır, 2013).

Following the Balta Limanı Treaty, the Ottoman Empire signed similar treaties with other European powers. While these free trade treaties themselves did not represent a turning point in terms of Ottoman foreign-trade policy, they contributed to further incorporation of the Ottoman economy into the European one as evidenced by foreign trade statistics: In the first half of the nineteenth century, British trade with the Levant (the total value of goods imported and exported) rose more than tenfold (Owen, 2009: 87). In the 1840s, France's industrialization took off and its import of raw materials, such as silk and cotton, rose substantially, leading to an almost 50 percent increase in the value of foreign trade with the Levant (Owen, 2009: 86–87). As Owen (2009: 87) notes, "[g]iven the fact that the price of most manufactured goods was falling during this period, the increase in European trade in volume terms was correspondingly larger." More importantly, "the move to liberal policies in the Ottoman Empire between the 1830s and the 1850s deepened the de-industrialization shock" (Pamuk & Williamson, 2011: 165).

By the 1850s, Ottoman markets were flooded with European manufactured goods. At the same time, foreign demand for Ottoman raw materials needed to produce these manufactures increased significantly. Domestic production, especially in sectors such as cotton and woolen textiles, was severely affected by foreign competition. Unable to adopt foreign technologies and preserve their privileged access to input markets, many traditional artisans such as spinners, weavers, and dyers were forced out of business. However, the literature provides some evidence challenging the portrayal of complete demise of traditional manufacturing in the wake of the influx of European manufactured goods (Owen, 2009: 93). There were areas which were exceptions to the strong deindustrialization pattern, such as the upland, mountainous areas of Ottoman Bulgaria, where the barriers of geography and local conditions favored domestic manufactures (Palairet, 1997: 66–84). Nevertheless, the long-term changes in the external terms of trade are consistent with the strong deindustrialization pattern until the late 1860s as the price of Ottoman manufactured imports fell far faster than the price of Ottoman exported primary products (Pamuk & Williamson, 2011: 165).[11]

Another indicator of deindustrialization is the dramatic collapse in the share of domestic consumption supplied by local sources (versus foreign imports) in textile manufactures. Looking at the share of domestic producers in textile production in a comparative framework, Pamuk and Williamson note that the Ottoman Empire had one of the most dramatic deindustrialization episodes among peripheral regions of the world economy until the 1870s (Pamuk & Williamson, 2011: 168). Moreover, this trend of deindustrialization was not evenly distributed across time and space. Penetration of foreign trade was confined mainly to coastal regions until railways expanded into the interior during the second half of the nineteenth century. Some parts, especially central and eastern Anatolia, remained quite unaffected, at least until the spread of railways later in the century. Also, deindustrialization slowed down and was even reversed to some extent in certain manufacturing sub-sectors in the later period, during which terms of trade deteriorated. For instance, the output of the weaving sector increased and factory production of yarn and cloth began to grow in certain regions of the Empire, such as Bulgaria and Macedonia (Lapavitsas, 2006; Palairet, 1997: 243–297, 346–356).

Nevertheless, deindustrialization was stronger compared to other regions during this period (Pamuk, 1987: 37).

The booming terms of trade clearly contributed to Ottoman deindustrialization as they pulled labor and other resources out of industry (and non-tradable sectors) and into the export sector. But, as Pamuk and Williamson (2011: 174) argue, the rise in the prices of exported consumer goods could also lead to a rise in the nominal wage, thus eroding competitiveness of domestic producers with foreign producers in import-competing sectors. In fact, Pamuk and Williamson (2011: 175) show that there was indeed a rapid rise in the wage in manufacturing, especially compared with the wage in commodity export sector, explaining the significant rise in the consumer price index (CPI) (dominated by foodstuffs) between 1800 and 1860. These figures support the argument that, along with global price movements, the supply-side conditions further diminished Ottoman wage competitiveness in manufacturing.

This deindustrialization trend seems to have slowed down starting with the 1870s. Per-capita exports from the Ottoman Empire expanded "at rates close to but lower than those of per capita world trade and per capita center-periphery trade" (Pamuk, 1987: 37). The importation of foreign techniques and availability of cheaper intermediary goods (such as yarn) might have partially contributed to the success of local industry in resisting the deindustrialization dynamics (Quataert, 1994: 889). But, the slowing down of deindustrialization closely followed the changes in the terms of trade, suggesting that the resistance of Ottoman manufacturing after the 1870s can be explained by the dynamics of world economy rather than successful attempts at catching up. After the 1870s, the external terms of trade moved against the Ottoman exports as the price of manufactures imports increased, reducing both the pull of domestic resources into agriculture and the competitiveness of the imported manufactures (Pamuk & Williamson, 2011: 170–175). Nevertheless, this slowing down of deindustrialization did not provide an opportunity for a significant repositioning of the Ottoman economy within the world economy, and there were several reasons for this lack of an upward shift.[12] First, the relief was temporary as it was driven by the rise of costs in the core regions; permanent improvements in the cost competitiveness of Ottoman manufactures seemed unlikely given both the factor endowments (low level of urban population and lack of domestic capital) and the technological upgrading in core regions. Secondly, the regions where indigenous industrial businesses frequently located (the regions which had the potential to benefit more from the favorable terms of trade along with other factors) would remain outside the borders of the Empire soon.

## The Era of FDI: 1860–1908

Along with the deterioration of external terms of trade, the second part of the nineteenth century witnessed two trends intensifying the Ottoman integration into the world economy. First, Ottoman reformers became more interested in introducing foreign institutions and laws during this period as they wanted to circumvent the interferences of the European states on the grounds of "institutional backwardness." Underlying these reforms was also the belief that emulating these institutions would help the Ottoman economy to catch up with the more developed countries. The legal and institutional reforms did not however level the playing ground, but rather served the interests of the foreign powers and domestic elite who were complicit in extending the realm of foreign domination. Secondly, the financial sector had been one of the major areas of growth in core countries during second half of the nineteenth century. In Europe, new institutions for mobilizing domestic savings emerged, and with their higher appetite for risk, many of these concentrated on foreign lending. Foreign investment in railways and steamships could also serve as a channel for expanding heavy industries that benefited most from economies of scale. This expansion of foreign financial resources coincided with the fiscal and military troubles in the Ottoman Empire, along with a desire to invest in public infrastructure. The results were the emergence of many foreign corporations with concessions in Ottoman lands, increasing indebtedness and financial insolvency of the Ottoman state, and the consequent loss of political autonomy over financial matters, like in many other peripheral regions. While these forces contributed to further and fuller integration of the Ottoman economy into the global one, this period also witnessed the rise of actors and ideas that dissented about the external dependency of the Empire. In a broad chronological narrative, three major trends are explained and discussed in this section: (i) the rise of foreign corporations with concessions, (ii) foreign borrowing and financial dependency, and (iii) the emergence of a reactive (developmental) discourse.

### *Foreign Corporations with Concessions*

During the second half of the nineteenth century, Ottoman government introduced modern institutions such as banks and corporations through legal reforms. These institutional innovations were part of a larger package of reforms (the Reform Decree of 1856), which was initiated as a result of the new turn in the relations between the Empire and Europe right after the Crimean War (1853–1856): In return for guarantees extended by France and England for the territorial integrity of the Empire and its admission into the league of European nations, the Ottoman state promised to introduce legal, administrative and financial reforms. Such integration of Ottoman polity with the European system, however, "was to be realized on western terms, and would entail the right of Great Powers to interfere in the internal matters of the Empire for the safeguard of the reforms, particularly protection of non-Muslims" (Eldem, 2005: 433). Rather than mobilizing domestic savings toward industry, these institutions became vehicles for FDI and external borrowing, paving the way for not only military modernization but also huge projects in transportation, communications, and public utilities sectors. A survey of corporate charters shows that most of the companies established during this period were European corporations, which secured special concessions such as monopoly power or profit guarantees from the Ottoman government to undertake public projects (Gökatalay, 2015; Toprak, 2012). Such practices were not unique to the Ottoman Empire. Income and loan guarantees were staple features of concessions to attract foreign capital for financing railroads (and other public projects) in many other developing economies, where domestic private savings were insufficient to undertake such large-scale investments (Bogart & Chaudhary, 2012; Eichengreen, 1995).

The Ottoman government viewed these public projects, especially transportation, as priorities to help national markets emerge and facilitate industrialization. Given the apparent lack of financial and entrepreneurial capital in the Empire, foreign investment was seen as the key to these objectives (Geyikdağı, 2011). Many foreign companies were backed by European governments that were interested in these projects for both economic and strategic reasons, given the background of rising competition among themselves, along with the objective of expanding their influence abroad. There were also many intermediaries involved in bribing or lobbying Ottoman officials in return for securing concessions. Ottoman subjects, mostly high-ranking Muslim bureaucrats and non-Muslim financiers, participated as board members in foreign corporations, but rarely established enterprises on their own.[13] There is little evidence that Muslim merchant families, who set up large-scale businesses, used these new legal institutions.[14] As Toprak (2012: 136) shows, Muslim merchants mostly preferred partnerships to joint-stock companies prior to 1908. Prominent Muslim businesspeople mostly acted as intermediaries between foreign companies and the government, for instance, by acquiring special concessions for these firms rather than creating their own (Cora, 2013). Their ability to participate in local politics and combine functions of an Ottoman official with that of an established businessperson provided them with a distinct advantage in such endeavors (Dimitriadis, 2013). As such, there were not many Muslim entrepreneurs who used novel forms of business organization and thus benefitted from improvements in company law. In contrast, those who could potentially set up large-scale enterprises had little need to do it under Ottoman law. The emergent capitalist-industrialist class of the Ottoman Empire, such as the family firms of Macedonia, was distinctly non-Muslim (Dimitriadis, 2013: 38–39; Lapavitsas & Çakıroğlu, 2019). But they continued to exercise their "exit" option extensively (Lapavitsas & Çakıroğlu, 2019: 132–134). As such, the continuation of extraterritorial privileges despite legal reforms undermined the demand for legal reform, especially by those who would be more likely to benefit from it (Ağır & Artunç, 2021).

An important result of the rising FDI was the expansion of railway networks. Although a large area remained without railways, the construction of railroad lines between one of the major ports of Anatolia and its hinterland (i.e., İzmir-Aydın and İzmir-Kasaba railways constructed by the French and the British from 1857 to 1872) contributed to the further integration of Ottoman Empire into the global economy. Since railroads depended completely on foreign investment, rather than serving the creation of a national market, they fostered links with the major European trade networks in line with foreign-trade interests (Coşar & Demirci, 2009). As such, they helped boost the expansion of agricultural production and commercialization, in particular in Western Anatolia. They also contributed to the widening of European presence in Ottoman economic life: "By the end of the 1860s, a third of the agricultural land around Izmir belonged to Europeans" (Owen, 2009: 113–114). With the opening of the Suez Canal in 1869 and the launch of the German ventures, the expansion of railroad networks started to move toward the Basra region, which was thus connected to the southern Anatolian ports such as Mersin and Iskenderun. Concessionary railway contracts signed with foreign corporations, along with the extraterritorial privileges, caused serious political concern on the part of the Empire. But their persistence and further expansion were inextricably linked to the Empire's integration to the world economy, albeit in an unequal manner. In the 1850s and 1860s, the Ottoman government was able to play the competing European interests against each other in negotiations and achieve relatively more favorable terms in concessions to foreign corporations. But, the financial dependence that resulted from external-debt accumulation would restrict what the Ottoman government could potentially achieve in its dealings with the European powers in the later period.

### *Financial Dependency*

The Ottoman government had already great difficulties in terms of fiscal matters prior to the nineteenth century. As Karaman and Pamuk (2010) show, due to the high shares of intermediaries, Ottoman fiscal revenues lagged behind those of the other states in the seventeenth and eighteenth centuries. However, the Ottoman administration responded to military defeats and achieved significant increases in central revenues through the creation of new fiscal tools during the nineteenth century. Nevertheless, the rising military pressures, along with the availability of opportunities to borrow at favorable terms, led to the first Ottoman foreign borrowing in the mid-nineteenth century.

When the government took its first external loan in 1854 during the Crimean War, the conditions of the borrowing were "exceptionally favorable" to the Ottomans due to "the political context of the time, with an awoved desire of Britain and France to finance their ally" (Eldem, 2005: 434). In a couple of years, however, the subsequent loans could only be ensured through a firm foreign control over the Ottoman finances (Eldem, 2005: 436). As the Ottoman statesmen perceived the risks involved in foreign financial control, they tried to maneuver in an effort to minimize the risk of being completely ruled by a European power. For instance, when the Ottoman government decided to grant a concession to the Ottoman Bank for a new loan in 1862, it required that an equal amount of French capital be included alongside the existing British capital (Eldem, 2005: 437). Nevertheless, continuing wars and the need to upgrade military technology led to an enormous rise in expenses, as a result of which foreign borrowing became a regular policy. In due course, the terms of the loans "signaled a gradual shift of Ottoman indebtedness toward a rather sterile and self-defeating pattern" as most of these new loans were used for financing the budget deficit and paying the interest on the previous debt (Eldem, 2005: 437–438).

The Ottoman government continued to borrow in increasing amounts and at even worse terms, given the rising cost of military campaigns and the local revolts, in addition to the Russian attacks during the second half of the nineteenth century. The increasing level of indebtedness eventually resulted in the formal "bankruptcy" of the Empire in 1875. The establishment of the Ottoman Public Debt Administration (OPDA, *Düyûn-ı Umûmiye*) in 1881 transferred state's major revenue sources to European management and enabled direct interventions with and investments in the Ottoman markets. The OPDA, which was mainly controlled by private European creditors, acted as the primary supporter of concessions.[15] Having lost its fiscal and economic discretion, the Ottoman state had little bargaining power. As such, the foundation of OPDA changed the nature of financial relations between the West and the Ottoman Empire in a radical way. Some scholars interpreted this change as a form of imperial control:

> A steady flow of western capital started to penetrate the Ottoman market at an increasing rate, and most of all, in ways that entailed a greater control over some of the most crucial sectors of the economy. In short, from the 1890s on, Ottoman integration with Europe had started to take a substantially different course, much akin to imperialism. (Eldem, 2005: 443)

The Ottoman case, characterized by huge indebtedness, fiscal bankruptcy, and the eventual loss of financial autonomy during this period, was not an exception at the level of the world economy. For most of the nineteenth century, many Latin American countries waged wars, which they also financed through heavy foreign borrowing. The availability of European investors, interested in the risky but lucrative bonds of these less-developed countries, was mainly the result of the financial expansion in the core countries. The new credit and finance companies in London and Paris were operating in a competitive framework, looking for new venues that promised higher returns to a wider range of investors (Owen, 2009: 102). As the indebted countries faced severe debt-service problems, however, they had to agree on new and more unfavorable terms for the settlement of their debts. Given the asymmetry of power between the debtors and creditors, the lenders went further and seized direct control of the fiscal revenues of many indebted countries, including the Ottoman Empire (Birdal, 2010: 1). In addition to the retrenchment of policy autonomy in fiscal matters, the creation of OPDA had significant implications for the Ottoman incorporation into the world economy. First, a significant portion of the loans managed by the OPDA was allocated to the infrastructural development of the Empire through the construction of railways, and hence contributed to the further integration of the Ottoman provinces into the world economy. Secondly, the OPDA also restructured the export-oriented sectors of the Ottoman economy and hence contributed to the gradual dissolution of subsistence production and boosted the external trade of the Empire during the1890s (Birdal, 2010).

While further integration through the management of the OPDA primarily served European economic interests, there were also some gains for the Ottoman government. There is no consensus among Ottoman economic historians regarding the economic benefits of the railways. Yet, taking a look at the data for the 1889–1914 period, Eldem (1994: 93) argues that the increase in taxes collected by the government due to the expansion of the railway system was substantially larger than the payments made to the Anatolian Railway Company. Secondly, the OPDA did not always act in line with the general policies of their governments. As the interests of their bondholders were closely tied to the performance of the Ottoman economy, sometimes they took positions in accordance with the interests of the Ottoman state: "For instance, while foreign merchants and governments pressed for lower tariffs on European goods and the extension of the tax privileges granted to foreign subjects, the OPDA asked for trade protection and the abolishment of tax privileges for foreigners" (Birdal, 2010: 175). Thirdly, as Birdal (2010: 173–174) shows, the OPDA initiated various administrative and technological transfers that contributed to the development and modernization of state entrepreneurship in the Empire, which would be later inherited by the Turkish Republic. In other words, the OPDA "brought about not only a weaker state apparatus but also a more efficient one in terms of facilitating the operations of the world economy" (Birdal, 2010: 9). All in all, however, the OPDA contributed to the intensification of unequal exchange between the core countries and the Ottoman Empire. The net capital outflow observed in the first decade of the 1900s was mostly "due to the high level of repatrieted profits following a major wave of investment," which indicated that the OPDA served to assure the transfer of resources from the periphery to the core (Birdal, 2010: 94–95).

Financial dependency had also some broader implications for the political and social structure of the periphery. In Western Europe, wars, or more broadly speaking interstate rivalry, had played a historical role in the institutional development of the state (Tilly, 1975); whereas in peripheral countries, they did not have the same effect. Because the peripheral states had alternative sources of finance as a result of their financial integration into the world economy, they could "escape the coerced extraction of resources from the domestic economy" (Centeno, 1997). What scholars suggest for Latin American states might also hold for other peripheral regions, including the Ottoman Empire: Due to the reliance on external debt, the rivalries and wars had little impact on promoting state capacity.[16] As a result, the constraints on the sovereign were not imposed by the internal dynamics of the country but rather from outside, enabling the state to regain access to foreign capital markets with lower risk premiums rather than achieving a sustainable rise in fiscal capacity.[17]

### *Emergence of a Protectionist Discourse*

External dependency had two legal-institutional pillars that undermined Ottoman sovereignty: the legal extraterritoriality and the foreign concessions. Both of these factors gave rise to serious concerns on the part of Ottoman statemen and intellectuals by the 1860s. The Ottoman state had challenged the normative basis of extraterritoriality as early as the Congress of Paris (1856), which admitted the Empire into the Concert of Europe. The Ottoman statesmen used this as the legal basis to make a case for repealing the capitulations (Ahmad, 2000: 6). Yet, European powers were reluctant to acquiesce (Ahmad, 2000: 7). In 1869, the Ottoman government communicated a memorandum to the foreign powers' diplomatic representatives in Istanbul, "referring to the capitulations as an impediment," while simultaneously passing a citizenship law that made it illegal for Ottomans to seek the citizenship (or protection) of another state (Ahmad, 2000: 7). Foreign embassies refused to respect the law and continued to provide protection and citizenship.[18] During

Abdulhamid II's reign (1876–1909), the negative perception of the capitulations became stronger.[19] In 1887, the state started requiring a permit for all foreign corporations before operating in Ottoman domains. European powers considered this requirement "a violation of the capitulations guaranteeing freedom of commerce" (Thayer, 1923).

Despite the Ottomans' attempts to balance British intervention by heading toward new players like German investors, foreign economic stranglehold on the Empire tightened further.[20] European powers successfully defended the interests of foreign monopolies; while extraterritorial rights became even more expansive at a time when Ottoman political sovereignty was highly curtailed (Ahmad, 2000: 9). The capitulations were criticized heavily by Ottoman intellectuals and policymakers. But the government failed to curtail or abrogate the capitulations given the fact that empire's financial and military dependency left little room for political action. The Ottoman political elite's resentment of privileges due to the capitulations was further fueled by the rising nationalism and anti-imperialist struggles against the European powers.[21]

During this period, Ottoman economic thought evolved in favor of what might be termed a naïve developmentalism "*alla turca*" (Özveren, 2001).[22] As of the last quarter of the nineteenth century, it was quickly cross-fertilized with Friedrich List's well-known doctrine of national political economy, which found its exemplary application in the German model that contested the British hegemony (Özveren, 2001). These protectionist ideas began to rise throughout Europe in an ad hoc response to the Great Depression of the nineteenth century (1873–1896). The point that List and his certain followers via the German Historical School made was that British political economy was by no means a general theory that was universally applicable irrespectively of the developmental levels of countries. It was in fact a product of its own time and place. Given its disguised but inevitable historical and spatial specificity, rival policies had to be: (i) developmentalist and protectionist in order to catch up with it, and (ii) consciously sensitive to the domestic and temporal circumstances that could be exploited for developmental advantage and institutional change. A national political economy for the purpose of economic development, thus, had to make the best use of existing resources and institutions in the broadest sense of the term, as well as introducing new institutions when needed.

These protectionist ideas were echoed by various Ottoman intellectuals in the last quarter of the nineteenth century. According to List, protection of infant industries through custom duties was crucial for an economy in its early stages of industrialization. Likewise, Ahmet Midhat Efendi, one of the most popular and influential intellectuals of the Ottoman late nineteenth century, underlined the importance of protectionist policies (including high tariffs) for overcoming economic backwardness. Despite their popularity, however, these policies were not put into effect until the eve of the First World War. Having lost its fiscal and economic discretion, the Ottoman state had little bargaining power vis-a-vis foreign powers to abolish Capitulations and put restrictions on foreign trade. As the next chapter shows, it was only after the Young Turk Revolution of 1908 that the creation of a national economy crystallized as the ultimate objective of policymakers. These ideas evolved into what was called the "national economy" (*milli iktisat*) on the eve of the First World War and underwent a process of learning-by-doing within the context of the war economy.

One particular aspect of the Ottoman "national economy" discourse was its concern with the economic discrepancy between Ottoman Muslims and non-Muslims. During the late nineteenth century, many influential Ottoman intellectuals, such as Namık Kemal and Ahmed Midhat, expressed their grievances against non-Muslims' dominance in the economic sphere. The widening commercial gap between Muslims and non-Muslims along with the spread of nationalist ideologies ignited a Muslim backlash, especially after the defeat in the Balkan Wars (1911–1912), in which the Empire lost most of its European territories. In the period following the Balkan Wars, the rising anti-foreign sentiment was coupled with an even stronger hostility against non-Muslims and motivated policies that discriminated against all non-Muslims through harassment, boycotts, and exclusion from employment. As such, the nationalist aspect of Ottoman protectionism aimed not only to protect Ottoman economy from foreign competition but also to replace non-Muslims with Muslim economic elites. In this respect, Ottoman "national economy" discourse diverged from the political liberalism of List, who advocated ethnic and religious diversity.[23]

## Conclusion

Much like other states with centralized governments, such as the Chinese Empire or Japan, the Ottoman Empire was not directly colonized. Instead, through various mechanisms of political-economic dependency, it was rendered into a peripheral country in the world economy from the mid-nineteenth century onward. The peripheralization process had several stages that were shaped by both domestic and external forces: (i) the demise of the guild-Janissary coalition, (ii) the expansion of extraterritorial privileges of the Europeans and non-Muslim communities, and (iii) the free trade agreements that reduced government's autonomy in trade policy. All these factors contributed to the expansion of European-Ottoman trade. Given the external terms-of-trade dynamics, the trade boom led to a strong pattern of deindustrialization, moving the labor force away from traditional industries toward agricultural production during the first half of the nineteenth century.

During the second half the nineteenth century, Ottoman integration with the world economy moved into another and more dynamic stage. Increasing FDI and external borrowing enabled the construction and spread of modern transportation networks, mainly railways, and further integration of the Ottoman economy. Eventually, high levels of external indebtedness resulted in the "bankruptcy" of the Empire and the foreign control of fiscal resources under the management of the OPDA. While deindustrialization slowed down during this period, the foreign management of fiscal resources opened up a new channel of foreign domination and external dependence, undermining the use of domestic resources in line with the long-term developmental goals of the state. It was also during this period that a protectionist and developmentalist discourse first emerged and became popular.

The integration with the world economy did not only bring about deindustrialization but also led to social and economic changes that had long-term impacts on Ottoman society. There was a sharp increase in the number of European merchants residing in Ottoman ports, who needed the collaboration of the indigenous merchants for establishing contacts with cultivators and state officials to enter interior parts of the Ottoman domain. Foreign language and religious identity that could enable forging international networks became an important asset for local actors. Access to extraterritorial (European) jurisdiction also made non-Muslims more familiar with the European legal institutions and commercial networks. As such, those who were able to play these intermediary roles, the "conquering Orthodox merchants of the Balkans, the Greeks and the Armenians of the western provinces, and the Arab, Persian, Armenian, Greek, and Jewish merchants of the eastern and southeastern provinces" survived and even thrived during the trade boom of the nineteenth century (Kasaba, 1993: 229–230).

While liberalization and deindustrialization undermined the already diminishing power of the artisans and small shopkeepers, these processes contributed to the enrichment of commercial intermediaries, creditors, and local powerbrokers, whose interests were aligned with those of the foreign merchants and investors. Given the absence of strong import-competing (protoindustrial or manufacturing) interest groups and the disorganized nature of export-dependent actors, the bureaucracy became the sole actor with stakes in a developmental agenda. The integration also deepened the cleavage between local Muslim and non-Muslim elites, favoring the ethnoreligious emphasis in the statist discourse and the use of extractive strategies to support "national businesses," which undermined both native capital accumulation and secure property rights. Lastly, integration into the world economy was accompanied by the modernization of economic institutions with certain characteristics that reflected the dependent nature of the development path. Legal institutions, for instance, ensured advantageous positions for the foreigners and non-Muslims in the commercial realm. The rise and overlap of protectionist and nationalist ideas, however, did eventually undermine the political weight and voice of non-Muslims, curtailing the indigenous capacity for further institutional reforms.

## Notes

1. The term "long nineteenth century" is often used by historians to refer to the period between the French Revolution (1789) and the First World War (1914). See Hobsbawm (2000).
2. Following Pamuk and Williamson (2011: 159), deindustrialization here is simply defined as "the movement of labour out of manufacturing and into agriculture." During the nineteenth century, most manufacturing in the Ottoman Empire (as in the rest of the periphery) was labour-intensive, home-based, and small-scale before the twentieth century. As economic historians argued, however, these traditional industries could have supplied the platform for the factory-based industrial revolution. As such, in the nineteenth-century context, the term usually refers to both cottage manufacturing and factory industry. Given the strong manufacturing activity in cotton and woolen textiles in the Ottoman Empire up until the 1820s, deindustrialization evidence mostly pertains to the decline of textile manufacturing. For studies that

use the concept of deindustrialization in the Ottoman context, see Issawi (1980), Quataert (2002), Pamuk and Williamson (2011), and Panza (2014).

3. This part is heavily based on previous research by the author (Ağır, 2018, 2020).
4. The question as to when the Ottoman economy was integrated into the world economy became a matter of debate among Ottoman economic historians especially from the 1980s onward. Some scholars dated the beginning of the peripheralization of the Ottoman Empire in the capitalist world economy as the late sixteenth and early seventeenth centuries (Wallerstein et al., 2004). It is well established that the European demand for Ottoman raw materials, in particular for raw silk and mohair yarn, rapidly increased during the late sixteenth and early seventeenth centuries. Indeed, these industries had come under the pressure of European competition by the second half of the sixteenth century (Çizakça, 1985). However, it is not so plausible to argue about the existence of a unidirectional and complete path of peripheralization prior to the nineteenth century. In fact, "the eighteenth century appears to have been a period of recovery for most Ottoman industries" (Çizakça, 1985: 373). Çizakça (1985), like Wallerstein et al. (2004), argues that the integration began in the sixteenth century and that it could have been completed at the end of the seventeenth century or at least by the middle of the eighteenth century had it not been for the channeling of the European pressure into the transoceanic regions.
5. This part is based on the findings presented in Ağır and Artunç (2021).
6. Selim III made the first serious attempt to curb extraterritorial "abuses" that arose from the capitulations. See Bağış (1983: 16) and Artunç (2015: 725).
7. French and British *berats* cost approximately 55 times the Ottoman GDP per capita (Artunç, 2015: 723).
8. Traditional industries usually refer to cotton and textile production in the periphery. See González et al. (2008), Clingingsmith and Williamson (2008), Pamuk and Williamson (2011), and Panza (2014).
9. As Cain and Hopkins (1986: 516) put it, in the 1830s, "[f]ierce competition and falling prices, both at home and abroad, meant

that rapid economic growth, while boosting the importance of mechanized industry in the economy, also contributed to a continuing crisis of excess capacity and low profitability."

10. *Inhisar* was already abolished by various decrees issued during the reign of Selim III, in the late eighteenth and early nineteenth centuries. The guild-imposed restrictions were also undermined during the reign of Mahmud II, who eventually abolished the Janissary corps.
11. The Ottoman Empire specialized in the export of primary products, while importing manufactures; therefore price of exports refers to an unweighted average of major primary products exported by the Ottoman Empire: wheat, wool, raisins plus figs, tobacco, opium, and raw silk. Price of imports refers mainly to manufactured goods and intermediate inputs, and it is proxied by the British export price index. See Pamuk and Williamson (2011: 171–172) for the details of terms-of-trade calculation.
12. As Frank (1979: 103) notes, "[t]he nineteenth-century international division of labor contributed to the development of underdevelopment in most of the world both when the terms of trade went in one direction and when they went in the other."
13. The evidence on the directors of corporations established during the 1850–1908 period is fragmentary. But available surveys of corporate charters indicate that there were some Ottoman bureaucrats, such as Hasan Fehmi Paşa, Osman Hamdi Bey, Tevfik Bey, Ottoman Jewish bankers such as the Allatinis, and Greek diaspora bankers such as Leonidas Zarifi, who were on the boards of several foreign corporations. See Pech (1906, 1911) for details.
14. Studies on Ottoman/Turkish trade networks and family businesses that depend on private archives are few and generally rely on the researcher's personal connections to the family. For instance, Mataracızade brothers, a prominent family business with overseas operations, were reluctant to rely on the new commercial courts to resolve disputes or establish corporations under the Ottoman code (Mataracı, 2016). Nemlizades, another elite family of mercantile background, did not try to form corporations until after 1914 (Cora, 2013).
15. As Birdal (2010: 98) argues, "the practice of kilometric guarantees was bound to raise disputes between the government and the

railway companies. In these disputes, the OPDA generally sided with the latter, since their interests often coincided."

16. For a summary of the classical and modified predatory theories of state building, see Lu and Thies (2013).
17. See Birdal (2010: 84) for a remark about how this process echoes the argument of D. North and B. Weingast (1989) on the economic consequences of the Glorious Revolution.
18. The Foreign Ministry had a subdivision for enforcing this law, but it was not successful (Findley, 1980: 188, 317–319).
19. This perception also reflected the Ottoman statesmen's move away from liberal ideas to protectionism. The capitulations also restricted the government's discretion over tariffs (Ahmad, 2000: 9).
20. Fleet (2015) describes the period of 1876–1908 as the "golden age of foreign concessions."
21. The newly independent countries, such as Bulgaria, were not subject to the capitulations, and they were recognized as equals by the European powers. Japan also became successful in acquiring an equal status with the West. These examples encouraged the Ottoman Turks to abolish the capitulations (Ahmad, 2000: 10–11).
22. There is little evidence on the negative impact of foreign trade on domestic industry prior to the nineteenth century, yet the late eighteenth century had already witnessed the emergence of what might be termed a "developmental discourse." During this period, various statesmen wrote about the need to catch up with the more advanced countries and suggested specific strategies to create a "national market." See Ağır (2017).
23. According to List, one of the reasons underlying the demise of the Spanish economy was the expulsion of Jews and Muslim from Spain along with lack of religious and political freedom. See Henderson (1983: 189).

## References

Ağır, S. (2013). The evolution of grain policy: The Ottoman experience. *Journal of Interdisciplinary History, 43*(4), 571–598.

Ağır, S. (2017). Osmanlı İktisat Düşüncesinde Bir Kalkınma Stratejisi Olarak Örnek Alma. In E. Özgür et al. (Eds.), *Türkiye'de İktisadi Düşünce* (pp. 13–49). İletişim.

Ağır, S. (2018). Rise and demise of *Gedik* markets in Istanbul, 1750–1860. *Economic History Review, 71*(1), 133–156.

Ağır, S. (2020). Institutions and business organizations in the late Ottoman Empire and early Turkish Republic. In A. M. Çolpan & G. G. Jones (Eds.), *Business, ethics and institutions: The evolution of Turkish capitalism in global perspectives*. Routledge.

Ağır, S., & Artunç, C. (2021). Set and forget? The evolution of business law in the Ottoman Empire and Turkey. *Business History Review*, 1–36. https://doi.org/10.1017/S000768052000094X.

Ahmad, F. (2000). Ottoman perceptions of the capitulations 1800–1914. *Journal of Islamic Studies, 11*(1), 1–20.

Artunç, C. (2015). The price of legal institutions: The *Beratlı* merchants in the eighteenth century Ottoman Empire. *Journal of Economic History, 75*(3), 720–748.

Bağış, A. İ. (1983). *Osmanlı Ticaretinde Gayrî Müslimler: Kapitülasyonlar, Avrupa Tüccarları, Beratlı Tüccarlar, Hayriye Tüccarları (1750–1839)*. Turhan Kitabevi.

Birdal, M. (2010). *The political economy of Ottoman public debt: Insolvency and European financial control in the late nineteenth century*. Bloomsbury.

Bogart, D., & Chaudhary, L. (2012). Regulation, ownership, and costs: A historical perspective from Indian railways. *American Economic Journal: Economic Policy, 4*(1), 28–57.

Cain, P. J., & Hopkins, A. G. (1986). Gentlemanly capitalism and British expansion overseas I: The old colonial system, 1688–1850. *Economic History Review, 39*(4), 501–525.

Centeno, M. A. (1997). Blood and debt: War and taxation in nineteenth-century Latin America. *American Journal of Sociology, 102*(6), 1565–1605.

Çizakça, M. (1985). Incorporation of the Middle East into the European world-economy. *Review (Fernand Braudel Center), 8*(3), 353–377.

Clingingsmith, D., & Williamson, J. G. (2008). Deindustrialization in 18th and 19th century India: Mughal decline, climate shocks and British industrial ascent. *Explorations in Economic History, 45*(3), 209–234.

Cora, Y. T. (2013). A Muslim great merchant [Tüccar] family in the late Ottoman Empire: A case study of the Nemlizades, 1860–1930. *International Journal of Turkish Studies, 19*(1–2), 1–29.

Coşar, N., & Demirci, S. (2009). Incorporation into the world economy: From railways to highways (1850–1950). *Middle Eastern Studies, 45*(1), 19–31.

de Beaujour, L.-A.-F. (1800). *Tableau du commerce de la Grèce: formé d'après une année moyenne, depuis 1787 jusqu'en 1797*. Renouard.

Dimitriadis, S. (2013). *The making of an Ottoman port-city: The state, local elites and urban space in Salonika, 1870–1912* (Unpublished PhD diss.). SOAS, London.

Eichengreen, B. (1995). Financing infrastructure in developing countries: Lessons from the railway age. *World Bank Research Observer, 10*(1), 75–91.

Eldem, V. (1994). Osmanlı İmparatorluğu'nun iktisadi şartları hakkında bir tetkik (Vol. 96). Türk Tarih Kurumu Basımevi.

Eldem, E. (1999). *French trade in Istanbul in the eighteenth century*. Brill.

Eldem, E. (2005). Ottoman financial integration with Europe: Foreign loans, the Ottoman Bank and the Ottoman public debt. *European Review, 13*(3), 431–443.

Findley, C. (1980). *Bureaucratic reform in the Ottoman Empire: The Sublime Porte, 1789–1922*. Princeton University Press.

Fleet, K. (2015). Geç Osmanlı Erken Türkiye Cumhuriyeti Döneminde Yabancılara Verilen Ekonomik İmtiyazlari. *Kebikec: Insan Bilimleri Icin Kaynak Arastirmali Dergisi, 39*, 343–362.

Frangakis-Syrett, E. (1988). Trade between Ottoman Empire and Western Europe: The case of Izmir in the eighteenth century. *New Perspectives on Turkey, 2*, 1–18.

Frank, A. G. (1979). *Dependent accumulation*. New York University Press.

Geyikdağı, N. (2011). *Foreign investment in the Ottoman Empire: International trade and relations 1854–1914*. I.B. Tauris.

Gökatalay, S. (2015). *The political economy of corporations in the late Ottoman Empire and early Turkish Republic (1908–1929)* (Unpublished Master's Thesis). METU, Ankara.

González, R. D., Galvarriato, A. G., & Williamson, J. G. (2008). Mexican exceptionalism: Globalization and de-industrialization, 1750–1877. *The Journal of Economic History, 68*(3), 758–811.

Henderson, W. O. (1983). *Friedrich list, economist and visionary, 1789–1846*. Psychology Press.

Hobsbawm, E. (2000). *Age of capital: 1848–1875*. Phoenix Press.

Hussin, I. R. (2016). *The politics of Islamic law: Local elites, colonial authority, and the making of the Muslim state*. University of Chicago Press.

Issawi, C. (1980). De-industrialization and re-industrialization in the Middle East since 1800. *International Journal of Middle East Studies, 12*(4), 469–479.

Karaman, K. K., & Pamuk, Ş. (2010). Ottoman state finances in European perspective, 1500–1914. *The Journal of Economic History, 70*, 593–629.

Kasaba, R. (1988). *The Ottoman Empire and the world economy: The nineteenth century*. State University of New York Press.

Kasaba, R. (1993). Treaties and friendships: British imperialism, the Ottoman Empire, and China in the nineteenth century. *Journal of World History, 4*, 215–241.

Kayaoğlu, T. (2010). *Legal imperialism: Sovereignty and extraterritoriality in Japan, the Ottoman Empire, and China*. Cambridge University Press.

Lapavitsas, C. (2006). Social and economic underpinnings of industrial development: Evidence from Ottoman Macedonia. *Journal of European Economic History, 35*(3), 661–710.

Lapavitsas, C., & Çakıroğlu, P. (2019). *Capitalism in Ottoman Macedonia: Industrialisation and modernity in the hinterlands*. Routledge.

Lu, L., & Thies, C. G. (2013). War, rivalry, and state building in the Middle East. *Political Research Quarterly, 66*(2), 239–253.

Mataracı, A. (2016). *Trade in wartime: The business correspondence of an Ottoman Muslim merchant family*. Libra Kitapçılık ve Yayıncılık.

North, D. C., & Weingast, B. R. (1989). Constitutions and commitment: The evolution of institutions governing public choice in seventeenth-century England. *Journal of economic History, 49*, 803–832.

Owen, R. (2009). *The Middle East in the world economy 1800–1914*. I.B. Tauris.

Özveren, E. (2001). Ottoman economic thought and economic policy in transition: Rethinking the nineteenth century. In M. Psalidopoulos & M. E. Mata (Eds.), *Economic thought and policy in less developed Europe: The nineteenth century* (pp. 129–144). Routledge.

Palairet, M. R. (1997). *The Balkan economies c. 1800–1914: Evolution without development*. Cambridge University Press.

Pamuk, Ş. (1987). *The Ottoman Empire and European capitalism, 1820–1913*. Cambridge University Press.

Pamuk, Ş, & Williamson, J. G. (2011). Ottoman de-industrialization, 1800–1913: Assessing the magnitude, impact, and response. *Economic History Review, 64*, 159–184.

Panza, L. (2014). De-industrialization and re-industrialization in the Middle East: Reflections on the cotton industry in Egypt and in the Izmir region. *The Economic History Review, 67*(1), 146–169.

Pech, E. (1906). *Manuel des sociétés anonymes fonctionnant en Turquie*. Gérard Frères.

Pech, E. (1911) *Manuel des sociétés anonymes fonctionnant en Turquie*. Gérard Frères.

Pepelasis, A. A. (1959). The legal system and economic development of Greece. *Journal of Economic History, 19*(2), 173–198.

Quataert, D. (1994). The age of reforms, 1812–1914. In D. Quataert & H. İnalcık (Eds.), *An economic and social history of the Ottoman Empire* (Vol. 2, pp. 759–943). Cambridge University Press.

Quataert, D. (2002). *Ottoman manufacturing in the age of the industrial revolution*. Cambridge University Press.

Singh, P. (2019). Of international law, semi-colonial Thailand, and imperial ghosts. *Asian Journal of International Law, 9*(1), 46–74.

Stoianovich, T. (1960). The conquering Balkan Orthodox merchant. *Journal of Economic History, 20*, 234–313.

Sunar, M. (2006). *Cauldron of dissent: A study of Janissary Corps, 1807–1826* (Unpub. Ph.D. thesis). State University of New York at Binghamton.

Thayer, L. E. (1923). The capitulations of the Ottoman Empire and the question of their abrogation as it affects the United States. *American Journal of International Law, 17*(2), 207–233.

Tilly, C. (1975). Reflections on the History of European State-Making. In C. Tilly (Ed.), *Formation of National States in Western Europe*, Princeton University Press.

Toprak, Z. (2020). *Atatürk – Kurucu Felsefenin Evrimi*. Türkiye İş Bankası Kültür Yayını.

Toprak, Z. (2012). *Türkiye'de "Millî İktisat" 1908–1918*. Doğan Kitap.

Ubicini, A. (1856). *Letters on Turkey: Turkey and the Turks*. United Kingdom.

Wallerstein, I., et. al. (2004). The incorporation of the Ottoman Empire into the world-economy. In H. Islamogu-Inan (Ed.), *The Ottoman Empire and the world-economy*. Cambridge University Press.

CHAPTER 3

# From Globalization to Deglobalization: Nationalism and Economics in the Making of Modern Turkey, 1908–1929

*Zafer Toprak*

## Introduction

Toward the end of the pre-modern period, the existing global trade network consisted of interlocking trade circuits that attached Eurasia and northeastern Africa. A new globalization initiative, as interpreted in Immanuel Wallerstein books, began around 1500 with the emergence of the Portuguese and Spanish colonial empires heralding the beginning of an irreversible process of worldwide integration (Wallerstein, 1997). Exploration, conquest, colonial expansion and regular trade relations put Europe, Africa, Asia and America in direct contact for the first time. These contacts had grown into a "stable" multilateral interdependency by the mid-eighteenth century. Finally, transcontinental networks had

Z. Toprak (✉)
Boğaziçi University, Istanbul, Turkey
e-mail: ztoprak@ku.edu.tr; toprakz@boun.edu.tr



E. Özçelik and Y. Özdemir (eds.), *Political Economy of Development in Turkey*, The Political Economy of the Middle East,
https://doi.org/10.1007/978-981-16-7318-4_3

been established, which were at least economically stable and potentially influential. Resulting from the new capacities in production, transportation and communication, created by the process of industrialization, the period between 1750 and 1880 was characterized by an unprecedented expansion of worldwide integration in terms of its intensity and impact. Politically, however, the same period witnessed retreats of Europe into itself, as *Pax Britannica* dominated the world. The structures of colonial empire in the Americas disappeared except for a few insignificant remnants. The outgrowth of the world economy took place under the conditions of predominant liberalism and free trade. At the same time, European institutions, including the nation-state, and European or Western dominant economic thought were exported throughout the world. In the 1860s and 1870s, economic spheres were deeply affected for the first time by truly global interdependencies. As a "long depression" started in the 1870s, globalization began to become politicized (Broadberry & Harrison, 2005). From then on, national states wanted to rein in the effects of global economic integration. The global economy was perceived as an integral part of world politics, shaped by national power. Soon conflicts arose among the world powers. Apart from Britain, most of the countries reverted to protectionism after 1878. While the first restrictions on immigration were established, segregation and racism gained ground. Modern interventionist states used import tariffs and social policy to steer globalization in a direction beneficial to "national" interests. Interventionism and regulation, hand in hand with global crises, heralded the age of economic deglobalization. The new era lasted until the end of the World War II. A new stage of globalization restarted as Western powers gathered in Bretton Woods in 1944 (Osterhammel & Petersson, 2005).

During the nineteenth and early twentieth centuries, Ottoman financial developments were accompanied by empire's general integration with European and world economies. In this process, one key factor was the rapid growth of trade between the Ottoman Empire and the leading countries of Europe. During the three-quarters of a century following the Free Trade Treaties, signed first with Britain in 1838 and then with other European countries, Ottoman exports increased by more than five times, measured in current prices, while imports, measured in current prices, expanded six and a half times (Quataert, 1993). Since the prices of the commodities involved in Ottoman foreign trade were considerably lower on the eve of World War I than in 1840, trade volumes increased even further because of an increase in productivity. In constant 1880 prices, Ottoman exports and imports increased, respectively, nine and tenfold during the 1840–1913 period. This rise in the volume of trade was achieved despite the loss of Ottoman territories and was a direct result of European industrialization, along with the free-trade era that was inaugurated in the middle of the nineteenth century (Pamuk, 1987).

## Globalization and Dependency: The Rule of Liberal Economics

The Ottoman economic structure witnessed great commercialization from 1839 onwards, during the years of the *Tanzimat*, or the Reform Period (1838–1876), and the growth in foreign trade had a positive impact on internal trade. The injection of money through foreign trade dismantled the self-sufficient, traditional and closed economic circuits, and created dual economic structures with a disintegrated, money-oriented and outward-looking market economy led by foreign and "native" bourgeoisie on the one hand, and a resistant, self-integrated and inward-looking "domestic" economy dominated by "petite" producers under traditional guild structure (*lonca*) on the other (Eldem, 1970). A second key factor in the integration of the Ottoman Empire with the outside world was the inflow of capital. With the modernization of the military and civil bureaucracy, the Ottoman demand for capital increased faster than the intake of revenues throughout much of the nineteenth and early twentieth centuries. The demand for capital and subsequent attempts to develop domestic sources of revenues through taxes was crucial for the Empire's structural changes in search of a modern state. There were drastic changes in commercial networking during the nineteenth century, which reverberated across Western Europe and Northern America. Commercial organizations were dominated by the growing importance of the joint-stock form of corporate financing. By the latter half of the nineteenth century, the Ottoman Empire too was caught up in this process. Financial institutions and techniques, based on European models, were actively developed, while the traditionally rigid Ottoman financial regime was gradually transformed into a dynamic and flexible European system. Much of these changes had been achieved through the acts of the Ottoman Public Debt Administration (OPDA, *Düyun-u Umumiye-i Osmaniye Varidat-ı Muhassasa İdaresi*), which was dominated by foreign powers. Set up in 1881 following on the Ottoman Empire defaulting on its debt, the OPDA was a major instrument in change, seen as a second Ministry of Finance within the Ottoman soil (Toprak, 1995).

The expansion of trade with Europe in terms of both imports and exports provided merchant capital for investment in Ottoman territory and encouraged the development of new financial networks and institutions to meet the rising demand for capital. This process, in turn, led to the creation of banks, the adoption of modern banking methods and the use of bond financing by the government and the private sector. However, most of these institutions were built up by European moneyed circles. The Ottoman government, partly due to capitulations, was losing the control of its own economy. Finance became the realm of foreign bourgeoisie settled in Istanbul (Karpat, 1985).

All these novelties of the Ottoman finances and economic structure went hand in hand with further dependency on European moneyed circles. The Ottoman Empire could preserve its political independence to a certain extent all these years. However, an alien bourgeoisie, settled in urban centers, was cherished within the borders of the Empire, challenging traditional and local economic units that were based on so-called provisionism, whose main purpose was to provide the urban population with daily necessities.

## Deglobalization and National Economy Under "Unionist" Young Turks

The rise of Turkish nationalism has frequently been ascribed to the literary and linguistic concerns of Ottoman intellectuals in the late nineteenth and early twentieth centuries (Lewis, 1977). Hence, most students of late Ottoman history have interpreted the "national literature" and "language reform" of the period as indicators of a "cultural nationalism" devoid of any social and economic content. Later on, however, this view has been challenged by scholars doing research on the rise of Turkish nationalism (Kushner, 1977).

The politics and ideology of the nineteenth-century world were styled mainly by the French. France pioneered the revolution against "*ancient regime*" and inspired the emerging nations with libertarian ideas. Tricolor flags became the emblems of the rising nation-states. In fact, world politics between 1789 and 1917 witnessed contentions for and against the tenets of 1789. The French Revolution provided the vocabulary and the essential qualities of liberal and radical-democratic politics for most of the newly emerging nation-states. France became the first great example of national identity, and the idea of nationalism disseminated from France throughout the world. Ottomanism or Ottoman nationalism was the main motto of the 1908 Revolution. Instigated by Young Turks organized as Committee of Union and Progress (CUP), the upheaval ushered in constitutional monarchy. In this regard, liberty, equality, fraternity and justice were the basic principles borrowed from the French Revolution (Toprak, 1997).

Nineteenth-century economic liberalism was still on the agenda of the Young Turk governments when they challenged Abdulhamid II's regime. The Young Turks fully recognized the importance of investment and capital accumulation. Indeed, they saw capital accumulation as a panacea for all economic ills of the country, just as the constitution was meant to cure all political ills. Initially, they espoused the *laissez faire, laissez passer* policies of classical economics. They encouraged foreign investment, but also tried to cultivate an Ottoman bourgeoisie through improved credit facilities and exemptions from tariffs and taxes. These concessions were equivalent to those enjoyed by the Europeans through the capitulations, the special privileges granted to foreigners. At the same time, the Young Turks tried to direct foreign investment into mining, agriculture and industry—the areas they saw as most beneficial to the Ottoman economy. Foreign investment, however, remained confined to financial and commercial enterprises and public works (Ahmed Emin, 1930). Meanwhile, guilds were officially banned in 1910 (Toprak, 2016). Chambers of commerce flourished all over the country. Agricultural and industrial pursuits were encouraged through parliamentary acts. Industrial disputes resulting from strikes all over the country were settled thanks to the intervention of the CUP (Quataert, 1983). In short, the 1908 political revolution heralded the libertarian atmosphere of the belated liberal age (Toprak, 2012).

The CUP liberalism was, in a sense, a continuation of the *Tanzimat* liberal thought. Its new version was the product of the commercial milieus in Salonika. Situated on the southern part of Balkan Peninsula, Salonika had always remained on the outskirts of Ottoman domain and had cherished European commercial culture. Therefore, as long as the Central Committee of the CUP stayed in Salonika and guided Ottoman economy from this commercial center, economic liberalism was pursued and the political apparatus in Istanbul stayed in harmony with the "men of commerce" of the Empire. But the loss of Salonika in 1912 and the shift of the political center to Istanbul marked a watershed in the economic perspectives of the Unionists. In the capital, the old-style corporations or trade guilds of Muslim artisans, as well as the obsolete transport sector, had always conflicted with non-Muslim commercial interests of the new alien bourgeoisie. The Chamber of Commerce, heavily dominated by non-Muslims and foreigners, complained incessantly of the restrictions and regulations imposed by the well-organized trade guilds.

## Class Structure and the Newborn Muslim-Turkish Bourgeoise

The CUP Central Committee tried first to reconcile the two sides. The renowned Minister of Finance Mehmed Cavid strived to make peace between the two parties, but in vain. Economic liberalism, with low customs duties regulated through capitulations, had always jeopardized the interests of the petite producers and Muslim guilds. Devoid of any protective measures and accumulated capital, Muslim merchants, too, complained of the unequal competition from foreign and non-Muslim commercial houses.

The Balkan Wars (1912–1913) between the Ottoman Empire and the Balkan states initiated a new era in the policy orientation of the CUP. After having lost the war, The Unionists faced the necessity of relying upon strata who had limited ties with the economically dominant imperial powers. Ottoman Greeks and Armenians were then identified as instruments of liberalism, and therefore "agents" of Western economic expansionism (Keyder, 1987). As long as the free-market mechanism ruled, and capitulations existed, they constituted the privileged strata of the Empire. Artisans and merchants of Muslim-Turkish origin fit the description and became the backbone of the new nationalist ideology, as the Ottoman Empire lost a large portion of its European territories in the Balkan Wars. In this endeavor, the Jewish community, too, satisfied to some extent the prerequisites of an "independent" economic power, and Jewish business milieu also became part of the rising Turkish nationalism. The Balkan Wars and the Muslim boycott of 1913 against non-Muslim trading interests were the crucial starting points in search for a national economic policy. Supported by the Turkish Hearths (*Türk Ocakları*), the intellectual clubs of the emerging Turkish nationalist movement, Muslims were advised to emulate their non-Muslim compatriots in the trades. Muslims were invited to embark upon commercial pursuits

(Çetinkaya, 2013). Following the Balkan War, in a few months, around 600 shops were opened in different districts of Istanbul, and Muslims were advised to purchase from their coreligionist shopkeepers. Pamphlets were distributed in support of the campaign. A "patriotic" literature guided by Unionists appealed to the national feelings of the Ottoman Muslim people (Toprak, 2013).

Meanwhile, a bye-law for the encouragement of industry was enacted in 1913. It was the time for launching a state-regulated economic model. Clubs associated with the CUP in the countryside provided the milieu for the establishment of joint-stock companies, cooperatives and banking institutions. Indigenous credit mechanisms were fostered through state funds. Industry started to benefit from protective tariffs, exemption of capital goods and intermediates from import duties, cheap credits, as well as direct government investment. This was the beginning of the process that would ultimately lead to state capitalism in Turkey in the wake of the War of Independence. A full-blown "import substitution industrialization" policy, however, had to await until the officially declared *etatism* (*devletçilik*) in 1930 (Boratav, 1988).

But the main turn came with World War I. Radical steps had to be taken in the early days of the war. Capitulations were abolished unilaterally in September 1914. Due to capitulatory rights, there were many foreign companies carrying out business on the Ottoman soil. These companies came under the jurisdiction of their own respective nations. Lawsuits between firms of different nationalities were decided in the court of the defendant's nation; those between foreign firms and Ottoman subjects by the Ottoman Mixed Tribunals. When the capitulations were abolished, the privileges of foreign companies were overridden, and they were rendered answerable to the Ottoman courts (Toprak, 2012). As for the Ottoman public debts, their regular payments were postponed. New customs tariffs brought about protective measures for the infant industries and local products. The employment of Muslims in economic and financial sectors was promoted through a "language reform." Turkish became the mandatory language in all business correspondence and official accounting.

The most spectacular development of the time was the commercial control of the CUP on basic food necessities. An allocation mechanism under the guidance of local CUP clubs was designed to suppress war speculation. In securing commercial supremacy, the CUP was greatly aided by its hold on various trade guilds of Istanbul. The practical effect of the new commercial movement was to create something like a Muslim monopoly of trade which resulted in huge profits (Ahmed Emin, 1930).

After the abolition of trade guilds in the early years of the revolution, artisans did not lose time in reorganizing their corporative structure under various societies (*cemiyet*). The 1909 Law of Societies provided them with further solidarity for their activities. In 1915, the new artisanal societies gathered and formed a central body under the name of The Society of Tradesmen (*Esnaflar Cemiyeti*). The new corporative structure under the official patronage of Ismet Bey, then the Prefect of Istanbul, was in harmony with the sociology of the era, namely, solidarism which was borrowed from the Third French Republic.

One of the side effects of the war economy was the increasing visibility of Ottoman women in society as the result of male labor shortage. Men were called under arms and moved to the fronts. Women were invited to enter professions hitherto regarded as the exclusive domain of men. They were employed as national governmental and municipal clerks, as factory workers, as street cleaners and even as barbers in many districts of Istanbul. Women from the outskirts of Istanbul brought their products to the city to market them. There was even a bazaar in Galata, earmarked exclusively for women merchants. The First Army in Istanbul initiated Women Workers' Brigades and trained them for support services. The Fourth Army in Syria organized a Women's Battalion to provide farmhands for agricultural production in the Çukurova Region. By the end of World War I, large numbers of women had been integrated into the social and economic life of the country. The poverty-stricken, isolated Ottoman women had no choice but to seek employment to survive as their men, who had hitherto provided for the household, were called to arms (Toprak, 2014).

## Panacea for Implosion: Sociology and Economic Solidarism

To understand the conceptual framework behind the restructuring during World War I, one must look at the Unionist intellectual milieu. A member of the central committee, Ziya Gökalp framed, in broad outlines, the "new life" (*yeni hayat*) of the Ottomans (Toprak, 2017). In fact, the Unionist economic policy was an amalgam of German "national economy" and French "solidarism," the latter being partly influenced by the German school of sociology. In this symbiosis, Ziya Gökalp played the

French part. He was a disciple of Durkheim and believed in the "division of labor" within the same ethnic entity, creating "outsiders" within the Ottoman society. As for the German ingredient, a Jew from Salonika brought the basic principles. Moiz Cohen, alias Munis Tekinalp, is one of the lesser-known Ottoman intellectuals who have contributed substantially to the development of Turkish economic nationalism in the early twentieth century (Landau, 1984). Jews in the Ottoman Empire seldom enjoyed foreign protection, and together with the Muslim elements, suffered heavily the consequences of European economic supremacy. The teaching of Tekinalp was in a way a challenge against liberalism. His main argument aimed at structuring the "nation-state" of the new era.

Tekinalp, under the guidance of his mentor Ziya Gökalp, and in line with CUP's ideological framework, conceptualized the economic prerequisites of a nation-state in a journal entitled Economics *(İktisadiyyat)*. He was strongly influenced by German "national economy" and "social economy" in the making since the second half of the nineteenth century. He advocated economic development and industrialization under state supervision. Gökalp's and Tekinalp's articles on solidarism and national economy heralded in the *etatist* and neo-mercantilist era in Ottoman-Turkish political, economic and social life.

But the crux of the problem was financial independence of the country. Credit mechanism had to fuel the new entrepreneurs. In the financial sphere, the CUP decided to run its own banks. The National Credit Bank (*İtibar-ı Millî Bankası*) was founded in January 1917 with a capital of 4 million Ottoman liras to replace the Ottoman Imperial Bank owned by foreigners. The General Bank (*Bank-ı Umumi*) was also a CUP enterprise, in which merchants, especially in the provinces, were invited to take shares. And finally, The National Bank of Economy (*Millî İktisat Bankası*) was the last CUP banking enterprise in Istanbul, run in conjunction with the Weighers' (*Millî Kantariye*), Produce (*Millî Mahsulat*) and Cloth (*Millî Mensucat*) Companies (Toprak, 2003). Meanwhile, Anatolian CUP notables did not lose time to form their own local banking institutions in different districts.

The war period also witnessed capital accumulation by small merchants of Muslim and provincial origins. Until then, the lot of the Muslim petty mercantile stratum depended on credit facilities extended by the well-established foreign and Christian merchants settled in commercial centers of the Empire. The CUP interfered in this one-sided interest network and provided the Muslim merchants with ways and means of accumulating their own capital. Local banking institutions were established under the aegis of the provincial CUP clubs. This was an example to the so-called primitive accumulation mentioned in classical textbooks (Toprak, 2019a).

## Provincial Notables and Primitive Capital Accumulation

Muslim provincial notables and moneyed men had every reason to support Unionist policies. They adopted the new economic model with self-confidence and in hopes of prospering. They responded to the call by establishing various economic organizations, such as the Entrepreneurs' Society, the Artisans' Society, the National Fabricants' Association, the Muslim Merchant Association, the Economics Society and Ottoman Farmers' Association (Gökatalay, 2020).

The CUP and the Ottoman Parliament did not lose time in promoting the economic fortunes of Muslim entrepreneurs. Some were businessmen themselves; others had invested heavily in commerce and agriculture; hence their eagerness to encourage "national economic" policy, their readiness to support indigenous capital and their insistence on "economic independence." The Muslim farmers and merchants who were integrated into the "national market" and who benefited from Turkish nationalism played a very significant role in the post-war national movement and in the making of Republican Turkey. As the national independence movement started, they joined Ankara and financed the war carried out under the leadership of Atatürk. "National economic policy," which became the motto of the single party era (1923–1946), was the product of the practices instigated by Unionist "economic rationality" (Toprak, 2013).

Unionists had discovered "economic rationality" thanks to their esteem for the German political union and development model. They repudiated nineteenth-century economic liberalism and attached their hopes to the late-comers' protectionist policies for industrialization (Kemp, 1983). In other words, the Young Turks discovered "economics" in the early years of the Revolution and mainly during World War I. Before the war, economics was taught in secondary and high schools, but most of the curriculum then consisted of word-by-word translations of the classical doctrine preached in Adam Smith's, Leroy Beaulieu's, or Charles Gide's textbooks. Economists of a non-classical trend, such as Friedrich List, Adolph Wagner, Gustav Schmoller and Eugen von Philippovich were unknown. The Ottomans discovered these economists thanks to the war and had consequently embarked upon a program for building up a "national economy." Friedrich List was the most important figure in the studies of national economy, pioneering in protectionism in Europe. Hailed as the "national economist," he elaborated the principles of economic redress in Germany. The unity of Germany accomplished under Bismarck's guidance had followed the path designed by List. Thanks to his contributions in the first half of the nineteenth century, Germany acquired supremacy in the economic field in the early twentieth century. Hence, Germans considered him a national hero. He was praised as the Bismarck of the economic world. In Unionist view, the Ottoman Empire had to emulate Germany which had become an industrial giant in a quarter of a century. Turks had to study carefully German economic development of the last forty or fifty years and learn from German experience how to build a national economy. In short, national economic theory bore German brand. And nationalism was the main spurt in the making of a national economic model.

Accordingly, the emerging Turkish nationalism required protectionism. The precepts of classical economic thought sponsored by Ottoman liberals for almost half a century since the *Tanzimat* era had resulted, in the view of the Unionists, in the dependence and dismemberment of the Empire. An economic model preaching "comparative advantages" dominated Ottoman economic literature until the Balkan War. That model had to be dismantled so as to pave the way for an autarkic national economy.

This was a challenge to classical economic taught. According to the national economic doctrine advanced by List and preached by the Unionists, the liberal economics of the British "Manchesterians" was not universal. It suited England's industrialized economy and imperialistic policies. England had already established its large-scale industry, so it was bound to export its manufactures and import raw materials. Therefore, free trade was the most beneficial policy for England (Hardach, 1977).

## "National Economy": A New Ideology for Economic Mind

The "national economy" had different connotations in the minds of Unionists. The CUP had a collegial yet heterogeneous structure. Different perspectives for the nationalist trend coexisted side by side. Ziya Gökalp's choice was for a "guild economy" or "guild socialism." His corporatist economic model was based on small crafts. A member of the central committee, Mehmed Cavid was a devoted liberal in economic thought. He never lost confidence in classical economic theory. He tried hard to reconcile "national interests" with the conceptual framework of the classics. As for Tekinalp, he never shared the corporatist interpretation of nationalism. Rather, he emphasized the importance of large-scale industry and an inevitable class society. The man who implemented economic nationalism was Kara Kemal, who later served as the inspector of the CUP for Istanbul and the president of the important Porters' Guild, and finally the Minister of Provision of Basic Necessities (*İaşe Nazırı*). He schemed his own "national economic" model on the rise of a Muslim commercial bourgeoisie made up of petite producers. To his initiative is ascribed the foundation of several "national" joint-stock companies in Istanbul. He convinced petty merchants and shopkeepers to buy the shares of the new companies and induced all the guilds in town to cooperate in the working of the new commercial network. The National Weighers' Company, The National Bakers' Company, the National Produce Company and the National Cloth Company were among the most important commercial institutions directed by Unionist nominees. As the CUP's commercial position grew stronger, its sphere widened, and other trading companies followed suit. Under the aegis of the CUP, a "national bourgeoisie," made up of petty producers, flourished.

However, due to the implosion of the Ottoman society in war years, economics and sociology had to go hand in hand with each other. Gökalp's economic thought associated Durkheimian sociology with List's economics. For him, "national economy" meant a market economy with advanced division of labor and organic solidarity. He thought that functional interdependence would defy class conflict. He propounded a nationalistic economy with no class tensions or economic egoism, which, he thought, were detrimental to the public interest (Parla, 1985). By contrast, Tekinalp criticized the sociological viewpoint of "national economy" and rejected Gökalp's occupational solidarity. He underlined the inevitability of classes in a capitalist system. For him, advance in civilization meant capitalist development, and nationalism as an ideology served to strengthen capitalism. Therefore, Ottoman society had to follow the same pattern. In his article entitled "Capitalist Era is Taking Off," written in 1917, he pointed out that the foundation of more than forty joint-stock companies in a single year and the establishment of the National

Credit Bank to replace the Imperial Ottoman Bank were concrete proofs of this transformation (Tekinalp 1917).

During the Second Constitutional Period (1908–1918), economics became one of the basic issues of intellectual life. Economic problems were discussed in the columns of the newspapers. Economic journals were published, while the parliamentary agenda was full of economic concerns. Textbooks, booklets, pamphlets on economic issues flooded the market. While welcoming the emergence of "national capitalism" in the Ottoman Empire, the Unionist intellectuals expressed great concern about its social consequences. As war speculation deepened, disparities in income widened. The bureaucracy and the army fell in destitute due to the vagaries of the war. The lot of the lower strata worsened. Individual interests endangered public well-being. Hence, it was left up to the state to protect the common interests of the nation. Since natural harmony that liberal thought assumed had lost its credibility, the state had to interfere on behalf of the have-nots. The new policy to be pursued was called "state economics" (*devlet iktisadiyatı*). This orientation, in fact, was, in a way, the prototype of Republican *etatism* (Toprak, 2019a).

Most of the Unionist intellectuals became mild *estatists* as the Ottoman society collapsed. Such *etatism* did not involve the suppression of the private sector. Rather, the state would act as an intermediary between public and private sectors. State economics would never endanger private entrepreneurs. On the contrary, the state would provide the appropriate milieu for the encouragement of private initiative so that maximum profits could be obtained from both sectors. But the making of a nation-state required more than economics. Hence, Unionist intellectuals felt that social unity necessitated "sociology." In fact, as a discipline in higher education and as a panacea for Ottoman social disintegration, sociology opened new vistas to Ottoman intellectuals. Indeed, solidarism turned out to be the basic creed of the Turkish Republic in the following decades. In the solidarist discourse, "populism" (*halkçılık*), later one of the six pillars of the Turkish Republic, took center stage.

"Populism" had been introduced into Turkish political literature by Gökalp. He used the term as a synonym for democracy. In the article entitled "*Halkçılık*," published in 1918, in *Yeni Mecmua*, he distinguished between political democracy ("*siyasî halkçılık*") and social democracy ("*ictimaî halkçılık*") (Ziya Gökalp, 1918). Populism based on solidarism would eradicate social Darwinism and install in its place what Tekinalp called "social politics," which would prevent imperialistic tendencies in the world as capitalism would follow "the New Path" ("*Yeni İstikamet*"—*The neue Orientirung*) (Tekinalp, 1918). Social revolution (*ictimaî inkılâb*) based upon "populist" precepts would spread over the whole globe and wipe out imperialism (Toprak, 2013).

As we shift to the 1920s, it can be argued that the Young Turk Era (1908–1918) harbingered the Republican Turkey. The "state economics" of the Unionists anticipated the neo-mercantilist policies in the early decades of the Republic. As for "populism," its brand was carried out by the Republican People's Party. Due to the emphasis given to the political and legal structure of the new republic, historians tend to underestimate the continuity between these two epochs. Without losing sight of the radical political steps undertaken in the early republican years, one must search for the social and economic continuities in the process of change (Boratav, 1988). In fact, the shaping of nation-state in Turkey was a response to the challenging nineteenth-century liberalism, and the Young Turks pioneered this dissent in the semi-periphery of global capitalism (Zürcher, 1984).

## Lausanne Treaty and Emancipation: The End of Capitulations

The post-war settlement was shaped by the Treaty of Versailles (1919) in the context of the Paris Peace Conference. However, it exacerbated the serious economic problems, failing to take account of economic realities. On the other hand, Turkey too had its own problems after the Lausanne Treaty. Several factors affected adversely the interventionist economic policy of the government. First and foremost, despite the official end of the capitulations, the Lausanne Treaty still imposed certain limitations on the government, especially about customs, taxation and concessions. Many complicated problems resulting from the population exchange, such as resettlement issues and financing the incomers, became the priority of the government. The early stage of nation-state making imposed many stumbling blocks upon the policy space. The feudal Kurdish riots against the unitary structure of the state popped up in several parts of Eastern Anatolia. The government had difficulty in finding the required capital for the start-up cost of reconstruction. Furthermore, Ankara had ignored several restrictions imposed upon it by the Lausanne Treaty, with respect to customs and concessions, along with the strict measures that deterred foreign companies. The problem of dealing with these issues was further compounded by an international economy which was undermined by the outcome of World War I and characterized by economic fluctuations and instabilities. Such ups and downs culminated in the Great Depression that struck at the end of the 1920s (Hershlag, 1968).

The intricate but fragile system of international division of labor had grown gradually in the century prior to the onset of World War I in August 1914, and brought unprecedented levels of well-being and even affluence to the populations of Europe and some overseas outposts. However, it suddenly disintegrated with the outbreak of World War I. After more than four years of the most destructive war the world had yet witnessed, world political leaders sought a "return to normalcy" but the world economy could not easily be put together again. Concentrated destructiveness of World War I surpassed anything in human history until the mass air raids and atomic bombings of World War II. Estimates of the direct money costs of the war (military operations) range from 180 to 230 billion dollars (1914 purchasing power), whereas indirect money costs because of property damage add up to more than 150 billion dollars (Broadberry & Harrison, 2005). Ankara had the mission of building a new nation-state under these catastrophic conditions. Several economic provisions of the Lausanne Treaty acted as constraints on Turkey during the 1920s. The most important were related to the tariff and tax structures. As the tariffs were frozen at the level of the adjusted specific scale of 1916, which approximately corresponded to the level of nominal protection prevailing on the eve of World War I, Ankara had to wait for the end of the "grace period" of the Lausanne Treaty for implementing protectionist trade policies. Differential rates of excise on imported and locally produced commodities were prohibited, the only significant exception being the government monopolies where higher prices could be charged for revenue purposes. Moreover, Turkey was obliged to eliminate existing quantitative restrictions on foreign trade and abstain from introducing new ones until 1929 (Tezel, 1994).

Reform acts, the main drive toward progress and development, speeded up dramatically just before and after the foundation of the Republic. The İzmir Economic Congress, held in February–March 1923 and the declaration of "economic independence" (*misak-ı iktisadî*), a replica of the "national independence" (*misak-ı millî*) act, which became the manifesto of the War of Independence in 1920, had a symbolic meaning for the pursuit of national economic policy. Delegates from most of Turkey's urban and rural areas, including representatives of capital and labor, were invited to the Congress. The resulting policies were not limited to urgent reconstruction projects, but also looked ahead to ambitious economic programs. The Congress laid down certain principles of industrial activity, which may be summarized as follows: Promotion of legislation for the encouragement of industry in basic necessities; changes in the customs tariffs according to the developmental needs of national industry; preference rates in land and sea transport for local produce; creation of better credit facilities for industry and agriculture; and technical education and training of engineers for industry (Ökçün, 1968). Through legislation and active entrepreneurship, the state attempted to initiate new patterns of economic development. The government's investment activities were reinforced by three national banks. The capital of the Agricultural Bank (*Ziraat Bankası*), which was established in 1888, increased to 20 million Turkish liras. Two new investment banks were founded: The Business Bank (*İş Bankası*) in 1924 and the Industrial and Mining Bank of Turkey (*Türkiye Sanayi ve Maadin Bankası*) in 1925. Both of these banks were established to finance the public and private initiatives of early republican years.

## Republican Mercantilism: Economy Under State Protection

War finance is a branch of defense economics or war economics. World War I was not only a military conflict, but also an economic war. In this context, financial mobilization played an important role. The macro logistics was on the side of the Allied Powers. In the first stage of the war, the Allies had access to five times the population, eleven times the territory and three times the output of the Central Powers. In terms of the resources as compared to either side, the Ottoman Empire did not seem to have much hope. If Germany, using surprise attack on the Western front with superior military qualities, could not win the war for the Central Powers in the first six weeks, then the chances of victory could only diminish over a longer span of time. With a protracted war, the balance of resources would become increasingly more decisive. In all belligerent countries, labor and material resources were shifted from civilian production to war-related purposes. A central planning system was established to organize production and distribution. This orientation heralded the age of regulation, or *etatism* in short (Supple, 2014).

The economics of financial mobilization involved three courses of action. First, a reasonable portion of the expenditure for troops, armaments, munitions and other war-related purposes was financed by taxes. In the second step, war loans were issued to fund the short-term government debt. As the third step, governments borrowed from the central banks, which practically meant printing money. The Ottoman Empire lacked flexibility in taxation, along with a lack of confidence for internal borrowing. Therefore, the third method of financing the war, the most unfortunate and dangerous option, was resorted to and implemented. As no more taxes could be collected at a time when the government's credibility was severely undermined, the only way to finance the war was to print money. The Ottoman government had no choice but shift from hard currency to paper money. Consequently, huge amounts of money were printed, adding up to 161,000,000 Ottoman liras in three years (Toprak, 2019a). Financing war expenditure through enormous increases in money supply did fuel price rises to a level unseen in world history. This course of action made the Ottomans the first to experience what might be called "hyper-inflation," as spiraling prices skyrocketed from the third year of the war. The cost-of-living index increased more than twenty times from July 1914 to the end of 1918. The annual inflation rate of 406% for 1917 remained unmatched in the economic history of Turkey. At the end of the war, prices in the USA averaged about 2.5 times higher than they were in 1914, in Britain about 3 times, in France about 5.5 times and in Germany more than 15 times. The great instability in Ottoman prices and consequently in the value of home currency caused severe social and political repercussions. The Ottoman society, creating its own haves and have-nots, imploded socially and lost the war much earlier than the armistice (Hardach, 1977).

On the positive side, however, it can be argued that wartime conditions, along with wartime government economic policies, changed the mentality of the Young Turks and "import substitution" helped pave the way toward a national economy. Republicans adopted basic tenets of the Young Turk government. "National economy" (*millî iktisat*) became the motto of the new republic. The period at least until 1927, and possibly until 1929, marked by decent rates of growth, should be interpreted as one of recovery and a return to pre-war levels of production.

The economic development of Turkey between the two world wars can be analyzed in two separate intervals: First, the period of rehabilitation from the ravages of the long years of wars with limited government intervention, mainly by administrative and legislative means; and secondly, the period of strict *etatist* policies from 1929 through the 1930s, characterized by energetic government intervention in the economic sphere, especially in the establishment of basic industrial units and financial institutions to replace the foreign ones. Those years altogether were mainly tilted toward the ideal of economic self-sufficiency on the part of Turkey, while the system of gold standard failed to restore itself to pre-war years in the world. The pressure of wartime finance had forced belligerent countries, except the USA, off the gold standard, which had served in the pre-war period to stabilize, or at least to synchronize, exchange rates and price movements. The disintegration of the gold standard brought the final dislocation in economies at both national and international levels, as divergent rates of inflation began to reign in countries (Hershlag, 1964).

After the dismemberment of the Ottoman Empire by the Allied powers and the three-year War of Independence, the Republic of Turkey was finally founded on 29 October 1923. It comprised a substantially smaller geographical area than the Ottoman Empire, containing only Eastern Thrace in Europe and Anatolia in Asia. Greater Syria and Iraq, and Western Thrace were lost. Total population dwindled from 24 to 13 million. The geographical boundaries of the new country and the nature of its political, economic, commercial and financial relations with the rest of the world were codified in the Lausanne Peace Treaty on 24 July 1923.

The Lausanne Treaty represented a major break for the new republic from the previous agreements of international legal framework that had governed the relations of the Ottoman Empire with the European powers. Three issues that caused a great deal of disagreement and conflict in Lausanne were particularly important for Ankara. First, the capitulatory system had opened the empire to arbitrary interpretations of the privileges granted to the capitulators. The second was the penetration of foreign interest and influence in economic and political fields, limiting the independence of the country. And thirdly, Ottoman foreign debts accumulated remarkably since the Crimean War (1853–1856). In the second half of the nineteenth century, the capitulatory system had facilitated the penetration of foreign capital. The government had granted an increasing number of concessions and privileges for the establishment and operation of a variety of economic enterprises in the Ottoman Empire. Concessions for railways, public utilities, banking, insurance companies and mining were, especially important.

The crucial issue at Lausanne was the settlement of the Ottoman debt, which had reached 142 million Ottoman liras on the eve of World War I (Toprak, 2019a). After protracted negotiations, Turkey assumed responsibility for the part of this debt that corresponded proportionally to its new geographical borders. As the Republic lacked financial resources, all payments on the outstanding debt, including interest payments, were frozen until 1929. Starting in 1929, however, this item became excessively important, partly because of the deflation in the 1930s. By that time, yearly payments accounted for 13–18% of total budget expenditures of the government. Meanwhile, under the pressure of the Allied Powers, an agreement was reached for the elimination all reparation payments arising from the War of Independence against Greece.

The Lausanne Treaty abolished capitulations and all privileges provided to foreign concessionaires, second time after 1914, this time multilaterally. It restored full sovereignty and freedom of action for the Turkish authorities. The treaty finally made it possible for the new government in Ankara to nationalize some of the more important foreign enterprises, particularly the railways, in return for compensation. Meanwhile, the government embarked on an expansive, long-term effort to build new railroads that would link eastern Anatolia with the rest of the country. This was an important step toward national security and the creation of an integrated domestic market within the borders of the new nation-state.

A closely related issue concerned the right of the country to pursue independent commercial policies. The free-trade treaties of the nineteenth century, signed with Western powers as an extension of the capitulatory system, ruled out government monopolies and committed the Ottoman state to low rates of customs duties, that is, 5% on imports and 12% on exports. Duties on exports were lowered and remained at 1% *ad valorem* until World War I. *Ad valorem* duties on imports were raised to 8% in 1861 and further to 11% in 1905. The most important aspect of the system was that tariff rates could not be changed without the consent of the European powers. As a result, Ottoman governments were unable to pursue protectionist trade policies until the outbreak of World War I (Issawi, 1980). At Lausanne, tariff rates on imports were fixed at levels comparable to those established by the Ottoman tariffs of 1916. After a grace period of five years, the new republic would be free to pursue independent commercial and tariff policies.

During World War I and the War of Independence, Turkey's losses were very large. Total population within republican territory appears to have declined by more than 30% between 1913 and 1923 (Toprak, 2017). Life expectancy declined to almost 30 years and literacy rate to 5%. Infant mortality rose to more than 60%. Animal husbandry dwindled to one quarter of the 1913 stock. There was a sharp fall in the urban population. The population exchange between Turkey and Greece, starting in 1923, further exacerbated the difficulties of economic redress, as new settlers had hard time to adapt themselves to their new environments. Agriculture also suffered heavily from the wars. Large segments of rural population were dislocated. Ethnic hostilities in different parts of Anatolia, along with the departure of Greek and Armenian peasants, affected the rural life adversely. The drastic fall in the number of draft animals reduced means of agricultural production. Areas under cereals cultivation decreased by as much as 50% between 1913 and 1923 (Pamuk & Toprak, 1988). Cash and tree crops were also hard hit. Levels of production of tobacco, cotton, raisins, ir branches of mining and industry were also severely affected. Railways, roads and ports were to a large extent destroyed.

However, in some branches of manufacturing, the disruption of imports, coupled with the rise in tariffs after 1916, encouraged the domestic production of imported goods. Not surprisingly, foreign trade had fallen sharply from its high levels in the years before World War I. In 1918, the value of exports was only 11% of the value in 1913 (Eldem, 1994).

## Major Targets of the Government Toward Self-Sufficiency

Meanwhile, the government laid down the major target of policies mainly as the protection of the national industry, of the local producers and their works and the utilization of domestic raw materials for industrial development. Balancing the budget and limiting the amount of money in circulation were also considered crucial, as the ravages of Ottoman economy haunted the minds of policymakers. First of all, the government had to avoid foreign aid on binding terms. "Balanced budget and strong currency" (*Denk bütçe, sağlam para*) became the motto of national economy. The amount of Turkish lira in circulation in 1923 did not change until 1939, leaving behind the dreadful and catastrophic price rises during World War I (Pamuk, 2018).

Measures were also taken in the field of industrial legislation. In April 1924, raw materials for export industries were exempted from duties.

1925 witnessed new regulations defining the legal status of professional associations of craftsmen, which were henceforth to be under the control of the Chamber of Commerce and the Ministry of Economy. The same year, the government published a decree which imposed on state institutions and those assisted by the state the duty of purchasing local produce if its price did not exceed that of foreign produce by more than 10% (Toprak, 2019b).

On the eve of World War I, attempts were made to encourage local industrial development through legislations issued in 1909 and 1913. They stipulated facilities for investors about acquisition of land and exemption from taxes and custom duties on imported raw materials, fuel and machinery. In the republican years, investment was further stimulated both by the Law for the Encouragement of Industry (*Teşvik-i Sanayi Kanunu*) of 1927 and the announcement of tariff reforms to be undertaken at the expiration of the "grace period" of the Lausanne Treaty. The 1927 Law reflected the government's decision to implement its own declarations and resolutions of the İzmir Economic Congress, concerning the encouragement of private initiative. Government intervention was restricted to those cases where private activity failed and capital-intensive investment was required. According to the industrial census taken in 1927, 44.30% of the enterprises were concentrated in food processing and 23.83% in textiles. The share of industries producing or servicing capital goods did not exceed 7–10%. The government owned at that time only the remnants of the pre-war state enterprises: The shoe factory in Beykoz, wood mills in Hereke and Feshane and a cotton-weaving mill in Bakırköy. These enterprises were transferred to the Industrial and Mining Bank of Turkey. Owned by the state, the Bank further aimed at facilitating the supply of credit to private initiatives and participated in 16 enterprises (apart from state-owned enterprises taken over by the military) until it became integrated, in 1933, with state-owned Sümerbank, the flagship of the industrialization in the thirties, within the framework of the First Five-Year Industrial Development Plan.

Lack of adequate initial capital was the main handicap of the slowly emerging industry. Great importance should therefore have been attached to the development of investment banking facilities. The initial step was taken by the establishment in 1924 of the Business Bank (*İş Bankası*). Although founded by the initiative of Atatürk, the president of the Republic, the Bank had a private character and reflected the then existing tendency of supporting private initiative for economic development. The tasks of the Bank extended over a wide range of activities, including investments in industry, mines and commerce; credit facilities in the organization of export activities; and stimulation of more extensive savings. In the early years of the Republic, the government encouraged the rapid growth of sugar industry, as Turkey suffered heavily during World War I due to the lack of sugar imports. The area of sugar beet cultivation increased, and the first sugar factory was established in Uşak, with the financial assistance of the Business Bank. Shortly afterward, a second factory was established at Alpullu in Thrace, and a third one in Eskişehir. Simultaneously, the government monopolized the import of sugar and regulated its price at home. Imports of sugar sharply dropped and disappeared completely in 1935. One of the concessions with lucrative income during the Ottoman years was tobacco. The government took over tobacco Regie in 1925, and at the end of the 1920s, it controlled the monopolies of tobacco, salt, alcohol and spirits, matches, sugar, oil and gasoline. The income from these essential goods did close the gap resulting from the abolition of the tithe (*aşar*), the land tax based on Sharia.

## Institutional Framework for National Economy

The reorganization of internal trade was of great importance for the future development of both agriculture and industry, as well as for the marketing of their products. Following the Greek exodus, commercial activities carried out by Turks increased and many new trading companies started up. The Law of Chambers of Commerce and Industry (*Ticaret ve Sanayi Odaları Kanunu*) enacted in 1925, regulated professional issues, made membership of Chambers compulsory for businessmen with a capital of more than 5000 Turkish liras and put the Chambers under government control. Commodities Exchange Markets were established in several cities; for hazelnuts in Trabzon and Giresun, for cotton in Adana and Mersin, for grapes and figs in İzmir and Manisa, for cereals and wood in Ankara, Konya and Eskişehir and for cereals and opium in Kütahya and Afyon. As for external trade, the tariff rates to be introduced were not known until 1929, but preparations for the reform had begun in 1925 and the general expectation was that the new tariff would be highly protective, with high rates for final consumption goods and low rates for imported inputs.

The government also changed the tax structure with the abolition of the traditional tithe of about 10% of output in agriculture and the animal tax (*ağnam*). To replace partially these sources of revenue, it increased the indirect tax levied on consumer goods, with a new 10% tax on the value of domestic industrial products, and raised the prices of commodities such as salt, sugar and kerosene sold by state monopolies. A first attempt to introduce income taxation was also made, with agriculture exempted. The abolition of the tithe has been viewed as the most important single change in policy affecting the agricultural sector during the interwar period. In 1924, the tithe accounted for 22% of the central government's budget revenue and 63% of the direct tax revenue. The abolition of the tithe, thus, involved the loss of the most important source of public revenue, and the newly instituted indirect taxes did not fully make up for the loss. The overall tax payments of the agricultural population were reduced considerably during the 1920s, shifting the burden on the urban population. But the internal terms of trade still made the rural populace vulnerable, as the price of non-agricultural goods increased faster than agricultural goods (Toprak, 2019b).

Close to one-third of the firms established in the 1920s were joint ventures of Turkish and foreign investors. The positive attitude toward foreign capital had a counterpart in government subsidization of domestic private enterprises (Keyder, 1981). The Law for the Encouragement of Industry offered a wide variety of incentives and subsidies to the new industrial establishments. Private investors also benefited from state monopoly of sugar, tobacco, oil, matches, harbors and other business areas. The government did not directly exercise its monopoly rights but allowed them to be held by domestic or foreign firms under favorable terms. The model of industrial development pursued by Ankara emphasized public financing with active participation of private local investors and capital contributions from foreign investors. Shortages of capital for financing industrialization and mining were met by the above-mentioned investment banks. They extended loans to the new industrial enterprises at low interest rates.

The years from 1923 to 1929 were characterized by the typical high growth rates of post-war periods. The estimated growth rate for GDP was 7.5% (Hansen, 1991). Terms of trade losses brought the rate of growth of gross national product down to 6.9%. The corresponding per-capita growth rates were 5.4 and 4.8%, respectively. Considering that these are growth rates for a post-war reconstruction period, they are respectable but not remarkably high. Behind the overall growth rates is an 8% annual increase in agriculture from 1923–1925 to 1927–1929. But construction and financing grew even faster, by 17 and 23%, respectively, and transport grew at a rate of 11%. The increases in manufacturing and government expenditures were less than average, but what held the overall growth rate not-so-high was the very low growth in housing and services (Hansen, 1991).

The increase in agricultural population is not known, but the exodus and exchange of population must have been a disrupting factor. The use of modern agricultural implements and machinery began expanding but data indicate a very low degree of mechanization, which was due to low level of education and lack of technical expertize. Turkey had labor shortages. Foreign labor had to be imported from Balkan countries for the construction of Ankara. Attempts in labor-intensive methods failed in most cases. The tractors imported from Italy ended up in tractor cemeteries as they were designed for Italy's soft soil and unsuitable for Turkey's harsh landscape. Furthermore, there was a lack of technical manpower required for the reparation of farm implements. The unusually rapid increase in yields may have been related to a return to pre-war circumstances and favorable weather conditions. Such a rise in yields was an important factor that should be emphasized in terms of the contribution of agriculture to the expansion of exports until 1929. Despite the exodus of rural Greeks and Armenians, who specialized in cash crops much more than their Muslim counterparts did, exports of tobacco, cotton, figs, raisins and hazelnuts to Europe and the United States rose steadily. By 1929, if not earlier, volumes of exports of these cash crops from the areas within the country's borders appear to have reached, if not surpassed, the levels of 1913. The share of manufacturing in 1923–1929 was by no means negligible, that is, almost 10% of GDP. Several factors should have served as a stimulus to industrial growth, but they were apparently slow to work. Post-war recovery in the urban areas led to the tripling of construction activity, thus generating substantial demand for building materials, timber, brick and cement. On the other hand, the high growth rate in agriculture must have generated a higher demand for consumer goods and possibly for agricultural inputs (Hansen, 1991).

## Concluding Remarks: The End of Dependency

The monetary and financial disorders caused by the war and aggravated by the peace treaties eventually led to a complete breakdown of the international economy. The 1920s were trial-and-error years of European powers. Unable to restore international trade to pre-war levels, they implemented a variety of restrictions, such as protective tariffs, physical import quotas and prohibitions, export subsidies and other measures to stimulate exports. Exaggerated economic nationalism resulted in lower levels of production and income. These drastic measures further deepened the crisis to such an extent that the protectionism of the 1920s may well be labeled as "neo-mercantilism." Each new restrictive measure provoked retaliation by other nations whose interests were affected. Volume of world trade had more than doubled in the two decades before World War I. It barely achieved the pre-war levels in the two decades that followed (Pamuk, 2018).

Turkish government's efforts toward reconstruction paid off. Toward the end of the 1920s, Turkey was able to meet its previous financial commitments and the economy recovered at least to its pre-war levels. The 1920s also saw radical economic and social reforms, however insufficient, in agriculture and in the public budget and taxation methods. These novelties, together with the beginnings of modern industry and real growth in traditional manufacturing, promised greater economic independence for the future (Pamuk, 2018). Gradually, the government reduced budget deficits and even registered a small surplus in 1928/1929 fiscal year, thanks to controlled expenditure and improvements in tax collection. Only in the depression episode of 1929/1930 did the deficit climbed once again. Then came the 1930s, when international upheavals and national responses and attitudes dramatically altered the economic setup both in Turkey and the world.

The post-tariff regulation policy took various forms. Foreign-exchange control was imposed in December 1929, following a huge demand for foreign currency for large imports in that year, causing a considerable depreciation of the Turkish lira. A system of quotas and restrictions on the import of certain commodities, along with a system of clearing and compensation agreements, constituted the measures taken by the government, bringing practically all foreign trade under government control. All these measures favorably affected Turkey's trade balance and increased the protection of domestic production. However, they hampered the development of a healthy and normal import–export policy. Meanwhile, Germany knew how to apply the clearing system and brought Turkey into its own international trading network, gaining effective control over Turkish foreign trade until World War II (Tekeli & İlkin, 1983).

In fact, apart from its cost in terms of the pitiable destruction of human life, the Great War was pyrrhic. Draining efforts of the war and commitments and the punitive peace designed in Paris in 1919–1920 led Europe and Turkey into profound economic difficulties and vicious political tragedies. The Austro-Hungarian, German, Ottoman and Russian Empires imploded. France was profoundly weakened. The United Kingdom lost its finance pre-eminence and trading strength to the USA and entered a prolonged and slow period of imperial twilight. The devastation was global. The costs and material destruction of war and the peace settlement, the huge overhang of public debt, and the consequent dislocation of trade, money and capital flow, all helped to destroy the basis of the pre-war gold standard and global economic and financial system. The profound misery of humanity's economic and social experience between the two great wars flowed directly from the Great War. Meanwhile, the capitalist system had temporarily accepted state intervention (Supple, 2014).

Turkey did survive under these dire conditions before establishing its nation-state in the 1920s. War finance for the first time in Turkish history challenged the Ottoman administration. This was a "total war." Home front had to sacrifice almost all its assets. High inflation created Ottoman's haves and have-nots. Ottomans lost the war in the fronts. But Ottoman society imploded before the end of the war.

The War of Independence was a watershed for the restoration of the national economy in Turkey. Despite the depressive milieu, the Republican economy fared reasonably well in the 1920s. The year 1929 was in several ways a turning point for economic development. This was the year of the beginning of the Great Depression when new strategies were called for at the level of the world economy. It was also the final year of the five-year grace period for customs tariffs of the abolished capitulations when, among other things, Turkey obtained tariff and tax autonomy. For both reasons, 1929 was the year from which new development efforts should have been expected as it heralded the last stage of what may be called "Turkish deglobalization." Finally, after the war economics of World War I and early republican endeavor for national-economy building, the third stage of Turkish self-sufficiency efforts, characterized by respectable industrialization in the 1930s, exhibited the highest growth rates in Turkish economic history, at a time when Ankara implemented economic planning as the second case in the world after Moscow (Yenal, 2003).

## References


Ahmed Emin. (1930). *Turkey in the World War*. New Haven.

Boratav, K. (1988). *Türkiye İktisat Tarihi 1908–1985*. Istanbul.

Broadberry, S., & Harrison, M. (2005). *The economics of World War I*. Cambridge University Press.

Çetinkaya, D. (2013). *The young Turks and the boycott movement: Nationalism, protest and working classes in the formation of modern Turkey*. I. B. Tauris.

Eldem, V. (1970). *Osmanlı İmparatorluğu'nun İktisadi Şartları Hakkında Bir Tetkik*. Türkiye İş Bankası Kültür Yayınları.

Eldem, V. (1994). *Harp ve Mütareke Yıllarında Osmanlı İmparatorluğu'nun Ekonomisi*. Türk Tarih Kurumu.

Gökatalay, S. (2020). *The political economy of corporations in the late Ottoman empire and early Turkish Repulic (1908–1929)*. Atatürk Araştırma Merkezi.

Hansen, B. (1991). *The political economy of poverty, equity, and growth*. Oxford University Press.

Hardach, G. (1977). *The First World War 1914–1918*. Allen Lane.

Hershlag, Z. Y. (1964). *The Modern Economic History of the Middle East*. Leiden: E.J. Brill.

Hershlag, Z. Y. (1968). *Turkey: The challenge of growth*. E.J. Brill.

Issawi, C. (1980). *The economic history of Turkey 1800–1914*. The University of Chicago Press.

Jurgen Osterhammel, J., & Petersson, N. P. (2005). Globalization—A short history. *Princeton University Press, 2005*, 28–29.

Karpat, K. H. (1985). *Ottoman population 1830–1914—Demographic and social characteristics*. The University of Wisconsin Press.

Kemp, T. (1983). *Industrialization in the non-western world* (2nd ed.). Longman.

Keyder, Ç. (1981). *The definition of a peripheral economy: Turkey 1923–1929*. Cambridge University Press.

Keyder. Ç. (1987). *State and class in Turkey: A study in capitalist development*.

Kushner, D. (1977). *The rise of Turkish nationalism*, 1876–1908.

Landau, J. M. (1984). *Tekinalp, Turkish Patriot 1883–1961*.

Lewis, B. (1977). *The emergence of modern Turkey*, 2nd ed.

Ökçün, G. (1968). *Türkiye İktisat Kongresi 1923-İzmir*. Ankara Üniversitesi Siyasal Bilgiler Fakültesi Yayınları.

Pamuk, Ş. (1987). *The Ottoman empire and European capitalism*. Cambridge University Press.

Pamuk, Ş. (2018). *Uneven centuries: Economic development of Turkey since 1820*. Princeton University Press.
Pamuk, Ş., & Toprak, Z. (1988) *Türkiye'de Tarımsal Yapılar (1923–2000)*. Yurt Yayınları and Türk Sosyal Bilimler Derneği.
Parla, T. (1985). *The social and political thought of Ziya Gökalp 1876–1924*.
Quataert, D. (1983). *Social disintegration and popular resistance in the Ottoman empire 1881–1908*.
Quataert, D. (1993). *Ottoman manufacturing in the age of industrial revolution*. Cambridge University Press.
Supple, B. (2014). War economies. In Jay Winder (Ed.), *The Cambridge history of the First World War*. Cambridge University Press.
Tekeli, İ., & İlkin, S. (1983). *1929 Dünya Buhranında Türkiye'nin İktisadi Politika Arayışları*. Orta Doğu Teknik Üniversitesi.
Tekinalp (1917). Kapitalizm devresi başlıyor. *İktisadiyyat Mecmuası, 67*, 1–2.
Tekinalp. (1918). Tesenatçülük—Yeni İstikamet. *Yeni Mecmua, 37*, 205.
Toprak, Z. (1995). *From imperial debt to global offerings*. İMKB Mepa.
Toprak, Z. (1997). Foreword. In R. Margulies (Ed.), *The proclamation of freedom in Manastir*. Yapı Kredi Yayınları.
Toprak, Z. (2003). *İttihat-Terakki ve Cihan Harbi—Savaş Ekonomisi ve Türkiye'de Devletçilik*. Homer Kitabevi.
Toprak, Z. (2012). *Türkiye'de Milli İktisat 1908–1918*. Doğan Kitap.
Toprak, Z. (2013). *Türkiye'de Popülizm 1908–1923*. Doğan Kitap.
Toprak, Z. (2014). *Türkiye'de Kadın Özgürlüğü ve Feminizm 1908–1935*. Tarih Vakfi Yurt Yayınları.
Toprak, Z. (2016). *Türkiye'de İşçi Sınıfı 1908–1946*. Tarih Vakfi Yurt Yayınları.
Toprak, Z. (2017). *Türkiye'de Yeni Hayat 1908–1928*. Doğan Kitap.
Toprak, Z. (2019a). *Türkiye'de Milli İktisat 1908–1918*. İş Bankası Kültür Yayını.
Toprak, Z. (2019b). Türkiye'nin Ekonomik Gelişimi (1923–2019). In Pegem Akademi (Ed.), *Modern Türkiye Tarihi* (pp. 238–258).
Tezel, Y. (1994). *Cumhuriyet Döneminin İktisadi Tarihi, 1923–1950*. Tarih Vakfi Yurt Yayınları.
Yenal, O. (2003). *Cumhuriyet'in İktisat Tarihi*. Homer Kitabevi.
Wallerstein, I. (1997). *The modern world system: Capitalist agriculture and the origins of the European world economy in the sixteenth century*. Academic Press.
Gökalp, Z. (1918). Halkçılık. *Yeni Mecmua, 32*, 102–104.
Zürcher, E. J. (1984). *The unionist factor: The role of the committee of union and Progress in the Turkish National Movement, 1905–1926*. Brill.

CHAPTER 4

# Turkey's Attempt to Break the Fetters Before the Ladder Was Kicked Away, 1929–1947

*M. Erdem Özgür and Eyüp Özveren*

## Introduction

There exists a rich tradition in political economy that takes either "imperialism" or "international division of labor" as a point of departure and attributes the ill fortunes of undeveloped or underdeveloped countries to this specific connection. It is argued that development is made difficult and distorted with obstacles placed on the way, if not outright impossible. More sophisticated formulations responding to the visible trends in the 1970s and 1980s without conceding from the earlier gains of dependency approach turned to seemingly oxymoron—but when

M. E. Özgür (✉)
Dokuz Eylül University, İzmir, Turkey
e-mail: erdem.ozgur@deu.edu.tr

E. Özveren
Middle East Technical University, Ankara, Turkey
e-mail: ozveren@metu.edu.tr



E. Özçelik and Y. Özdemir (eds.), *Political Economy of Development in Turkey*, The Political Economy of the Middle East,
https://doi.org/10.1007/978-981-16-7318-4_4

thoroughly considered, meaningful—specifications such as "dependent development" (Evans, 1979). Underlying these approaches are graded notions of a "dependency" that characterizes the connection between developed countries and the rest of the world as basically of an asymmetric nature. Various studies conceived with this basic perspective in mind, depending on where they stand along the optimism–pessimism axis, spell out strategies for "breaking the fetters" to "unbound the Prometheus" once more *pace* David Landes (1969), borrowing the title of his now-classic study of European industrialization, on one end, and to resonating Albert O. Hirschman (1970) to specify the possibilities as "voice and exit" by recourse to "exit" as "de-linking" after Samir Amin (1990) on the other. In this chapter, with this "dependency" literature in mind, we are concerned first and foremost with how close Turkey came to "breaking the fetters" in the wake of the Great Depression.

As of the 1970s, with the seemingly contradictory observation of industrialization in developing countries, there has accumulated a new critical literature from within the development economics. Development could no longer be treated synonymously with industrialization as had been the case until then with both mainstream and heterodox approaches. It became increasingly clear that industrialization itself was subject to geographical relocation from "center" to "periphery," just like any other entity on which the principle of Vernon's (1966) product life cycle applied. The shift in itself did not suffice to tell a success story about the country on the receiving end. More often than not, it showed the degrading of the activities involved in the relocation. Critical scholars thus had to adopt a subtler analytical framework that took into consideration the deeper dynamics at work beyond mere dependency, as well as measuring development in both absolute and relative terms. This critical literature serves as a safeguard to the excesses of modernization theory, as well as a constructive criticism to some of the lacunae in dependency formulations. It not only shoulders the nineteenth-century lessons of Friedrich List and the German Historical School, but also emphasizes that institutions matter as the other leg of the context. The best-known example of this kind of development economics is advocated by Ha-Joon Chang (2003).[1] He has repeatedly argued that now-developed countries developed by doing exactly the opposite of what they, along with international organizations such as the World Bank and the IMF, recommend today as best policies and practices to developing countries. It is not only that they recommend different policies, but they actually make sure, by changing the "rules of the game" when necessary, that the newcomers cannot replicate their experience. His path-breaking work that captures the specification of this deliberate obstruction, *Kicking Away the Ladder* (2002), provides us with the second component of our title.[2] We formulate our argument concerning Turkey's attempt as seen from a window of opportunity that was shortly opened by the Great Depression when the ability of those who kicked away the ladder was considerably eroded by a set of circumstances, and it was later to be closed by a new round of "kicking away the ladder," as witnessed with the construction of the postwar world under Bretton Woods international order. So much for the parameters of our deployed analytical scheme as summarily expressed in our title.

A few words on identifying the motivating problems for our work in existing literature remain in order. It is always useful to put ideas in perspective by use of (very) long-term observations with respect to greater spatial units of analysis. A recourse to economic history will help highlight them more easily. Let us do to Roger Owen the same honor he did to Charles Issawi at the very end of his now-classic *Middle East in the World Economy* (1981):

> In post-war Turkey, the regime established by Atatürk and the Republican People's Party *remained embarassingly dependent* on foreign capital and foreign enterprise even during the period of étatist policies in the 1930s. Neverheless, by 1914, the beginnings of *a movement directed against the structure of dependence established in the nineteenth century can dimly be discerned*. On this subject let Charles Issawi have the last word. Writing in 1961 he noted:
>
> In the *last forty years*, and more particularly *in the last ten*, three main shifts of power have taken place in the Middle East: from foreigners to nationals; from the landed interest to the industrial, financial, commercial and managerial interests; and from the private sector to the state. (Owen, 1981: 293, emphases added)

Owen speaks of the persistence of an embarrassing dependence in the long term. Issawi qualifies this further in terms of timing and changing forms across the Middle East. Forty years back from 1961, we get to the early republican Turkish experience, and ten years back, we get to the more general postwar spread of "economic development" in the rest of the Middle East. In one of the best studies of political economy of the Middle East by Alan Richards and John Waterbury, we see this point worked out in greater detail:

> Turkey serves as bellwether for the region in this process. It is *one generation in advance* over all its neighbors in the Middle East, having begun in economic policy and state building in the 1920s what most other countries would not attempt before the 1950s. (Richards & Waterbury, 1996: 43; emphases added)

They go on to speak of a "Turkish paradigm," and of "replicating the paradigm," with Turkey as "an example if not a model" for the other countries in the region, and argue that "Turkey showed what could be done to thwart imperialism," launching on an experimentation with import-substituting industrialization (ISI) strategy as early as in the interwar period (Richards & Waterbury, 1996: 175–176, 180). The authors opine that, after the 1950s, when a "liberal" economic phase was experienced, "[o]nly after a military takeover in 1960 did Turkey *return* to etatism. By that time it had been joined by another half-dozen states in the region" (Richards & Waterbury, 1996: 179–180; emphasis added). They felt obliged to note that the dissemination concerned was not the consequence of voluntary emulation but of broader forces of convergence at work on a world scale: "In fact, state-led ISI spread throughout the developing world in the years after 1945 and, as a strategy, had a logic independent of any single country's efforts" (Richards & Waterbury, 1996: 180). Notwithstanding the question of whether or not it was the same etatism to which Turkey returned in the 1960s, we need to emphasize in our narrative how Turkey's role in this respect as an outlier and a pioneer-trendsetter in the 1930s[3] was "normalized" so as to become one among the many in the postwar context. Such "normalization" was nothing less than an erosion of the global significance of the Turkish experience with the shifting context. This normalization process, moreover, possessed an out-of-the-ordinary attribute that begs for further scrutiny. Not only was Turkish economic development "normalized," but also Turkey got stuck or "trapped" at a certain stage of economic development, to use a more fashionable term:

> The case by case periodization of growth according to the stages formulated by a leading modernization theorist indicate that Turkey and Argentina are exceptional as far as persistence within an early phase is

concerned (Rostow 1978). Both countries, which had made an early entry into the path of development were now being taken over by late-latecomers in their political economic environment. (Özveren, 2000: 15)

This empirical demonstration by W. W. Rostow (1978), the development economist who previously authored a "noncommunist manifesto" of economic growth that left a deep mark on mainstream modernization theory, suggests how the early success of Turkey may have been arrested because of changes in international economic climate that benefitted the very forces economic development and the war economy cultivated in the first place. This concern lies behind our periodization of this chapter into two phases. Before going into that in the next section, however, several historical reminders are in order.

The Ottoman Empire yielded its heartland territories to the Turkish Republic as the major heir, after a decade of successive wars, the last of which was a national liberation struggle (1919–1922). This national liberation movement inspired many future leaders of the Third World, including Mahatma Gandhi and Jawaharlal Nehru of India, not to mention Sun Yat-sen of China. It was the first example of a country defeated in the First World War rejecting what John Maynard Keynes called a "Carthaginian Peace" imposed by the winners at the Paris Conference in Versailles by way of a resounding victory in the War of Independence. Not only was the effect of this event of potential worldwide significance, but also the making of this victory at both the battleground and the peace talks depended on a correct reading of the international context and exploiting conveniently the circumstantial opportunity created by the Soviet Revolution. By forging a mutually beneficial strategic alliance with their northern neighbor, the Kemalist regime in Ankara could turn the table upside down to its advantage.

The newly formed state inherited a huge international debt from its predecessor, which was negotiated during the peace talks leading to the Treaty of Lausanne (1923). Some economic clauses of the peace treaty put certain limitations[4] on state-led economic policy in terms of the trade regime and monetary policy. In addition to the massive debt burden, the expenses of reconstruction due to physical destruction by warfare in the more developed market-oriented regions of the country, and the costs incurred by resettlement of refugees from Greece and Bulgaria upon the agreements of population exchange compounded economic difficulties. The new regime, despite its strong developmental aspirations it inherited from the last decade of the Ottoman Empire, was thus confined to a "liberal" economic policy until the start of the Great Depression in 1929. The 1920s can best be understood as a period of "reconstruction under open economy conditions" (Boratav, 1993: 37; 2008: 311). The distinguishing characteristic of the era was international market-led agricultural development. The new regime compromised from ideological and doctrinal commitments and "adopted a relatively free trade and finance policy." For Keyder (1981: vii), the 1920s were "a period of full integration into the world economy despite the constitution of an independent nation-state, and it exhibited an almost exemplary structure of a dependent economy."

The far-reaching changes the national economy underwent in the 1930s, will be presented in the next section. We will see how this transformation in structure and purpose had one foot in the world economic trends of the time and the other in the specificities of national conditions and the resulting institutional "embeddedness" thereof. It should be noted that the reinforcement of the one-party (Republican People's Party; hereafter RPP) regime inherited from the 1920s, as first of a number of institutional innovations inaugurating the era, was also the precondition for the emergence and success of a national economic model of development just as its postwar dismantling would herald the end of our period of study.

## The First Phase (1929–1939): The Great Depression & the Innovative Turkish Response

The Turkish Republic changed the track of its economic policies during the Great Depression, the most serious economic crisis that the world economy had ever faced, a crisis which dwarfed all previous crises in size and intensity. In *General Theory*, John Maynard Keynes suggested that the instability of investor confidence, which affected the level of business investment, was a major reason for the collapse of industrial production in the developed world (Keynes, [1936] 1964: 315–320). While Eichengreen (1996) denounced the gold standard, Friedman and Schwartz (1993: 299–301) blamed contractionary monetary policy implemented in the US. In their view, this policy made the crisis more severe in the US and contributed to the spread of depression throughout Europe. Bernanke (1983: 258), in a similar vein, argued that the effects of the credit squeeze "helped convert the severe but not unprecedented downturn of 1929–1930 into a protracted depression." The credit squeeze in the US also affected Europe adversely. Capital flows from the US had fueled the economic boom of the 1920s in Europe; however, those flows declined significantly after 1927, causing a severe credit shortage. All in all, international lending declined by over 90% between 1927 and 1933 (Hobsbawm, 1996: 89).

Whether the Great Depression was triggered from within the US economy is important because in the course of the process US was on the way to become the primary global actor in the world economy and ultimately rise as the world hegemonic power promoting its custom-tailored postwar international order. Whereas John Kenneth Galbraith (1961: 182–191) focused on the internal structural problems of the US economy to do with the unequal distribution of income, investment deficit, and the role of luxurious consumption, Kindleberger (1986: 289) turned his attention to the greater picture with Britain unable, and the US unwilling, to assume responsibility for managing the financial flows of the world economy. The crisis in the developed world spread to the underdeveloped world swiftly, as the advanced countries hit by the crisis held a large share of world trade. Protectionism was seen as the best way to defend national economic interests against the vagaries of the world market. Such policy, however, was easier said than done, as national state-capacity in the economic sphere was required to implement protectionism (Polanyi, [1944] 2001: 216–217).

The deflation that followed the crash in 1929 hit primary-good producing countries harder than the industrial ones, owing to deteriorating terms of trade resulting from the sharper decline in the prices of agricultural and primary goods. Be that as it may, when the Great Depression hit Turkey through mainly reductions in agricultural export revenue, the country was nevertheless in a better position than many other equally vulnerable peripheral economies, as it possessed full political independence and a corresponding capability to shape its own economic policy at a time when such autonomy was a rare phenomenon in what would become the Third World only after the Second World War. With the expiration in 1929 of certain important economic clauses of the Treaty of Lausanne, such as the customs policy stipulations, the new regime could proactively adopt an interventionist and protectionist developmental policy, thereby, transforming the unfolding international economic crisis into a national developmental opportunity. Yet, this economic orientation would emerge neither easily nor spontaneously. Competent policymakers were needed throughout this trial-and-experience process.

The year 1929 was the beginning of a heavy storm that reshaped the world economy, but at the same time it was a window of opportunity for developing countries (Frank, 1967). During that short period of time from 1929 to the beginning of the Second World War, the policy decisions made by peripheral countries could break the fetters of dependency. Turkey was among the countries that could take advantage of the weakened power relations between the core and the periphery, originating from the aggravated internal problems of the former. Political and economic independence was the motto of the new regime in Turkey from the very beginning, but the 1920s were tough years, because of the economic reconstruction underway as well as the temporary economic provisions of the Treaty of Lausanne, for the state to assume the role of an autonomous policymaker. The obvious weakness and inability of national bourgeoisie to initiate the much desired industrialization, along with the adverse conditions generated by the Great Depression, steered the policymakers toward a major shift in economic course of action. Starting from 1929, the state began to take pronounced measures to increase its control over the economy, including foreign trade. The "revolution from above" type of intervention in the sociopolitical sphere, pertinent to the 1920s, was introduced with a new vigor into the economic sphere in the 1930s. Possessing a certain degree of policy autonomy, the state, controlled by a strong bureaucracy situated somewhat above—if not equidistant to—social classes, launched protectionist measures along with an early version of import-substitution industrialization (ISI) policy. One should keep in mind, though, that the inward-oriented policy framework of the time was by no means peculiar to the Turkish case.

Prime Minister İsmet İnönü declared the character and pronounced the name of the new economic policy in 1930: Etatism. However, etatism in this context was not synonymous with economic planning. It meant more than that, and "how much more" was the main subject matter. Etatism suggested that the state go beyond "a handmaiden role" vis-à-vis the private sector so as to "to seize the 'commanding heights' of the economy" (Richards & Waterbury, 1996: 178), controlling the key sectors. Yet, this augmented role of the state did not indicate a diminished role for private entrepreneurship, because a zero-sum game was not conceived between the two. State power and scope would be expanded via more active involvement in the economy, and the private sector could also benefit from this state-led economic framework through profits. Indeed, the policymaking elite of the period believed that private entrepreneurship would be protected and fostered in the playground set by the government (Kuruç, 1987: 53). Increasing public investment expenditures were not meant to crowd out private investments.[5] Instead, by undertaking investments that the private sector usually shied away due to reasons of scale or profitability, the state would show its support for private entrepreneurs and its underlying commitment to capitalism. As a matter of fact, the emerging bourgeoisie prospered through "etatism by obtaining marketing monopolies through the state economic enterprises, exclusive import licenses, credit from state controlled banks under very favorable terms and lucrative contracts from state firms to undertake major construction projects" (Pamuk, 1981: 26). In a sense, etatism helped create early segments of a national bourgeoisie within the broader "national economy" framework. Before delving into the developments that followed the initial phases of the Great Depression, we should take a look at its effects on society.

The Great Depression had varying effects on different social groups. Agricultural population was affected negatively in general, but large land-owners, despite their political strength, suffered more than the medium-sized, non-mechanized farms and peasants with self-sufficient family holdings because of the severe contraction of the export markets. Moreover, input prices did not decline as much as product prices resulting in another source of strain for large, market-oriented farms. The Land tax, which replaced the tithe, forced small- and medium-sized farmers to market a certain portion of their products, making life more difficult particularly for small family farms whose surplus production was quite limited. Landless laborers in rural areas lost their employment opportunities in large farms, but road construction schemes of the government provided them with an alternative job opportunity. In short, the Great Depression affected the overall rural population adversely in varying degrees. Merchants, industrialists, bureaucrats, and urban laborers that compose the urban population were not immune to the effects of the Depression either. Merchants who were in direct contact with agricultural producers suffered from declining revenues, yet usurer/trader type of merchants benefited from the negative rural conditions through appropriating the lands of peasants unable to pay their debts. Large exporters were definitely affected negatively, while small local traders were not influenced much. Foreign trade restrictions shifted internal demand toward domestic goods. Hence, the industrialists benefited from the

Depression conditions, thanks to lower agricultural prices accompanied by stable manufacturing prices. Civil servants were also among the beneficiaries, as their real incomes increased. Similarly, urban laborers enjoyed new job opportunities created by developing small- and medium-scale industrial enterprises. The consensus on the necessity of industrialization between the bureaucracy and large landowners, who wanted a stable internal demand for their products independently of the conditions of the world economy, was a significant consequence of the Great Depression (Tekeli & İlkin, 1983: 216–223).

Economic development through industrialization had been the strongest aspiration of the Republic since its foundation. The Great Depression, along with the uncertainties it created in the international milieu, provided Turkey with a historical opportunity to run after this aspiration. Core countries of global capitalism found themselves in the midst of an unexpectedly deep and long crisis, which forced them to renounce the premises of liberal capitalism such as free trade and the gold standard (Polanyi, [1944] 2001). Preoccupied with their own problems, the core countries lost their grip on the periphery, providing the latter with a window of opportunity for developing their own national industries (Berend & Ránki, 1974), through imitation as well as ad hoc trial and error, in response to the unfavorable primary commodity export trends, "and the attendant balance of payment crises" (Bagchi, 1987: 167).

With a swift policy change, and with one-party system in place, Turkey seized this opportunity by preparing its First Five Year Industrialization Plan (FFYIP) as the major vehicle of etatism. The FFYIP aimed at building up an independent and industrialized economy that is immune to wartime and peacetime crises. In this process, Turkey benefited considerably from Soviet guidance, which did not involve any strings attached, political or otherwise. Soviet economic experts arrived to Turkey in August 1932 and submitted their report titled "Turkish Cotton, Linen, Flax, Chemical and Iron Industries" (*Türkiye Pamuk, Keten, Kendir, Kimya, Demir Sanayi*) in November 1932. Not all suggestions of the Soviet experts accorded with the wants and needs on the Turkish side, but they still provided an important source of inspiration for the industrialization plan and even for longer-term industrialization attempts[6] (Tekeli & İlkin, 1982: 158–168). Because of the Soviet role in the Turkish planning process, the First Plan would have a compulsory dimension that went further than the characteristic incentive planning of the postwar mixed-economies, and even in the 1960s, after the mainstream retrenchment, Turkish economic planning would remain compulsory for the public and incentive for the private sector. Except for the loan from the Soviet Union, with a value of 10.5 million Turkish Liras and used for textile investments exclusively, and the loan from Britain, which was worth 16 million pounds and used to finance Karabük Iron and Steel Factory; the industrialization plan was financed with government's budgetary funds, especially through indirect taxes levied on consumption goods. There was no substantial increase in internal or external debts during the 1930s (Kepenek & Yentürk, 1994: 59, 61). Although the planners did not have much control on the technology of production, the industries covered by the plan would employ domestically available inputs eliminating concerns that could arise from the availability of raw materials. Hence, although technological dependence was an unavoidable aspect of the period, the authorities tried to minimize the dependence on external financial resources and the problems associated with raw material availability in the implementation of the Plan.

The FFYIP began to be implemented in 1934 and covered the period between 1934 and 1938. It involved the establishment of state-owned factories within a coordinated framework. The priority was given to consumer goods, such as textiles, sugar and food processing, and also to intermediate goods, such as paper, cement, glass, iron, and steel. The locations picked for these new enterprises were medium-sized urban centers on the existing railway lines (Arnold, 2012: 367; Pamuk, 1981: 26).[7] Industrialization was a development path with increasing returns and the FFYIP was a success.[8] Dependence on foreign producers (and also on "comprador" importers) of basic consumer goods declined considerably. Industrialization not only created new employment opportunities, but also helped to attain a relatively balanced budget on the part of the government. The next step was to launch a more ambitious second Plan in 1938, which covered such areas as mining and construction of power plants for electrification. Nonetheless, the outbreak of the Second World War in 1939 prevented its implementation.

One major indicator of the success of planned economic development via industrialization was the high growth of national output, as reflected in its annual average growth rate of 9% between 1933 and 1939 (Kepenek & Yentürk, 1994: 70), though this figure is suspect of a certain overestimation. Be that as it may, even if it were less, qualitative significance of the change underway far outweighed its numerical measure. Various reports and studies about the second and third plans reflect an orientation toward a more comprehensive approach to economic development by establishing growth poles around Zonguldak-Karabük and Kütahya (Tekeli & İlkin, 1992: 47). Such orientation indicates an awareness of the significance of "industrial districts" as a vital catalyst to growth and development via spillover effects. There was also a growing concern for the "microeconomic" aspects and efficient management of state economic enterprises in terms of cost-conscious and rational decision making. This turn of mind could serve as a check for the common problem of fostering internationally uncompetitive high-cost industries in the context of the early version of ISI. In this way, an important bottleneck could be resolved by raising prospective export earnings that would then sufficiently finance the imports of technology, machinery, and certain necessary inputs.

The contributions of Dr. Max von der Porten, a consultant employed by the Ministry of Economy and a protégé of Celal Bayar, the last Prime Minister of Atatürk, are important in this respect. Recourse to the viewpoint of outsiders reflects the outward-looking attitude of policymakers at a time when the collapse of world markets encouraged autarchic aspirations. At first, the best technologies available were sought for the new state economic enterprises (Kepenek & Yentürk, 1994: 61). It did not take long to see, however, that the best technology was not always the same as the "economically" best choice. *Kadro*[9] economists had practically recommended that second-hand machinery be imported from bankrupt businesses in Europe during the process of building up new plants. Von der Porten went further and pointed out how the best technology could fail to fit the existing organization and factors of production by raising costs and reducing efficiency (Tekeli & İlkin, 1992: 23–24). Instead, he suggested functional combinations of equipment and workforce. The fact that these issues were taken seriously demonstrates the intellectual sophistication behind the development efforts underway.[10]

On the one hand, the FFYIP itself was a major innovation that would later serve as an archetypal scheme to instruct postwar latecomers. On the other hand, its success as a specific course of action should be evaluated in connection with certain formal institutions, such as the newly organized Ministry of Economy, the "Supreme Economic Assembly" (*Âli İktisat Meclisi*, an advisory board established to help design economic policies), the Central Bank (established in 1930, only a few years prior to the Plan), the Foreign Trade Office (established in 1934), and Sümerbank and Etibank[11] as the two major entities responsible for establishing and operating state economic enterprises covered in the Plan. *Türkiye İş Bankası* ("Business Bank of Turkey"), the first national bank founded in 1924, also played a supplementary role in financing the Plan during the 1930s. The fact that *İş Bankası* was founded by the prominent figures of the time[12] for supporting the private sector indicates that the Plan did not intend to impose an absolute state control upon industrialization.

There was also a steady drive to inculcate the urban consumers with a sense of duty to buy domestically produced goods, such as the annual exhibitions organized in Istanbul and Ankara to display and promote "native products" (*Yerli Malı Sergileri*) and a nationwide festivity week with the "native products" theme (*Yerli Malı Haftası*). Yet, another institutional endeavor to develop saving habits at national level was the establishment of the National Economy and Saving Society (*Millî İktisat ve Tasarruf Cemiyeti*), headed by Kazım Özalp, the then president of the National Assembly (Tör, 1999: 15, 16). This Society, as an umbrella institution, also organized a "Congress of Industry" (*Sanayi Kongresi*) in 1930 and a "Congress of Agriculture" (*Ziraat Kongresi*) in 1931. It was in these two congresses that a consensus on state-led and planned national economic development was reached. Moreover, this Society also took part in fairs and expositions in Budapest and Leipzig in 1937, on behalf of the Ministry of Economy (Tör, 1999: 17). All these development-oriented organizational efforts constituted a single institutional matrix that aimed to generate the desired economic outcomes at national level. In 1937, etatism, as one of the six basic principles of the Republican People's Party, was incorporated into the Constitution, and was retained as a constitutional principle until the Constitution of 1961.

Agricultural sector, on the other hand, is a slightly different story. The fall in agricultural prices with the Great Depression affected a large portion of the population, as more than 80% of the total population lived in rural areas in the 1930s (Pamuk, 2018: 189). The existing property relations and distributional patterns, lack of transportation network, and scarcity of physical and human capital prevented profitable agricultural production, hence capital accumulation in agriculture. In 1933, an Austrian geographer described Turkey's peculiar agricultural structure as follows:

> The rule that of all grains wheat obtains the best soil, generally holds true throughout the world; nevertheless, in Turkey it is practicable only for regions so situated that they have connections with the world market. But

> when a region is so poorly connected to the main streets of commerce that its agricultural production cannot be exported, then it applies such agrarian laws as it deems best, producing those grains and products in demand in its own neighborhood and in adjacent territories. (Stratil-Sauer, 1933: 328)

Despite unfavorable price developments, agricultural output increased and its strong performance turned agriculture into a source of economic growth during the 1930s. Despite all negative conditions generated by the Depression, the agricultural sector managed to grow at an annual rate of 4.4% during the 1930s (Pamuk, 2018: 158). One of the primary reasons for this performance was the demographic recovery coupled with the expansion of cultivated land. The number of family farms and the average amount of land cultivated by each family farm increased. In order to cope with the declining prices, the amount of family labor in production was increased. Another reason was the improvements in the transportation network. Construction of railways linked central and eastern Anatolian lands to urban markets, and by the end of the decade, Turkey became an exporter of not only traditional cash crops but also of a major staple food, wheat. Beyond any doubt, the manufacturing sector owed its strong performance to the resilience of the agricultural sector (Pamuk, 2018: 189–190).

Improvements in transportation and communication networks, and health and education services, along with a more stable financial system, were on the agenda of the government. Given the fact that an overwhelming majority of the population still lived in rural Turkey, modernization attempts were not confined to urban areas. Nation-state building required the elimination of backwardness, in the widest sense of the term, in the countryside, by borrowing from examples observed in a wide range of countries along the political spectrum ranging from the more obvious Soviet Russia to Mussolini's Italy (Muşat, 2015: 542–543). Whereas the earlier "model village" project was put into action in 69 sites by 1934 (Örmecioğlu, 2019: 734–735), the establishment of village institutes (*Köy Enstitüleri*) gained momentum in the second half of the decade. These institutes were designed to educate, both practically and politico-culturally, the rural population by recruiting teachers from the rural youth. The project was quite innovative and certainly brought some change to the countryside after centuries of neglect.

The economic policy followed by the government during the 1930s was a successful mix of orthodox and Keynesian policies. Orthodox elements of economic policy involved strict fiscal discipline and tight (strong) money; while the Keynesian elements were reflected through government intervention, regulation, and planning. Fiscal discipline implied that deficit-financing of the industrialization process would be ruled out in principle. The government chose to implement such a hybrid policy because of the lessons learned from the past, while common sense also necessitated it. The Ottoman experience with external debt and public deficit had left such traumatic scars on the civil and military bureaucracy of the time that they had no tolerance whatsoever for debt- or deficit-financing. Expansionary fiscal and monetary policies were, thus, out of the picture throughout the 1930s. Yet, according to available estimates, both GDP and GDP per capita rose during the 1930s with average annual growth rates of 5.2 and 3.2%, respectively (Pamuk, 2018: 158).

As an important indication of "monetary independence," the Central Bank of the Republic of Turkey was established in 1930 and became functional in 1931. Founded as a joint-stock company, it enjoyed a certain degree of autonomy during the 1930s, reflected in relatively low inflation rates. Naturally, the authority of issuing money belonged exclusively to the Central Bank, which could set discount rates and regulate the money market, but nominal money supply did not change during the decade, and the Turkish Lira appreciated against major currencies. In this environment, export revenues as a ratio of GDP declined "from more than 11 percent in 1928–29 to less than 7 percent in 1938–39" (Pamuk, 2018: 187). On the other hand, the measures taken to maintain a balanced foreign trade through import tariffs, quotas, and foreign exchange controls resulted in a fall in imports in terms of both quantity and value (Tekeli & İlkin, 1983: 217). Indeed, these measures "sharply reduced the import volume from 15.4 percent of GDP in 1928–29 to 6.8 percent by 1938–39" (Pamuk, 2008: 278).

Hale (1980: 108) noted that, in 1928, basic consumer needs, textiles, clothing, and sugar "accounted for 44.7 per cent of total imports, compared with 20.2 per cent for metals, machinery and vehicles. By 1939 these percentages had been virtually reversed to 19.2 per cent and 42.5 per cent respectively." Turkey managed to spare a higher proportion of its foreign exchange earnings to finance imports of capital goods, which had a positive effect on economic growth. A combination of external and internal conditions created a suitable environment for the flourishing of small- and medium-scale enterprises in the country. Although prices of manufactures declined in international markets, they remained more or less constant within the country (Tekeli & İlkin, 1983: 219). Fall in imports resulted from protectionist policies, and the strong-money policy, coupled with low wages and low raw material prices, enabled private entrepreneurs to increase their investments and profits (Pamuk, 2018: 189).

A crucial outcome of the Great Depression in Turkish economic thought was the *Kadro* movement. Indeed, an early version of the "dependency approach" emerged in Turkey during the first half of the 1930s with the publication of *Kadro* journal. For *Kadro* economists, the Great Depression heralded the imminent collapse of capitalism as they knew it. They perceived the Depression as an exceptional opportunity for the underdeveloped world to severe their dependency ties to a certain degree (at least on consumption goods) with the core countries. Importing relatively cheap capital goods was the shortest way of creating a national industry under crisis conditions. Turkey, as the leader of national liberation movements in the early twentieth century, should have set yet another example of independence—this time in the economic sphere. A spurt of industrialization through state intervention, regulation, and planning would not only make the Turkish economy strong enough to compete with the core countries, but also prevent social class formations that vitiated developed capitalist societies, according to the *Kadro* authors (Aydemir, 1932: 24; Belge, 1932: 39). To this effect, they argued that the key sectors of the economy had to be controlled by the government. Their views were rather extremist for the mainstream ruling elites and quite disturbing for the societal groups whose faith in liberal capitalist development was unshakeable. Expansionary monetary and fiscal policies they proposed were not heeded as an alternative to the orthodox policies of the government. For a regime that was far from willing to burn bridges with capitalism, the "renegade" Şevket Süreyya and Vedat Nedim, and perhaps even İsmail Hüsrev, remained suspect of crypto-communism. Policymakers, unlike the *Kadro* authors, believed that etatist policies were not meant to ultimately build a state-controlled economy, but aimed at nurturing private initiative as a side-effect along the course of economic development (Boratav, 2008: 325). After the publication of its 36$^{th}$ issue, the *Kadro* journal was closed in January 1935.

During the 1930s, Turkey's relations with Germany and Soviet Russia improved as a result of increasing foreign trade and economic cooperation. The share of clearing agreements in foreign trade increased during the 1930s, and Germany became an essential partner in these agreements.

Likewise, the feedback of Soviet experts in the preparation of the FFYIP was essential. Diversifying external economic relations was another way of diminishing the level of economic dependence. Turkey's dependence on its traditional partners, Britain and France, decreased along with the improving relations with Germany, Soviet Russia, and also the United States (Ahmad, 1993: 100). Intensification of political-economic rivalries among these countries created exceptional opportunities. As a major heavy-industry investment through British credit, iron-and-steel plant in Karabük started operation in 1939 (Kepenek & Yentürk, 1994: 59, 66). In an international conjuncture where Britain collaborated, behind the scenes, with its rival, Germany, to reject assistance to Greece and obstruct their attempts for a similar project as part of an ambitious industrialization program,[13] Turkey's relative success in getting a favorable response was of major significance as it reflected the ability of the government two achieve "milking two cows at the same time"—a phrase the popularity of which is generally attributed to Joan Robinson (1903–1983), the influential British economist, who campaigned for unorthodox economic development in the 1960s and 1970s. Robinson conceived this option some twenty-thirty years later, in a world where the Western and Soviet Blocs sought to expand their spheres of influence at the expense of one another, and their rivalry served to strengthen the hand of Third World countries that desperately needed foreign aid and credit for their economic development projects. Toward the end of the war, Turkey would symbolically declare war against Germany with an eye to admission to the United Nations; and later on, Soviet Russian territorial demands would push the country to the North Atlantic coalition in the making, with the United States expanding its sphere of influence so as to include Turkey. Before these developments took place, however, there was yet another phase for Turkey, during which the world was "burning up in the horrors of an inter-imperialist war",[14] while the future of the Turkish economy hung in the balance.

## The Second Phase (1939–1947): Wartime Derailing of the Turkish Political Economy

High growth rates and low inflation that Turkey enjoyed during the 1930s, along with the experimentation of an early version of ISI, came to an end with the outbreak of the Second World War. The implementation of the ambitious Second Five-Year Industrialization Plan (1939–1943), which sought to deepen and spread industrialization, was indefinitely postponed. Even before the war began, resources were switched to military ends. Turkey did not participate in the war, yet suffered from severe economic downturns as a result of diminishing imports and increasing defense spending financed by monetary expansion and resources extracted from the peasantry. On the other hand, one of the main measures taken to increase government revenues, the Wealth Tax (*Varlık Vergisi*), quite common elsewhere, turned out to be a contentious issue in Turkey ever since its introduction in 1942 because of the disproportionate burden it practically generated for the non-Muslim bourgeoisie (Pamuk, 1981: 26, 2008: 280).

During the Second World War, both agricultural and industrial production declined, but paradoxically, war conditions speeded up the process of creating a national bourgeoisie. In an environment characterized by scarcities and shortages, black markets flourished, opening a new way for capital accumulation in private hands in the form of excessive earnings. Wartime inflation contributed to such accumulation.[15] Imports decreased by half during the early years of the war, and the intense shortage of imported machinery and spare parts triggered a fall in domestic industrial output. Agricultural output also decreased severely because of the rising military conscription and the prolongation of compulsory service. The production of the major staple food, wheat, dropped by 50% during the war years (Boratav, 2008: 333).

The incumbent governments during the war faced more or less the same problems. Shortages and high inflation hit large masses. At the same time, serious problems emerged in meeting the needs of the urban population, such as the provision of food, clothing, and heating. During the first two years of the war, the government attempted to solve the problems by taking harsh interventionist measures and imposing price controls; but rather than solving the problems, these measures aggravated them by leading to black markets, hoarding, and bribery. After 1942, such interventionist policies were replaced by relatively more market-oriented alternatives, and price controls were largely abolished. The immediate effect of this policy shift was a hike in prices, rendering 1942 and 1943 the years with the highest wartime inflation rate (Boratav, 2008: 335). Because of the high inflation rates, the real wages that had not changed significantly during the 1930s declined by around 30 percent during the war. Indeed, the real wages did not catch up with their prewar levels until 1948 (Pamuk, 1981: 26).

In 1944, just before the end of the war, the Turkish government decided to prepare a postwar development plan. As of May 1945, the program summary was ready, sharing significant similarities with the Second Five-Year Industrialization Plan that had been put on the shelf because of the war. The industrialization program consisted of two parts: The first was the urgent one (hence the resultant Urgent Industrialization Plan), and the second part included industrialization schemes that would be phased out. In this plan, infrastructure projects, such as railroad and highway construction, ports, irrigation, and electrification works, were proposed along with a comprehensive industrialization package. Since two members of the *Kadro* movement, Şevket Süreyya Aydemir and İsmail Hüsrev Tökin, were actively involved in the preparation of the plan, it carried the features of thorough "work plans" depicted in various articles in the *Kadro* journal a decade earlier. The state was given a chief role in the plan for preventing the emergence of a parasitic social stratum dependent on foreign capital and avoiding antagonisms among social classes (Tekeli & İlkin, 1981: 1–4).

Nevertheless, the postwar domestic and external conditions forced the government to put aside this plan and prepare a new one in line with foreign expectations and internal demands in 1947. The most powerful internal reason was the pressure posed on the governing RPP through the formation of a rival political party by a splinter group, the Democrat Party (DP), in conjunction with the transition to a multiparty system in 1946. The DP embraced a liberal stance, opposed the land reform that had been on RPP's agenda since the 1930s, and had certainly more pro-business leanings. In order not to fall behind in the race for adapting to the new postwar international climate, the RPP government, after winning a disputed election in 1946, switched to a more moderate pro-market position by scaling down the interventionist content of the economic plan. The main external reason was the unwillingness of foreign circles to tolerate, let alone extend financial and technical support for an ambitious industrialization program. Seeking security under the Western alliance and adopting a multiparty regime, the Turkish government was then deprived of any Soviet support. Therefore, there was no foreseeable alternative than yielding to the Western external pressure. The result was a new plan, that is, the Vaner Plan[16] prepared mostly by the more liberal-minded bureaucrats of the day (Kepenek & Yentürk, 1994: 82). Expecting to receive foreign financial support, the new plan focused on agriculture and agriculture-related transportation and energy projects. In order to look eligible for the Marshall Plan, the new plan was called the "Turkish Recovery Program." Having remained practically neutral during the war, with no physical destruction, Turkey was initially considered ineligible as a country in need of urgent reconstruction when the Marshall Plan was first launched in 1947. In return for a more liberal, more open, and more agricultural economic structure, Marshall Plan was extended to Turkey in 1948 (Kepenek & Yentürk, 1994: 84, 122; Pamuk, 2018: 206). The favorable revision of attitude to Turkey in this respect was helped by the urgent need to provide aid during the Greek Civil War (1946–1949) that made US increasingly aware of the Soviet threat hanging over the Balkans and the Straits.

The result was further pruning of the 1947 Vaner Plan, which was itself a curtailed version of the original 1945 plan. In the new version, agriculture was accentuated as the principal sector and singled out as the prospective engine of economic development. In addition, private initiative was allowed to invest freely in any area of economic activity. Foreign pressure, thus, forced the ruling party to follow a liberal path, prefer private enterprises over public ventures and prioritize agricultural development over industrial development. In retrospect, the significance of this unimplemented plan lies in mirroring the reorientation of the Turkish economy at a crossroads (Tekeli & İlkin, 1981: 1–26). After the war, etatist policies based on planning were already being strongly criticized by liberal circles within the country. However, the last nail in the coffin came from what is widely known as the Thornburg Report and remains beyond the scope of this chapter (Thornburg et al., 1949). In short, because the original industrial growth strategy could not be pressed forward as originally intended, sideward economic outgrowths via the black market and smuggling as well as other rent-seeking activities distorted the existing political economy and cultivated social forces waiting for their turn in the wings.

## Conclusion: *Erken Öten Horozu Keserler!*[17]

Through etatist planning and inward-oriented policies, a great deal of industrial and infrastructural investments was undertaken during the 1930s with a sincere desire for creating an independent economic structure. By the end of the decade, Turkey was already producing basic consumption goods it had previously imported. Despite unfavorable changes in prices, agricultural sector also exhibited a noteworthy performance, contributing to the growth of national income rather than becoming a bottleneck for the further progress of an early version of ISI. It is true that the capitalist core found itself preoccupied with its own problems, providing a critical window for peripheral countries like Turkey to develop their own industries, yet, the dependency relations established and forged during the nineteenth century, which continued until the Great Depression, were not easy to break in a decade.

An extremely powerful external factor, the Second World War, interrupted, and the emergent and profoundly different postwar political-economic order reversed the tide of what may be called "Turkish exceptionalism." The combined effect of the cost of maintaining a large army, armament expenditures, declining output in manufacturing and agriculture, diminishing imports (especially of capital goods, spare parts, and raw materials), rising inflation, deteriorating internal economic conditions as a result of hoarding and black-marketing, and profiteering was to compound domestic distress during the war years. Foreign trade surpluses and the concomitant accumulation of gold and foreign reserves were positive developments of the war years. Joseph Stalin's postwar territorial demands and the gloomy psychology of domestic groups[18] pushed the government to the Western bloc forged under the US leadership. Turkey became a member of the International Monetary Fund and the International Bank for Reconstruction and Development (the World Bank) in 1947. The path chosen after the war restrengthened dependency relations which had tended to take a different course during the 1930s.

The vindictive attack by foreign experts like Thornburg and his associates on the Turkish attempt to set up heavy industries reflected not only a mainstream economic criticism based on a static notion of efficient resource allocation, but also the cumulative frustration in the West with Turkey's out-of-the-ordinary development strategy that could have had a dangerous demonstration effect on late latecomers waiting in the line. Even if the example of securing British finance for an iron-and-steel plant project in Karabük was "uneconomic" by standard "economic" criteria, it manifested a benchmark performance by its "political economic" quality. If Turkey, by exploiting great-power rivalry to its own advantage in the 1930s, could do what others could not, this was proof of developmental success of the international political-economic kind. Such an attainment had to be prevented at all costs. The window of opportunity that made "milking two cows at the same time" possible had to be closed. Achievement of this end was only a matter of time in a postwar world where international neutrality was no longer possible, and where geopolitics dictated that a multiparty democracy be adopted immediately in return for international security.[19] It is no wonder why the Turkish planning experience of the 1960s, dissociated from etatism in tune with mainstream ISI spreading all over the world, would not measure up to the etatist planning of the 1930s in terms of producing "differential gains" that hold the key to the improvement of the relative position of a country in international political economy.

The determination to erase the memory of Turkish exceptionalism became an understandable self-reinforcing trend ever since the Survey of Thornburg and his company. The question as to why Turkey serving as a laboratory for economic development during the 1930s, with not only Turkish economists but also genuinely interested German and Russian experts, did not actually leave a strong mark in postwar institutionalization of development economics has been raised (Tekeli & İlkin, 1992: 59). While this remains a legitimate question as far as mainstream development economics is concerned; within a broader perspective, we would like to bring to the notice of the reader the insufficiently recognized legacy of the *Kadro* movement. The effect of the *Kadro* movement remained limited in pushing Turkish etatism ahead in a radical direction. But its contribution into the interactive intellectual environment in which the Turkish model took shape was greater. To put it differently, it played a greater role, albeit indirectly. By theorizing economic development in relation with dependency along the way, it was of worldwide significance as a precedent of the Latin American *Dependencia* school. As such, the originality of *Kadro* economic thought deserves credit as one further indicator of Turkish exceptionalism during the 1930s. It remains as testimony to the deliberately carved void in collective memory, at home and abroad, concerning the highly original Turkish political-economic experience of the interwar period. The Turkish experience itself, came too early, before the Third World emerged within decades as an unintended consequence of the postwar order reaping the benefit of bipolar balance of power. This gives historic significance to the Turkish case as a pioneer of what was yet to come, though at a high price, because the unfavorable context prevailing in the meantime undermined its chances for survival.

## Notes

1. See his edited volume with a wide range of contributions for a good sample of critical work in this direction.
2. The originator of the term is Friedrich List who stated: "It is a very common clever device that when anyone has attained the summit of greatness, he kicks away the ladder by which he has climbed up, in order to deprive others of the means of climbing up after him" (List, [1841] 1885: 295).
3. "Turkey became first among the backward countries to conduct an experiment in planned development with its first five year plan in 1934" (Hershlag, 1968: 74).
4. "At Lausanne, the Turkish delegation was forced to make economic concessions in return for the abolition of the political and legal capitulations. As a result, tariffs were frozen at the 1916 rates, with prohibitions on differential rates for imported and locally produced goods. These restrictions came to an end at the beginning of 1929; until then Turkey forfeited her right to protect her already ailing economy" (Ahmad, 1993: 94).
5. In 1938, after the completion of the First Five-Year Industrialization Plan small-scale private enterprises still provided 75% of employment in manufacturing (Pamuk, 2008: 278).
6. In 1933 and 1934, a group of American experts also prepared a survey on the Turkish economy (the Report of the Hines-Dorr-Kemmerer Mission). Whereas Tekeli and İlkin (1982: 173–174) argue that this survey did not have any influence on the FFYIP, Trask (1964: 76) asserts that it "contributed much to Turkish economic planning and development".
7. Arnold (2012: 367) notes: "Twenty-one enterprises were planned, including a paper mill in İzmit, a cement plant in Sivas, an iron and steel plant in Karabük, and brimstone and copper factories in Keçiborlu (Isparta) and Ergani (Diyarbakır)....cotton textile mills at Nazilli and Kayseri....cotton textile factories were established in Kayseri (1935), Ereğli (Konya, 1937), Nazilli (1937), and Malatya (1939).... A rayon plant at Gemlik (1938) and wool factory at Merinos (1938) in Bursa completed the array of textile investments".
8. Boratav (2008: 328) states that annual average growth rate of the industrial sector was 11.6% between 1930 and 1939, and it

has been the highest rate ever in Turkey. The reader should be cautioned that higher rates are nonetheless easier to attain by also arithmetic necessity at lower stages of growth when one starts with a "base" little more than nothing.

9. A movement formed by a group of economists organized around the Kadro Journal, short-lived yet influential.
10. Only as of the 1960s did development economists like Joan Robinson, through theoretical insights gained from the "Cambridge capital controversies" and the "switching of techniques" debate, recommend "unorthodox" combinations of factors to the less-developed countries in compliance with the Chinese principle of "walking on both legs." Robinson believed that the coexistence of old and new techniques "was consistent with rapid accumulation without imposing an intolerable sacrifice of consumption." (Harcourt & Kerr, 2009: 149–150).
11. Sümerbank and Etibank were critical institutions of the etatist era. The former was established in 1933, both as a bank and a primary institution responsible for the execution of investment plans. The latter was established in 1935 together with the General Directorate of Mineral Research and Exploration (*MTA*) and was responsible for mining operations.
12. Mustafa Kemal (Atatürk) himself was one of the founders and provided one fourth (250.000 TL) of its initial capital.
13. Greek attempts to circumvent the obstacles by recourse to buying used equipment from the US also failed, and the Metaxas regime had to renounce its plan in 1937. We thank Soner Aytek Alpan for drawing our attention to the details of this parallel process, and to a source in Greek (Chatziiosif, 1993: 165–174).
14. "Before humanity chokes (or basks) in the dungeon (or paradise) of socialism it may well burn up in the horrors (or glories) of imperialist wars". An original footnote clarifies that the section was written in 1935, before the war broke out (Schumpeter, [1942] 1976: 163n).
15. "From a base of 100 in 1939, the Istanbul cost of living index had risen to 354 by 1945, an average rate of increase of around 23 percent per annum" (Hale, 1980: 110).
16. This plan was conveniently named after the chairperson of the council that prepared the plan, Kemal Süleyman Vaner.

17. Popular Turkish proverb that can literally be translated as "They cut off the early crowing rooster".
18. Wartime taxation and the burden of urban provisioning upset the rural population, especially the poor peasantry. Large landowners were already disturbed by the land-reform plans of the ruling party, and the bourgeoisie (despite their increasing revenues thanks to lucrative opportunities) started to demand less government regulation and more private initiative (Pamuk, 2008: 281).
19. Spain and Portugal under the dictatorships of Franco and Salazar, respectively, also faced a similar pressure for adopting multiparty democracies, but because they were not under threat from a disproportionately powerful neighbor, they could resist until the Cold War forced the West to reconcile with them as they were.

## References


Ahmad, F. (1993). *The making of modern Turkey*. Routledge.

Amir, S. (1990). *Delinking. Towards a polycentric world*. Zed Books Ltd.

Arnold, C. E. (2012). In the service of industrialization: Etatism, social services and the construction of industrial labour forces in Turkey (1930–1950). *Middle Eastern Studies, 48*(3), 363–385.

Aydemir, ŞS. (1932). Tabiata Tehakküm. *Kadro, 1*(3), 19–24.

Bagchi, A. K. (1987). Industrialization. In J. Eatwell, Murray Milgate & Peter Newman (Eds.), *The new Palgrave: Economic development*. Macmillan.

Belge, B. A. (1932). Cihan Buhranı Bitti mi? *Kadro, 1*(10), 28–39.

Berend, I. T., & Ránki, G. (1974). *Economic development in East-Central Europe in the 19th & 20th centuries*. Columbia University Press.

Bernanke, B. (1983). Nonmonetary effects of the financial crisis in the propagation of the great depression. *The American Economic Review, 73*(3), 257–276.

Boratav, K. (1993). *Türkiye İktisat Tarihi*. Gerçek Yayınevi.

Boratav, K. (2008). İktisat Tarihi (1908–1980). In S. Akşin (Ed.), *Türkiye Tarihi 4 Çağdaş Türkiye 1908–1980* (pp. 295–380). Cem Yayınevi.

Chang, H.-J. (Ed.). (2003). *Rethinking development economics*. Anthem Press.

Chang, H.-J. (2002). *Kicking away the ladder: Development strategy in historical perspective*. Anthem Press.

Chatziiosif, C. (1993). *Η γηραιά σελήνη—Η βιομηχανία στην Ελλάδα 1830–1940* [I giraia selini—I Viomichania stin Ellada 1830–1940]. Themelio.

Eichengreen, B. (1996). *Golden fetters: The gold standard and the great depression, 1919–1939*. Oxford University Press.
Evans, P. B. (1979). *Dependent development: The alliance of multinational state and local capital in Brazil*. Princeton University Press.
Frank, A. G. (1967). *Capitalism and underdevelopment in Latin America: Historical studies of Chile and Brazil*. Monthly Review Press.
Friedman, M., & Schwartz, A. J. (1993). *A monetary history of the United States, 1867–1960*. Princeton University Press.
Galbraith, J. K. (1961). *The great crash, 1929*. Houghton Mifflin.
Hale, W. (1980). Ideology and economic development. *Bulletin (British Society for Middle Eastern Studies), 7*(2), 100–117.
Harcourt, G., & Kerr, P. (2009). *Joan Robinson*. Palgrave Macmillan.
Hershlag, Z. Y. (1968). *Turkey: The challenge of growth*. E.J. Brill.
Hirschman, A. O. (1970). *Exit, voice and loyalty: Responses to decline in firms, organizations and states*. Harvard University Press.
Hobsbawm, E. (1996). *Age of extremes: The short twentieth century, 1914–1991*. Abacus.
Keynes, J. M. [1936] (1964). *The general theory of employment, interest and money*. Harcourt Brace & Company.
Kepenek, Y., & Yentürk, N. (1994). *Türkiye Ekonomisi*. Remzi Kitabevi.
Keyder, Ç. (1981). *The definition of a peripheral economy: Turkey 1923–1929*. Cambridge University Press.
Kindleberger, C. (1986). *The world in depression 1929–1939*. University of California Press.
Kuruç, B. (1987). *Mustafa Kemal Döneminde Ekonomi*. Bilgi Yayınevi.
Landes, D. (1969). *The unbound prometheus: Technological change and industrial development in Western Europe from 1750 to the present*. Cambridge University Press.
List, F. [1841] (1885). *The national system of political economy*. Longmans, Green, and Company.
Muşat, R. (2015). Lessons for modern living. Planned rural communities in interwar Romania, Turkey and Italy. *Journal of Modern European History, 13*(4), 534–548.
Owen, R. (1981). *The Middle East in the world economy, 1800–1914*. Methuen.
Örmecioğlu, H. T. (2019). Cumhuriyetin İlk Yıllarında Köycülük Tartışmaları ve Numune Köyler. *Belleten, 83*(297), 729–752.
Özveren, E. (2000). The scope of Turkish 'Semiperipherality. *Ekonomik Yaklaşım, 11*(36), 1–24.
Pamuk, Ş. (1981). Political economy of industrialization in Turkey. *MERIP Reports, 93*, 26–32.
Pamuk, Ş. (2008). Economic change in twentieth-century Turkey: Is the glass more than half full. In R. Kasaba (Ed.), *The Cambridge history of Turkey*

*volume 4 Turkey in the modern world* (pp. 266–300). Cambridge: Cambridge University Press.

Pamuk, Ş. (2018). *Uneven Centuries: Economic Development of Turkey Since 1820*. Princeton University Press.

Polanyi, K. [1944] (2001). *The great transformation*. Beacon Press.

Richards, A., & Waterbury, J. (1996). *A political economy of the Middle East*. Westview.

Rostow, W. W. (1978). *The world economy: History and prospect*. University of Texas Press.

Schumpeter, J. A. [1942] (1976). *Capitalism, socialism and democracy*. Harper.

Stratil-Sauer, G. (1933). Cereal production in Turkey. *Economic Geography, 9*(4), 325–336.

Tekeli, İ., & İlkin, S. (1981). *Savaş Sonrası Ortamında 1947 Türkiye İktisadi Kalkınma Planı*. Orta Doğu Teknik Üniversitesi.

Tekeli, İ., & İlkin, S. (1982). *Uygulamaya Geçerken Türkiyede Devletçiliğin Oluşumu*. Orta Doğu Teknik Üniversitesi.

Tekeli, İ., & İlkin, S. (1983). *1929 Dünya Buhranında Türkiye'nin İktisadi Politika Arayışları*. Orta Doğu Teknik Üniversitesi.

Tekeli, İ., & İlkin, S. (1992). *Dr. Max von der Porten'in Türkiye'deki Çalışmaları ve İktisadi Devlet Teşekkülleri Sisteminin Oluşumu*. Friedrich Ebert Stiftung.

Thornburg, M. W., Spry, G., & Soule, G. (1949). *Turkey, an economic appraisal*. The Twentieth Century Fund.

Tör, V. N. (1999). *Yıllar Böyle Geçti*. Yapı Kredi Yayınları.

Trask, R. R. (1964). The United States and Turkish Nationalism: Investments and technical aid during the Atatürk Era. *The Business History Review, 38*(1), 58–77.

Vernon, R. (1966). International investment and international trade in the product cycle. *The Quarterly Journal of Economics, 80*(2), 190–207.

CHAPTER 5

# Transition to Dependent Development, 1947–1960

*Yakup Kepenek*

## Introduction

The period between 1947 and 1960 is of crucial importance in order to understand Turkey's economic development. What makes the period under inquiry very important and unique is that it is the initial phase during which the Turkish Republic, having been founded after an anti-imperialist Independence War (1919–1922), withdrew hastily and indisputably from its determination for independent decision making.

In the post-1945 period that began with the Cold War, establishing close ties with the United States of America (US) within the fields of foreign relations and defense, Turkey experienced a drastically sharp shift in economic policy, along with critical changes in domestic political and intellectual realms. All of these developments took place in interplay with each other. Yet the analyses provided in this chapter will focus mainly on the issues surrounding the economy. The "great transformation" of

Y. Kepenek (✉)
Middle East Technical University (METU), Ankara, Turkey



E. Özçelik and Y. Özdemir (eds.), *Political Economy of Development in Turkey*, The Political Economy of the Middle East,
https://doi.org/10.1007/978-981-16-7318-4_5

the economy toward external dependence and agricultural specialization under the aegis of private capital is important due to its decisive role in shaping the social, political, and later on, cultural developments not only in the period under inquiry here, but also in the decades that followed.

This chapter is organized as follows. First, the rapprochement process between Turkey and the US, with an eye to two reports prepared by the US experts, is scrutinized. Second, the transformation of the economy is analyzed in detail, along with a particular emphasis on agricultural specialization in terms of both its "shining" and "stumbling" trends. Third, the "great social transformation" is examined in conjunction with contemporaneous political developments. Fourth, ideological and cultural processes are very briefly elaborated by underlining the "economy-versus-democracy" dilemma. All of these are followed by concluding remarks.

## The Radical Shift in Economic Policy

After World War II, it was vital for the US, by far the greatest power and the undisputed hegemon of global capitalism, to strengthen the war-torn Europe, and to prevent, or at least contain by all means, the expansion of the Union of Soviet Socialist Republics (USSR) into Western Europe and the Third World (Halle, 1967, 120). This rift between two countries led to the Cold War, which was extremely comprehensive, involving not only the domains of ideology and military, but also the political, economic, cultural, and administrative fields (Cohn, 2012: 61–62; Halle, 1967: 109; Örnek, 2015: 65; Özkan and Gürakar, 2020).

The US managed to reshape the capitalist world economy and politics as well with the help of newly established institutions like the United Nations (UN), the World Bank (WB), and the International Monetary Fund (IMF). Moreover, the dollar was establishing its place as the "soundest currency," becoming the international means of payment and reserve money, while the dollar-pegged system was to characterize the so-called Bretton Woods era (Panitch & Gindin, 2012: 69–80; Peet, 2009: 36–65). Such an institutional setting aimed at preventing developed economies from drifting into crisis and enabling developing countries to take the capitalist path. When the World War II ended with the breaking up of colonial empires and political emancipation of colonies, economists were challenged by the urgent problems of development. As their investment opportunities, access to markets and sources of raw materials were at stake, the "grave danger" for major capitalist countries was that those newly independent countries could fall under communist domination (Meier & Seers, 1984: 8).

Post-war conception of economic development from an international perspective rested upon an "uneasy compromise between neo-classical and Keynesian theory" (Kiely, 2005: 49); while the former was grounded on private entrepreneurship, the domination of the free market and the international division of labor based on specialization, the latter was the architect of the Bretton Woods order consisting the WB and the IMF. Of these two regulatory financial institutions, the WB was created to oversee global investments, and thus production processes; whereas the IMF dealt with exchange rates as well as international monetary and capital flows, facilitating international trade in goods and services (Rodrik, 2011: 67–88). In addition, the worldwide price stability of raw materials and agricultural products would be achieved with the General Agreement on Tariffs and Trade (GATT). These three institutions would manage full employment, freer and expanding world trade and stable exchange rates. Thus, a kind of "international" public sector or macro-economy, so to speak, was created. In other words, that is how ***dependent economic development*** was born at this juncture.[1]

The question of "Why Turkey?" is, thus, meaningful in this context. Turkey–US relations were not so close in the years during and following the Turkish War of Independence (Trask, 1971). Yet what laid behind the excessive rapprochement beginning with the Cold War was the desire of the US to subordinate Turkey, which stemmed from its extraordinary geostrategic importance due to the long borders it shared with the USSR, as well as its possession of the Straits and a strong army that stayed out of the World War II. Moreover, Turkey could make important contributions to the containment of the USSR by building defense alliances with its neighboring countries (Hale, 2000: 78, 111). Also, Turkey could become a role model for the post-colonial countries that were gaining their political independence (Doster, 2020: 303). For Turkey, it was rather for security reasons than economic ones to choose sides within the context of the Cold War. Furthermore, Turkey could contribute food and raw materials to the recovery of Europe as well. It also had the potential to become a market for US-made weapons, durable household goods, and gradually, cultural products (Örnek, 2015). Lastly, petroleum was then the main source of energy, and Turkey's historical and cultural affinity with, and geographical proximity to, the oil-rich Middle Eastern countries could well be utilized to benefit the US. In short, with the onset of the Cold War, the most decisive external factor that determined Turkey's political, economic, and cultural transformation was, by its full appellation, the USA! The US scripted and directed this process by exploiting every possible opportunity. Turkey was thus becoming subordinated into a comprehensive dependency relationship with the US, losing its independent policy making power accordingly (Aybar, 1968: 5–188; Kepenek, 2019: 43; Örnek, 2015: 43).

The first unequivocal step toward the US–Turkey post-war rapprochement was the Truman Doctrine, which was announced on March 12, 1947, with the justification that Greece and Turkey needed to be protected from "the perils of communism" (Hale, 2000: 115–116). As a matter of fact, shortly after the Truman Doctrine, Turkey was also included in the Marshall Plan in July 1948, which was designed by the US for the reconstruction of war-torn Europe (Hale, 2000: 16; Price, 1955: 37). Since Turkey was not affected by the war in terms of physical destruction, it was, in fact, not meeting the criteria for inclusion in the Marshall Plan. The main reason behind Turkey's inclusion was the widespread opinion held by the American foreign aid networks, according to whom the country could contribute to the reconstruction of Europe via its agricultural and mining products (Harris, 1972: 31; Hershlag, 1968: 150) . Such inclusion in the Plan meant not only making Turkey an integral part of the US-led capitalist world, but more importantly acknowledging that Turkey was a European country.

Thus, unlike the former colonies, Turkey had already completed the process of nation-building and was fit to become a founding member of the Organization for European Economic Cooperation (OEEC; or OECD since 1961), which was formed in 1948 to implement the Marshall Plan, and a member of the Council of Europe, which was founded in 1949 for promoting human rights, democracy, and the rule of law in Europe. Turkey was also admitted to the North Atlantic Treaty Organization (NATO) as its thirteenth member in 1952, upon sending troops to the Korean War. As an expected outcome of these developments, in the summer of 1959, Turkey applied to join the European Economic Community, which was established by six founding members after the Treaty of Rome in 1957, constituting the basis of the present-day European Union.

For a full analysis of the dependency process of Turkey, a more detailed account of two reports, which are the backbone of the US recommendations, will be examined pointedly: Thornburg-Spry-Soule report (1949; hereinafter TSS report) and the World Bank Report of 1951 (WB, 1951; also known as the *Baker Report*). In accordance with the purpose and scope of this chapter, only industrial policy recommendations of these reports are underlined. To start with, both reports were attempts to concretize the approaches put forward by the Truman Doctrine and the Marshall Plan. More importantly, if the recommendations were not implemented, the reports explicitly held, Turkey would be deprived of military, technical, and economic aids from the US (TSS, 1949: viii). As a matter of fact, the great discord and the near-rupture in Turkey–US relations, which emerged in the second half of the 1950s, was mainly due to Turkey's efforts to defy the reports' recommendations on industrial policy.

*The TSS Report*, with the subheading "An Economic Appraisal," was commissioned by the Twentieth Century Fund, which "chose Turkey for the subject of this study even before the announcement of the 'Truman Doctrine' in 1947—with the strategic significance of that country. … Turkey was a key bastion in any defense that may be required against further Communist encroachment" (*Foreword* by Evans Clark). The report investigated the background of US-Turkey cooperation, the subsectors the US firms could invest in, and the conditions for the US foreign aid.

*The WB* report was written after the Democrat Party (DP) assumed office, between the summer of 1950 and May 1951, and complemented the TSS report in the sense of its implementation. The WB report not only outlined the economic situation in the country, but also investigated such issues as national education, health, and public administration. In compliance with the main function of the WB, the report recommended long-term development policies. Interestingly, it was the Republican People's Party (RPP) government that requested the preparation of the report, yet the DP was in power when it was completed.

### *Concrete Proposals: "Specialize in Agriculture" and "Stay Away from Heavy Industries"*

Both reports, especially the WB report, relied on the theory of international division of labor and specialization, adopted as the foundation of the neoclassical model of trade: Turkey needed to specialize in labor-

and land-intensive agricultural production rather than in capital-intensive sectors. As it was spelled out in the TSS report, "the major objective at the beginning must be to increase the efficiency and productiveness of agriculture" (TSS, 1949: 22). Arguing that "industrial development has been overemphasized at the expense of agriculture" (1951: 32), the WB suggested a similar development path: "Our Report has stressed the importance of agriculture. We believe that agricultural development should have top priority in allocation of public investment resources because it provides the greatest opportunity for increased productivity and because it is an essential prerequisite for industrial development" (WB, 1951: 264). The US, having become industrialized by defying this theory just as many other industrialized countries did, was imposing it on Turkey "in the name of science" after World War II (Mason & Asher, 1973: 303).

Turkey's specialization in agriculture could perhaps be defended for two presumable reasons. First, according to the General Census of 1945, Turkey's population was approximately 20 million, and 80% of it was in the agricultural sector. On this account, it could be proposed that Turkey should have prioritized the role of agriculture in development. Secondly, with the transition to the multi-party political system in 1946, prioritizing agriculture in pursuit of votes would seem politically "natural" to the parties that started to strive for electoral success. What was not "natural," though was that the US-imposed proposals threatened with sanctions, and excluded any give-and-take. Thus, Turkey was being situated in the international division of labor of global capitalism, based on a coerced specialization in agriculture.

Proposals of the reports to prioritize agricultural development are concluded with assertions on industrialization. In both reports, Turkey was suggested to steer away from heavy industries, and focus instead on developing light industries. Starting its recommendations with an emphasis on American aid to Turkey, the TSS report (1949: 205) puts Turkey's national pride into question.[2] Thus, the report suggests that "[the] urgent need is for small and light industries ... [such as] plants for the assembly and repair of agricultural, road building and other essential machinery, the manufacture of building materials. A great opportunity exists in industries for food processing and preservation" (254). The report concludes that attention should be "...concentrated on the most efficient production of most widely needed goods ... [in which case] Turks will be able to make good use of their rich resources or Americans will be able to offer them effective help in doing so" (255).

In comparison with the TSS report, the WB report lays a much stronger claim on the issue of industrialization. The report underlines the scarcity of capital as a factor of production, in contrast with the overabundance of labor, asserting that industrialization policy should be formulated in such a way to prioritize labor-intensive sectors. Not contented with this recommendation, the report does not even leave the decision to Turkey regarding the sub-sectors that should be prioritized. To be precise, eight such sectors are pointed out: (i) processing of agricultural products; (ii) light machinery; (iii) building materials; (iv) leather; (v) woodworking; (vi) light chemicals; (vii) ceramics and pottery; and (viii) village handicraft (WB, 1951: 100). Interestingly enough, the report goes beyond counting the priority areas, and also enumerates the sub-sectors that should *not* be prioritized: (i) luxury goods of all kinds; (ii) heavy machinery and metalworking industries; (iii) heavy chemical industry; and (iv) cellulose and paper industry (WB, 1951: 102).

Both reports notably pick out the issue of the shortage of skilled labor force in Turkey. While the WB report insists that "the shortage of responsible managers is still acute" (WB, 1951: 28), the TSS report elaborates this issue in greater detail. Identifying that Turkey would need "general consultants, experts in public works, technical specialists, agricultural experts, experts in public and education economics" (TSS, 1949: 213–216), the report proposes explicitly and at length how they could be acquired from the US in the section entitled "Methods of Obtaining Advisers" (216). As with capital, skilled labor too would come from the US. In fact, Turkey had worked with foreign experts before World War II, nonetheless, it had then chosen them on its own in accordance with the needs of national-economy building. After World War II, on the contrary, patterns of dependence with regards to educated workforce were being formed; and the national policy of raising own experts was set aside.

Among the policy proposals made by the US, one is an example of inconsistency *par excellence*, while another one is of deliberate ignorance. The first is related to the issue of roadways. The US experts had started to work in Turkey to develop railways, with allocated resources and a plan, at the outset of the rapprochement between Turkey and the US in 1946 (TSS, 1949: 81). However, only within a year, a new delegation headed by the deputy commissioner Harold Hilts of the US Bureau of Public Roads called for putting a definite priority on the construction of roadways (Hershlag, 1968). Turkey, still ruled by the RPP government that attached a special importance to the railways, could neither question this sudden change in the transportation policy, nor coordinate it with other means of transportation.

Secondly, the US needed to assert Turkey's underdevelopment for building up ties of dependence. As if they decided to speak with a single voice, both reports emphasized that the Turkish economy was on the whole in a pretty good shape, yet also concluded that, with much still remaining to be fixed, "[it was] 'largely underdeveloped' (TSS, 1949: 253) … judged by Western European or American standards, … but a fair evaluation of progress [was] made since the establishment of the Republic in 1923" (WB, , 1951: 27). Hence, the fact that Turkey had achieved a "take off" by around 1937; the industrialization and institutionalization processes with which it gained great success (Rostow, 1956: 25–48; Singer, 1977: 5; Meier & Seers, 1984: 238); and the foundations of all those, namely the institutional infrastructure, rule of law, modern and scientific education, peaceful foreign policy were all deliberately ignored. The industrialization strategy, that constituted the main axis for these accomplishments, was thus said to be wrong, without showing signs of consistent reasoning in any manner.

All in all, according to the US proposals that were formulated in these reports, Turkey was an underdeveloped country, and it could overcome underdevelopment only with the US foreign aid, i.e., through "dependent development" by specializing in agriculture with more market-oriented and private-capital-dominated approaches.

### *Developments in Domestic Political Sphere*

With Turkey's transition to the multi-party system,[3] the party in power, the RPP, changed its economic-policy stance accordingly. First, in the government program announced in the Parliament on August 14, 1946, an agenda for state-private sector partnerships was set forth (Öztürk, 1968, 294). That attempt was the first step toward a mixed economy. Secondly, a "new etatist" approach was announced, which defined the main role of the state as supporting private entrepreneurship. Thirdly, another step of crucial importance was taken with the preparation of the Turkish Economic Development Plan (EDP) of 1947 (Tekeli & İlkin, 1974). The EDP relied upon the same logic that was underlined above in the context of US reports. Arguably, the EDP was the first domestic economic-policy document that bounded the country by "dependent development." Fourthly, as a complementary act, the first drastic home-currency devaluation in the history of Republic was implemented in order to adapt the Turkish economy to "free-market" conditions. On September 7, 1946, Turkish lira (TL) was devalued from 1.30 to 2.80 TLs per US dollar. The aim was to regulate the trade balance through the market mechanism in an increasingly liberalized foreign-trade regime. Another important reason for the devaluation was the expected membership to the IMF, whose member countries were not allowed to devalue their currencies by more than 10% without permission (Kepenek, 2020: 118).

On the other side, the DP in the main opposition started to get stronger from 1947 onwards, with the explicit support of the US and thanks also to President İsmet İnönü's unbiased attitude toward both his RPP and the DP. On May 14, 1950, the DP, with its election slogan "Enough! The nation has the say!" (*Yeter! Söz milletindir!*), rose to power after winning 55% of the votes and gaining 85% of the seats in the Parliament (Ahmad, 1976: 66). One can argue that this was solely a shift from one single-party regime to another with similar features, since both parties were united against the same external danger, i.e., the USSR (Harris, 1972: 23).

The change of power with the 1950 elections, also known as the *white revolution* (Huntington, 1968: 433–463), carries a historical significance for at least two reasons. First, unlike the 1946 general elections, the first of multi-party elections, which was heavily criticized due to systematic irregularities (Ahmad, 1976: 23; Karpat, 1959: 164), the single-party system was terminated peacefully in 1950 by free and fair elections. Secondly, the fact that the people held onto their vote and overthrew the RPP government was indeed "revolutionary" (Boran, 2016: 92–107). For that was the first time that an election could bring about a change in government. This change in government left a true and lasting impact on the collective memory of all segments of society (Kaynar, 2015, 296; Kepenek, 2019: 60).

## The Great Transformations in the Economy

The policy foundations of the period had already been laid out by 1947, as summarized above. For a proper and realistic analysis, however, the period will be parted into two sub-sections: first the *shining* and then the *stumbling* years.

### *The Shining Years with the Rise of Agriculture*

Capital accumulation process is generally the key concept to understand aspects of economic policy in less-developed countries. The first half of the period, until 1954, was a process of what can conveniently be called "capital explosion" in both quantitative and qualitative terms. It can be seen in Table 5.1 that expansionary trends were observed in money, budget, and credits; and with the contribution of the US aid and loans, a good amount of increase in investment, and high rates of growth were also achieved. In the second half, between 1954 and 1960, on the other hand, the stability measures marked the period in response to the foreign-exchange shortages and rising inflation, as well as capital contraction. As Table 5.1 shows, foreign trade decreased to around one fourth of its peak and credits shrank acutely while the inflation rate almost doubled; all leading to a drastic fall in the rate of growth. From a bird's eye view of the period, it can be observed that the DP ran the economy like a racing horse that was first speeding but then getting out of control, expediting economic and social transformations (Kepenek, 2020: 84–136).

Ascending to power in 1950, the DP put aside altogether the previous decades' politics of achieving balance in the triad of money, budget, and foreign trade. Money supply was increased disproportionately to the output growth, while balanced-budget requirements were entirely abandoned and the balanced-trade approach was forgotten. In addition to the monetary expansion, the US foreign aid and loans, as well as the reforms implemented to secure guarantees to foreign capital, contributed to the remarkable expansion of budget and credits in the early 1950s. Moreover, the US military assistance to Turkey as "deliveries and expenditures" was amounting to 1,781,5 million dollars during the 1948–1960 period (Harris, 1972: 155). Lastly, as stated by W. W. Rostow, the defense support provided by the US was vital to compensate abnormal military outlays proving an effective instrument of development assistance (Meier & Seers, 1984: 248).

As a result of the developments indicated above, the DP government provided full support to the agriculture. The agricultural output skyrocketed initially, with the exponential increase in the main inputs. First, the number of *tractors* increased from 1556 in 1947 to more than 9000 in 1949, and then above 40,000 and 42,000 in 1955 and in 1960, respectively. Secondly, the amount of *cultivated land* significantly increased from 113.6 million hectares in 1947 to 14.5 million hectares in 1950,

**Table 5.1** Main economic indicators, 1945–1960

| | *Growth rate*[a] | *Investment*[b] | *Money*[c] | *Budget*[c] | *Credits*[c] | *Prices*[d] |
|---|---|---|---|---|---|---|
| 1946 | – | – | 6.1 | – | | –3 |
| 1947 | 4.1 | | –29.2 | 53.5 | 38.5 | 1 |
| 1948 | – | | 5.0 | –10.4 | 9.3 | 3 |
| 1949 | 5.0 | – | –13.8 | 12.1 | 10.0 | 11 |
| 1950 | 9.4 | 9.6 | 7.3 | –6.7 | 21.7 | 10 |
| 1951 | 12.8 | 10.3 | 16.8 | 7.7 | 36.7 | 6 |
| 1952 | 11.9 | 12.8 | 9.6 | 41.4 | 47.3 | 1 |
| 1953 | 11.3 | 12.4 | 16.5 | 2.0 | 30.9 | – |
| 1954 | 3.0 | 14.7 | 3.1 | 11.9 | 25.7 | 11 |
| 1955 | 7.9 | 14.3 | 31.5 | 29.0 | 17.4 | 8 |
| 1956 | 3.2 | 13.4 | 29.2 | 5.4 | 16.3 | 20 |
| 1957 | 7.8 | 13.2 | 26.6 | 19.4 | 33.3 | 26 |
| 1958 | 4.5 | 14.0 | 3.6 | 19.6 | 11.3 | 25 |
| 1959 | 4.1 | 15.6 | 11.5 | 35.2 | 8.9 | 37 |
| 1960 | 3.4 | 15.9 | 12.3 | 8.8 | 1.4 | 12 |

| | *Imports*[e] | *Exports*[e] | *External Trade Balance*[f] | *Terms of Trade*[g] | *Foreign Capital*[h] | *Foreign Trade*[i] |
|---|---|---|---|---|---|---|
| 1945 | 126 | 219 | +93 | | | |
| 1946 | 224 | 432 | +208 | | | 9.6 |
| 1947 | 685 | 625 | –60 | | | 17.4 |
| 1948 | 770 | 551 | –219 | | | 13.9 |
| 1949 | 813 | 694 | –119 | | | 16.6 |
| 1950 | 780 | 738 | –42 | 0.98 | – | 15.9 |
| 1951 | 1126 | 879 | –247 | 0.90 | 1.2 | 17.7 |
| 1952 | 1557 | 1016 | –541 | 0.88 | 1.1 | 19.2 |
| 1953 | 1491 | 1109 | –382 | 0.88 | 0.4 | 16.7 |
| 1954 | 1339 | 938 | –401 | 0.89 | 2.2 | 14.3 |
| 1955 | 1393 | 877 | –516 | 0.91 | 1.2 | 11.9 |
| 1956 | 1140 | 854 | –286 | 0.97 | 3.4 | 9.5 |
| 1957 | 1112 | 967 | –145 | 1.00 | 1.3 | 7.1 |
| 1958 | 882 | 692 | –190 | 0.75 | 1.1 | 4.5 |
| 1959 | 1316 | 991 | –325 | 0.75 | 3.4 | 5.3 |
| 1960 | 2219 | 1721 | –498 | 0.89 | 1.9 | 8.4 |

[a]Annual percentage change in Gross National Product (GNP) at fixed prices, base year=1948
[b]Ratio of Fixed Capital Investment to GNP (percentage)
[c]Annual percentage rate of change
[d]Inflation (Wholesale Price Index, WPI, 1953=100); annual percentage rate of change
[e]In millions of Turkish Liras (TL)
[f]In millions of TL; Surplus (+), Deficit (–)
[g]The ratio of export price index over import price index, Px/Pm; calculated from Singer (1977: 393)
[h]Foreign investment in millions of US dollars. During the period, a total of $1177.1 million was obtained from the US; of which $824.2 million was donated, and $352.9 million was loaned. A loan of $320.4 million dollars was obtained from other institutions, mainly from the World Bank and the OECD
[i]Volume of Foreign Trade (Exports + Imports) / GNP (percentage)
*Sources* Kepenek (2020: 98) and Hershlag (1968: 369)

and then to 21 million in 1955 and 23.3 million in 1960 (SIS-TIS, 1973: 165). Agricultural loans were also raised accordingly (SIS-TIS, 1973: 361). In addition, the share of the agricultural sector in total employment was 80.8% in 1955 and 77.7% in 1960. However, total employment in agriculture increased by more than three percent, from 9.4 to 9.7 million people even in the 1955–1960 period (OECD, 1970: 185).

The increase in cultivated land was largely due to freely occupying publicly owned pasture lands. In this respect, it was a free direct transfer of wealth to those who were able to occupy these lands. However, this remarkable expansion did not lead to a significant change in the economies of scale in agriculture, as can be observed in the agricultural surveys of 1950 and 1963. For one reason or another, the US did not urge Turkey to design a land reform. Small farming was still dominant; of all cultivated land, 61.7% in 1950 and 68.7% in 1963 were still owned by those who were cultivating an area between 1–50 decares (1000–50,000 square meters). It should also be mentioned that entrepreneurs cultivating 25 decares of land on average were cultivating around 18.9% of all cultivated land in 1950; whereas these figures were 19 decares and 24.3%, respectively, in 1963 (Kepenek, 2020: 107).

The mechanization in agriculture and the increase in the quantity of cultivated land were complemented by price and loan supports. Swift proliferation of the *roadways* also contributed to agricultural expansion. Concrete roads were exponentially increased from 1624 kilometers in 1950 to 7046 kilometers in 1960, with a rate of increase by 334% (Singer, 1977: 221). This highway program was rightly described as "success on wheels" (Harris, 1972: 79). Similar expansions in other types of roads precipitated the process of rural commercialization. Irrigation and storage infrastructures were also built. Domestic and foreign conditions, boosting the demand for agricultural products, also generated a boom in agricultural output. Consequently, the main crop, wheat, production nearly doubled; while industrial inputs from agriculture, such as cotton, sugar beet, and tea, exhibited significant increases (Singer, 1977: 229).

As the national-income accounts show, agricultural production considerably surpassed the pre-War values in 1948, having increased by 40% until 1953, and in 1960 it was 60% above its 1948 level—that is, nearing to twice of its pre-War figures. Indeed, "the expansion in this period [1948–1960] of cultivated lands and of agricultural output is unprecedented in the past 200 years of Turkey" (Pamuk, 2014: 289). As a result, the agrarian sector in the period under inquiry underwent a substantial change from self-sufficient, closed village farming to production for sales in the market rather very rapidly. This transformation undoubtedly benefitted mostly the large landholders, yet the agricultural sector as a whole largely retained its small farming features.

In general, labor and capital are inseparable in small farming. In terms of its structural features, small farming tends politically toward conservatism. Agrarian economic policies of the DP government restructured the rural sector as its own sociopolitical basis. Regardless of how it is called, *populism*, or the *golden years*, as some scholars would call it; the objective truth is that the DP government caused Turkey to undergo a "great transformation" in agriculture. And, such transformation left a long-lasting mark in the country's politics, both quantitatively and qualitatively, not only in the period under scrutiny, but also in the decades that followed (Keyder, 1987: 117). Hence, this agrarian transformation sparked truly a radical social change. Above all, with the commercialization of the closed and self-sufficient village economy, millions of people rapidly moved away from pre-capitalist socioeconomic dependency relations and began to enter a market-dependent process in the broader context of global capitalism.

The manufacturing industry also grew fast as a result of agricultural development, along with urbanization and increasing domestic demand. Two factors were decisive for the expansion of the supply side of the industry in the period under consideration. First, the Industrial Development Bank of Turkey (IDBT) was founded; and secondly, state economic enterprises (SEEs) were revived by the pro-entrepreneurship DP government.

The IDBT was founded in 1950, with the support of the WB, as an exemplary experiment for underdeveloped countries in accordance with the mission of the Bank. For this purpose, the Bank aimed at supporting the development of private industry by establishing domestic and foreign partnerships and empowering private-ownership structures (Mason & Asher, 1973: 166–167). The IDBT provided approximately one tenth of all bank loans in the period, at a time when private banking was also flourishing. Nevertheless, its support was primarily reserved for consumption-good industries. The goal was to situate the Turkish manufacturing industry in its "appropriate" place within the global division of labor, in terms of its development trajectory and business management (Keyder, 1987: 139). Lastly, since the IDBT loans were mostly allocated to projects located in the Marmara region, the rest of the private industrial capital also gravitated prominently toward this region. Consequently, a great inequality emerged in the regional distribution of industrial development, which concentrated within the Istanbul-Bursa-Kocaeli triangle (Kepenek, 2020: 108–109).

In the decade of the DP's rule, the SEEs, despite the promises in the first government program, were not privatized. Furthermore, the DP government needed to expand the SEEs especially when domestic production plus imports did not meet domestic demand. The production capacity of the SEEs in such goods as cement, paper and sugar was increased, and some new SEEs were also established (Kepenek, 1993: 33). Thus, the SEEs moved on a *sui generis* development path with their support to the private sector.

The SEEs supported private capital accumulation through three main channels. First, the SEEs directly transferred resources by establishing either partnerships or subsidiaries with the private sector. (For the full list of public–private partnerships, see Ministry of Finance, 1977: 522–524). Secondly, the SEEs provided the private sector with inputs that were way underpriced with regards to their production costs. The losses incurred by the SEEs were then registered as "duty losses," which were compensated from the state budget. Thirdly, the SEEs also indirectly provided skilled labor force with experience to the private industry by their eventual transfers, as a result of large public–private wage gaps, or in response to the bureaucratic problems occurring within the SEEs (Kepenek, 1993: 111). Thus, private capital, back then, preferred exploiting the SEEs rather than purchasing them (Buğra, 1994).

In this period, the domestic production of basic consumption goods, such as food, textiles, and apparels grew adequately to meet the domestic demand. Yet, increased import difficulties during the second half of the period still created a stimulus for domestic industrial production. Thus, an implicit import-substituting industrialization (ISI) process, so to speak, was realized. This process paved the way for the planned and much more systematic ISI strategy of the 1960s and 1970s. Expansion of domestic markets with the commercialization of rural production, as well as economic externalities that emerged thanks to public infrastructural investments in road haulage, energy, and infrastructure, contributed vastly to the increase in fixed capital formation in the private industry (Kepenek, 2020: 109).

Another main feature of the period under examination was the rapid expansion of the services sector. The share of services in GNP rose from 39% in 1946 to 45% in 1960, so as to surpass the share of agriculture. Interestingly enough, the services grew independently of the developments in agriculture and industry. Especially, such sub-sectors as the retail trade, construction, financial institutions, and transportation grew rapidly. Moreover, the rapid expansion of roadways and the spread of services, such as transportation, maintenance-repair, and tourism, changed the face of the economy by facilitating the growth of the market for motor vehicles, especially in terms of the use of private cars and fuel consumption (Kepenek, 2020: 115).

### *The Stumbling Years and Beyond*

Very high rates of steady growth lasted until 1954. From that year on, painful consequences of the "populist" policies started to surface. Domestic demand exploded as a result of expansionary monetary, fiscal and credit policies, along with the contribution of rapid urbanization. However, it was impossible to meet this surge in demand, given the internal constraints of the Turkish economy. Although the foreign exchange and gold reserves at the initial phases enabled an easy increase in imports; supply shortages especially in industrial products and raw materials emerged with the lapse of time, as the 1946 devaluation had not encouraged exports relative to imports. Moreover, exports fell with the ending of the Korean War in 1953, widening the trade deficit even more. As a result, the volume of foreign trade, which was approximately around 15% of GNP until 1954, decreased remarkably to values less than 10% in the second half of the 1950s. Throughout this process, the problem of foreign-exchange shortage intensified further at a time when significant growth slowdowns were accompanied by widening trade deficits, as can be seen in Table 5.1, aggravating the dependence of the Turkish economy on external borrowing (Kepenek, 2020: 118).

The supply shortages, arising both from the decrease in agricultural yield due to the drought in 1954 and the fall in imports due to the foreign-exchange bottleneck, led to a situation of unsatisfied excess demand. The ratio of exports to imports fell drastically to 63% in 1955 from 92% in 1950, alongside a sharp rise in the annual inflation rate to over 20% from around 10%. Not surprisingly, this combination of economic difficulties resulted in a major crisis, bringing the economy to a near halt.

The DP government looked for a solution to the supply-side problems by means of even more expansion and higher growth; that is to say, it wanted to ride the horse even faster. There were two conditions for such a solution: First, increasing the production of goods and services at home; and secondly, utilizing external resources through foreign borrowing. The government tried both but failed, especially in the latter. Therefore, the DP government had to accept the implementation of an IMF-designed stabilization program in 1958, which was initiated for the first time in the history of the country.

As it was pointed out above, a "covert" and ad hoc import-substitution process could have been implemented via the utilization of the SEEs, without openly clashing with the US requests. An obvious supporter of private entrepreneurship, the DP government implemented a SEEs-based industrialization policy due mainly to the imperatives of objective conditions (Kepenek, 1993: 32). Insofar, as domestic production could not meet domestic demand, the ruling party followed a policy that prioritized the domestic production of industrial products, especially that of intermediate and durable consumer goods, which could not be purchased from abroad due to the scarcity of foreign exchange. Under these circumstances, the DP government aspired to benefit from the SEEs as much as possible. In a sense, it had to take a compulsory yet implicit and partial step toward the etatism of the 1930s.

The DP government took some measures to prevent the economy from drifting into depression. For instance, it paid more than the official exchange rate (2.80 TLs per US dollar) for some of the dollar-denominated monetary receipts; began to implement multiple exchange rates in imports as well as price controls in the domestic market; raised interest rates and limited commercial loans. However, all these measures remained insufficient to overcome the financial bottleneck. Two further developments, moreover, aggravated the crisis: Prime Minister Menderes resisted the recall of a WB delegation on the grounds that "they were intervening the country's internal affairs by making inflation a subject of debate" (Krueger, 1974: 69), and the US refused Turkey's $300 million request for supplementary aid.[4]

Given these conditions, and in line with the requests of the IMF, on August 4, 1958, the government decided to devalue the TL; liberalize imports; limit the money supply; restrict public spending; schedule investments according to a specific program; and increase the prices of goods and services supplied by the SEEs. The dollar rate was gradually yet drastically increased from 2.8 TLs to over 9 TLs. Measures were also taken for facilitating imports and easing the terms of foreign-debt obligations. Consequently, a foreign credit of $359 million could be obtained from abroad. Thus, Turkey was, for the first time, paying the heavy price of drifting away from its determination to implement independent economic policies, as the consequence of the crisis experienced from the mid-1950s onwards. As a matter of fact, covering imports with short-term external borrowing had started to generate problems in debt repayment as early as 1952. Eventually, Turkey became the first country both to use funds in excess of its IMF quota and to request an extension of its repayment deadline (Horsfield, 1969: 347).

It is not easy to assess the economic consequences of the stabilization measures because of the political crisis that occurred in 1960. But one major conclusion can be derived: The dependence of the economy on foreign capital reached an unprecedented level at the end of the ten-year period of DP government. Turkish economy was highly integrated with the US-led capitalist world, and Turkish policymakers were no more able to take independent steps without the IMF approval. In a sense, domestic economic stability was tied to elements of external dependence.

## The Great Social Transformation

A distinct and unprecedented social transformation is the primal characteristic of the period. First, the total population of the country increased from 19 million to 27.5 million, or by 44.7%, with a 2.98% annual average during 1945–1960. The share of urban population in the total also increased from 18 to 25%, with an annual increase of about 5%. Population growth and mobility rates were, in other words, exceptionally high.

Second, a rapid acceleration of internal migration and urbanization took place (Karpat, 1976). Urban migration was primarily caused by impressive mechanization, that is, the use of tractors in agriculture and facilitation of road transportation in rural Turkey. It must be underlined rather emphatically that this unprecedented population mobility, which we call *physical emancipation*, was a result of the dissolution of pre-capitalist formations. As the precondition of all other types of freedoms, physical emancipation here refers to the disintegration of the age-old, self-subsistent, and stagnant village structures due to the increasing share of marketed crops and the use of money, as well the substantial weakening of people's traditional familial, squirarchical (*ağalık*), and tribal ties all across the country.

Rapid urbanization brought about not only new problems, but also *sui generis* solutions. Besides unemployment in the cities, the process raised two important problems, namely accommodation and transportation. Rather practical solutions found for these two problems were squatter housing (*gecekondu*; literally meaning "built overnight") and shared minibuses (*dolmuş*s), respectively. Though the relative effects of *dolmuş*s were limited, the *gecekondu* question rather became a crucial one from legal, economic, and social points. Constructed via the *de facto* seizure of publicly owned lands, the *gecekondu* neighborhoods thus became not only a subject of various sociopolitical problems and controversies, but also the backbone of the urban construction sector. In fact, the share of urban population living in *gecekondu*s increased from 1.4% in 1945 to 12.8% in 1950, and to 17.9% in 1960, underlining its extraordinary dynamism (Danielson & Keleş, 1980: 273).

Physical emancipation also brought about two further significant changes that need to be briefly touched upon here. First, the demand for education, historically one of the most important tools of vertical social mobility, resulted in a surge along with the additional effect of emerging economic necessities (Kepenek, 2020: 133). Second, as a response to the burgeoning political and economic liberalization, a series of institutional measures in the labor market were undertaken, such as establishing the Ministry of Labor and the Labor Employment Office (LEO), in order to coordinate the supply of and demand for labor. With the increasing pressures for enhanced labor rights, labor unions were established, albeit without the enactment of the right to strike. Accordingly, the first government Program of Menderes stated that "we will legalize the right to strike ... which we recognize as a natural right in accordance with the principles of democracy" (Öztürk, 1968: 330). However, no further steps were taken in this direction, even in the years when the economy was growing rapidly. By 1960, the number of unionized workers and the number of socially insured workers were each around 10% in non-agricultural employment, which proves that the DP's class preference was *not* on the labor side (Koç, 2019: 238). The LEO statistics, the only source regarding the labor market of the period, also indicates a striking social development of the day: as a result of the rapid migration to cities, the job applications of *women* increased at a rate that cannot be compared with the subsequent years (Kepenek, 2020: 126).

Lastly, from the available data limited to the unionized workers, it is seen that the real wages increased until 1955, but fell in the following years. Although similar figures can be observed for agricultural incomes, it should also be noted that the government was already supporting the agricultural sector both directly and indirectly. Salaries of the civil servants, on the other hand, were generally increasing below inflation. The wage-salary differentiation process is indeed one of the indicators of the DP's class base (Boratav, 2019: 93; Keyder, 1970).

## Ideological and Cultural Developments Leading to the Great Dilemma

Ideological, political, and cultural aspects of the period should also be summarized briefly here, since they were the mirror images of subsequent developments. To start with, the DP came to power by creating a "revolutionary" culture of freedom and democracy, although limited by a heavy Cold War atmosphere. As soon as the party took office, however, more conservative thoughts, especially Islamism, gained momentum. Accordingly, attempts to erode the Reforms, which were initiated after the establishment of the Republic, surged (Eligür, 2010: 48; Kısakürek, 1959; Tuğtan, 2020).

Two important points should be underlined. First, as the following short quote concisely sums up, the Marshall Plan in Turkey resulted in the "*strengthening of the Political Islamist movement under the umbrella of 'democracy'*" (Teazis, 2010: 46). Secondly, anticommunism became the primary and decisive factor shaping not only national politics, but also the short- and long-term developments in the country's intellectual life, via its negative impacts on creative thinking (Karpat, 1959: 138). Concomitant institutional restructuring, created within the framework of cooperation with the US, was accompanied by cultural convergence, that is, "the American way of life," which is detailed elsewhere (Örnek, 2015). The rapprochement in the early 1950s focused especially on public bureaucracy, including the drafting of some important economy-related laws (Kara, 2006). As for education, as well as social and cultural relations, the US replaced Europe. English became the dominant foreign language, replacing French. Moreover, the likes of *Chicago Boys* in Latin

America started to become prominent in the country (Boratav, 2015: 100; Kepenek, 2011: 159). As stated elsewhere, the WB allied itself with the "development minded" figures in the country (Mason & Asher, 1973: 648).[5] Likewise, as the cost of sending people to the US were becoming high, similar educational institutions were being established in Turkey (Harris, 1972: 76–79). The aim was not only to make up for the qualified labor force of the country. Rather, it was a total change in thought and culture.

Meanwhile, Prime Minister Menderes hardened his attitude toward the intra-party opposition by limiting participation and expelling those who criticized his leadership. Increasing monopolization of the selection process of parliamentary candidates by the party president not only diminished the effectiveness of the Turkish Grand National Assembly (TGNA), but also strengthened the one-man, top-down structure of the DP (Cerrahoğlu, 1996; Eroğul, 2014: xi). In fact, such leader-dependent restructuring of the party set a precedent as a wrong legacy not only for other political parties, but also for all other types of associations that followed (Kepenek, 2019: 82). Accordingly, the DP government, which had already become well identified with the leader, was beginning to take a hardline stance against the opposition especially after the 1957 elections (Mert, 2007: 21–22). Notwithstanding, the opposition made its voice stronger and louder in its battle for fundamental rights and freedoms, such as demanding freedom of the press, autonomy of the universities, economic and social rights, etc., which influenced the developments in the following years (Ahmad, 1993: 102; Kepenek, 2019: 120).

It should be underlined that the main reason for the tightening up of the dress of democracy emerged primarily due to the economic crisis, while the ruling party was dragged into what we can call a big dilemma of the "economic advancement-versus-democratization." As underlined repeatedly, the DP leadership was firmly determined for achieving more growth, even at the cost of disregarding all possible destructive consequences.[6] Ironically, the "top defender" of freedoms and the "free world," the US, was nevertheless not showing any sensitivities about further limitations of rights and freedoms in Turkey, at least not until the country ran into political turmoil in May 1960 (Armaoğlu, 1996: 216; Kepenek, 2019: 99).

The changing nature of the Cold War, especially after the launch of the first satellite by the USSR, namely Sputnik, in October 1957, as well as the political upheavals in the Middle East, drove the US–Turkish relations to even a more vulnerable situation, as observed by Rostow (Meier & Seers, 1984: 259). The Turkish–US relations harbor various unknowns to this date in many aspects (Armaoğlu, 1996: 208, 212). What we know, though, is that, when the DP could not obtain funds for industrialization from the US,[7] it turned its gaze toward the USSR. The decision of Menderes to visit the USSR with two ministers in mid-July 1960 *would* mean the unilateral termination of the dependency relationship that had started with the Cold War. As the Turkish Ambassador to Tehran, Mahmut Dikerdem summarized lucidly: "*In 1960, the US had serious reasons to overthrow the Menderes-Zorlu duo... Since 1947... the country's government... was attempting an action on its own for the first time ... without first receiving a permission from the US. ... This could not be left unpunished*" (Dikerdem, 1977: 23–24).

Not surprisingly, as a result, during the second half of the period, the honeymoon between Turkey and the US came gradually to an end due to deep disagreements over industrialization. The DP's attempts to find foreign loans for industrialization in some vital sub-sectors were constantly blocked by the US, which acted consistently in line with the TSS and WB reports analyzed above. Even Menderes himself expressed his confusion for why Turkey's allies opted to oppose those industries that would process agricultural products; he thus simply stated: "I do not understand" (Yavuzalp, 1991: 89).

## Conclusion

The period of 1947–1960 analyzed in this chapter was truly path-breaking, characterized by great changes and transformations. Furthermore, this period underlay the steppingstones for the following decades. Initially, Turkey found itself in the midst of a global restructuring process, led by the US as the hegemonic power of the capitalist world, within the Cold War environment that started after World War II. Turkey underwent radical changes in this period, starting especially in the domains of foreign affairs, defense policy, and economic restructuring. Eventually, the country lost its ability to determine, design and implement an independent policy.

Taking the path of dependent development with the urgings of the US, Turkey started rather abruptly to specialize in agriculture and participate in the international division of labor accordingly. With the change in government upon the will of the people for the first time in the country's history in 1950, the more "liberal-leaning" DP, backed by the US, commercial capital and landowners, came to power. Afterward, socioeconomic mobility and transformations gained an unprecedented momentum.

With the help of its past acquisitions, along with the US economic and military aids and loans, as well as increasing volume of foreign trade thanks to favorable external conditions, the economy grew immensely at a rate of 11.4% on average per year between 1950 and 1953. This success was the outcome of combined effects of the commercialization of rural areas, which were previously both economically and socially closed and self-sufficient, the rapidly increasing use of tractors in agriculture, construction of new roads and the swift expansion of the cultivated areas, which, more or less, provided economic well-being to all segments of society. This extraordinary process stimulated internal migration remarkably by *freeing* the rural population and prompting rapid urbanization, notwithstanding the new problems it generated. Nevertheless, this impressive economic expansion, along with prominent social change, was not accompanied by democratic development. Instead, the DP government restricted the rights and freedoms with a staunch anti-communist bias. The result was a combination of an unleashed liberal market economy with circumscribed political rights and freedoms.

However, the remarkable episode of economic expansion could not be perpetuated after 1954, due to the slowdown in agricultural production, foreign-exchange bottlenecks and concomitant supply shortages. The DP turned to the SEEs in order to boost domestic production and supply; yet this effort failed to save the situation. The government, which eventually turned to market controls, as a result, had to accept stringent stabilization measures and a substantial devaluation of the Turkish lira in line with the IMF recommendations in order to obtain foreign aid and loans. Thus, the country, having already devalued its currency by its own will in 1946, was doing the same in 1958, but this time according to IMF conditionality. Such conditionality started to become increasingly more binding in the decades to come.

With an even more definitive and impressive electoral victory in 1954, the DP started to gain a leader-dependent character by narrowing intra-party participation and began to constrain political rights and freedoms, especially after the 1957 snap elections when it fell below the majority of the popular vote. While implementing the IMF stabilization measures of 1958 rather reluctantly, the government decided to overcome the "unacceptable" economic stagnation by expanding on agriculture-based industries and producing some industrial intermediate goods domestically. Simultaneously, though, the DP government was trying to further curtail existing rights and freedoms. Thus, the DP opted for prioritizing economic development in the midst of a great dilemma of "economy-versus-democracy." Nonetheless, the DP could not obtain the foreign capital support it desperately strived for. Its attempts to receive the hand of the Soviet Union also remained futile, as that ran into the wall of the US.

To sum up, the process started with a shift in economic policy toward specialization in agriculture, as formulated by the US. It encompassed all of the major policy domains over time. In a very short period of ten years, economic and social mobility increased tremendously, and Turkish society became economically more responsive and politically more conservative. Accordingly, the independent policymaking processes, along with the previous legal and institutional infrastructure, secular education, peaceful foreign policy, that is, the essential backbones of the Atatürk Reforms have entered a period of erosion.

As a matter of fact, the DP government had begun to put its signature to immense socioeconomic transformations. Nonetheless, it failed to put into operation and carry forward the democratic processes through which it had risen to power, while also running into a deadlock in its relatively more successful field, that is, the economy. The upshot of this failure was the military takeover of 1960, which was unfortunate not only with its dire consequences immediately for the party, but in the long-run, also for the country.

**Acknowledgements** I thank Feriha Tunçay of the Presidency of Library and Archive Services at Turkish Grand National Assembly and Gönül Arslan of the METU Library for providing the sources for this article; Prof. Dr. Fikret Şenses for his invaluable comments; Dr. Emre Özçelik and Dr. Yonca Özdemir for their editorial help; and Dr. İhsan Ercan Sadi for his translation and editing.

## Notes

1. The literature on development economics, with its various notable contributions from theoretical and applied research, initially began to grow at a time corresponding to the period under scrutiny in this chapter. Some pioneering examples were Lord Bauer, Colin

Clark, Albert O. Hirschman, Sir Arthur Lewis, Gunnar Myrdal, Raul Prebisch, Paul N. Rosenstein-Rodan, Walt Whitman Rostow, H. W. Singer, and Jan Tinbergen. Their works put forward important concepts and theses within the areas such as "unlimited supply of labor" (Lewis); the theory, strategy, stages, and patterns of development (Myint; Hirschman; Rostow; Chenery and Syrquin), foreign trade (Prebisch; Emmanuel), and a critique of proposed liberal policies (Joan Robinson). For a succinct collection of the pioneering figures in development economics of the day, see Meier and Seers (1984).

2. Interestingly, the TSS Report states that "the Karabük steel mill and its related plants present more than a problem of efficient management. In no proper sense of the word is there an 'industry' here to be managed. The problem of Karabük is one of large-scale salvage operation" (1949: 227), and "the greatest need which Turks themselves cannot yet fill is that of trained advisers, good managers, competent technicians, industrial and commercial know how. This is a need which Americans can supply, provided that the opportunity is offered to them to exercise their talents" (1949: 254).
3. Transition to the multi-party system is of crucial importance for a proper understanding of the period, yet its full analysis falls beyond the scope of this chapter. A few brief remarks should suffice. The multi-party system that started almost simultaneously with the beginning of the Cold War, which divided the world into two camps—"free" and "unfree,"—remained largely limited in terms of democratic development, especially in the sphere of freedoms of thought, expression, and association. Moreover, a new development occurred in the context of the rapprochement between Turkey and the US. Two right-wing political fractions, namely political Islamists and ultranationalists that had until then been experiencing disaccords with the regime, formed an alliance to fight against communism. The anticommunist campaign that united the Turkish right accorded with the US intentions. This harmony became increasingly prominent and influential after 1946, shaping the habits of thought and political climate in the country on the one hand, and leading to a corrosion of the foundational values that defined the *sui generis* modernization project of the Republic, that is, Atatürk Reforms, on the other (Kepenek 2019: 44). For more details, see Tekeli and İlkin (2014).

4. See Harris (1972: 49–84) for an extensive analysis of the cooperation as well as the rifts between the two countries, not only in economic policies but also on all issues, during the "Menderes Decade."
5. Indeed, Demirel and Özal are perfect examples in this regard. After obtaining their engineering degrees in a public university in Turkey, they were both sent to the US for further education in the 1950s. They both joined the ranks of bureaucracy, after Menderes was overthrown. Becoming the leading US-backed politicians of the center-to-the-Islamic right, along with their emphasis on economic liberalism, they served for over three decades, roughly from 1965–2000, as prime ministers and presidents of the country (Heper & Sayarı, 2002: 87–105, 163–180).
6. Challenged by economic difficulties, Prime Minister Menderes stated that, if necessary, democracy could be given a break or postponed for the sake of economic progress; while President Celal Bayar had a sharper attitude than Menderes in this regard (Ahmad, 1993: 110; Eroğul, 2014: 214, 217). Thus, with Prime Minister Menderes, economic development gained momentum, but not in the direction of enhancing democracy. Yet, this approach has frequently been resorted to in the subsequent decades.
7. For instance, despite Prime Minister Menderes's persistent insistence starting from 1954, foreign credits needed for Ereğli iron and steel mill, among other projects, could not be obtained until 1960, when an agreement was eventually reached for the WB's provision of $129 million. Other technical and financial problems aside, the main difficulty arose from the "condition of US assistance" that "the majority of shares must be *privately owned*" (Harris, 1972: 99). The Ereğli case should be considered as a concrete example illustrating the limits of Turkey's independent decision-making abilities.

## References

Ahmad, F. (1976). *Çok Partili Demokrasi Dönemi Kronolojisi*. Bilgi Yayınevi.
Ahmad, F. (1993). *The making of modern Turkey*. Routledge.
Armaoğlu, F. (1996). Amerikan belgelerinde 27 mayıs olayı. *Belleten, 60*, 203–226.
Aybar, M. A. (1968) *Bağımsızlık, Demokrasi, Sosyalizm*. Gerçek Yayınevi.

Boran, B. (2016). *Türkiye ve Sosyalizm Sorunları*. Sarmal Yayınları.
Boratav, K. (2015). *Türkiye'nin Faşizmleri ve AKP*. İmge Kitabevi.
Boratav, K. (2019). *Türkiye İktisat Tarihi 1908–2009*. İmge Kitabevi.
Buğra, A. (1994). *State and business in modern Turkey a comparative study*. SUNY Press.
Cerrahoğlu, P. B. (1996). *Demokrat Parti Masalı*. Milliyet Yayınları.
Cohn, T. H. (2012). *Global political economy*. Longman.
Danielson, M. N., & Ruşen Keleş. (1980) Urbanization and income distribution in Turkey. In E. Özbudun & A. Ulusan (Eds.), *The political economy of income distribution in Turkey* (pp. 269–309). Holmes & Meier Publishers.
Dikerdem, M. (1977). *Üçüncü Dünyadan Bir Büyükelçinin Anıları*. İstanbul Matbaası.
Doster, B. (2020). Soğuk Savaş Döneminde Türkiye-ABD İlişkileri. In Ö. Gürakar (Ed.), *Türkiye'nin Soğuk Savaş Düzeni* (pp. 288–334). Tekin Yayınevi.
Eligür, B. (2010). *The mobilization of political İslam in Turkey*. Cambridge University Press.
Eroğul, C. (2014). *Demokrat Parti Tarihi ve İdeolojisi*. Yordam Kitap.
Hale, W. (2000). *Turkish foreign policy, 1774–2000*. London: Frank Cass.
Halle, L. J. (1967). *The Cold War as history*. Chatto & Windus.
Harris, G. S. (1972). *Troubled alliance: Turkish-American problems in historical perspective, 1945–1971*. American Enterprise Institute for Public Policy Research.
Heper, M., & Sayarı, S. (2002). *Political leaders and democracy in Turkey*. Lexington Books.
Hershlag, Z. Y. (1968). *Turkey: The challenge of growth*. E. J. Brill.
Horsfield, K. (1969). *The International Monetary Fund*. IMF.
Huntington, S. P. (1968). *Political order in changing societies*. Yale University Press.
Kara, B. (2006). Türkiye'de Personel Reformu Reformu Tartışmalarının Alt Yapısı:1930–60 Yılları Arasında Yabancı Uzmanların Hazırladıkları Raporlar. *Cumhuriyet Üniversitesi Sosyal Bilimler Dergisi, 30*(2), 149–162.
Karpat, K. H. (1959). *Turkey's politics: The transition to a multi-party system*. Princeton, New Jersey: Princeton University Press.
Karpat, K. H. (1976). *The Gecekondu: Rural migration and urbanization*. Cambridge University Press.
Kaynar, M. K. (Ed.). (2015). *Türkiye'nin 1950'li Yılları*. İletişim.
Kepenek, Y. (1993). *Türkiye'de Kamu İktisadi Teşekkülleri (KİT)*. Gerçek Yayınevi.
Kepenek, Y. (2011). *Development & structure of the Turkish economy*. Ankara: METU Press.

Kepenek, Y. (2019). *Cumhuriyet Çağdaşlaşmasından Günümüze Türkiye'nin Değişimi*. Yeni Kuşak Köy Enstilülüler Derneği.
Kepenek, Y. (2020). *Türkiye Ekonomisi*. Remzi Kitabevi.
Keyder, Ç. (1987). *State and class in Turkey*. Verso.
Keyder, N. (1970). Türkiye'de Tarımsal Reel Gelir ve Köylünün Refah Seviyesi. *ODTÜ Gelişme Dergisi, 1*, 32–52.
Kısakürek, N. F. (1959). Amerika, Dünya ve Biz. *Büyük Doğu, 10*(20), 1.
Kiely, R. (2005). *The clash of globalisations: Neo-liberalism, the third way and anti-globalisation*. Brill.
Koç, Y. (2019). *Türkiye İşçi Sınıfı Tarihi Osmanlı'dan 2019'a*. Türkiye Gıda ve Tarım İşçileri Sendikası.
Krueger, A. O. (1974). *Foreign trade regimes & economic development: Turkey*. Columbia University Press.
Mason, E. S., & Asher, R. E. (1973). *The World Bank since the Bretton Woods*. Brookings Institution.
Meier, G. M., & Seers, D. (1984). *Pioneers in development*. Oxford University Press for the World Bank.
Mert, N. (2007). *Merkez Sağın Kısa Tarihi*. Selis Yayınları.
Ministry of Finance. (1977). *Kamu İktisadi Teşebbüsleri ve İştirakleri Yıllığı 1977*. Ankara.
OECD. (1970). *Labor force statistics, 1957–1968*. OECD.
Örnek, C. (2015). *Türkiye'nin Soğuk Savaş Düşünce Hayatı Antikomünizm ve Amerikan Etkisi*. Can Sanat Yayınları.
Öztürk, K. (1968). *Türkiye Cumhuriyeti Hükümetleri ve Programları*. Ak Yayınları.
Özkan, B., & Gürakar, T. (2020). *Türkiye'nin Soğuk Savaş Düzeni, Ordu, Sermaye, ABD, İslamizasyon*. Tekin Yayınevi.
Pamuk, Ş. (2014). *Türkiye'nin 200 Yıllık İktisadi Tarihi büyüme, kurumlar ve bölüşüm*. İstanbul: Türkiye İş Bankası Kültür Yayınları.
Panitch, L., & Gindin, S. (2012). *The making of global capitalism*. Verso Books.
Peet, R. (2009). *Unholy trinity: The IMF, World Bank and WTO*. Zed Books.
Price, H. B. (1955). *Marshall plan and its meaning*. Cornell University Press.
Rodrik, D. (2011). *The globalization paradox*. W. W. Norton.
Rostow, W. W. (1956, March). The take-off into self-sustained growth. *Economic Journal, 66*, 25–48.
Singer, M. (1977). *The economic advance of Turkey, 1938–1960*. Turkish Economic Society.
SIS-TIS [State Institute of Statistics-Turkish Institute of Statistics; DİE-TÜİK]. (1973). *Türkiye'de Toplumsal ve Ekonomik Gelişmenin 50 Yılı*. T.C Başbakanlık Devlet İstatistik Enstitüsü (DİE).
Teazis, C. (2010). *İkincilerin Cumhuriyeti*. Mızrak.

Tekeli, İ., & İlkin, S. (1974). *Savaş Sonrasi Ortamında 1947 Türkiye İktisadi Kalkınma Planı*. ODTÜ.
Tekeli, İ., & İlkin, S. (2014). *İkinci Dünya Savaşı Türkiye'si I, II, III*. İletişim.
Thornburg, M. W., Spry, G., & Solule, G. (1949). *Turkey, an economic appraisal*. The Twentieth Century Fund.
Trask, R. R. (1971). *The United States response to Turkish nationalism and reform, 1914–1939*. University of Minnesota Press.
Tuğtan, M. A. (2020). Soğuk Savaş ve Türkiye'de Siyasal İslam'ın Yükselişi: 1945–1975. In Ö. Gürakar (Ed.), *Türkiye'nin Soğuk Savaş Düzeni* (pp. 71–122). Tekin Yayınevi.
WB [World Bank / (IBRD-International Bank for Reconstruction and Development]. (1951). The *economy of Turkey, an analysis and recommendations for a development program*. IBRD.
Yavuzalp, E. (1991). *Menderes'le Anılar*. Bilgi Yayınevi.

CHAPTER 6

# Import-Substituting Industrialization Strategy and Planning Experience in Turkey, 1960–1980

*Ümit Akçay and Oktar Türel*

## Introduction

This chapter reviews the import-substituting industrialization (ISI) strategy and economic planning experience in Turkey in the 1960s and the 1970s, with due consideration for its international boundary conditions. It comprises six sections. Following the first introductory section, the second one starts with the description of the institutional framework established after World War II (WW-II) and the roles of its main constituents in the governance of the global economy. This institutional

Ü. Akçay (✉)
Berlin School of Economics and Law, Berlin, Germany

O. Türel
Middle East Technical University, Ankara, Turkey



E. Özçelik and Y. Özdemir (eds.), *Political Economy of Development in Turkey*, The Political Economy of the Middle East,
https://doi.org/10.1007/978-981-16-7318-4_6

framework was geared toward a gradual yet definite liberalization of international trade and investment throughout the 1960s and the 1970s. The second section then proceeds with a concise survey of the characteristic features and policy instruments of ISI, which turned out to be the preferred strategy in many developing countries (DCs), including Turkey, in those years. ISI was sometimes supplemented with indicative economic planning in DCs, albeit with varying degrees of effectiveness. New patterns of industrial specialization along the "primary" stages of ISI and/or recourse to indicative planning in DCs were compatible with the political-economic interests of the advanced countries (ACs) till the early 1970s.

The third and fourth sections deal with specific aspects of indicative economic planning and the political economy of ISI in Turkey, respectively. At the onset of Turkish planning experience in the early 1960s, two basic problems confronting the planners were: (i) the reorganization of state economic enterprises (SEEs) which had a large share in industrial activities, and (ii) raising domestic savings *via* a tax reform. It is debatable whether the political compromise reached in the 1960–1963 period on these issues provided satisfactory answers to the basic problems faced. In the 1960s and the early 1970s, Turkey's large business groups supported the ISI strategy of the government due to the prospects of high profits it offered through protection from international competition and various pecuniary incentives provided by the state without reciprocal commitments. Workers in large enterprises were another group supporting the ISI strategy. Apart from its importance in providing basic necessities to consumers and inputs to consumer-goods industries, the agricultural sector had a limited role as a provider of export revenue. In view of some industrial deepening in consumer durables and intermediates, Turkish version of ISI during the 1960–1980 period resembled the "secondary" phase of ISI in major Latin American countries in the 1955–1968 period. This analogy was observed in the policy space as well.

In the fifth section, the crisis of ISI in the 1970s is examined in two different contexts. At the international level, the "over-accumulation" crisis of 1968–1971 in ACs and the ensuing economic instabilities throughout the 1970s indicated that the implicit social contract between capital and labor envisaged by the Keynesian economic paradigm was no longer sustainable. Besides, the dialogue between ACs and DCs to establish a just and more equitable world order was moving toward a deadlock. Irrespective of geography and international political affinities, capital at the "center" could no longer tolerate ISI and indicative planning at the "periphery." At the national level, after the first oil crisis in 1973, industrial productivity slowed down, inflation rate accelerated and balance of payments deteriorated in Turkey, leading to insolvency in international transactions of the country in 1977. The government under Bülent Ecevit's premiership, which had come to power in January 1978, failed to manage the crisis and had to resign in November 1979. Its successor, Süleyman Demirel's government, announced an economic policy package in January 1980, effectively bringing the Turkish ISI experience to its end. Lastly, the sixth section concludes this chapter.

## International Conditions

### *Institutional Framework for the Governance of the World Economy*

Policy orientations of major actors within the institutional framework for the governance of the world economy are summarized below. The post-war decades were characterized by the political-economic prominence of the International Monetary Fund (IMF), the World Bank (WB), the General Agreement on Tariffs and Trade (GATT), and the United Nations Conference on Trade and Development (UNCTAD).

***IMF***: In the 1950s, IMF mostly lent to the ACs which suffered from "dollar shortage," and administered relatively moderate exchange-rate alignments. The pattern of lending changed significantly in the following two decades: In the 1960s, about two fifths of the total approved lending were extended to the DCs, and that proportion went up to about two thirds in the 1970s. Furthermore, the conventional form of IMF lending, that is to say, Standby Arrangements (SBAs), started to become longer in duration and more articulate in terms of the economic assessment of debtor countries and "conditionalities" attached to the loans (Reinhart & Tresbesch, 2015: 2–10).

As the economic boom enjoyed by many DCs in the first half of the 1970s turned into a protracted slump later, both the number and the total volume of IMF lending arrangements started to increase very rapidly till 1983. What was more disturbing was that, from the mid-1970s onward, IMF support programs usually went beyond the original mission of providing liquidity to countries in distress, and started to involve broader intervention in national economic policies and resource allocation.

***WB***: Notwithstanding a tardy start, the WB gradually turned into a major international investment bank over the 1950–1968 period, lending mostly to the DCs outside the socialist block. In that period, the WB adopted a market-friendly, pro-growth and pro-private sector policy stance, emphasizing export promotion, and liberalization of international trade and investment. However, the WB management was flexible enough so as not to categorically oppose: (i) ISI, (ii) protectionist practices and administrative controls in the economy, if these were moderate, and (iii) public ownership of productive enterprises in the borrowing countries. It was also tolerant of the adverse distributional impacts of pro-growth policies, being a firm believer in "trickle-down" processes of economic development.

Two other important institutions under the WB's umbrella were established in that period: International Finance Corporation (IFC) in 1956 and International Development Association (IDA) in 1960. The former was entrusted with the task of lending to or participating in the private ventures in the DCs. The latter was expected to provide long-term, concessional finance to the poorer DCs.

The next period of 1968–1978 almost fully coincided with the demise of the Keynesian paradigm, the breakdown of the Bretton Woods system and the global crises following it. By a major overhaul in policy priorities, the WB management tried to: (i) enlarge the volume of its lending, (ii) increase the effectiveness of the WB in international relations, (iii) set up a new system of country programs so as to better guide the policies of member countries, and (iv) place greater emphasis on reduction of poverty, protection of environment, population control, urban development, and reforming macroeconomic policies (Kapur et al., 1997: 488–503). The global swing toward economic orthodoxy made a definite impact on WB headquarters in the 1978–1981 period, as manifested by the announcement of the idea of Structural Adjustment Loans (SALs) in 1979, which would further narrow the room for maneuver in the policy space of the DCs.

***GATT***: GATT's code of conduct was drawn up with reference to three trade-related principles which had been staunchly defended by the US governments since the mid-1930s, that is to say, non-discrimination, reciprocity, and free trade as the ultimate objective.

Non-discrimination essentially meant adherence to the "most favoured nation" (MFN) principle. However, a number of exceptions that were legitimized under the GATT clearly violated the MFN principle, for instance, (i) preferential trade agreements, (ii) customs unions, and (iii) free trade areas (Barton et al., 2006: 38–41; Van der Wee, 1987: 349–350). Besides, some flexibility in interpreting the principle of reciprocity was needed in order to make trade liberalization acceptable to the DCs. A meaningful step in this direction was taken rather lately in 1971, when the Generalized System of Preferences (GSP) developed by UNCTAD's efforts was incorporated into GATT's regulations, and its validity was confirmed by the Enabling Clause of the GATT Decision (1979).

A series of trade negotiations organized by GATT from 1947 to 1961 were concluded with modest, but meaningful tariff reductions.[1] In the history of GATT, the most important and comprehensive rounds of trade negotiations were the Kennedy Round (1963–1967) and the Tokyo Round (1974–1979). Both of these rounds were set forth by the initiative of the US, which reacted to changing patterns of trade and competitiveness across major trading blocks, that is, the US, the European Economic Community (EEC) and Japan. By and large, DCs were passive onlookers with regard to these rounds.

***UNCTAD and the New International Economic Order***: Resolution 1710 (XVI) by the United Nations (UN) General Assembly in 1961, which proclaimed the 1960s as the "First Development Decade," was an indication of growing sensitivities over the pressing problems of the DCs. In 1962, the General Assembly decided to convene UNCTAD I (Resolution 1785, XVII).

In the *Final Act* adopted by UNCTAD I in 1964, a strategy of reform for the governance of global economy was put forward, which included three basic policy proposals: (i) preferential and concessionary entry of DC exports to the ACs, (ii) attainment of an equitable and satisfactory stability in primary commodity prices, and (iii) increasing unconditional aid to the DCs (Bello, 2000; Taylor & Smith, 2007: 10–13).[2] Shortly, after this conference, UNCTAD was granted a formal organizational status by Resolution 1995 (XIX).

ACs effectively resisted to the translation of these three policy proposals in their entirety into concrete international commitments. Nevertheless, some modest and patchy steps were taken. In the context of the first proposal, deliberations in and studies undertaken after UNCTAD II (1968) convinced AC governments to incorporate GSP into the GATT regulations (see above). In the context of the second, ACs somehow supported the measures for providing *stability* to commodity prices and export revenues of poor countries; but they were against measures that would affect their *trends* and *levels*, which could help overcome the problem of "unequal exchange." The compromise out of differing policy positions found its expressions in: (i) *Integrated Program for Commodities* prepared for UNCTAD IV (1976), which paved the way for a few international commodity agreements from 1977 to 1981, (ii) *Stabex* scheme to be applied by the EEC to the exports of African, Caribbean, and Pacific (ACP) countries (1975), and (iii) compensatory financing facility provided by the IMF to DCs in case of a sudden and drastic fall in their export revenues. As we will accentuate later, these measures were insufficient responses to the demands and expectations of the DCs for a more just and equitable world.

After the initiatives of Movement of Non-aligned Nations and G-77, the Sixth Session of the UN General Assembly adopted Declaration 3201 (S-VI) on the establishment of a New International Economic Order (NIEO) in 1974, which was complemented with its Plan of Action (Declaration 3202 (S-VI). In the preamble of Declaration 3201 (S-VI), members of the UN stated their determination to establish a NIEO based on "equity, sovereign equality, interdependence, common interest and cooperation among all states." The vision of NIEO was by no means confrontationist, and envisaged the reduction of inequalities between Global North and Global South by negotiation and mutual consent of the parties concerned (Boratav, 1976: 75).

Despite efforts by the UN bodies to further qualify and improve the policy content of NIEO objective, it became clear in the second half of the 1970s that the dialogue between ACs and DCs were moving toward dead ends: The Conference on International Economic Cooperation (1975–1977) initiated by the French president Valéry Giscard d'Estaing could not produce any concrete result; and the Common Fund to finance UNCTAD's *Integrated Program for Commodities* could not be made operational. Under such circumstances, UNCTAD V in 1979 produced no significant improvement in North/South negotiations, signaling the eventual demise of the NIEO idea.

### *Characteristic Features of the Post-War ISI*

Following Hirschman (1968: 4–6), four impulses which stimulated ISI in DCs can be identified as follows: (i) wars and depressions leading to a breakdown in international division of labor, (ii) serious balance of payments difficulties, (iii) growth of domestic markets, and (iv) a deliberate policy choice. The first three of these impulses had been observed in some DCs (including Turkey) prior to the WW-II, but the rise of ISI to the status of an official development strategy and thus the transformation of "infant industry" argument into an "infant economy" argument (Bruton, 1989: 1605) were post-WW-II phenomena. Both non-Marxian development economists and supporters of ISI argued that new patterns of industrial specialization can be shaped by negotiation and consent so as to yield mutual gains to the DCs and the ACs (Hirschman, 1981: 3–5).

The post-WW-II ISI in the DCs turned out to be a highly *sequential* or *staged* process, starting primarily with the manufacture of finished consumer goods that were previously imported, and later proceeding to "higher" stages, that is, the production of intermediate and investment goods through backward linkages.[3] In practice, these backward linkages did not work as rapidly and smoothly as expected for a number of reasons related to market size, entrepreneurial behavior, government policies, and technological capabilities of individual countries (Hirschman, 1968: 13–24; Schmitz, 1984: 3–4). In many countries, such failures led to a secular rise in imports-to-GDP ratios. Since export revenues were generally insufficient to pay for the import bills, followers of the ISI strategy frequently encountered sizable trade deficits toward the end of their medium-term cycles, culminating in balance of payments crises and macroeconomic instabilities.

Trade protectionism implemented under an ISI strategy can be grouped into three categories: (i) trade policies (tariffs, quantity restrictions on imports, import licenses, etc.), (ii) foreign exchange policies (setting the exchange rate, controls on current account and capital account transactions), and (iii) indirectly protective policies (interest rate and wage policies). Here, some explanatory notes on these policies may be useful.

In the period under our study, nominal tariffs were generally set on the basis of *ad hoc* economic considerations (Bruton, 1988: 912), leading to diffuse structures both in tariffs and effective rates of protection (ERsP).[4] In conformity with the logic of ISI, tariffs on imported inputs were usually set at lower rates relative to those applied to imports of finished products. This practice could be expected to make (and actually made) the ERsP higher than nominal rates in industrial sectors. Observed ERsP were definitely higher in comparison to those in the ACs, showing also a large variance across DCs on the one hand, and across industries on the other (Bruton, 1988: 912; Schmitz, 1984: 6–7).[5] Nominal and effective protection by tariffs were complemented with various quantitative restrictions and administrative controls on imports. These policies aimed to attain some specific sectoral ISI targets and to handle balance of payments difficulties. Import licenses were essentially used as instruments to safeguard imports of basic necessities and/or machinery and equipment for key industrial investments.

Undoubtedly, the most important one in the second group of policy instruments was the exchange rate. The dominant tendency in ISI was to keep domestic currency overvalued, basically for the following reasons: (i) to promote capital accumulation by keeping imported investment goods cheaper, (ii) to control "imported inflation," and (iii) to suppress domestic prices of traditional export goods so as to transfer real income from their producers and exporters to other strata of society (Türel, 2017: 208). In order to offset the disincentive of an overvalued currency, non-traditional (mostly industrial) exports were supported with various pecuniary incentives.

Interest rate subsidies for promoting output growth and capital accumulation were mostly selective and frequently resulted in negative real interest rates. On the other hand, wages in the more organized segments of the economy were above the rates that would be attained under competitive labor market conditions, putting some parts of the industrial workforce to a disadvantaged position; but the DC governments generally did not regard such stratification of the labor market as a negative phenomenon (Türel, 2017: 208–209).

Not surprisingly, the proponents of mainstream economics, on grounds of efficiency, objected to all these price "distortions" and the anti-export, anti-agriculture and anti-employment biases they may have generated. An OECD-sponsored comparative study by Little et al. (1970) offered a sophisticated critique of the ISI in line with mainstream economic thinking, which was later repeatedly referred to by many international organizations. Some other critical studies in the 1970s reflected growing sensitivities on the problems of employment, reducing inequalities and poverty, and meeting basic needs (Arndt, 1987: Chap. 4).

The attitude of DC governments toward foreign direct investment (FDI) as an external resource and a channel for transferring technology and know-how differed widely. At one extreme, there were countries that were fully open to and supportive of FDI, such as Brazil. At the other extreme, there were countries like India, which did not encourage FDI at all (Bruton, 1989: 1619–1633). Turkey was a case between these two extremes.

Toward the late 1960s, ISI strategy began to lose its earlier attractiveness due to the failures of its adherents in: (i) generating sufficient export revenues, and (ii) raising domestic savings needed to finance the advanced stages of industrialization. A new policy orientation in such major Latin American countries as Brazil, Mexico, and Argentina involved the avoidance of excesses committed in the past, concerning protection, negative real interest rates, and substantial overvaluation of domestic currency. Such a revision of policy agenda did not receive much political support in India and Turkey till the 1980s, apart from policies for the promotion of manufactured exports (Türel, 2017: 210–211).

The brief survey above is focused upon the common characteristics of ISI in DCs from the early 1950s to the early 1970s. The political economy of Turkey's ISI experience in the 1960s and the 1970s, which had many similarities to the general outlook summarized above, will be specifically dealt with in the fourth section below.

### *Planning in DCs*

Although development plans and related programs prepared by non-socialist countries abound in our period of study,[6] most of these were formal exercises devoid of functional significance; because the structure and traditions and/or the competence of public administration in many DCs were not conducive to the incorporation of plans into the political decision-making process. Of course, there were exceptions; India, Turkey, and Korea stood out as archetypes of countries which carried out central, comprehensive, and indicative national planning effectively, the former two being the adherents of ISI strategy, and the latter one shifting to export-led industrialization (ELI) in the 1960s.[7]

## The Making of Planning in Turkey

The main trends in the world economy in the post-WW-II period resonated with Turkey as well. Turkey's experience with ISI and economic planning went back to the Great Depression era, when Turkish policy-makers launched industrialization programs under the leadership of the public sector. Nevertheless, the integration to the US-dominated Western system in the post-WW-II era resulted in the introduction of multi-party system in Turkey in 1946; and the Democrat Party (DP) governments, which positioned themselves against the *statist* orientations of the 1930s, dominated the 1950s. The uncoordinated and fragmented public investments undertaken by the DP governments were criticized not only by opposition parties (Simpson, 1965), but also by international institutions such as the WB (Maxfield & Nolt, 1990). Although it was reluctant, the DP government invited Professor Jan Tinbergen, a well-known Dutch economist, to consult on the establishment of a planning institution as well as its planning model in 1959 (Mıhçıoğlu, 1988). After a balance of payments crisis led the government to devalue the national currency in 1958, the DP government also established a Coordination Ministry to manage public investments in order to meet the demands of both international institutions and domestic business groups (Akçay, 2007). Yet, the ISI framework and indicative planning became official only after the military coup of May 27, 1960. Shortly, thereafter, the military government announced that economic affairs would henceforth be organized within a planned framework, and Cemal Gürsel, the leader of the coup and later President of the Republic, declared that "the government is determined to support the planning activities in every possible way" (DPT, 1960: 26).

After the establishment of the State Planning Organization (SPO) (Torun, 1967: 58), the central trajectory of the planning system in Turkey was determined by the High Planning Council (HPC), as laid out in the 1961 "Objectives and the Strategy of the Plan." According to the document, "a development plan will be prepared to attain the highest possible rate of growth and to achieve social justice within the democratic system which is the preferred way of life of the Turkish people" (SPO, 1961: 1). Based on the Strategy Document, planners then embarked on the formulation of the first five-year development plan that covered the 1963–1967 period.

The period between the formation of the SPO in 1960 and the implementation of the first five-year plan in 1963 was a critical juncture, in which the main characteristics of the development planning and the ISI regime were determined by negotiations among planners, bureaucracy, industrialists, merchants, agricultural interest groups, and politicians. Planners' attempt to form a coherent planning regime depended upon two reform proposals, namely the reorganization of the SEEs and the tax reform. These were not only important for building a policy framework compatible with the ISI strategy, but also vital for improving the "extraction capacity" of the state to finance the plan.[8]

### *The Reorganization of the SEEs*

The reorganization of the SEEs constituted the main pillar of the restructuring project as envisioned by the planners.[9] Since Turkey had the largest public sector in the non-communist world in 1960 (Amsden, 2001) and public sector investments constituted 55% of total investments that year (DPT, 1963: 74–75), the planners considered the SEEs as the main engine to increase savings and thus to attain their target growth rate. More importantly, while private sector operations generally concentrated on light industries in such traditional sectors as food stuffs, textiles, and construction, the SEEs focused on heavy capital-intensive industries in the manufacturing, mining, energy, steel, and petrochemical sectors (Walstedt, 1980: 31–32). In comparison to private enterprises, the SEEs generally utilized more advanced technologies at larger scales with higher fixed capital formation.[10]

That being said, the investment strategies of the various SEEs were neither managed nor even coordinated by a central authority; in fact, "there [was] no system of Turkish state enterprises" (OECD, 1961: 11). Instead, each SEE was governed under the supervision of a different ministry. This fragmented structure posed two main problems: overlapping investments and insufficient data collection. From the perspective of the planners, the reorganization of the SEEs was thus of paramount importance for two interconnected reasons: first, a united and strong instrument—which covered half of the whole economy under the control of the SPO—was needed to meet the targets of the plan; and secondly, the operational costs of the SEEs and the government's budget deficits were to be eliminated, while additional funds for the financing of the plan would be created (DPT, 1963: 54). In response, the planners designed two crucial restructuring schemes at the organizational and operational levels.

At the organizational level, the restructuring blueprint envisaged that the investment decisions of the SEEs would be managed under the auspices of the SPO in order to steer public investments according to the priorities of the plan. The State Investment Bank (*Devlet Yatırım Bankası*) (SIB), which was expected to serve as a link between the SPO and the SEEs, was the institution proposed for the centralization of investment decisions. The planners wanted all public investments to be coordinated and monitored by a single institution, namely the SIB, which was designed to be under the control of the SPO. The SIB would determine the criteria, fields, and scopes of investments, in addition to its authority to approve the investment projects coming from the SEEs. However, the SIB would not only manage the investment policies of the SEEs, but also provide cheap credit when needed for the realization of investments (Bulutoğlu, 1961a). In short, through this organizational restructuring, the planners aimed to correct the fragmented nature of SEEs so that, collectively, SEEs would become a more integrated, coherent and strong instrument operating under the control of the SPO.

The operational restructuring was as important as the organizational changes. As organizational centralization provided the SPO with enormous capacity to conduct state investment, the planners anticipated that operational restructuring would insulate the SEEs from political influence and intra-bureaucratic conflicts. The main aim of the operational restructuring was to ensure the productivity and profitability of the SEEs. Thus, the SEEs would be utilized to reach investment targets by contributing to the financing of the plan under the management of the SPO (SPO, 1962: 9–10). Changing the management patterns of the SEEs toward a more market-oriented outlook meant that their pricing policies could not be manipulated by political intervention or by the strategy of selling at a loss in order to subsidize private enterprises (Bulutoğlu, 1961b: 1). Instead, by subjecting the SEEs to competitive market forces, prices would be governed by the profit motive so as to make the earning of "normal profits"the regulating principle of each SEE (Bulutoğlu, 1961b: 4; DPT, 1962a: 49; SPO, 1960a: 1). In other words, the SPO intended to create a dynamic and competitive domestic market in which public and private production units were incentivized to rationalize their investments through a process that would ultimately lead them to increase their levels of productivity.

### *The Tax Reform*

The tax reform proposal depended on the establishment of a new taxation system in the agricultural sector, which had previously been untaxed,[11] and the realignment of the taxation system to both the priorities of the plan and the requirements of the ISI regime. During the formulation of the proposal, the SPO invited Professor Nicholas Kaldor, a well-known development economist, to prepare guidelines on agricultural taxation in 1962. Kaldor (1963: 13) believed that "taxation of the agricultural sector has a vital role to play in accelerating economic development," and his subsequent report concluded that taxation of the agricultural sector would allow two aims to be fulfilled simultaneously: increases in both productivity and tax revenues (Kaldor, 1962). In this sense, the Kaldor report showed that potential output could be used as a taxation base and suggested a progressive taxation policy, aiming at creating an incentive structure for the efficient use of land based on the taxation of large landowners. Accordingly, it recommended that only 15% of the total agricultural sector, namely large landowners with 50 hectares of land or more, be taxed in proportion to their agricultural output (Üstünel, 1962: 5).

More importantly, however, alongside the objective of creating an additional resource for financing the plan, the planners expected that the tax reform proposal would also support land reform (DPT, 1962b) by creating an incentive structure for large landowners to sell their lands in order to avoid paying higher taxes. In this way, land redistribution would take place, while idle land would be transformed into productive units (Üstünel, 1962: 6). In short, taxation of the agricultural sector was expected to lead to three improvements: agricultural productivity increases; additional resources for financing the development plan; and strong incentives to facilitate land reform.

The second major adjustment of the taxation system in line with the planning framework was to introduce new incentives and disincentives. The proposal intended to use taxation as a tool to channel private investment into desired sectors. Specifically, it aimed at heavier taxation in unproductive fields, along with investment allowances for favored areas. For example, it recommended "the revision of building tax to render the construction of dwellings economically less attractive, [so that] more resources would then be available for investment in directly productive activities" (Öngüt, 1967: 157). As previously mentioned, the new tax allowances were also expected to increase levels of investment in the private sector (Bulutoğlu, 1967: 192).

### *The Exclusion of the Reform Proposals*

The SPO's proposal to reorganize the SEEs and initiate a tax reform sparked a vocal opposition, consisting of industrialists and merchants, the traditional bureaucracy, and the right-wing political elite. The main conflict between planners and industrialists originated from their differing priorities: On the one hand, the investment strategy of the Turkish capitalist class traditionally concentrated on "economically less productive but easier, safer and more profitable fields, notably real estate" (Cohn, 1962: 8). On the other hand, planners aimed at channeling resources into more productive areas such as industry. In return for changing their investment patterns in accordance with these new priorities, major business groups demanded profit guarantees from the government. The industrialists also saw the reorganized SEEs as a potential competitor in the domestic market and thus demanded the elimination of any possible competitive pressures from the SEEs (SPO, 1960b). The industrialists also rejected the SPO's tax proposals, insisting that the corporate tax rate be lowered to its previous level of 10% (Union of Chambers, 1962: 13), that the cost of, and earnings from, new investments be exempt from taxation (Union of Chambers, 1962: 23), and that—instead of considering it a method of revenue collection—the entire taxation system be seen as a means to encourage private enterprise.

Similarly, the traditional bureaucracy's resistance to the SPO's proposals was also "rational" insofar as it wanted to secure its own position within the state system. If the SPO's proposals were implemented, all the SEEs would be united under the control of the SPO, which is to say that not only would all ministries lose their most important agents, but also their very position in the state system would be downgraded.

Finally, the political elites also turned hostile to the SPO's reform program for two reasons. First, along with the SPO's reform programs (which meant, in practice, the de-politicization of economic management in general), there was a strong possibility that the political elite would lose at least some of their discretionary power and ability to maneuver in determining economic policies. Secondly, the political elite did not want to lose their authority over the SEEs, because they saw them as a means to create new employment opportunities for their voters and to increase their electoral potential through the choice of investment locations.

The trajectory of the planning regime in Turkey was determined during the 1962 HPC meetings. The most significant outcome was the realignment of the plan document in response to the demands of the opposition bloc. As a result, the SPO's two key reform proposals, namely the reorganization of the SEEs and tax reform, were deleted from the original document (Akçay, 2007: 200; Forum, 1962: 4). As Deputy Prime Minister Hasan Dinçer stated, "our statism is not socialism. Instead of undermining each other, the public sector will complement the private sector" (*Milliyet* 27 June 1962: 7). The government thus rejected the SPO's proposal on SEEs, which constituted the backbone of the reform program (*Milliyet* 28 June 1962: 1). Although the capitalists agreed with the state during the HPC meetings on the implementation of the ISI, they rejected the SPO's reform proposals and demanded new incentive measures to encourage private sector investment (*Milliyet* 18 June 1962: 7). The tax reform proposal was assessed as "absolutely unacceptable" by the political elite. Indeed, Ekrem Alican, another Deputy Prime Minister, clearly stated that "those who want to change the tax laws are those who want to change the democratic regime as well" (Yön, 1962: 5). After the exclusion of the reform proposals, business circles were assured of two matters: they would not be faced with competition (and there would thus not be any direct or indirect state intervention in investment decisions) and the SEEs would continue to hold a complementary status in the economy. Hence, the failed attempt to establish a coherent planning regime paved the way for the dependent development of Turkish capitalism.

The capitalist influence over the planning regime was further consolidated after the introduction of a new incentive scheme, which was regulated through Law No. 933, via forming a new body within the SPO, namely the Incentive and Implementation Department (IID), in 1968. Although the IID was initially formed to orient private investments through the establishment of a new resource allocation mechanism according to the SPO's priorities, the SPO itself became a battleground of various capital fractions, which were lobbying to alter the incentive scheme according to their interests (Akçay, 2007). Hence, the installation of IID further undermined the SPO's relative autonomy, which was a requisite for successful economic planning (Milor, 1990).

## Political Economy of Turkey's ISI Experience

Not only did international institutions actively promote ISI in the post-WW-II period, but also this strategy was compatible with the internationalization of capital—mainly in the form of FDI (Eralp, 1981: 618). Therefore, as Evans (1979) described in the Brazilian case, the ISI strategy was key to the process of "dependent development," whose main actors were multinational companies, states and domestic business groups. In addition to the international components, the ISI strategy necessitated a cross-class alliance at the national level.

At the beginning the 1960s, Turkey's large business groups began to demand an ISI strategy since it would provide industrialists with a shield from international competition. Conversely, the same business groups successfully lobbied against disciplinary planning and aimed to separate the planning framework from the ISI strategy. For capitalists, ISI and the implementation of "indicative planning" offered a huge opportunity to increase their profits through subsidies and incentives. What was crucial for them, however, was that those subsidies and incentives should not have been seen as a rationale for state intervention aimed at stepping in and changing the investment decisions of private firms. In other words, the business community did not want a reciprocal deal; rather, they tried to gain access to the opportunities of the planning regime as a kind of "giveaway." This attitude was not unique to Turkey. As Chibber (2003: 34) observes for the Indian case, the "capitalists therefore had an interest in supporting the subsidizing side of ISI, while strenuously opposing the state's power to regulate and monitor the flow and utilization of investment." Amsden (1989: 89) also argues that, in the South Korean case, "although profit maximization and growth maximization [were] not antithetical, neither [were] they necessarily synonymous." Therefore, for the Turkish business class, securing existing investment patterns—or, in other words, resisting the plan—was not only desirable but also rational from their own viewpoint.

The planners continuously criticized the bourgeoisie for being narrow-minded and short-sighted, because they believed that if capitalists had followed the plan's direction, they would have benefited from it (Karaosmanoğlu et al., 2003: 47–48). Nonetheless, the capitalists never opted for that alternative. Their priorities for profit maximization did not fit with those of the plan, as investment in industry required higher rates of capital accumulation and a longer horizon. Moreover, for investing in industry, uncertainties need to be eliminated for the foreseeable future and necessary financial opportunities must be made available to entrepreneurs. Unless these two requirements are met, profit-maximizing capitalists always prefer to invest in projects that offer quick and secure returns (Wade, 1988: 153). Particularly, after the elimination of the reform proposals, the industrialists enjoyed unchallenged profit opportunities in addition to state incentives and tax rebates (Saybaşılı, 1985: 102). As a result, Turkey's planning regime became merely a resource transfer mechanism to domestic firms that were not required to make any commitments in return. This particular nature of the ISI regime, therefore, shaped the dependent development trajectory of Turkish capitalism between 1960 and 1980. After the initial wave of resignations of the planners,[12] the business community's "doubts about the character of the Turkish planning were settled" (Buğra, 1994: 136). From the vantage point of big business, having defeated the SPO, planning was no longer seen as a threat. What is more, the sustainment of the existing structure of the SEEs was the most significant gain for business groups from their two-year struggle with the SPO (Keyder, 1987: 160). Indeed, the support of the Turkish business community for this "domesticated" version of the ISI regime can be clearly discerned in a survey dated 1974, according to which, 86.7% of businessmen believed that the SPO had been functioning in a pro-developmental way, fostering the Turkish economy (Şaylan, 1986: 145).

Along with business groups, industrial workers were another significant and growing group that was included in the ISI strategy—insofar, as the industries were producing primarily for the domestic market. Industrial workers quickly improved their organizational capacity after the passing of the 1960 amendments to the Constitution regarding collective rights, including unionization. Between 1960 and 1980, they subsequently became a powerful social class. Thanks to the workers' struggle, real wage increases were no less than the increases in real income per capita between 1962 and 1976 (Karacan, 1983–1984: 84). However, toward the end of the ISI period, which was characterized by a balance of payments crisis between 1977 and 1980, the conflicts between industrialists and workers manifested itself through an increasing number of industrial strikes and decreasing rates of capacity utilization in the manufacturing sector.

The agricultural sector was the third component of the ISI strategy, although a rather limited role had been assigned to it. Since the main target of ISI was to speed up industrialization, the planning model took the agricultural sector into account only insofar as it generated export revenue, which was necessary for industrial deepening. It was also important for keeping the prices of consumer goods low and stable—the main rationale for providing extensive subsidies for the agricultural sector. In addition, it became a strategic sector for political parties, since more than two thirds of the population still resided in rural areas (Keyder, 1987).

Sustained and relatively low-conflict interaction among business groups, industrial workers, and agricultural interests was possible only when the economy grew rapidly. As Table 6.1 indicates, during the first and the second five-year plan periods, average GNP growth was close to the targeted rate. However, from the third five-year plan period onward,

**Table 6.1** Growth rate targets and realization in plan periods (annual average percentage changes)

| | *1st plan (1963–1967)* | | *2nd plan (1968–1972)* | | *3rd plan (1973–1977)* | | *1978 program* | | *4th plan (1979–1983)* | |
|---|---|---|---|---|---|---|---|---|---|---|
| | *Target* | *Realization* | *Target* | *Realization* | *Target* | *Realization* | *Target* | *Realization* | *Target* | *Realization* |
| Agriculture | 4.2 | 3.0 | 4.1 | 1.8 | 3.7 | 1.2 | 4.1 | 2.8 | 5.3 | 0.3 |
| Industry | 12.3 | 10.9 | 12.0 | 9.1 | 11.2 | 8.8 | 8.8 | 3.4 | 9.9 | 2.4 |
| Services | 6.8 | 7.2 | 6.3 | 6.6 | 7.7 | 7.3 | – | 0.1 | 8.5 | 2.6 |
| GNP | 7.0 | 6.6 | 7.0 | 6.3 | 7.9 | 5.2 | 6.1 | 1.2 | 8.0 | 1.7 |

*Source* Türkiye Cumhuriyeti Cumhurbaşkanlığı, Strateji ve Bütçe Başkanlığı (*Presidency of Turkey, Presidency of Strategy and Budget*), (accessed on: 14 January 2021, https://www.sbb.gov.tr/ekonomik-ve-sosyal-gostergeler/#1540021349004-1497d2c6-7edf

Turkey's ISI strategy reached its limits, and the internal contradictions of the dependent development model manifested themselves in a slowing down of the economic growth rate, which paved the way for increasing conflicts between social classes and groups.

## Crisis of the ISI

### *The Global Outlook: Structural Crisis of Capitalism*

After the great post-WW-II boom (1951–1968) of the world economy, ACs started to exhibit signs of an "over-accumulation" crisis in the 1968–1973 period. Their labor markets were getting tighter in the mid-1960s; so, in order to sustain the high rates of growth of the boom years, capital accumulation had to be accelerated to pave the way for increased productivity. Notwithstanding the high propensities to invest, labor productivity growth slowed down after 1968, while workers could maintain past rates of product-wage growth for some years, thus lowering the share of capital in output. Accompanied by a declining output-to-capital ratio, this process implied a fall in profit rates, which eventually had adverse effects on investment, generating recessionary tendencies. In contrast to the earlier experience, these tendencies were concomitant not with falling, but rising prices (Armstrong et al., 1991: 172–191, Glyn et al., 1991: 51–52, 77–84). Especially, in Western European countries, strikes and other labor disputes peaked in the 1968–1971 period, indicating that a transformation in capital-labor relations was under way.

Aggregate demand management of the 1970s in ACs brought about a stop-go cycle of output change.[13] As far as the entire 1970s were concerned, average growth rate of GDP was substantially lower and the rate of inflation was substantially higher in comparison to those in the great boom years of 1951–1968. Profit rates had a tendency to decline over the 1970s. In order to overcome economic instability, almost all governments in the ACs got gradually closer to the views that: (i) the implicit post-WW-II social contract between capital and labor must have been abandoned, and (ii) economic recovery must have been based on a broader reliance on markets and restoration of profit rates (see, *inter alia*, Streeck, 2014: Chs. 1–2). As we will note again below, the year 1979 was a decisive turning point toward these directions.

The structural crisis in ACs was also related to the limitations of the Fordist work organization, which was predominant in the period under study. A greater *involvement* of workforce in production was then needed, which, in turn, implied an increase in the *intensity of work*. Attempts of "lean production" by Japanese industrialists in the 1970s were steps taken in this direction, which were emulated by other countries in the next decade (Moody, 2001: 85–113).

In the 1970s, labor unions in ACs resisted the pressures for greater corporate control over shop-floor, deskilling labor force and increasing intensity of work. Facing higher unemployment and devoid of a strong political support, their efforts were not that effective. Besides, there was an additional problem due to the internationalization of production: less skill-intensive industries with fairly standardized technologies started to move to new locations in the DCs that offered lower wages. Transnational corporations and their local subsidiaries were the active agents of this process. Such a pattern of industrialization caused job losses at the "center," and intensified exploitation of labor at the "periphery," along with deterioration in living standards (Fröbel et al., 1981: Chaps. 1–2).

From our observations above, it is clear that in the 1968–1979 period, ACs were very far from a "social psychology" that could respond positively to the aspirations of the DCs for an equitable and just global economic order. However, the problem was not confined to the lack of such a "social psychology" on the part of the ACs. In the second half of the 1970s, negotiating capabilities of DC governments were seriously eroded, because DCs experienced: (i) increased economic and political differentiation, (ii) changing class structures in support of articulation with international capital, and (iii) policy failures in offsetting external shocks (Türel, 2017: 334–335).

A brief note on the upheaval in world monetary order in the 1970s must be added to our narrative of structural crisis. Following the collapse of the Bretton Woods system in 1971, it took about five years to reach a compromise on Second Amendment (April 1976) to IMF's Articles of Agreement, which legitimized floating exchange rates and conferred greater freedom on member countries in managing their international reserves.[14] The new "system," or the "non-system," as Ocampo (2017) calls it, was, in fact, a dollar standard. The mechanisms foreseen in the Second Amendment for institutionalizing international cooperation and coordinating national policies in an increasingly interdependent world economy were rather weak and fragile (Spero & Hart, 2010: 26). Although its adverse effects on trade and investment were limited, the regime of floating rates substantially increased exchange-rate volatility among major international currencies. After renewed speculative attacks on the US dollar in 1978–1979, which jeopardized its status as an international reserve currency, the US government switched to a very tight monetary policy, starting from the last quarter of 1979. This move, which was later followed by other ACs, was one of the striking harbingers of the neoliberal world economic order to be established in the 1980s and beyond.

### *Crisis of the Turkish Economy, 1977–1980*

Our summary of the political economy of ISI in Turkey above suggests that this strategy was unlikely to end up with an under-consumption crisis, as in a developed capitalist economy, since it put a strong emphasis on the expansion of domestic markets. But it resulted in a crisis due to the falling rates of profit and the declining income-share of capital, in conjunction with the dissolution of implicit social contract that supported ISI. These factors were interwoven with Turkey's balance of payments difficulties in the late 1970s (Keyder, 1987: Parts VII–VIII).

In Turkey, the ratio of current account deficit (CAD) to GDP was within the interval of 0.5–2.1% during the 1960s. The CADs in these years were financed mostly by "program and project credits," while FDI accounted for a lesser part. Starting from 1964 and rapidly increasing to 1.2 billion US dollars in 1973, "workers' remittances" turned out to be very helpful in keeping the CADs at moderate levels. These inflows, combined with the effects of August 1970 devaluation and the commodity boom of 1972–1973 in international markets, contributed to the exceptional surplus in the current account around 1.3% of the GDP (Ministry of Development, 2012).[15]

However, this situation abruptly changed in 1974–1976: (i) The first oil price hike in 1973 and the end of 1972–1973 commodity boom led to a serious deterioration in Turkey's terms of trade, (ii) the growth of volume of world trade slowed down, and (iii) workers' remittances tended to fall due to the recession in EEC countries (from 1.4 billion US dollars in 1974 to 1.1 billion US dollars in 1976). Thus, Turkey started to run sizable and rising CADs (1.4% in 1974 and 2.8% in 1976 as a proportion of GDP). Helleiner (1986: 905–907) notes that the adverse effects of the external shock were not offset by domestic policy responses (that is to say, changes in imports-to-GDP and exports-to-GDP ratios, and reductions in domestic absorption in 1973–1975). Rather, the Turkish governments in the 1974–1977 period relied heavily on borrowing from international banks either through the "convertible Turkish Lira deposits" (CTLD) scheme or through trade credits, which together accounted for about two thirds of the net capital inflow in 1973–1977 period (SPO, 1979: 71).[16]

By the end of 1977, Turkey was unable to repay its external debts overdue or close to being due, amounting to about 6.5 billion US dollars. Approximately, 3.0 billion US dollars of this sum was private debt (a large part of which was extended by 8 major banks) to be repaid to a motley group of 230 international banks. Loans extended to the public sector (or loan repayments guaranteed by the state) amounted to 1.5 billion US dollars; while non-guaranteed commercial debt (acceptance credits, etc.) totaled 2.0 billion US dollars. The external debt burden, which had been around 5% of GNP in 1960, approached 20% in 1977. It was then clear that, with an export revenue of 2.3 billion US dollars and an import bill of 6.2 billion US dollars, Turkey was insolvent in international transactions.[17]

There were other signs of growing instability in the Turkish economy over the 1975–1977 period. The ratio of public sector borrowing requirement (PSBR) to GDP was on a rising trend (3.6% in 1975, 5.1% in 1976, and 6.1% in 1977), and a high proportion of public sector deficit was financed by the Central Bank's credits to the Treasury. The annual rate of increase in monetary base was also substantial and rising (23% in 1976 and 57% in 1977), indicative of a loose monetary policy. Moreover, the annual increase in wholesale price index (WPI) in 1977 (36%) exceeded the annual average rate of increase in the same statistic in that year (24%) by a wide margin, which was a definite sign of growing inflationary pressures.

During the first two five-year plan periods (1963–1972), policymakers in Turkey had been prone to conceive industrialization led by the large enterprise sectors as a process of "dynamic efficiency" (Boratav et al., 1996: 40–43), whereby output, employment, and average productivity might have risen; and in parallel with productivity growth, real wages might have also increased. The wage share could remain unchanged or decline, because, if workers regarded real wage increases as satisfactory, they might not have cared much about the distributive shares. But in the third five-year plan period (1973–1977), it gradually became clear that such a process was no longer sustainable due to: (i) the signs of a slowdown in productivity growth, (ii) the increasing wage demands by better organized labor, and (iii) the growing tensions in sectoral and functional distribution of income. All in all, a revision of industrial strategy was urgently needed.

Thus, the Republican People's Party (RPP) government, which took office in January 1978, had a policy agenda with three urgent and interconnected issues: (i) restructuring external debt, (ii) stabilizing the economy, and (iii) revising the strategy of industrial development. Its performance in these issues is summarized below.

*External debt:* Under the favorable impressions generated after the SBA with the IMF (April 1978) for two years, negotiations for debt restructuring were initiated. However, the gap between the expectations of the two sides could not be bridged: Turkish policymakers were expecting that, after the debris of the "road accident" was cleared, they would attain freedom of action in economic management in the medium run. In contrast, Turkey's creditors were inclined to consider major changes in economic-policy orientation as an essential complement to debt restructuring (Wolff, 1987: 68–71). This difference in expectations was the basic reason why the SBA of April 1978 was suspended first (September 1978) and officially terminated later (December 1978).[18]

The growing political and economic instability in Turkey convinced both parties on the need to reopen negotiations in the spring of 1979. The outcome of this change in attitude was a new SBA with the IMF (July 1979), which facilitated a partial settlement: (i) official debts were restructured, (ii) "fresh money" (about 0.4 billion US dollars) was extended to Turkey by international banks, and (iii) the EEC and the WB also provided some credit support (100 million and 150 million US dollars, respectively). However, these attempts, as of 1979, were rather late and insufficient to make a substantial improvement in the Turkish economy, which was deeply shaken by the second oil shock. It must be noted that the second SBA with the IMF also had to be suspended in October 1979.

*Stabilization:* As a prelude to the agreement with the IMF, Turkish Lira was devalued by 23% in March 1978. In the SBA of April 1978, the Turkish government made commitments on a tighter monetary policy, reduction of public sector deficits and a better management of external debt in order to reduce the CAD-to-GDP ratio and lower the rate of inflation.[19] Although some meaningful steps were taken in these directions, this SBA was suspended in September 1978 on the grounds of arguments put forward by the IMF that limits concerning the monetary base, the public deficits, and the use of external resources were violated.

Nevertheless, the efforts to stabilize the economy did not fail completely in 1978. Acceleration of inflation was avoided (annual rates of increase in WPI were 38% in January 1978, 57% in July 1978 and 49% in December 1978). The PSBR-to-GDP and CAD-to-GDP ratios were brought down by 3.7 and 2.5 percentage points, respectively. Events took a turn for the worse in 1979, however: The annual rate of inflation rose to 81%, the PSBR-to-GDP ratio increased by 3 percentage points, CAD in nominal US dollar terms grew by about 11%, real GDP stagnated, and serious shortages occurred in intermediate goods and basic necessities. Before the second SBA in July 1979, the government devalued the Turkish Lira once again in June 1979 by 40% to offset its real appreciation from March 1978 onward, but the new SBA was also short-lived, as noted above.

*Revision of Industrial Strategy:* There were three strategic and internally consistent options with regard to industrial orientation possibilities: (i) initiating ELI, (ii) deepening ISI, and (iii) reconstructing populism (Türel, 2010: 412–415).[20] Each of these options was expected to be implemented not in its "pure" form, but in combination with the other options. Such a mix of options eventually involved a political choice in the context of class relationships. Key international organizations and business communities were in favor of ELI, which would be combined with some elements of the "soft" variant of the second option, that is, ISI in consumer durables.[21] On the other hand, Turkey's fourth five-year plan (1979–1983) envisaged the "hard" variant of the second option, emphasizing the production of machinery and equipment, and also incorporating some elements of the third.

Turkey's major segments of industrial bourgeoisie, which had been a constituent and beneficiary of ISI in its earlier stages, did not provide much political support to the deepening of ISI, hence to the fourth five-year plan. In 1978, they adopted a "wait and see" attitude; and after mid-1979, their dissatisfaction with the economic policies of the RPP government became evident.[22] Apparently, they were more sensitive to external financial and political support they might have received, together with the predictability of economic environment, and less sensitive to prospective profits of a deepened ISI. In contrast, unionized part of the labor force was mostly supportive of the government policies because of the introduction of the "social contract" formulated in 1978, which aimed to prevent real wage erosion. Small- and medium-sized industrial enterprises, small artisans and tradesmen, non-unionized labor employed in private sector, civil servants and agricultural producers were the losers of the 1978–1979 stabilization efforts. The story ended up with the resignation of the RPP government in December 1979 (following the RPP's loss of parliamentary by-elections in October 1979 in all five provinces); and a major policy shift was announced on January 24, 1980 by the new minority government led by Süleyman Demirel.

## Conclusions: A Balance Sheet

This chapter provides an overall assessment of Turkey's ISI experience from a critical political economy perspective. First, it analyzes the international conditions for the expansion of ISI strategies in the (semi)periphery by focusing on the post-WW-II international institutional design as the global governance framework of world economy. It also indicates that the comprehensive and indicative national planning frameworks were considered as parts of the ISI strategy in this period. The current chapter then applies this framework to the Turkish case particularly focusing on two critical junctures: (i) formation of the development planning framework in the early 1960s, and (ii) crisis of ISI strategy in the late 1970s. For a fair assessment of ISI as a development strategy, the following points should be taken into consideration:

1. To criticize ISI on grounds of deviation from "optimal" resource allocation by "free" markets is not much convincing, because it is by no means certain that a developing economy without these deviations could grow and industrialize faster. In fact, the emphasis placed by ISI (and also by ELI) on augmenting markets rather than conforming to them (Johnson, 1982), and getting relative prices deliberately wrong whenever necessary (Amsden, 1989: Chap. 7) made better sense for economic development.
2. Protection against international competition in a haphazard manner and the stop-go pattern of growth this generated were not intrinsic features of ISI (Bruton, 1989: 1614).
3. Building the capability to transfer and learn to use advanced technologies has always been a multifarious process in the case of DCs. Hindrances to this process were not specific to ISI; but ISI was not necessarily superior to other strategies in that respect (Bruton, 1988: 903–904, 1989: 1609–1613).

4. Although country studies referred to in Bruton (1989: 1619–1633) suggest that some late industrializers in East Asia enjoyed higher growth rates of total factor productivity in the 1960s and the 1970s, those observations could hardly be generalized to argue that that ISI was inferior in comparison to ELI.

Notwithstanding these arguments, the severity of 1977–1979 crisis in Turkey was often adduced by many circles as evidence for the inferiority of ISI *vis-à-vis* alternative strategies. However, the overall economic performance in the 1960–1980 period gives a somewhat different impression:

1. Average annual rate of growth of GDP in the 1960–1980 period was 4.7%, which was close to the DC average in that period (cf. Maddison, 2006).
2. United Nations Industrial Development Organization (UNIDO) defines five sub-categories, i.e., low, lower-middle, intermediate, upper-middle, and high income countries within the DC category. Average annual rate of growth of industrial value added in Turkey (7.6%) was also close to the DC average for the same period. This rate was higher than those of the DCs in low and high income groups. In the case of a comparison with DCs in lower-middle, intermediate, and upper-middle income groups, the picture was not so clear (UNIDO, 1985: Chap. 2).
3. The structure of manufacturing value added (MVA) changed considerably toward intermediates, and a relatively modest development took place in engineering industries as well. Shares of consumer goods, intermediates and engineering industries in MVA (in current prices) in 1960 were, approximately, 52, 33, and 15%, respectively. Corresponding figures for 1980 in the same order were 34, 48, and 18%.[23]

In short, Turkey was neither a brilliant star nor a laggard among the DCs as far as its economic performance in the 1960–1980 period was concerned. This chapter argues that two failed attempts shaped the overall trajectory of Turkish ISI experience. Inability to establish a coherent planning framework in the early 1960s and failure to deepen the industrialization in the late 1970s resulted in consolidation of "dependent development" of Turkish capitalism.

## Notes

1. These negotiations took place in Geneva (1947), Annecy (1948), Torquay (1950–1951), and Geneva (1956, 1960–1961). Tariff cuts agreed upon in Torquay were relatively higher in comparison to the others.
2. Also, the formation of G-77 as a coalition of DCs in the UN coincided with UNCTAD I.
3. This sequential process was in contrast with the experience of early industrializers and their followers like Japan. When these countries were essentially at the stage of producing "light" consumer goods, they were also producing their own capital goods by "artisan" methods and trying to innovate and improve their technologies (Hirschman, 1968: 6–8).
4. Effective rate of protection (ERP) is an indicator that measures how domestic value added in an industry under the existing set of nominal tariffs is proportionally greater than the value added that would be produced under no protection at all. In the case of traditional exports of the DCs, the ERP can be negative.
5. According to mainstream economic thinking, such a variance was a manifestation of inefficient resource allocation; and DCs were advised to apply lower and uniform tariff rates for the sake of efficiency (see Balassa et al., 1971; Corden 1971).
6. From 1950 to the early years of the 1980s, more than 300 development plans were prepared by the governments of DCs (Agarwala, 1983: 5).
7. For a brief review of Indian and Korean national planning experiences for the period under our study, see Türel (2017: 228–235).
8. The basic problem that planners had to deal with was finding additional resources for financing the development plan. In the context of the plan, an almost 50% rise in domestic savings rate was expected (Aren, 1961).
9. There were several attempts to reorganize the SEEs. For a discussion of one of the earliest attempts, see Hanson (1960).
10. At that time, total profit of 220 public enterprises was equal to that of 5,200 private firms. As for their organizational structures, the SEEs used more advanced management techniques and employed more skilled and highly-qualified workers and managers (DPT, 1963: 75, 77).

11. The Ottoman tax system regarding the agriculture sector, which was based to a large extent on the tithe [*aşar*], was abolished by the new Republic of Turkey in 1925. Although this tax was briefly "restored in the form of a 'payment-in-kind tax' on agricultural produce" during the WW-II (Ahmad, 1993: 74), planners believed that a new modern agricultural tax was necessary for both increasing state revenues and increasing productivity in agriculture.
12. After the rejection of the SPO's original proposal, Osman Nuri Torun, Undersecretary of the SPO, Attila Karaosmanoğlu, Head of Economic Planning Department, Necat Erder, Head of the Social Planning Department, and Ayhan Çilingiroğlu, Head of the Coordination Department, resigned collectively (*Cumhuriyet*, 27 September 1962: 1).
13. Efforts to contain the inflationary impact of nominal-wage increases in the late 1960s led to a minor recession in 1970–1971, which was followed by a short-lived upturn in 1972–1973. The "crash" of 1974–1975 following the first oil shock was managed through the necessary relative price adjustments, leading to a recovery in 1976–1978. Although conjunctural movements coincided with each other, the choice and use of macroeconomic policy instruments differed widely across the ACs. Despite some hesitations concerning their effectiveness, Keynesian demand management policies were often used in the 1970s.
14. For the sake of brevity, here we do not elaborate EEC's response to the world monetary disorder. The EEC moved further toward economic and monetary union, which, obviously, had a major historical significance (see Swann, 2000: 199–208). On the survival of the Bretton Woods institutions, see section "International Conditions" in this chapter.
15. Unless otherwise stated, numerical estimates for some economic indicators given in this section are taken or calculated from Ministry of Development (2012: Parts 1 and 3).
16. Although the CTLD scheme had been made effective in 1967 by a Communique of the Ministry of Finance, its widespread use started in 1975. For procedural details of this borrowing scheme and its serious drawbacks, see Artun (1980: Part 7).
17. It was tragic that a full and reliable account of Turkey's external debt became available in the late 1979.

18. The differences of opinion peaked in mid-1978 after the announcement of numerical exercises on macroeconomic magnitudes of the Fourth Plan (June 1978) and the Strategy of the Fourth Plan (August 1978) (Türel, 2010: 435).
19. In the agreement, it was foreseen that the CAD-to-GDP ratio would fall by 4 percentage points in 1978 and the annual rate of inflation in that year would be lowered to about 20%.
20. The third option, which would prioritize the production of wage goods and basic necessities, was preferred and implemented by some governments in Latin America in the 1960s and the 1970s.
21. An articulate and quantitative presentation of this option was offered by Derviş and Robinson (1978).
22. An unusual announcement by the Turkish Association of Industrialists and Businessmen (*TÜSİAD* in Turkish acronym) in May 1979 was strongly critical of government's economic policies.
23. Calculated from Uygur (1990: Appendix).

## References


Ahmad, F. (1993). *The making of modern Turkey*. Routledge.

Agarwala, R. (1983). *Planning in developing countries: Lessons of experience* (World Bank Staff Working Papers No 576). Washington, DC: The World Bank.

Akçay, Ü. (2007). *Kapitalizmi Planlamak: Türkiye'de Planlama ve DPT'nin Dönüşümü* [Planning of capitalism: Planning in Turkey and transformation of state planning organization in Turkey]. SAV Press.

Amsden, A. (1989). *Asia's next giant: South Korea and late industrialization*. Oxford University Press.

Amsden, A. (2001). *The rise of 'the rest.'* Oxford University Press.

Arndt, H. W. (1987). *Economic development: The history of an idea*. The University of Chicago Press.

Aren, S. (1961). Yatırım Politikası [Investment Policy]. *Planlama, 1*, 83.

Armstrong, P., Glyn, A., & Harrison, J. (1991). *Capitalism since 1945*. Oxford: Basil Blackwell.

Artun, T. (1980). *Banking in Turkey: Its functions, development, characteristics and problems* (in Turkish). Tekin.

Balassa, B., and associates. (1971). *The structure of protection in developing countries*. Johns Hopkins University Press for the WB and IADB.

Barton, J. H., Goldstein, J. L., Josling, T. E., & Steinberg, R. H. (2006). *The evolution of the trade regime: Politics, law, and economics of the GATT and the WTO*. Princeton University.

Bello, W. (2000, January). *UNCTAD: Time to read, time to challenge the WTO* (Focus on Trade, 44). www.tni.org/en/archives/act/708

Boratav, K. (1976). Basic commodities and the new international economic order (in Turkish). *METU Studies in Development* (Special Issue), 59–79.

Boratav, K., Türel, O., & Yentürk, N. (1996). *Adjustment, distribution and accumulation (research report prepared for UNCTAD (second draft)*. mimeo., 71pp. + appendices.

Bruton, H. J. (1988). A reconsideration of import substitution. *Journal of Economic Literature, 36*(2), 903–936.

Bruton, H. J. (1989). Import substitution. In H. Chenery & T. N. Srinivasan (Eds.), *Handbook of development economics* (Vol. II, pp. 1601–1644). North Holland.

Bulutoğlu, K. (1961a). *İktisadi Devlet Teşekkülleri ve Devlet Planlama Teşkilatı* [State Economic Enterprises and State Planning Organisation]. DPT, Archive No: 3.5.5 BULİ.

Bulutoğlu, K. (1961b). *İktisadi Devlet Teşekküllerinin Fiyat Politikası* [Pricing Policy of State Economic Enterprises]. SPO, Archive No: 3.5.5 BUL-FİYAT.

Bulutoğlu, K (1967). Financing Turkey's development plan. In S. İlkin & E. İnanç (Eds.), *Planning in Turkey* (pp. 181–202). SPO.

Buğra, A. (1994). *State and business in modern Turkey: A comparative study*. State University of New York Press.

Chibber, V. (2003). *Locked in place: State-building and late industrialization in India*. Princeton University Press.

Cohn, E. (1962). *Private sector survey*. SPO, Archive No: 3.12.3. COH.

Corden, W. M. (1971). *The theory of protection*. Claredon.

Cumhuriyet. (1962, September 27), p. 1.

Derviş, K., & Robinson, S. (1978). *The foreign exchange gap, growth and industrial strategy in Turkey, 1973–83* (World Bank Staff Working Papers No. 306). Washington, DC: The World Bank.

DPT. (1960). *Planlama Uzmanı Dr. Koopman ile Devlet Başkanı Cemal Gürsel arasındaki görüşme tutanakları* [Minutes of Meeting between Planning Expert Dr. Koopman and President Cemal Gürsel] (K. Klasörü, Ed.). DPT, Archive No: 338.95.61.KOOs.

DPT. (1962). İktisadi Devlet Teşekküllerinin Reorganizasyonu [Reorganisation of State Economic Enterprises]. *Planlama Dergisi, 1*.

DPT. (1962a). *Toprak Reformu Kanun Tasarısı* [Land Reform Law Proposal]. DPT, Archive No: 4.1.1.3.1/1.2.

DPT. (1963). *Birinci Beş Yıllık Plan* [First Five Year Development Plan]. DPT.

Eralp, A. (1981). Türkiye'de İzlenen İthal İkameci Strateji ve Yabancı Sermaye [Import substitution industrialisation strategy in Turkey and the foreign capital]. *ODTÜ gelisme dergisi*, Özel Sayı: Türkiye'de planlı gelismenin yirmi yılı [ODTÜ Journal of Development, Special Issue: 20th year of Planned Development in Turkey], 613–631.

Evans, P. B. (1979). *Dependent development: The alliance of multinational, state, and local capital in Brazil*. Princeton University Press.

Forum. (1962, December 1), p.1

Fröbel, F., Heinrichs, J., & Kreye, O. (1981). *The new international division of labour*. Cambridge University Press.

Glyn, A., Hughes, A., Lipietz, A., & Singh, A. (1991). The rise and fall of the golden age. In S. A. Marglin & J. B. Schor (Eds.), *The golden age of capitalism: Reinterpreting the evidence* (pp. 39–125). Clarendon.

Hanson, A. H. (1960). *A law for Turkish state enterprises*. SPO, Archive No: 3.5.5.1/1.3.

Helleiner, E. (1986). Balance of payments experience and growth prospects of developing countries: A synthesis. *World Development, 14*(8), 877–908.

Hirschman, A. O. (1968). The political economy of import-substituting industrialization in Latin America. *The Quarterly Journal of Economics, 82*(1), 1–32.

Hirschman, A. O. (1981). *Essays in trespassing: Economics to politics and beyond*. Cambridge University Press.

Johnson, C. (1982). *MITI and the Japanese miracle: The growth of industrial policy, 1925–1975*. Stanford University Press.

Kaldor, N. (1962). *Report on the Turkish tax system, a confidential report to the prime ministry of Turkey*. SPO.

Kaldor, N. (1963, March). Taxation for economic development. *The Journal of Modern African Studies, 1*, 7–23.

Kapur, D., Lewis, J. P., & Webb, R. (1997). *The World Bank: Its first half century* (Vol. 1). Brookings Institution.

Karacan, N. (1983–1984). Türkiye'de Popülizm Üzerine Bir Not [A Note on the Populism in Turkey]. *Yapıt, 2*, 83–89.

Karaosmanoğlu, A., Sönmez, A., Çilingiroğlu, A., & Erder, N. (2003). *Planlı Kalkınma Serüveni: 1960'lı Yıllarda Türkiye'de Planlama Deneyimi* [Planned Development Experiment: Planning Experience in Turkey in the 1960s]. Bilgi Üniversitesi Yayınları.

Keyder, Ç. (1987). *State and class in Turkey: A study in capitalist development*. Verso.

Little, I., Scitovsky, T., & Scott, M. (1970). *Industry and trade in some developing countries: A comparative study*. Oxford University Press for OECD.

Maddison, A. (2006). *The world economy, Vol. 2: Historical statistics*. OECD Development Centre Studies.

Maxfield, S., & Nolt, J. H. (1990). Protectionism and the internationalization of capital: U.S. sponsorship of import substitution industrialization in the Philippines, Turkey and Argentina. *International Studies Quarterly, 34*(1), 49. https://doi.org/10.2307/2600405

Mıhçıoglu, M. (1988). Yine Devlet Planlama Teskilatının Kurulusu Üzerine [Again, on the Formation of State Planning Organisation]. *AÜSBF Dergisi, XLII*(1–2), 113–146.

Milliyet. (1962, June 18), p. 7.

Milliyet. (1962, June 27), p. 7.

Milliyet. (1962, June 28), p. 1.

Milor, V. (1990). The genesis of planning in Turkey. *New Perspectives on Turkey, 4*, 1–30.

Ministry of Development. (2012). *Economic and social indicators (1950–2010)* (in Turkish). T. C. Kalkınma Bakanlığı. http://www.kalkinma.gov.tr

Moody, K. (2001). *Workers in a lean world: Unions in the international economy*. Verso.

Ocampo, J. A. (2017). *Resetting the international monetary (non)system*. Oxford University Press.

OECD. (1961). *SOEs in Turkey (Consolidated Report)*. Ankara: State Planning Organization, Archive No: 3.5.5./3STA.

Öngüt, İ. (1967). The private sector in the five-year plan. In S. İlkin & E. İnanç (Eds.), *Planning in Turkey* (pp. 159–165). SPO.

Reinhart, C., & Trebesch, C. (2015). *The international monetary fund: 70 Years of reinvention* (Harvard Kennedy School Faculty Research WP Series 15-077). https://research.hks.harvard.edu/publications/workingpapers/Index.aspx .

Saybaşılı, K. (1985). *Devletin Ekonomiye Müdahalesi* [State Intervention to the Economy]. Birey ve Toplum Yayınları.

Şaylan, G. (1986). *Türkiye'de Kapitalizm Bürokrasi ve Siyasal Ideoloji* [Capitalism, Bureaucracy and Political Ideology in Turkey]. V Yayınları.

Schmitz, H. (1984). Industrialization strategies in less developed countries: Some lessons of historical experience. *Journal of Development Studies, 21*(1), 1–21.

Simpson, D. J. (1965). Development as a process: The Menderes phase in Turkey. *Middle East Journal 19*(2), 141–152.

Spero, J. E., & Hart, J. A. (2010). *The politics of international economic relations* (7th ed.). Wadsworth Cengage Learning.

SPO. (1960a). *Guiding the private sector*. SPO, Archive No: 3.12.3.GUI.

SPO. (1960b). *The meeting between J. Koopman and Istanbul chamber of industry*. In Koopman's Folder. SPO.

SPO. (1961). *Objectives and the strategy of the plan*. SPO, Archive No: 3.1.1DPT.

SPO. (1962). *Notes for the colloquium on the technical aspects of Turkey's long-term plan*. SPO, Archive No: 3.1.1./2DPT.

SPO. (1979). Fourth five-year development plan (in Turkish). Ankara: DPT.

Streeck, W. (2014). *Buying time: The delayed crisis of democratic capitalism*. Verso.

Swann, D. (2000). *The economics of Europe: From common market to European Union*. Penguin Business Library.

Taylor, I., & Smith, K. (2007). *United Nations Conference on Trade and Development (UNCTAD)*. Routledge.

Torun, O. N. (1967). *The establishment and structure of the state planning organization*. In S. İlkin & E. İnanç (Eds.), *Planning in Turkey* (pp. 44–70). SPO.

Türel, O. (2010). The crisis of 1978–9 in Turkey and central economic planning. In E. Türkcan (Ed.), *Festschrift to Attila Sönmez: The rise and fall of planning in Turkey, 1960–80* (in Turkish) (pp. 411–441). Bilgi University.

Türel, O. (2017). *A short global history, 1945–79* (in Turkish). Yordam Kitap.

UNIDO. (1985). *Industry in the 1980s: Structural change and interdependence*. United Nations.

Union of Chambers. (1962). *Some regulations in the taxation system that obstacles to capital accumulation and development of industry and proposed solutions*. SPO.

Uygur, E. (1990). *Policy, productivity, growth and employment in Turkey 1960–1989 and the prospects for the 1990s (first draft)*. mimeo., 46p. + Appendix.

Üstünel, B. (1962). *Plan Hedefleri, Kalkor Raporu ve İç Finansman Problemleri* [Plan Targets, Kaldor Report, and Domestic Finance Issues]. DPT, Archive No: 3.4.0.1.ÜST.

Van der Wee, H. (1987). *Prosperity and upheaval: The world economy, 1945–1980*. Pelican.

Wade, R. (1988). The role of the market in overcoming the market failure: Taiwan, Republic of Korea and Japan. In H. Hughes (Ed.), *Achieving industrialization in East Asia* (pp. 129–163). Cambridge University Press.

Walstedt, B. (1980). *State manufacturing enterprise in a mixed economy: The Turkish case*. The Johns Hopkins University Press.

Wolff, P. (1987). *Stabilization policy and structural adjustment in Turkey, 1980–1985: The role of the IMF and World Bank in an externally supported adjustment process*. German Development Institute.

Yön. (1962, August 15), p. 5.

CHAPTER 7

# Turkey's Encounter with Neoliberal Globalization and the Logic of Washington Consensus, 1980–1990

*Ziya Öniş and Fikret Şenses*

## Introduction

Turkey's overall economic strategy before 1980 was characterized by state interventionism and protectionist trade and industrialization policies. There were occasional and short-lived periods of deviation from this policy stance toward an increased role given to the private sector and trade liberalization, such as the early 1950s and early 1970s. However, the strategy, embraced by major political and economic actors, remained

Z. Öniş (✉)
International Political Economy, Koç University, İstanbul, Turkey
e-mail: zonis@ku.edu.tr

F. Şenses
Department of Economics, Middle East Technical University (METU), Ankara, Turkey
e-mail: fsenses@metu.edu.tr



E. Özçelik and Y. Özdemir (eds.), *Political Economy of Development in Turkey*, The Political Economy of the Middle East,
https://doi.org/10.1007/978-981-16-7318-4_7

intact. For example, the period between 1963 and 1980 can best be described as arch-typical import-substituting industrialization (ISI) with the state playing a dominant role in drawing the main direction of economic change through five-year plans. This orientation meant that the private sector, while growing in stature, was, along with foreign investors, very much in the sidelines at the beginning but gradually reinforced itself as an equal partner in the development process. To draw an international comparison, Turkey's economic strategy during this period bore a close resemblance to those of Brazil and Mexico in Latin America and India and Pakistan in South Asia.

January 24, 1980 signaled the beginning of the most important transformation of economic policies in Turkey, aimed basically at gradually reducing the economic role of the state and moving toward an open foreign trade regime, which can be summarized as a move toward a market-based outward-oriented strategy. In this regard, Turkey was one of the first developing countries to adopt the policies which were soon described aptly as the Washington Consensus policies. These represented in the Turkish case a radical and yet gradual and stage by stage approach to neoliberal restructuring. The important steps taken in this direction in the 1980s, such as foreign trade and financial liberalization, have continued in subsequent decades and spread to most spheres of economic and social life, such as labor markets and agricultural, health, and education sectors, with little sign so far of being reversed after more than forty years of continuous implementation.

The main objective of this chapter is to provide a retrospective political-economy analysis of this transformation of economic strategy and its initial impact, taking into consideration external as well as domestic factors. A related objective is to draw comparisons between this transformation in Turkey and similar transformations in other cases with an emphasis on Latin American and East and South East Asian countries. Although our main period of analysis will be the 1980s, we shall also dwell on the period immediately preceding it and make occasional references to the current state of economic and political life in Turkey by reflecting on the changes in these spheres in the initial phase of this transformation.

The chapter aims to address itself to the following questions: What were the main domestic political and economic factors that underlay these "sudden" steps taken toward this radical transformation in January 1980? How significant was the role of external elements, most notably the IMF and the World Bank and the brutal military intervention on 12 September

1980, in terms of the sustainability of this transformation during the crucial initial years in the face of mounting domestic opposition? What was the role of critical political figures such as Turgut Özal in this transformation and how similar was this role as compared to his counterparts in Latin America? What were the reasons behind the initial export success in the 1980s and the failure to sustain it? How important was the decision of capital-account liberalization in August 1989 in shaping the future economic course of the economy, in particular, the subsequent economic crises in 1994 and 2000–2001 with a devastating socio-political as well as economic impact. What were the main medium and long-term political and economic outcomes of this transformation that began in the 1980s? How important were these economic and political changes in the 1980s in the economic bottlenecks and democratic deficits facing Turkey at present? More importantly, given the overall negative impact of this transformation in the 1980s, what were the domestic and external factors behind its sustainability over more than forty years with little sign of an alternative approach in sight? What are the counterfactual arguments that can be put forward pertaining to this transformation to draw attention to the missed opportunities and mistakes made in the 1970s and 1980s, which can be held responsible for the current economic and political problems facing the country?

The chapter is organized as follows. In the section after this introduction, we present an overview of the economic and political conditions in Turkey together with the geopolitics and other elements of the international environment just before the start of the transformation in January 1980. This overview is followed by a descriptive presentation of the main components of political and economic changes and the role of external factors in this transformation. The next section carries out an assessment of the main impact of this transformation in the 1980s, while the following one is devoted to an analysis of the Turkish case together with the Latin American and East and South East Asian experiments during the 1980s in a "compare-contrast" framework. The section before the conclusion addresses itself to the counterfactuals to provide a better understanding of past developments and shed light on our recommendations pertaining to the future course of the economic and political process in the country. The last section summarizes and concludes.

## Background: Political and Economic Setting Just Before the 1980 Transformation

The 1980 transformation of economic policies requires a brief description of the most influential political and economic factors and conditions in the second half of the 1970s, as they had strong ramifications for subsequent developments in the 1980s. On the domestic front, Turkey was characterized by very deep and increasing political and economic instability. There was a sharp division in Turkish politics between the right-wing block comprising mainly the center-right Justice Party (JP, *Adalet Partisi*), Nationalist Action Party (NAP, *Milliyetçi Hareket Partisi*), and the Islamist National Salvation Party (NSP, *Millî Selamet Partisi*) on the one hand, and the block headed by the center-left Republican People's Party (RPP, *Cumhuriyet Halk Partisi*) and several splinter left-wing parties on the other. The rule of the right-wing coalition, which had been in office during the 1975–1977 period under the name of "Nationalist Front," came to an end in 1977 when they lost their majority to the left-wing block in the general elections. To form a government, however, the RPP needed to transfer a group of eleven (right-wing but highly heterogeneous) deputies, some of whom were granted ministerial posts. The slim and controversial majority of the RPP government was instrumental in increasing the challenges of the opposition and contributed to the aggravation of deep divisions in the Parliament, augmenting the polarization of Turkish society at large.

A major factor in this polarization was the violent clashes between right-wing and left-wing youth groups, concentrated initially at universities, then at high and even junior-high schools, and soon spreading throughout the country and claiming the lives of hundreds of young people. The death of 42 demonstrators in the 1977 May Day celebrations in İstanbul, incidents such as the one in Kahramanmaraş in December 1978 which led to the death of more than one hundred Alewite citizens resulted in the declaration of Martial Law in 13 provinces, including İstanbul and Ankara. These as well as the assassination of a number of academics, journalists, trade union leaders, and other public figures were clear manifestations of the breakdown of law and order on a large scale.

The deep political instability was accompanied and strongly reinforced by economic instability of similar proportions. Encouraged by the sharp increase in export revenues and workers' remittances under the spurt of the massive (66%) devaluation of the Turkish Lira in August 1970,

Turkish planners had drawn ambitious targets for the Third Five Year Plan (1973–1977), envisaging high rates of growth and perhaps more significantly pushing ISI toward intermediate and capital goods. The planners did not find it necessary to make any major revisions to these targets despite the sharp increase in international oil prices, sluggish export revenues and faltering workers' remittances in the face of stagflation in Turkey's major economic partners across Europe.

This attitude of planners continued even when the Fourth Five Year Plan (1978–1982), comprising similar ambitious targets, was drawn in the face of the high and rising oil prices under the second oil shock of the late 1970s. Given their preoccupation with medium and long-term issues to the neglect of short term problems, Turkish planners were also oblivious to the sharp increase in public sector deficits[1] and the sharp increase in the rate of inflation. The twin pressures on the balance of payments and the domestic price level as aggravated by high and growing public sector deficits signaled the beginning of a major economic crisis.[2] Although both pressures were behind the emergence of the crisis, it was the former, namely the payments crisis which gained prominence in the eyes of both domestic and external observers as well as the public at large. Turkey's foreign exchange shortage became so acute that it was unable to meet the import requirements of existing domestic production, let alone the requirements of new investment envisaged under the five-year plans. The result of economic difficulties reaching crisis proportions was shortened working weeks and acute shortages of basic consumption goods such as cooking oil and various petroleum derivatives. These difficulties as well as the declining real wages led to an increased trade union activity and sharp criticism of the government by big business, and most significantly to the erosion of much of the popular support for the government.

The government's response to this deep payments crisis and its inability to service its external debt was spending much time to convince donors for debt rescheduling, undertaking some policy changes such as increased interest rates, devaluation of the Turkish Lira at shorter intervals, and increased export incentives which fell far short of likely IMF demands. These efforts by the government failed to bring the much-needed foreign exchange resources. In a way, reform attempts by the government were too weak and too late. The by-elections held in late 1979 resulted, as expected, in the heavy defeat and resignation of the RPP government and its replacement by a minority government formed by the JP.

The political and economic instability on the domestic front was accompanied and, in many senses, reinforced by the volatility and uncertainty in the external environment. The Cold War was very much in force with the Middle East and its vicinity, constituting one of the main play grounds of the two super powers and catching Turkey in the middle of the competition between them. Turkey continued to enjoy a key position as a NATO member in the Western Alliance. The Soviet invasion of Afghanistan and the Iranian Revolution in 1979 were instrumental in increasing Turkey's geopolitical importance in the eyes of the West. This favorable change, however, did not enable Turkey to get meaningful financial support from them (*before* the neoliberal transformation) either directly through national governments or indirectly through the IMF. Indeed, financial assistance became available only following a major debt crisis and as part of policy conditionality, which effectively meant that Turkey was constrained by and dependent upon the path chosen by the key external actors.

There were several other events in the late 1970s that have played a crucial role in preparing the ground for the economic transformation in Turkey. Margaret Thatcher's rise to power in the UK in 1979 and Ronald Reagan's election as president in the US in 1980 were clear manifestations of a sharp and final turn away from Keynesian welfare-state policies which had given the state a pivotal role. Chinese economic reforms around the same time (while preserving a central role to the state in the commanding heights of the economy) in the direction of free markets constituted another significant yet oft-neglected event in this context. The World Bank and the IMF, which until then had occupied separate spheres of activity, began to act in cohesion based on a common agenda comprising the twin programs of structural adjustment and stabilization.[3] Finally, the backlash created by penetration of neo-Marxist and other leftist approaches into the development discourse and the increasing challenge presented by the newly-industrializing countries to the established global industrial structure, as well as the international debt crisis of the early 1980s requiring indebted countries to increase their export revenues may also have contributed to the emergence of neoliberalism as a new development paradigm. Turkey was one of the first countries to implement these programs which were instrumental in the spread of neoliberal economic policies to many other countries in the 1980s and 1990s.

In explaining the setting of Turkey's transformation at the outset, one other factor that should not be neglected is the developments on the academic front. The sharp criticism of economic policies implemented in many developing countries (with the exception of a few in East and South East Asia, headed by South Korea), whose roots could be traced back to the early 1960s, gained a new momentum in the 1970s. Research projects and country case studies conducted under the auspices of international institutions, such as the OECD and World Bank, carried a strong message that those policies, based on state-led ISI, were wrong in almost all their aspects and everything was going to be fine under an alternative policy regime.[4] What was intended with the alternative was, in a nutshell, no more and no less than what emerged as the Washington Consensus policies, succinctly described as "stabilize, liberalize, and privatize."

## Political and Economic Components of the 1980 Transformation and the Role of Domestic and External Factors

Several weeks after coming into office, the minority government formed by the Justice Party announced the 24 January 1980 package of economic policies, signaling the start of Turkey's neoliberal transformation. The initial package consisted of, *inter alia*, price decontrol resulting in a substantial rise in the prices of goods and services produced by the State Economic Enterprises (SEEs), and a massive 33% devaluation of the Turkish Lira to be followed by the decision in May 1981 to move to a flexible exchange rate regime. Decontrol of interest rates in July 1980, leading to a sharp increase, was a major initial move toward financial liberalization in a country which was characterized by financial repression throughout the 1970s. The steps toward foreign trade liberalization were initiated by the abolition of quotas in 1981 and gained momentum with more substantial policy changes in December 1983 and January 1984.[5]

Most observers agree that these measures represented a kind of "shock therapy" at the initiation stage, to use the terminology that was much in vogue at the time and during the gradual transition thereafter. However, there is one question that remains unanswered after so many years. How could a minority government take such radical measures without giving any hint to the electorate during the by-election campaign in which economic, along with law- and order-related issues were at center stage?

This question becomes all the more significant if one takes into account the fact that, even in the late 1970s, major influential sections of the population ranging from academics to big business did not express much discontent with the previous economic regime based on ISI.[6] One would have thought that, under an open political regime, admittedly bedeviled by important shortcomings, the electorate deserved some information about the contents and nature of the government's proposals for taking the country out of a deep economic impasse.

With the benefit of hindsight, we can provide two possible answers to this question. The crisis was so deep, and shortages were so grave that some segments of society were ready to accept such measures, as commodities in short supply soon became available albeit at much higher prices. This reasoning, in the Turkish case, justifies to some extent the "crisis as an instigator of reform" argument. The second answer to the above question, linked closely with the first, lies in the fact that most sections of the electorate were under the impression that the initial measures were of a short-term nature to deal with the immediate economic problems and were unaware that these were the beginning of a major transformation involving extensive medium and long-term structural changes.

These two factors may go a long way in explaining how a minority government could, in the absence of a supporting constituency initially, take the radical measures in the early 1980s without informing the electorate beforehand. This lack of information, however, did not prevent major actors from strongly opposing these measures. In the face of galloping inflation under the influence of price decontrol and the erosion of real wages accompanying it, trade unions and other civil society organizations together with the main opposition party (RPP) took the lead in this opposition. For example, the number of strikes and working days lost through strikes reached new peaks during the January–September 1980 period. Moreover, the political support that the minority government enjoyed in parliament was fast waning. By early September the government faced a strong possibility of being pushed out of office and the radical policies it introduced earlier in the year being reversed (Şenses, 1983).

How could then these policies be sustained beyond September 1980? There were again two factors at work in this context; namely, the role of external factors, most notably the IMF and the World Bank, and the military takeover on 12 September 1980.

First, international donors headed by the IMF, World Bank, and the OECD, which were reluctant to provide financial support for the RPP government to realize the Fourth Five Year Plan targets and to deal with the deep payments crisis, turned out to be very generous in their support of the new program.[7] This change in the attitude of international donors must have increased the confidence of the military leaders regarding the sustainability of the program. The provision of much needed foreign-exchange resources, however, increased the leverage of foreign donors over domestic policies. While the signing of a three-year stand-by agreement with the IMF subjected the domestic policy space to strict conditionality in the spheres of fiscal and monetary policies, the World Bank through its structural adjustment loans was behind policies with a greater medium- and long-term impact, such as the abolition of a large number of industrial projects, financial liberalization, and trade liberalization on a large scale. It is interesting to note here that it was the IMF which received most of the criticism, while the more essential changes undertaken through agreements with the World Bank went unnoticed. Similarly, although the main spheres of domestic economic policy space were captured by the neoliberal agenda of the Bretton Woods Institutions (BWI), policies undertaken through agreements with these institutions were skillfully presented to the domestic audiences as Özal's policies (Şenses, 1983, 1991).

Second, the rapid erosion of law and order that started in the 1970s and reached new proportions in 1980 resulted in the military takeover on 12 September. One of the first actions of the military government was to declare its support for the radical measures introduced in the January of that year. In fact, it was public knowledge that Özal who played a major role as Undersecretary at the Prime Minister's office in the introduction of the program had close contacts with the military officers during the January–September 1980 period. There is also circumstantial evidence that the US establishment was indirectly involved in the coup. The military regime was brutal in suppressing all opposition, most notably the labor movement. Activities by trade unions, political parties, and civil society organizations were banned and some of their leaders imprisoned (Şenses, 1993). The period under the military regime was characterized by human rights abuses of the worst kind.

New labor legislation introduced in 1982 imposed severe restrictions on the activities of trade unions. A new constitution reflecting the highly restrictive political spirit of the time came into effect in 1982 after being accepted by a huge "yes" vote (around 91%) in a murky referendum. Major political parties, whose roots went back to many years ago, were closed and replaced by new ones with their candidates in the upcoming general elections closely scrutinized by the military council. The general elections resulted in the victory of the Motherland Party (MP) established by Özal. The period between 1983 and 1987, during which the head of the military regime General Kenan Evren remained as President and Özal served as Prime Minister, was aptly described at home and broad as a guided democracy.

The second half of the 1980s witnessed political liberalization to some extent. Mounting pressures on the government resulted in the lifting of the restriction on the political activities of the leaders of previously banned political parties in September 1987 when the "yes" voters in the referendum gained a slim majority. Somewhat shocked by this result, Özal called a snap election and retained power albeit with an eight-percentage point drop in the support for his party. Toward the end of the decade, organized labor, squeezed by the twin pressures of a severe fall in real wages and restrictions on its activities, started to make its presence felt through nationwide demonstrations.

One of the first measures undertaken by the Özal government that came to power in late 1983 was extensive liberalization of the foreign-trade regime. Except for a handful of goods whose importation was prohibited, all goods could be imported which in effect meant a move from protection of the domestic market through quantitative restrictions to protection through price measures as imports were made subject to tariffs and other taxes. Tariff revisions later in the 1980s involving reductions on a large scale created further liberalization of the import regime. These tariff reductions were accompanied by extensive export incentives such as tax rebates and subsidized export credits. These export incentives were so generous that they led to fictitious exports reaching as high as one-fifth of total exports.[8] These incentives and continuous depreciation of the Turkish Lira on the exports side together with substantial liberalization on the imports front were instrumental in gradually removing the bias of the trade regime away from import-substitution toward export orientation.

By far the most important development on the economic sphere was the controversial capital-account liberalization decision taken in August 1989. The controversy was centered on two interrelated issues: the extent to which it was a domestic or externally imposed decision and its timing.

On the first issue, one can at the outset argue that capital-account liberalization, considered an integral component of neoliberal policies, was sooner or later going to be a part of the Turkish policy framework which was under heavy IMF influence. However, most observers agree that it was Özal, renowned for blunt decision-making, who was behind this decision. He was no doubt prompted by the recessionary tendencies in the economy and the foreign exchange requirements of the infrastructural investments in the face of faltering export revenues (Gemici, 2012). On the second (timing) issue, on the other hand, there is almost unanimous agreement that it was a premature decision (Rodrik, 1990). Inflation, after reaching a peak of 101.4% in 1980 under the spurt of the sudden and sharp price decontrol and then falling to an average of 31.3% in the following three years had begun to accelerate, reaching as high as 73.7% and 63.3% in 1988 and 1989, respectively.[9] Taking such a decision under heavy inflationary pressures was against even the "stabilization first" dictum of the timing-and-sequencing literature that had emerged from BWI quarters. Likewise, the fact that the decision was taken before the establishment of an appropriate regulatory framework carried with it the potential of severe problems ahead, as successive crises in the following years have shown.

Most observers, not familiar with the Turkish political economy, would be rightly puzzled by the lack of significant progress in the privatization sphere in the 1980s with steps in this direction confined only to the sale of two telecommunication facilities in 1989.[10] The reasons behind this delay can be found in the strong *etatist* tradition in Turkey and the reluctance of the government to confront the likely strong opposition from society. Instead, the government chose a strategy of initially depriving the State Economic Enterprises of necessary investment, presenting them as a loss making burden on the Treasury, thereby skillfully shielding their positive socioeconomic role and gradually preparing the public opinion for privatization, that is, "creeping privatization" *par excellence*.

There were two other developments that need to be highlighted in this overview of main economic and political events of the 1980s. The first was the establishment in June 1986 of the Fund for the Encouragement of Social Assistance and Solidarity (*Sosyal Yardımlaşma ve Dayanışmayı Teşvik Fonu*) as a poverty alleviation device. This scheme can be regarded as Turkey's response to the adverse impact of structural adjustment policies in spheres like health, education, and child nutrition, as effectively expressed in 1985 in a UNICEF document, *Adjustment with a Human*

*Face*. Like their counterparts in Latin America under the title of Social Funds, this device in its Turkish version in effect comprised some in-kind and cash benefits to disadvantaged groups but fell short of making a real dent on the extent of poverty in Turkey and was criticized for its non-participatory nature, unstable financial structure, and vulnerability to political pressures.[11]

The second crucial development was Özal administration's lax attitude toward Turkey's established bureaucratic practices and more significantly toward the rule of law. In the name of reducing red tape, Özal removed the Treasury from the Ministry of Finance and re-established it as a separate entity. Such practices along with the establishment of extra-budgetary funds and decision-making by decrees rather than through laws enacted by the parliament, while introducing some flexibility in public administration, were also instrumental in eroding well-established regulatory norms, paving the way for loopholes for corruption. The decision to confine punishment for financial crimes to pecuniary penalties only and the exemption of so-called "black money" from legal investigation if sent back to Turkey were clear manifestations of this lax attitude toward established norms and practices in the legal and administrative spheres. This tendency found its expression in such statements by Özal himself as "My civil servants are shrewd in their daily dealings with the general public"[12] and "Violating the constitution once does not matter at all."[13]

## The Main Impact of the Transformation in the 1980s

Neoliberal transition in Turkey, as in other countries, has had medium- and long-term impacts, extending far beyond the economic realm to almost all spheres of social and political life. Here we shall confine ourselves to its main economic impact in the 1980s.

As expected, following the sharp price decontrol, inflation accelerated and reached new heights with 101.4% in 1980. However, tight monetary and fiscal policies under the IMF program yielded quick results. Inflation fell from 101.4% to an average rate of 31.3% during 1981–1983 period. However, even this lower but still high rate could not be sustained, as the latter part of the decade showed signs of much deeper instability. While the budget deficit (as percent of GNP) rose from an average of 1.7% during 1981–1983 to 3.2% during 1988–1989, inflation jumped to 68.5% in the latter period. Both the domestic and external debt stock increased substantially, from an average of 12.5% of GNP during 1981–1982 to 20.1% during 1988–1989, and from 22.7 to 41.9% during the same period, respectively. On a brighter spot, as the share of agriculture in GNP declined from 22.7 to 17.5%, there was a corresponding increase in the share of industry from 21.7 to 25.5%.[14] The ratio of external debt service to GNP increased nearly three-fold from 3.4% in 1981 to 10.1% in 1988 (Şenses, 1991: 222).

On the labor front, limited reliable information available indicates that real wages declined sharply, prompting trade union activity toward the end of the 1980s after being at a standstill during much of the decade. The lack of evidence prevents us from passing a firm judgment on income distribution and poverty. What little information we have indicates is that inequality in income distribution was deep and remained so during much of the decade with a Gini coefficient of around 0.5, while the ratio of the income shares of the top 20% to the poorest 40% stood intact at around 5 (Şenses, 1991: 227).

Looking back on it all, probably the main achievement of the 1980s was the ability to increase and diversify exports in the early 1980s and initiate the process of Turkey's integration to the global political economy. There was a notable rise in the share of exports in GNP, which increased from an average of only 2.9% during 1977–1979 to 11.9% during 1987–1989. This surge was accompanied by a change in the composition of exports toward manufactured goods whose share increased from 32.5% to a massive 78.7% during the same period.[15] This was a significant achievement for a country whose previous experience under the ISI model was extremely inward-oriented and characterized by considerable "export pessimism." Meanwhile, the share of imports in GDP increased from an average of 7.4 to 15.7% during the same period, indicating that Turkey made important strides to becoming an open economy.

Several factors can explain this early and sharp improvement in export performance, which includes an aggressive devaluation (and almost daily currency depreciation) strategy, provision of generous export subsidies, dramatic decline in real wages, compression of domestic demand due to IMF-induced austerity measures, and a favorable Middle Eastern market in the context of the Iran-Iraq War. Because of the extraordinary circumstances of the early 1980s, the industrial capacity that had been built up during the ISI years of the 1960s and the 1970s could be channeled to exports.[16]

Yet, Turkey could not maintain the momentum of this export drive by building an investment boom. A comparison with successful cases like South Korea is important in this context. Countries like South Korea have been able to achieve the degree of macroeconomic stability and low inflation rates necessary to turn the initial export boom to an investment boom, which created a virtuous cycle of more exports leading to more investment and to more exports. Consequently, the more successful East Asian style economies have been able to achieve growth on a continuous basis, avoid costly financial crises and increasingly upgrade their exports to medium and high technology product ranges. In the Turkish case, as Dani Rodrik aptly describes, "incomplete stabilization" during the 1980s acted as a serious barrier to carrying the initial export boom to a subsequent investment boom (Rodrik, 1990). Indeed, apart from the withdrawal of the state from investment in manufacturing, both private domestic investment in this sector and foreign direct investment in general remained stagnant. It is rather ironic that the principal investment drive in a neoliberal setting originated from public enterprises in infrastructural areas such as motorways and telecommunications.

In terms of longer-run consequences, the full liberalization of the capital account in August 1989, at Özal's discretion, in the face of strong opposition by some of the bureaucrats of that time, such as the Central Bank Governor, Rüşdü Saraçoğlu, deserves serious emphasis (Gemici, 2012). Dani Rodrik terms this as "premature liberalization" since Turkey in 1989 lacked the preconditions for full capital account liberalization, such as a high degree of macroeconomic stability and a tightly regulated banking and financial system (Rodrik, 1990). The capital account liberalization decision allowed the Turkish economy to grow based on short-term capital inflows in the early 1990s. Possibly this decision enabled Turkey to avoid a financial crisis at the end of the 1980s. Yet, the decision also paved the way for the significant instability that followed in the subsequent era, with two consecutive crises in 1994 and 2000–2001 in a timespan of less than a decade. Dependence on highly volatile short-term capital flows in an environment of endemic macroeconomic instability and under-regulated banking system was at the core of the new wave of crises associated with the neoliberal era. There is a tendency among observers of the Turkish economy to regard the second decade of Washington Consensus policies in Turkey as an inferior decade, in fact even as a "lost decade" as compared to the 1980s. We should not forget, however, that the 1980s and 1990s were strongly inter-connected.

The key decisions taken toward the end of 1980s have helped to shape the highly unstable macroeconomic environment of the 1990s.

Another problem in this context was the failure to curb corruption and rent-seeking behavior. Again, a comparison with successful East Asian cases is relevant in this regard (Öniş, 1998). In East Asian cases, export success was dependent on a combination of state-led support and discipline. Exporters received support on a selective basis, but they also faced a penalty if they did not act in line with the policy requirements. In the Turkish context, exporters received significant subsidies, which indeed constituted an "unorthodox" element of the program. Yet, the discipline element was weak. As mentioned before, one of the striking highlights of the period was the misuse of export subsidies, known in popular terms as "fictitious exports." The Özal government was quite lenient to such "economic crimes." The rise of corruption during the 1980s, in an environment where the rule of law and the importance of strong institutional checks and balances were underemphasized, in fact, was carried over to the post-Özal era of the 1990s and beyond.[17]

## The Turkish Transformation: An International Perspective Based on Latin American Examples

Turkey's neoliberal restructuring in the Özal era involved the implementation of key elements associated with the logic of the Washington Consensus. As mentioned above, Turkey was one of the first countries during the 1980s, which applied a joint IMF-World Bank Program of stabilization and medium-term structural adjustment in line with the principle of "cross conditionality." We need to recognize that geopolitics also mattered in the implementation of neoliberal reforms. Turkey, because of its key geopolitical position, was able to draw on significant funding from international financial institutions, which clearly helped Turkey to adjust more smoothly than would otherwise have been the case, in the aftermath of the major economic and political crises of the late 1970s, signifying the end of the ISI era. Given its peripheral importance in terms of the overall security structure of the Western alliance in the ongoing Cold War context, it was not surprising that the BWI were more generous to Turkey as compared to many other cases. Turkey was able to draw on a three-year extended fund facility by the IMF (1980–1983) and five consecutive structural adjustment loans by the World Bank (1980–1984) (Kirkpatrick & Öniş, 1991).

By 1985, the Turkish economy had recovered from the crisis. The BWI also tried to present the Turkish experience as a success case of the new paradigm of the Washington Consensus in action. Observers from BWI circles, for example, identified Turkey as a successful case of adjustment,[18] pointing out its experience as a reference for other countries undergoing structural adjustment along neoliberal lines.

Although the Turkish program was a multi-dimensional program, it was also a gradual stage-by-stage program in its orientation. Trade liberalization, for example, started in 1980 and continued at discrete intervals in 1983–1984 and 1987–1989. The final step in trade liberalization occurred following the Customs Union agreement with the European Union in December 1995, and membership of the World Trade Organization in March of the same year. Similarly, capital-account liberalization proceeded in terms of discrete changes in 1980, late 1983 and early 1984. The final step in this direction was taken by the famous and controversial cabinet decree in August 1989, leading to full convertibility of the Turkish lira. Again, in the realm of privatization, one of the main pillars of neoliberal reforms, the process was quite protracted. In the early 1980s, the emphasis was put on reforming the state economic enterprises through restricting their operations and introducing price flexibility in their decisions. Although privatization came relatively late on the policy agenda in 1986 and started in the late 1980s, progress was slow—a pattern that continued during the subsequent decade. Indeed, Turkey's experience with "hyper-privatization" is a predominantly post-2001 phenomenon, gaining significant momentum in the early years of the Justice and Development Party government after 2002.

Hence, we can observe sharp contrasts between some of the key Latin American experiences with neoliberal restructuring and the Turkish case. Chile, for example, constitutes a good counter-example of a program, which was both radical and involved a dramatic "shock treatment style" restructuring. The Chilean economy, under the authoritarian regime of Augusto Pinochet and management by the "Chicago Boys"[19] experienced a dramatic opening of the economy in 1974, with massive reductions in trade protectionism, capital account liberalization and large-scale privatization of public enterprises right from the inception of the program (Valdes, 1995). Turkey also had its military interlude during 1980–1983 and its own brand of US trained technocrats[20] who also played an important part in Turkey's neoliberal restructuring in the 1980s. Yet the Turkish experience was nowhere near as abrupt and extreme as the Chilean case.

Similarly, one could argue that the Argentinean neoliberal experiment during the presidency of Carlos Menem in the 1990s and the Mexican case during the presidency of Carlos Salinas in the context of Mexico's NAFTA membership (becoming effective in January 1994) were more dramatic instances of reform, which embodied significant "shock treatment" elements (Teichman, 1997). Both the Argentinean and Mexican experiences involved massive waves of dismantlement of trade protectionism, capital account opening, and privatization during the 1990s. In Turkey, privatization started almost a decade earlier than both Argentina and Mexico but was delayed and then tended to proceed at a much slower pace.

Yet another striking feature from a comparative perspective involves the role of transnational policy actors or "policy entrepreneurs." Key transnational actors played an important part in establishing a dialogue with the key Washington institutions and legitimizing a radical program of economic restructuring in the context of domestic politics, often portraying the program as a national scheme of the country, as opposed to a program imposed by external actors. In Turkey, Özal was clearly the key transnational policy actor whose influence was quite dramatic throughout the 1980s. His role was quite extraordinary in the sense that he managed to play a dominant role and provide a significant element of continuity in Turkey's neoliberal restructuring in a period marked by dramatic political shifts. He was the key technocrat in the minority but democratically elected government that inaugurated the famous 24 January 1980 measures signaling the beginning of the neoliberal economic reforms in Turkey. His role as the key technocratic figure continued during the military interlude, following the military intervention of September 1980. Özal was able to resume his role as the Prime Minister and the leader of the Motherland Party, following the return to parliamentary democracy with the elections of November 1983. Özal, this time as a key political figure, was again the dominant personality in shaping the course of neoliberal reforms from 1983 to the point where he became the president in late 1989 (Öniş, 2004).

In retrospect, there is no comparable figure to Özal in the principal Latin American cases, in the sense of a single person enjoying this extraordinary dual role as a key political figure and a key technocratic figure at the same time, which was visible mostly during the 1980–1983 period. In Argentina, for example, Carlos Menem, as the key political figure, played a similar role to Özal's role during the 1980–1983 period in Turkey, as the democratically elected president in Argentina.[21] As a popular political figure, Menem played an important role in terms of generating widespread political support for a drastic program of neoliberal restructuring, which also found support from the Argentine trade unions (Öniş, 2006). However, the key technocratic figure, who was instrumental in the implementation of the program was a US-educated economist, Domingo Cavallo. In fact, the Argentine program is often referred to as the "Cavallo program" (Teichman, 1997). Hence, there was a division of responsibility between Menem and Cavallo. While Menem was the politician, Cavallo was the implementer or the technocrat. In the Turkish context, Özal played both roles, which is rather unique and dramatic by international standards.

Looking at the Mexican example, we see a pattern rather like Argentina. Carlos Salinas was the key political figure as the president who pushed for Mexico's NAFTA membership program and the drastic neoliberal transition associated with it. However, key technocratic figures such as Pedro Aspe who played a key part in Mexico's massive privatization drive[22] were responsible for actual implementation. Finally, Pinochet provided the degree of political space and autonomy needed for the implementation of Chile's massive shock treatment, while technocrats acted as the key transnational policy actors. Hence, in a nutshell, Özal was an unusual transnational policy actor in terms of combining key technocratic and political roles.

Another interesting parallel that we can draw between the Turkish and the key Latin American cases during this period relates to the presidential system of government. In sharp contrast to the presidential systems in Western settings such as the United States and France, presidential systems in Latin America allowed key presidential figures like Menem in Argentina and Salinas in Mexico to capitalize on concentration of executive authority and relatively weak checks and balances. This enabled the latter to push through massive programs of neoliberal reforms and override significant opposition from powerful interest groups in the process. While Menem was able to accomplish this in a relatively more democratic context in Argentina, Salinas utilized his presidential powers under a semi-authoritarian, one party regime in Mexico (Aspe,1993; Teichman, 1997).

In Turkey, parliamentary system of government was the norm. However, the 1982 Constitution, established during the military regime interlude, enhanced the powers of the executive relative to the legislature.

Following the return to free elections, Özal tried to govern the country under a de facto presidential system, at times disregarding the restrictions of the parliamentary regime. Many of the key decisions, such as the one on capital account liberalization in August 1989, among others, were taken as cabinet decrees, thereby by-passing parliamentary approval. In fact, Özal actively pushed for a transition to a formal presidential system in Turkey, which he believed would be instrumental in taking major economic decisions on issues like privatization, to which serious opposition existed on the part of both key segments of economic bureaucracy and the business community. As an end note, it was ironic that Özal was elected the President in November 1989 and remained in that position until his death in April 1993. In retrospect, he was a more powerful figure, at least in the realm of economic policy, as a de facto president in his role as the Prime Minister during the 1983–1989 period than as the president. Although he formally became the President toward the end of his career, the presidency he occupied was more of a symbolic nature compared to its Latin American counterparts. The fact that his Motherland Party had lost the elections in 1991 meant that his role in guiding the economic policy process became quite marginal.

## The Turkish Transformation in the Light of Some Counterfactuals

In discussing the possibility of alternative scenarios or counterfactuals, we may shift the comparative axis from Latin America to East Asia. Arguably, a major opportunity was missed in Turkey in the early 1970s, *before* the neoliberal transition decade of 1980s.[23] If Turkey had been able to accomplish a policy shift in the early 1970s or in the context of the Third Five Year Plan (1973–1977) in the direction of export-oriented industrialization with selective import-substitution in intermediate and capital goods, the developmental impact would have been significantly better. The comparison with South Korea in the context of the 1960s and 1970s is quite telling in this context. South Korea was able to move swiftly in the 1960s from the successful first and easy phase of ISI to export-orientation accompanied by selective import-substitution (Haggard et al., 1991). As a result, it was able to avoid Turkish or Latin American style ISI crises, with costly economic consequences and associated democratic breakdowns. Hence, South Korea was able to grow on a continuous basis, which meant that it was one of the few countries that was able to break "the middle-income trap" that many developing economies, including Turkey, continue to face, and reach high income status within the timespan of a few decades.

Instead, Turkey continued with prolonged ISI and experienced a deep economic and political crisis in the late 1970s. Turkey was able to shift to export-oriented policies only after a major breakdown of the democratic system, a costly military interlude, and under the pressure of key external actors with a time lag of at least a decade. Furthermore, the neoliberal reforms were implemented in a top-down fashion in the absence of a broad social and political consensus. Key segments of society, such as labor and agricultural interests, were excluded from the decision-making process. As a result, the return to democracy during the decade resulted in resistance by organized labor to severe distributional imbalances, which, in turn, contributed to severe macroeconomic instability. Such instability acted as a key constraint blocking Turkey's ability to generate high rates of domestic and foreign direct investment needed to achieve high rates of economic growth on a sustained basis (Öniş, 1992).

Obviously, one needs to bear in mind that South Korea had managed to accomplish such a dramatic policy shift in an authoritarian political environment characterized by state autonomy vis-à-vis key business actors, which allowed the policy makers to carry out the required policy shifts in a relatively swift and smooth manner (Amsden, 1989). In Turkey or in similar Latin American settings, in contrast, the underlying political economy was such that the states enjoyed lower levels of autonomy and, hence, lacked the political and institutional capacity to engineer dramatic changes in incentive structures to allow them to shift smoothly from domestic market-based to export-oriented paths of development. One can conjecture that if Turkey was able to achieve the policy shift to an export-oriented model at an earlier stage, in a predominantly democratic environment, it could now have been in a much better position in terms of its economic development and established itself as a case of successful democratic development among the developing economies.

It is pertinent to ask at this stage why this option was not taken in the early 1970s. The answer to this question has both domestic and international dimensions. Internationally, ISI, although receiving increasing criticism from academic circles, was, except for a handful of countries in East and South East Asia, very much the norm. Moreover, international organizations were not yet raising their voices against it and were instead turning a blind eye to the Third World countries implementing it. In this process, the emergence of the Third World as a unified force in the international political and economic arena has no doubt played an influential role.

In the specific Turkish case we can identify several factors. The big devaluation of the Turkish Lira in 1970 led to a large inflow of foreign exchange resources through exports and remittances of Turkish migrant workers abroad. This inflow created the false impression in the eyes of planners and policy makers as well as the public at large that Turkey's chronic foreign exchange bottleneck was over and done with. Moreover, due to the dominance of "export pessimism," there was a general belief that exports were not responsive to exchange rate depreciation and other incentives, given Turkey's dependence on a handful of traditional exports headed by cotton, tobacco, hazelnuts, figs and raisins, characterized by low elasticity of demand in world markets. The military-backed government at the time, unlike the military regime of the early 1980s was in support of ISI. There was a general willingness not only among planners and policy makers but also on the part of the business community and academic circles to go ahead with ISI in pursuit of the objective of extending it into intermediate and capital goods. To replace the ISI by export orientation, difficult as it was given the above reasons, was even more difficult to go hand in hand with democracy under the brutal military backed government of the time, characterized with widespread human rights abuses.

There are two other counterfactuals that we can consider at this stage. What would have been the level of industrialization in Turkey if the bountiful resources that were made available to it by international donors in support of its neoliberal transformation were made available to support the Third Five Year Plan targets? Could the severe economic crisis of the late 1970s be avoided if these donors could provide Turkey sufficient financial assistance to enable it to ride through the severe foreign exchange shortages storm of the late 1970s? These two counterfactuals like the previous one runs against the *Realpolitik* of the time. International organizations as the main source of such support and assistance were, although not openly hostile to ISI, were ideologically reluctant to support it financially.

This leaves us with the third counterfactual, which is somewhat more plausible than the first two. Although the Third Five Year Plan targets were set in a period of foreign exchange glut, one would have expected planners of a country heavily dependent on imported oil to revise these targets downward and pay more attention to short-term stability to avoid public sector deficits and the ensuing galloping inflation. Such a revision of targets would have provided planners and policy makers with a wider policy space free of the straitjacket likely to be imposed by international donors and given them more leeway to save ISI and implement it selectively in combination with export orientation.

As our discussion in this chapter has shown, all three scenarios remained as counterfactuals and what emerged instead was full-scale transformation of Turkey's economic policies in a neoliberal direction in the early 1980s when the objectives of international organizations and the Turkish government matched each other, and the thorny road ahead cleared forcefully by the military regime, shortly after the first steps in that direction were taken.

## Concluding Observations: Broad Reflections on the Possible Legacy of the 1980s

Turkey was one of the first countries to adopt a neoliberal program in 1980, which radically changed the direction of economic policies away from state-led ISI toward market-based export orientation. The transition in this direction began rather abruptly but proceeded gradually, in contrast to Latin American cases where shock treatment constituted the dominant approach. While neoliberal programs display certain common characteristics, the Turkish experience also illustrates that specific national contexts are important in terms of explaining the variations of the sequencing, speed, and relative effectiveness of various neoliberal programs put into action. The Turkish case also demonstrates the importance of the geopolitical context. In retrospect, Turkey clearly benefited from its geopolitical position in terms of attracting a sizable assistance from the BWI, an option which was not equally available in other developing country contexts such as Mexico in 1982 and Argentina in 1989.

The Turkish case has shown that initiating such transformations in the absence of domestic stability and taking steps like the capital account liberalization in 1989 before establishing an adequate regulatory framework can have wider repercussions. Such steps can lead to a situation in which instability becomes embedded in the economic sphere and pave the way for devastating crises in subsequent periods.

There is no doubt that the neoliberal policies implemented in Turkey during the "Özal era" of the 1980s have had a deep impact on Turkey's developmental trajectory of the subsequent decades. A full-fledged analysis of the impact of the profound economic and political transformations of the 1980s on developments in the subsequent era is beyond the scope of the present chapter.[24] Nevertheless, from Turkey's rich body of experience in the 1980s a few observations can be derived for its present-day political economy.

A central point to emphasize is that neoliberal norms introduced in the 1980s continued to remain intact in the subsequent decades. However, the nature of neoliberalism also changed in line with domestic and external developments. The first crucial turning point came in the aftermath of the twin crises of 2000–2001. The period from 2001 to roughly 2011, starting with the "economy program" of Kemal Derviş under the coalition government and continued to be implemented by the Justice and Development Party (*AKP*) government (in its early years), may be regarded as Turkey's encounter with the logic of "Post-Washington Consensus." The emphasis during the early 2000s shifted to a modified version of neoliberalism, which could be characterized as "social and regulatory neoliberalism." In this modified version, more emphasis was given to social assistance and strong regulatory institutions in the realm of banking, finance, and competition. Yet, certain key elements of the neoliberal program remained intact (Öniş, 2009). Indeed, the early AKP period was characterized by a major privatization boom, a process which was at its infancy and was firmly resisted in the early neoliberal phase of the Özal era (Öniş, 2011; Öniş & Şenses, 2009). The post-2011 period, arguably represents a gradual shift toward a new hybrid developmental model, where neoliberal elements continued to co-exist with "state capitalist" features (Kutlay, 2020; Öniş, 2019). During the post-2011 period, Turkey as a "reactive state" (Öniş & Şenses, 2007) is once again deeply affected by global shifts in terms of the increasing challenge by authoritarian models of capitalism, represented by the Russia-China axis.

It is often argued that the origins of the current presidential system, which was formally established in the late 2010s, may be a legacy of the 1980s.There is no doubt that the 1982 constitution instituted under the auspices of the military regime has deeply shaped political developments in Turkey in the subsequent decades and has constrained Turkey's democratic progress ever since its inception. Nevertheless, the parallels between Özal's vision of a presidential system and the existing presidential regime instituted during the late AKP era should not be exaggerated. Although, neoliberal policies in Turkey were implemented in a de facto presidential system, with government decrees constituting a dominant form of decision-making, the domestic political environment, especially after the transition to democracy in 1983 was quite different to the present context. Moreover, Özal's vision of a presidential system, which could not be implemented, was more in line with the democratic presidential systems, despite their major flaws, of the United States or key Latin American cases such as Argentina and Brazil. One should also note that Özal became the President in 1989 in an essentially parliamentary system of government. Indeed, his influence in the economic realm appears to have waned after November 1989, as his concerns increasingly shifted to domestic politics and foreign policy issues. The current presidential system, in contrast, is much more in line with a more authoritarian, Russian style presidential regime.

From the perspective of the present chapter, neither the neoliberalism of the 1980s, nor its hybrid versions such as the Post-Washington Consensus approach of the early 2000s or the authoritarian state capitalist neoliberal synthesis provides an adequate response to Turkey's fundamental problems, including low domestic savings and a lop-sided pattern of development based on a combination of the construction sector, consumption expenditures, and foreign borrowing, which, in turn, raises fundamental difficulties in terms of long-term sustainability. Turkish economic performance in the recent era continues to display some fundamental deficiencies involving low investment, heavy dependence on external resources and technology imports, high level of external indebtedness, widespread rent-seeking activities, low level of employment creation, and high levels of unemployment and inequality (Güven, 2016; Şenses, 2012).

What is required as an alternative is a model of "democratic developmentalism" where an active industrial policy aiming at industrial diversification would play a key role in breaking up the "middle-income trap" based on a broad democratic consensus and supported by strong and meritocratic institutions. The fact that Turkey is still confronted with the "middle-income trap" constitutes a clear sign that, after four decades since the inception of neoliberal reforms, the country failed to match the kind of success that countries like South Korea have managed to accomplish. The South Korean comparison is quite telling for illustrating the possibility that significant industrial and developmental success can be achieved, as South Korea has proven to be one of the very few countries to break down the middle-income trap in the contemporary context, along with an increasingly democratic environment. South Korea has successfully emerged from its authoritarian past and is clearly presenting itself as a successful Asian democracy and a role model for the rest of the world, along with significant lessons also for the current Turkish context. The possibility of achieving a shift to such a model of "democratic developmentalism" will crucially depend on domestic political transformations and the broader global context. On both counts, we cannot be very optimistic in the present historical juncture.

**Acknowledgements** We thank Oktar Türel, Emre Özçelik and Yonca Özdemir for their useful suggestions. We would also like to thank Uğur İlker Darıcı and Özge Yüksekkaya for their valuable assistance. All remaining errors are ours.

## Notes

1. The public sector borrowing requirement (as percent of GNP) increased from 2.0% in 1973 to 10.6% in 1979. Figures in this paragraph come from State Institute of Statistics, *Statistical Indicators, 1923–2009*.
2. The annual rate of inflation (Consumer Price Index) increased from 15.8% in 1973 to 22.5% in 1977 and further to 53.3% and 62.0% in 1978 and 1979, respectively. The current account balance deteriorated from 2.8% of GNP in 1973 to –6.1% in 1979. The payments crisis was so severe that the debt service obligations were nearly three times the revenue obtained from merchandise exports. State Institute of Statistics, *Statistical Indicators, 1923–2009*.

   The government was unable to pay the salaries of its diplomatic mission abroad.
3. See Wolff (1987) for details.
4. See, for example, Little, Scitovsky and Scott (1970). For a case study on Turkey, along very similar lines, see Krueger (1974).
5. For details, see, for example, Şenses (1983), and Aydın and Oyan (1987).
6. For details on this point, see Ebiri (1980) and Kepenek and Yentürk (2009).

7. European Economic Community, European Settlement Bank, and the Islamic Development Bank were among other sources of financial support for the program. According to Boratav (1987), gross capital inflow during the 1980–1984 period amounted to 13.8 billion dollars.
8. See Celasun and Rodrik (1989) on this point. Fictitious exports referred to false declaration by exporters of the contents of their export package with the intention of benefiting from the generous export tax rebate scheme.
9. State Institute of Statistics, *Statistical Indicators, 1923–2009.*
10. In fact, privatization came on the agenda as late as the mid-2000s, in the aftermath of the severe 2001 crisis and consisted of mostly mergers and acquisitions by foreign investors, and sales of real estate, various services like banking as well as distress sales of some manufacturing enterprises to external buyers. See Öniş (2012) and Kazgan (2017) for the analysis of Turkey's privatization experience.
11. For a critical assessment of the Fund, see Şenses (1999), Boratav (1995) and Ulagay (1987).
12. This saying in Turkish (*'Benim memurum işini bilir'*) implies that civil servants do and may readily take bribes. Özal's inspection of a team of soldiers in holiday wear with shorts, a t-shirt, and slippers was also seen as a manifestation of his lax attitude and caused sharp criticism from wide sections of society.
13. To be fair, it was also Özal's administration which opened the way for some of the political exiles to return to homeland and implemented reforms in the penal code for liberalizing the clauses pertaining to some religious and left-wing activities.
14. Figures in this paragraph, unless otherwise stated, come from State Institute of Statistics, *Statistical Indicators, 1923–2009.*
15. Figures in this paragraph come from State Institute of Statistics, *Statistical Indicators, 1923–2009.*
16. See Şenses (1990) and Pamuk (2016) for analyses of Turkey's export performance in the 1980s.
17. Apart from fictitious exports, corruption episodes that first come to mind are the so-called bankers' crisis involving the bankruptcy of a group of 'bankers' who laid their hands on large sums of money from the public by utilizing basically Ponzi-type financing in the early 1980s, the corruption scandal surrounding Istanbul Municipality in the 1990s, banking scandals in the early 2000s,

and finally the resignation of three government ministers amidst bribery allegations in the 2010s.

18. See, for example, Balassa (1988: S288–S289). Turkey's increased credit-worthiness on the basis of its economic performance during 1981–1984 was praised by an IMF staff member with the following statement: "It is difficult to find another example of another country which has had such a major turnaround in such a short spell of time". See Roy (1984: 1).
19. This term refers to key economic technocrats trained in the tradition of free market economics at the University of Chicago as students of academics like Milton Friedman and Arnold Harberger and characterized by their organic links to the Washington institutions as well as by the political space they enjoyed to implement their policy paradigm in their domestic political settings.
20. These were referred to as 'Özal's princes' representing the Turkish counterpart of Chicago Boys, consisting mostly of technocrats trained in the US and befriended by Özal's elder son.
21. One wonders whether the fact that he was referred to as 'El Turco' due to his Middle Eastern roots was a reflection of the influence of the Turkish reform experience on the Argentinean case.
22. See Aspe (1993).
23. See Tekin (2006) and Öniş (1998).
24. See Şenses (2012) and Donat (1987) for the overall examination of Turkey's experience under neoliberal polices since 1980.

## References


Amsden, A. H. (1989). *Asia's next giant: South Korea and late industrialization*. Oxford University Press.

Aspe, P. (1993). *Economic transformation the Mexican way*. MIT Press.

Aydın, A. R., & Oyan, O. (1987). *İstikrar Programından Kur Ekonomisine*. Verso Yayınları.

Balassa, B. (1988, April). The lessons of East Asian development: An overview. *Economic Development and Cultural Change, 36*(3, Supplement).

Boratav, K. (1987). *Turkey: Stabilization and adjustment policies and programmes*. Country Study 5, World Institute for Development Economics Research of the United Nations, Helsinki.

Boratav, K. (1995). *1980'li Yıllarda Türkiye'de Sosyal Sınıflar ve Bölüşüm*. Gerçek Yayınevi.

Boratav, K. (2019). *Türkiye İktisat Tarihi, 1908–2015*. İmge Yayınları.

Celasun, M., & Rodrik, D. (1989). Debt, adjustment, and growth: Turkey. In J. D. Sachs & S. M. Collins (Eds.), *Developing country debt and economic performance, in Volume 3: Country studies—Indonesia, Korea, Philippines, Turkey* (pp. 615–616). University of Chicago Press.

Donat, Y. (1987). *Özal'lı Yıllar*. Bilgi Yayınevi.

Ebiri, K. (1980). Turkish apertura. *METU Studies in Development, 7*(3–4), 209–254.

Gemici, K. (2012). Rushing toward currency convertibility. *New Perspectives on Turkey, 47*, 33–55.

Güven, A. B. (2016). The political economy of Turkish democracy. In C. Erişen & P. Kubicek (Eds.), *Democratic consolidation in Turkey: Micro and Macro challenges* (pp. 184–203). Routledge.

Haggard, S., Byung-Kook, K., & Moon, C. (1991). The transition to export-led growth in South Korea: 1954–1966. *The Journal of Asian Studies, 4*(50), 850–873.

Kazgan, G. (2017). *Tanzimattan 21. Yüzyıla Türkiye Ekonomisi*. Bilgi Üniversitesi Yayınları.

Kepenek, Y., & Yentürk, N. (2009). *Türkiye Ekonomisi*. Remzi Kitabevi.

Kirkpatrick, C., & Öniş, Z. (1991). Turkey. In P. Mosley et al. (Eds.), *Aid and power: The World Bank and policy based lending* (Vol. II). Routledge.

Krueger, A. O. (1974). *Foreign trade regimes and economic development, Turkey*. National Bureau of Economic Research.

Kutlay, M. (2020). The politics of state capitalism in a post-liberal international order: The case of Turkey. *Third World Quarterly, 41*(4), 683–706.

Little, I. M. D., Scitovsky, T., & Scott, M. (1970). *Industry and trade in some developing countries*. Oxford University Press or the OECD Development Center.

Öniş, Z. (1986). Stabilization and growth in a semi-industrial economy, an evaluation of the recent Turkish experiment, 1977–84. *METU Studies in Development, 13*(1–2), 7–28.

Öniş, Z. (1992). Redemocratization and economic liberalization in Turkey: The limits of state autonomy. *Studies in Comparative International Development, 27*(2), 3–23.

Öniş, Z. (1998). *State and market, the political economy of Turkey in comparative perspective*. Boğaziçi University Press.

Öniş, Z. (2004). Turgut Özal and his economic legacy: Turkish neo-liberalism in critical perspective. *Middle Eastern Studies, 40*(4), 113–134.

Öniş, Z. (2006). Varieties and crises of neoliberal globalisation: Argentina, Turkey and the IMF. *Third World Quarterly, 27*(2), 239–263.

Öniş, Z. (2009). Beyond the 2001 financial crisis: The political economy of the new phase of neo-liberal restructuring in Turkey. *Review of International Political Economy, 19*(3), 409–432.

Öniş, Z. (2011). Power, interests and coalitions: The political economy of mass privatisation in Turkey. *Third World Quarterly, 32*(4), 707–724.

Öniş, Z. (2019). Turkey under the challenge of state capitalism: The political economy of the late AKP era. *Southeast European and Black Sea Studies, 19*(2), 201–225.

Öniş, Z., & Şenses, F. (2007). Global dynamics, domestic coalitions and a reactive state: Major policy shifts in post-war Turkish economic development. *METU Studies in Development, 32*(2), 251–286.

Öniş, Z., & Şenses, F. (Eds.). (2009). *Turkey and the global economy: Neoliberal restructuring and integration in the post-crisis era*. Routledge.

Pamuk, Ş. (2016). *Türkiye'nin 200 Yıllık İktisat Tarihi*. İş Bankası Kültür Yayınları.

Rodrik, D. (1990). *Premature liberalization and incomplete stabilization: The Özal decade in Turkey* (NBER Working Paper: No: 3300). National Burau of Economic Research.

Roy, J (1984). *Structural adjustment program in Turkey, mimeographed, World Bank Europe, Middle East and North Africa Region*, Washington, DC.

Şenses, F. (1983). An assessment of Turkey's liberalization attempts since 1980 against the background of her stabilization program. *METU Studies in Development, 10*(3).

Şenses, F. (1990). An assessment of the pattern of Turkish manufactured export growth in the 1980s and its prospects. In T. Arıcanlı & D. Rodrik (Eds.), *The political economy of Turkey: Debt, adjustment and sustainability*. Macmillan.

Şenses, F. (1991, September). Turkey's stabilization and structural adjustment program in retrospect and prospect. *The Developing Economies*, XXIX-3.

Şenses, F. (1993). Turkey's labour market policies in the l980s against the background of her stabilization program. In B. Yeşilada, M. Tünay & A. Eralp (Eds.), *Political and socioeconomic transformation of Turkey since 1980* (pp. 97–109). Praeger.

Şenses, F. (1999). Yoksullukla Mücadele ve Sosyal Yardımlaşma ve Dayanışmayı Teşvik Fonu. *METU Studies in Development, 26*(3–4), 427–451.

Şenses, F. (2012). Turkey's experience with neoliberal policies since 1980 in retrospect and prospect. *New Perspectives on Turkey*, Special Issue on Turkey's Experience with neoliberal Policies and Globalization, No. 47, Fall.

Teichman, J. (1997). Mexico and argentina: Economic reform and technocratic decision making. *Studies in Comparative International Development, 32*(1), 31–55.

Tekin, A. (2006). Turkey's aborted attempt at export-led growth strategy: Anatomy of the 1970 economic reform. *Middle Eastern Studies, 42*(1), 133–163.

Ulagay, O. (1987). *Özal Ekonomisinde Paramız Pul Olurken Kim Kazandı Kim Kaybetti*. Bilgi Yayınevi.

Valdes, J. G. (1995). *Pinochet's economists: The Chicago school in Chile*. Cambridge University Press.

Wolff, P. (1987). *Stabilization policy and structural adjustment in Turkey, 1980–85, the role of the IMF and World Bank in an externally supported adjustment process*. German Development Institute.

CHAPTER 8

# The Era of Speculation-Led Growth and the 2001 Crisis, 1990–2001

*A. Erinç Yeldan*

## Introduction: Setting the Stage

The 1990s can be termed as the "lost decade" for the Turkish economy. The stage was set by the completion of "external liberalization" in August 1989 with the announcement of the *Decree No. 32*, which opened up the capital account of the balance of payments and gave rise to a whole set of new modes of macroeconomic adjustments for the domestic economy. Perhaps in its entire history, Turkey suddenly confronted a new era in which the "constraints" of the "external gap" was eliminated and the domestic economy met with a new instrument: the ***real interest rate***. Short-term financial flows, lured by the arbitrage opportunities of a new emerging market, seemed to have alleviated the external imbalances once and for all. This new process meant significant reallocation of investments, along with realignment of the main macroeconomic prices, namely, the

A. E. Yeldan (✉)
Department of Economics, Kadir Has University, Istanbul, Turkey
e-mail: yeldane@bilkent.edu.tr; erinc.yeldan@khas.edu.tr



E. Özçelik and Y. Özdemir (eds.), *Political Economy of Development in Turkey*, The Political Economy of the Middle East,
https://doi.org/10.1007/978-981-16-7318-4_8

rate of interest and the exchange rate. There was also significant reorientation of the parameters of distribution, as the sphere of finance commenced to ascend against the "real sectors" in general, and industrial labor in particular.

The decade was one of extreme volatility, characterized by narrowing of the time horizon. Volatility of the flow of foreign finance led to deeper adjustments in the exchange rate, which, in turn, resulted in severer turbulences in the traded sectors, and warranted ever more inflows of foreign capital, leading to higher volatilities in the external finances. Consequently, mechanisms of income distribution had to be readjusted, new forms of rent-seeking were enacted, and new coalitions had been formed across the bureaucracy, industrial conglomerates, and the banking sector.

This chapter accounts for these observations. It is organized under four additional sections. The first section following this Introduction analyzes the main elements of change in the global commodity and finance markets, elaborating the rise of speculative growth and the new nature of the business cycle. Then, the following section discusses Turkey's mode of adjustment to the new global order and documents the context of capital account liberalization in 1989, studying also the effect of this move on the "real economy." The section before the Concluding Comments focuses on the elements of the IMF-induced, exchange-rate-based disinflation program that was initiated at a time when the decade came to a close by setting the stage for the eruption of one of the most severe crises of Turkish economic history in November 2000 and February 2001. The last section concludes with an overview and discussion over new forms of dependency across the developing world.

## The Changing Global Context: "Financialization" of the Third World

The 1990s can be understood as a case of "*financialization redux*" at the level of the global economy. The decade opened up with trumpets echoing "*the end of history*" à la Francis Fukuyama. The Soviet system of "real socialism" collapsed, and all the global markets, with the exception of labor, were started to be integrated under one logic: free mobility of capital—especially "finance capital." Removal of barriers over international finance has granted it with extensive deregulation, while labor was trapped within national borders.

Deregulation of finance capital was in the making since the early 1970s. Limits of the "golden age" of Bretton-Woods era were already reached with the decline in the rate of profits in the manufacturing industries of the developed countries. Technologies matured, capital intensities increased, and easy gains in productivity along the assembly line and the scale economies were exhausted. These developments led to the collapse of the gold-exchange standard in 1971, and along with excess accumulation of petrodollars and pension funds in the hands of few western banks searching for lucrative speculative deals, regulations on the mobility of financial capital could not have been sustained any more. Financial deregulation meant dismantling the rules and interventions of the nation states. Any regulation inhibiting the quest for financial profit across the globe was cursed as backwardness. Furthermore, along with a severe and sudden reorientation of priorities of capital accumulation away from industry to finance and banking, the process of *deindustrialization* has intensified and industrial labor has been caught within the confines of short-term speculative capital flows under national constraints.

All of this was referred to as *globalization*, which was hailed as an unstoppable planetary motion toward global "civilization." Thereby we can deduce three interlinked aspects of global capitalism in the juncture of the 1990s: *neoliberal restructuring*, *neoliberal globalization*, and *financialization*. Neoliberal restructuring had been propagated with the counter attacks of monetarism and supply-side economics during the 1980s in the hands of Ronald Reagan in the USA, Helmut Kohl in Germany, Margaret Thatcher in the UK, and Turgut Özal in Turkey. The assault reached its zenith in the 1990s with the rhetoric of "the end of history," when all political-economic questions were declared to be resolved, all unknowns were behind, and the world was on a sustained path toward global bliss. The states would now allegedly assume the role of a bystander, a referee, setting the rules of the game and ensuring that the rules were obeyed.

This idea of a *neutral* state, *standing at an equal distance* from all participants in the workplace, however, was far from reality. The state apparatus has, in fact, was reorganized to ensure the supremacy of capital over labor; and any dissent was brutally suppressed with accusations of backwardness and/or outright military force against labor organizations. The neoliberal state was actually a *stronger* state, given its new instruments of control over society, such as the newly formed regulatory bodies, committees, task forces that typically consisted of a handful of "technicians" and were most often enacted with powers outside the parliamentary jurisdiction.

What lied at the heart of this restructuring was the ascendancy of finance over industry, characterized by a global process of *financialization* imposing its logic of short-termism, liquidity, flexibility and immense mobility over the objectives of long-term industrialization, sustainable development and poverty alleviation with social welfare states. *Financialization*, as it stands, is a loose term and no consensus yet exists among economists on its definition. However, starting from David Harvey's seminal observation that "something significant has changed in the way capitalism has been working since about 1970" (Harvey 1989: 192), a set of distinguishing characteristics of the concept can be unveiled. Krippner (2006: 174), in line with Giovanni Arrighi's *The Long Twentieth Century,* defines it as a pattern of accumulation in which profits accrue primarily through financial channels rather than through trade and commodity production. According to Epstein (2005: 3), "financialization means the increasing role of financial motives, financial markets, financial actors and financial institutions in the operation of domestic and international economies." In a broader way, we can consider "financialization" as a phenomenon that can be described as increasing financial motives, and increasing volume and impact of financial activities within and among countries. As Duménil and Lévy underline:

> What is at issue here, are not markets and states per se, but the stricter subjection of these institutions to capital: on the one hand, the freedom of capital to act along its own interests with little consideration for salaried workers and the large masses of the world population, and, on the other hand, a state dedicated to the enforcement of this new social order and the confrontation to other states. (Duménil & Lévy, 2004: 3)

Over the decade, waves of financial crises were witnessed. The first of these waves typically erupted in the "emerging market" economies of Mexico in 1994, Turkey in 1994 and then again in 2001, Brazil and Russia in 1998, Argentina in 2001, and of course, the "Asian Flu" of 1997. Almost all of these financial crises were explained, one way or another, by a form of *moral hazard*—lack of "prudential" regulation and biased incentives emanating from the assumption that the risk-takers were *too large to fail.*

Under this new episode, crises erupted mainly due to premature financial liberalization, lack of governance, lack of rule of law, etc. Typically, countries, which were lured into the trumpets of "***end the financial repression; hail to the free financial markets***" (à la McKinnon, 1973; Shaw, 1973), liberalized their financial sectors too prematurely and too hastily without paying attention to their macroeconomic fundamentals. In these economies, capital-account deregulation often led to increased interest rates. Based on the motive to combat the "fear of capital flight," this commitment stimulated further foreign inflows, and the domestic currencies appreciated inviting an even higher level of short-term capital and "hot money" inflows into the often shallow domestic financial markets.

The experience of the 1990s was thus a new global order of instability. One can trace out the main mechanics of this instability as follows: with (prematurely) opening up of the capital account, short-term foreign finance (hot money inflows) pour in with an attempt to take advantage of the speculative financial arbitrage opportunities. Currency appreciates, import costs fall and the domestic agents enjoy a sudden relaxation of their budget constraints. The initial bonanza of debt-financed public spending (e.g. Turkey) or private spending (e.g. Mexico, South Korea) escalates rapidly and worsens the fragility of the shallow domestic financial markets. Eventually, the bubble bursts out and a series of severe and onerous macroeconomic adjustments are enacted through very high real interest rates, sizable devaluations, and a harsh entrenchment of aggregate demand accompanied by the short-term "hot money" outflows. Elements of this vicious cycle are further studied by Adelman and Yeldan (2000), Calvo and Vegh (1999), Dornbsuch et al. (1995), and Diaz-Alejandro (1985). This cycle is more recently referred to as the *Diaz-Alejandro-Taylor cycle* in Köse et al. (2007), following Diaz-Alejandro (1985) and Taylor (1998). A schema of this cycle is portrayed in Fig. 8.1.

Figure 8.1 discloses main features of what I will term as the *Alejandro-Taylor Cycle*. As this is a closed system, one can initially start from any point of this cycle. Suppose that given the threat of capital flight, or any lucrative expectation of short-term gain from capital inflows, the domestic rate of interest is increased. Speculative arbitrageurs storm in, given the absence of any regulation and the currency appreciates due to the bonanza of foreign exchange. Imports expand, current account widens, and most probably foreign indebtedness rise as well. All these mean increased external fragility and thereupon a more intensified interest hike is warranted. The cycle recommences, as the country is set into a trap

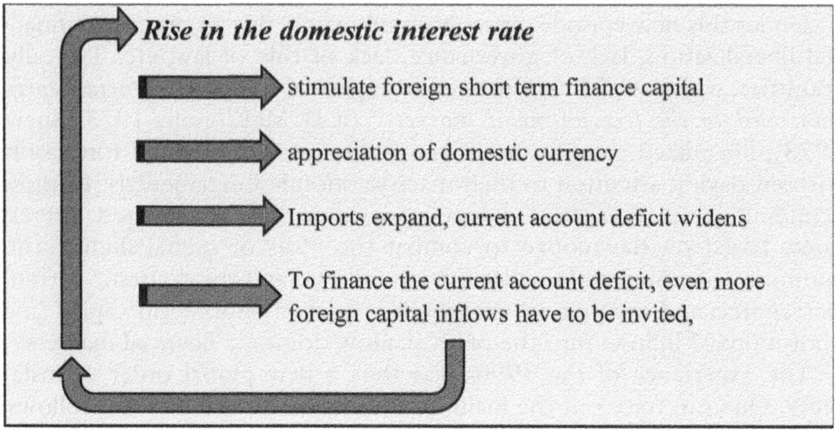


**Fig. 8.1** The Alejandro-Taylor cycle: vicious cycle of capital flows & macroeconomic disequilibria

of high interest rates, appreciating currency and collapse of the domestic import-competing industries. The end result is an unsustainable path of speculation-led growth.

Historical evidence suggests that the main characteristics of this variety of crises typically involved the following:

i. International capital market has been the major source of shocks;
ii. Flows have largely originated from and been received by the private sector;
iii. The financial crises have mostly hit emerging market economies that were considered to be highly credible and successful;
iv. The rise of capital inflows has been characterized by a lack of regulation, on both the supply and the demand sides.

Under these conditions, many developing countries have suffered from premature de-industrialization, serious informalization, and consequent worsening of the position of wage-labor, resulting in a deterioration of income distribution and increased poverty. Many of these phenomena have occurred under the neoliberal "conditionalities," imposing rapid liberalization of trade, privatization of public enterprises, and premature deregulation of the indigenous financial markets. Thus, across all economies, industrialized or peripheral, wage incomes collapsed; income share of wage labor in aggregate domestic product fell; and the appropriated surpluses fed the rising corporate profits. Turkey's experience with capital account liberalization and financial deregulation over the 1990s disclosed almost all of these key attributes. It is to these issues that I now turn attention.

## The Decade of Speculation-Led Growth

The decade of the 1980s was marked by the reorientation of the Turkish economy to integrate with the global markets. A series of reforms and structural adjustment conditionalities were enacted, resulting in tariff liberalization, export promotion and a severe wage repression for labor incomes. The economy, however, entered a period of *reform fatigue* by 1988 and slowed down significantly in 1988. Realizing that the "fruits" of export promotion and globalization were "delayed," Özal government initiated the liberalization of the capital account in order to access international finance capital.

The *Decree No. 32* was the main policy document leading to the full liberalization of the capital account. In a nutshell, it covered the following:

- All the residents of Turkey, including private persons, corporations and banks can bring and take out foreign exchange in any magnitude to and from Turkey without any restrictions.
- Nonresidents can purchase any form and quantity of assets from Turkey, bring in and take out their yields in any form of denomination, Turkish Lira or foreign exchange.
- Residents are free to introduce any type of assets to be sold domestically as well as abroad, and free to transfer the returns in and out freely.
- Nonresidents are free to bring in any foreign credit, or purchase domestic credit from within and transfer monies in any denomination to and from Turkey.

Historically speaking, the elements of this maneuver were quite liberal, even more so than the advanced economies of Europe at the time, and Turkey was severely criticized for not creating the necessary institutional infrastructure to oversee the flow of funds in a very narrow domestic financial system. Main indicators of this episode involved mostly a new division of responsibilities and rent-seeking opportunities among the banking sector, the industrial bourgeoisie and the state. First of all, it was clear that, as a ratio of GDP, Turkey indeed experienced significant *financial deepening*. Securities issues in total rose from 6.5% of the GDP in 1990 to 40% by the end of the decade (Yeldan, 2001). Time deposits also rose by almost two-folds as a ratio, taking advantage of the increased rate of return, that is, the real rate of interest. Banking sector credits and the volume of transactions both in the primary and secondary financial markets expanded feverishly.

Nevertheless, much of this transition relied on mainly two factors: issuance of Government Debt Instruments (GDIs) and significant dollarization of domestic deposits. In fact, financial deepening can be argued to have led the residents to switch to foreign currencies (dollarization), paving the way for a new form of deficit financing by the government.

With the advent of financial liberalization, Turkey experienced, perhaps for the first time in its entire republican history, a substantial alleviation of the foreign-exchange constraint. The foreign-exchange scarcity disappeared, and Turkish credit and money markets experienced a sizeable inflow of foreign exchange within a few months' time, releasing all concerns about the *external deficit*.

A direct effect of this process was the onerous adjustments forced by the so-called *open-economy trilemma*, according to which, in an open economy, only two out of the following three can be chosen and implemented by the authorities: independent monetary policy (conduct of money supply), the foreign exchange regime (free float or fixed exchange rates) and the capital account regime (open or closed). Yet, in a developing, emerging market economy such as Turkey, what actually happened with an open capital account was that Turkey could have control over neither monetary policy, nor the foreign exchange regime. Simply put, the rate of interest and the exchange rate collapsed into a single price and constituted the main operational indicator for the inflows and outflows of foreign exchange—the "hot" component of foreign finance. Thus, the *impossible trilemma* had been observed to work even under more stringent conditions where the emerging market economies that had opened up their capital account to international flows of finance, had actually lost their control over *both* the independent monetary policy and the foreign capital mobility. The implications were a structurally constrained economy to yield ever increasing real rates of interest and monetary deflation under the threatening conditionalities of international speculative finance.

Table 8.1 introduces the critical economic indicators of this transition. Here, along with the pre-1989 period, the "lost decade" of the 1990s is divided into four main episodes: uncontrolled financial liberalization (1989–1993); the 1994 crisis; return to "hot money" driven growth (1995–1997); and the contagion of the Asian crisis (1998 and 1999). All of these episodes can be contrasted against the export-orientation era of the 1980s. The first of these episodes (1989–1993) is characterized by ad hoc and often politically-motivated interventions aiming at deregulation of the financial asset markets. As noted above, the *Decree No. 32* had been introduced with an eye on foreign "hot money" inflows. The unavoidable home-currency appreciation under this foreign-exchange boom led to the 1994 crisis, the first full-fledged financial-cum-real crisis in Turkey. After 1994, domestic economic policies were realigned for hot-money driven, speculation-led growth. Yet, the contagion of the Asian crisis hit the Turkish economy under these prolonged structural imbalances. This episode was finally cut by the introduction of the IMF-led disinflation program under the exchange rate-based *tablita*.[1] The end result would be the November 2000 and February 2001 crises, which are narrated in detail below.

Reading from Table 8.1, recovery of GDP growth from the 1988 deceleration is clearly visible. Fueled by inflows of short-term foreign finance, investment expenditures continued on their expansionary path; yet, as discussed in detail by Yeldan (2001), their share as a ratio to the GDP has not revealed a structural shift. One of the main reasons of this was the switching of destined investments away from industry, to one-time expenditures such as construction and housing (Boratav and Yeldan, 2006; Yeldan, 2001). Both of these were non-traded sectors and led to the widening of the current-account deficit by 1993 and reaching its climax in 1994 as the balance of payments crisis exploded.

The adjustment experience of the real sector to financial liberalization had been one of boom-and-bust cycles. As documented in Table 8.1, the post-1988 performance of GDP revealed intensified short-term business cycles, along with rates of annual growth ranging between 8% (1993) and −5.5% (1994). Following the production cycle, both consumption and investment demand fluctuated sharply over the same period. Similarly, the external economy was in turbulence with the balance on current account

**Table 8.1** Macroeconomic adjustment processes: Turkey, 1983–1999

| | *Export oriented growth* | *Exhaustion of reform process* | *Uncontrolled financial liberalization* | *Financial crisis* | *Return to short-term capital driven growth* | *Demand contraction due to Asian crisis* | |
|---|---|---|---|---|---|---|---|
| | *1983–1987* | *1988* | *1989–1993* | *1994* | *1995–1997* | *1998* | *1999* |
| *I. Production and accumulation (real annual change, %)* | | | | | | | |
| GDP | 6.5 | 2.1 | 4.8 | –5.5 | 7.2 | 3.1 | –5.0 |
| Agriculture | 0.8 | 7.8 | 0.1 | –0.7 | 1.3 | 8.4 | –4.6 |
| Manufacturing | 8.6 | 1.6 | 6.0 | –7.6 | 10.2 | 1.2 | –5.7 |
| *Fixed investment* | | | | | 0.0 | 0.0 | 0.0 |
| Private sector | 14.1 | 19.2 | 11.9 | –9.6 | 9.5 | –4.2 | –11.0 |
| Public sector | 12.0 | –2.3 | 5.2 | –39.5 | 15.8 | 4.6 | 7.4 |
| *% of GDP:* | | | | | | | |
| Savings | 19.5 | 27.2 | 21.9 | 23.0 | 21.1 | 23.1 | 19.8 |
| Investment | 20.9 | 26.1 | 23.7 | 24.4 | 24.8 | 24.3 | 23.8 |
| Public sector borrowing requirement | 4.7 | 4.8 | 9.1 | 7.9 | 7.2 | 9.2 | 14.3 |
| *II. Prices and distribution* | | | | | | | |
| Inflation rate (CPI) | 40.7 | 68.8 | 65.1 | 106.3 | 85.0 | 90.7 | 70.5 |
| Annual depreciation of the Exc rate | 39.7 | 66.0 | 50.4 | 170.0 | 72.0 | 71.7 | 60.6 |
| Real interest rate on government debt securities[a] | – | –5.8 | 10.5 | 20.5 | 23.6 | 29.5 | 36.8 |
| Manufacturing industry real wages[b] | –3.9 | –7.1 | 10.2 | –36.3 | –2.8 | 1.0 | 1.0 |

| | *Export oriented growth* | *Exhaustion of reform process* | *Uncontrolled financial liberalization* | *Financial crisis* | *Return to short-term capital driven growth* | *Demand contraction due to Asian crisis* | |
|---|---|---|---|---|---|---|---|
| | *1983–1987* | *1988* | *1989–1993* | *1994* | *1995–1997* | *1998* | *1999* |
| Share of wage income in manufacturing value added (%) | 20.6 | 15.4 | 21.8 | 16.1 | 16.7 | 17.0 | 17.5 |
| *III. Internationalization* | | | | | | | |
| Rate of growth manufacturing exports | 12.5 | 14.0 | 5.1 | 18.0 | 14.2 | 3.2 | −5.5 |
| *% of GDP:* | | | | | | | |
| Imports[c] | 15.9 | 15.8 | 14.6 | 17.8 | 23.2 | 22.5 | 21.7 |
| Exports[c] | 10.8 | 12.8 | 9.1 | 13.8 | 15.8 | 13.2 | 14.2 |
| Current account balance[c] | −1.9 | −1.7 | −1.3 | −2.0 | −1.4 | 1.0 | −0.7 |
| Foreign debt stock | 37.8 | 44.8 | 35.1 | 49.6 | 45.6 | 50.9 | 55.7 |

[a]Annual compounded interest rate on Government Debt Instruments (GDIs), deflated by the CPI

[b]Private Manufacturing Industry data belong to businesses employing 10 or more people

[c]Including "luggage trade" from 1996 onwards

***Data sources*** State Planning Organization, Main Economic Indicators; Undersecretariat of Treasury and Foreign Trade, Main Economic Indicators; Turkish Statistical Institute (TURKSTAT), Manufacturing Industry Annual Surveys suffering from severe fluctuations between US $ −6.4 billion in 1993 and US $ 2.6 billion in 1994, and again US $ −2.3 billion in 1995. Domestic rate of inflation reached the plateau of 70–80% per annum and displayed strong resistance at this threshold.

In fact, inflation could never be kept under control. Hovering around the plateau of 70–80% per annum caused serious appreciation of the real exchange rate (see Fig. 8.2). Indeed, in the early decade, Turkish Lira appreciated significantly, by as much as 15% per annum. Such appreciation meant worsening of the current account balance together with the deceleration of the export revenues. Exports as a share of GDP dwindled to less than 10% from its peak of 12.8% in the late 1980s. Import expansion continued in an intensified manner over the whole decade.

Early years of the "lost decade" also witnessed real increases in manufacturing wages. This was the end of a period of secular decline over the 1980s. Led by the "spring uprisings" of the late 1980s, wage remunerations of industrial labor increased at an annual rate of 10% in real terms, halting back the losses of the Özal decade. Yet, all of this increase in real wages would be taken back in 1994 with the eruption of the financial

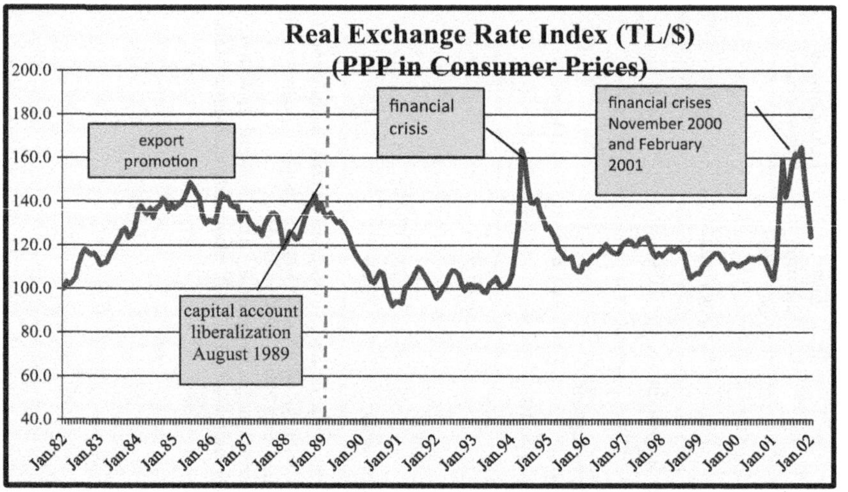


**Fig. 8.2** Real exchange rate index (TL/USD), purchasing power parity (PPP) in consumer prices (*Data source* Annual reports of the Central Bank of the Republic of Turkey [Author's calculation])

crisis, along with the rapid escalation of inflation and depreciation of the Turkish Lira. Wage data are scarce and often not reliable in Turkey, especially for the period considered. In what follows, wage data in Table 8.1 is limited only to the employees in the manufacturing sector through the official data of the Turkstat (then the State Institute of Statistics). The relative position of wage labor in the global realm can further be examined through the unit wage costs denominated in foreign currency. Such costs are calculated by taking into account the (average) productivity of labor, deflated by the exchange rate. In this way, unit wage costs account for the degree of competitiveness of the industrial sector across the global economy. Adjusting for the competitive devaluations of 1994 and 2001, the unit wage costs remained roughly 25% lower than their value in 1993. As Table 8.1 attests, manufacturing industry wage share in value added receded to 16.1% as a result of the wage suppression led by the devaluation of 1994. From 1994 onward, this share stayed more or less stable around this rate up to the end of the decade.

The impact of financial liberalization had been sudden and deep. Theoretical expectations of this maneuver were ***deepening of the financial system*** and thus to achieve a higher savings ratio supporting fixed investments. Financial deepening, as measured by the ratio of financial assets to the gross domestic product, would be the key element of this transition.

Data reveals that such a deepening did in fact occur. As a ratio to GDP, total financial securities expanded, for instance, from a ratio (to the GDP) of 7.8% in 1988 to 24.8% in 1994 (Balkan & Yeldan, 2002; Boratav and Yeldan, 2006; Yeldan, 2001). However, this increase was predominantly explained by securities issued by the public sector to cover its expanding fiscal deficits. Public securities issued rose from 6.9% in 1988 to 22.7% in 1994 to reach 38.7% in 1999; whereas private sector securities issued stayed at 2.1% of the GDP in 1994, rising only marginally from its miniscule level of 0.9% in 1988. By the end of the decade the share of private securities had fallen to 1.1%.

Total deposits, likewise, expanded. The ratio of total deposits was 15.7% in 1988 and reached 39.5% by 1999. Again, this was problematic since the major expansion came from foreign-exchange deposits, as their ratio rose from 4.2% in 1988 to 22.4%. This was mainly due to agents' preferences for dollarization, in an attempt to protect against the inflationary losses. As credibility of the Turkish Lira was lost, economic agents tried to protect their assets by shifting into dollar-denominated deposits. In fact, banking sector credits to the enterprise sector fell, as a ratio to the GDP. These stood at 17.6% in 1988; and fell to 13.3% in 1994, averaging around 18% over the remaining years of the decade (Boratav and Yeldan, 2006).

All of these were contrary to the expectations of ***financial deepening***. The realization of financial deepening meant a new round of formation of coalitions in the Turkish socio-economic structure. The government continued to run fiscal deficits as was dictated by high interest costs under the high interest rate trap enforced by the threat of capital out-flight. The banking sector, on the other used this opportunity to borrow cheap abroad and extend these foreign monies as domestic credit to the government sector. The high interest burden unavoidably led to expansion of the "public sector borrowing requirement" (PSBR) as a result of the high interest burden. The government debt instruments (GDIs) were critical in financing the budget deficit of the public sector (the central budget as well as the state economic enterprises, including the social security administration deficits). The stock of securitized domestic debt grew rapidly and the stock of GDIs reached 22% in 1994 from 6% of the GDP in 1989. Interest costs on domestic debt grew to 10.6% of the GDP by 1994, and then continued viciously to increase by almost ten-fold in real terms over the decade. As a further comparison, interest costs on servicing the debt reached 1,010% of public investments, and 481% of the transfers accruing to social security institutions in 1998 (Balkan & Yeldan, 2002).

As these were being realized in the government accounts, the banking sector was lured by the real interest rate exceeding 30% per annum, and evolved into arbitrageurs of "hot money" finance. The banks continued their borrowing from abroad and channeled "hot money" flows to the public sector to cover the PSBR. In so doing, there were significant pressures to run *open positions* in the banking sector balance sheets (see Fig. 8.3). With the bonanza of foreign exchange, Turkish Lira appreciated (see Table 8.1) giving rise to current account deficits. These twin deficits (fiscal and external) were financed by external borrowing of the banking sector and the debt instruments of the public sector. This was a fragile environment and the bubble burst in 1994; when the interest rate rose to unprecedented levels and yet could not sustain the inflows of foreign capital as desired.

Thus, the episode was set with the completion of the ***triumvirate***; the foreign capital centers would be bringing in "hot money" to the domestic banking sector, which, in turn, was channeling these to the public sector. In the meantime, the rate of return on speculative financial arbitrage

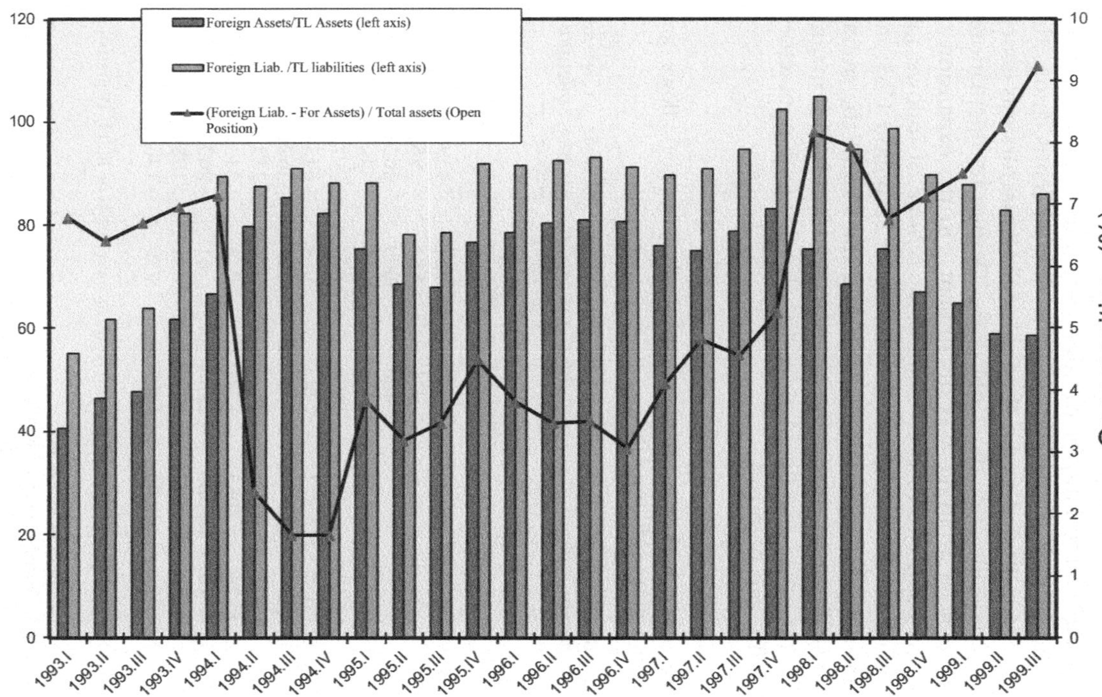


**Fig. 8.3** Assets, liabilities and open position of the banking sector (%) (*Data source* Annual reports of the Central Bank of the Republic of Turkey)

would reach to almost 30% just before and immediately after the 1994 crisis (see Table 8.2).

The instruments and consequences of this process are portrayed in Table 8.2. Measured as the ratio of the domestic interest rate (approximated by the rate of return on GDIs) to the rate of depreciation, the domestic rate of return offered to the "hot money" transactors was generally around 30% especially after the 1994 crisis. Despite its fluctuations, the size of the financial arbitrage was instrumental in the expansion of the banking sector's short-term borrowing. The *volume* of inflows and outflows of banking sector foreign credits reached 122 billion US$ and 118 billion US$, respectively, in 1993, exceeding the size of the overall GDP. Given the shallowness of the domestic financial sector, this magnitude, no doubt, meant severe fluctuations for the financial transactors, creating uncertainty and high risk.

**Table 8.2** Speculative short-term foreign capital (hot money) flows and selected financial indicators (Million US$)

| | *Domestic return on hot money*[a] | *Banking sector foreign credits* | | *Balance of payments net errors & omissions*[b] | *Short-term net capital movements*[b] | *Current account balance*[b] | *Currency substitution*[c] |
|---|---|---|---|---|---|---|---|
| | | *Inflow* | *Outflow* | | | | |
| 1988 | −0.073 | | | 515 | −2281 | 1596 | 27.0 |
| 1989 | 0.236 | | | 971 | −584 | 961 | 23.0 |
| 1990 | 0.293 | | | −468 | 3000 | −2625 | 22.5 |
| 1991 | −0.038 | 43,186 | 42,523 | 948 | −3020 | 250 | 29.5 |
| 1992 | 0.154 | 64,767 | 62,363 | −1190 | 1396 | −974 | 39.9 |
| 1993 | 0.045 | 122,053 | 118,271 | −2222 | 3054 | −6433 | 50.2 |
| 1994 | −0.315 | 75,439 | 82,040 | 1769 | −5127 | 2631 | 53.0 |
| 1995 | 0.197 | 76,427 | 75,626 | 2354 | 3713 | −2339 | 54.8 |
| 1996 | 0.329 | 8824 | 8055 | −1781 | 5945 | −2437 | 50.9 |
| 1997 | 0.278 | 19,110 | 18,386 | −2755 | 1761 | −2638 | 48.6 |
| 1998 | 0.254 | 19,288 | 19,225 | −1985 | 2601 | 1984 | 45.1 |
| 1999 | 0.298 | 122,673 | 120,603 | 1899 | 759 | −1364 | 45.2 |

[a] $[(1 + R)/(1 + E)-1]$; R: The highest interest rate in domestic financial markets; E: TL Depreciation Rate

[b] Including "luggage trade" from 1996 onwards

[c] Foreign Exchange Deposits/Total Deposits of Residents

*Data sources* Central Bank of the Republic of Turkey, Balance of Payments Balance Sheet Statistics; State Planning Organization, Main Economic Indicators

It should to be noted that one must consider the *gross* magnitudes of such flows rather than *net* amounts, because that is where the destabilizing consequences of speculative short-term capital movements prevail. In columns 2 and 3 of Table 8.2, the gross inflows and outflows of "hot money" to the domestic financial markets for the post-1990 period are reported. For the purposes of this chapter, "hot money" is identified as the foreign exchange credits brought by the banking system, so as to distinguish it from the net errors and emissions in the balance of payments statistics (which mostly account for the so-called "unrecorded" transactions).

The gross inflows grew rapidly from US $43 billion in 1991 to reach US $122 billion in 1993. After a brief deceleration during 1996 and 1998, they again reached US $122 billion in 1999. This magnitude was almost two-thirds of the size of the overall Turkish GNP. Clearly, the domestic financial system, under a severe pressure exerted by international speculative centers, was no longer in a position to conduct an independent monetary and foreign exchange policy. Furthermore, those centers constituted the major reason behind short-termism and volatility of the real business cycles, leading to increased fragility of the financial and the external position of the domestic economy and worsening of the distribution of income (Balkan & Yeldan, 1998, 2002; Yeldan, 2001). These issues are examined in more detail in the following section.

Thereby emerged a vicious circle: as the budget deficit expanded, the government had to issue GDIs with substantial returns on its securities, propelling the banking sector to bring in higher volumes of foreign credit so as to augment its indebtedness. The risk and uncertainty involved at the background, coupled with the widening trade deficit, resulted in even higher rates of interest for the government during the next round of the cycle.

The cycle was abruptly broken in 1994, when the sources of foreign finance dried up and Turkey experienced a *sudden stop*, perhaps the first of its kind in retrospect. The behavior of the real exchange rate turned out to be the dominant driver of macroeconomic adjustment (See Fig. 8.2).

The exchange rate was on a real depreciation trend over the 1980s. The strategy of export promotion necessitated a depreciating Turkish Lira. The success or failure of this choice left aside, the adjustments entailed by real depreciation implied contraction of wage incomes, as explained above. As also shared within the common history of late industrializers attempting to pursue an export-led industrialization strategy amidst a darkening external environment, Turkey's strategy of export promotion over the 1980s based on intensive currency depreciation failed. Lira depreciated in real terms by as much as 45% by mid-decade; and real wages were severely suppressed to generate a domestic surplus to be exported abroad (Yeldan, 1995). Suppression of wages were also the end result of the repressive conditions of the military regime through its dismantling of the trade unions and the changes imposed in the Labor Law, banning of the right to strike and restricting collective bargaining. Yet against all this, Turkish industry failed to pick up as a structural leader of expert-led growth, and Turkey entered the 1988 deceleration referred to as the *reform fatigue* (Yeldan, 2001).

By 1990, however, these dynamics changed. Ensuing capital liberalization caused the Lira to start to appreciate strongly. Given high gains of arbitrage, speculative foreign hot money flew in and gave rise to the trap of high interest rates and appreciating domestic currency (cheap foreign exchange) whose dynamics were discussed above. Figure 8.2 attests that, compared to 1988, the Lira enjoyed real appreciation by as much as 40%. The 1994 devaluation reversed the trend. After then, there emerged a brief episode of *stable real exchange rate*. At a time of very high inflation, the central bank was successful in maintaining the competitiveness of the Lira. It is clear from the Fig. 8.2 that, over 1995–1999, the real exchange rate was almost stable. This could be mentioned as a "successful" strategy on the part of the Central Bank, which at the time of significantly high rates of inflation, could nevertheless maintain a "competitive" exchange rate by aligning the nominal value of the spot exchange rate through a series of mini-devaluations and monetary accommodation.

The high risk element of these operations was, nevertheless, the banking sector. At a time of significant appreciation in early part of the decade, the banks' foreign exchange liabilities exceeded their foreign exchange assets, creating substantial "open positions." The risk contained in maintaining such high rates of open positions, reaching as much as 10% of total assets by the end of the period, began to take its toll from 1994 onward. Figure 8.3 portrays the magnitudes involved.

The distribution of the open positions across the banking sector revealed that, not surprisingly, the private deposit banks were the key actors of the operations. In 1993, just before the eruption of the financial crisis, the tensions were already setting in. As a ratio to "paid capital," banking sector's cumulative open position was already at its peak at 178%.

After a brief fall due to the 1994 crisis, the open positions were sustained at ratios approaching to 80% of paid capital, or to almost 20% of the GDP.

As such, new coalitions had been re-grouped throughout the period; the banking sector came to the forefront of financial speculation; and the main macroeconomic prices—rates of interest and foreign exchange—were restructured under a new set of equilibrium relationships. All this process generated severe repercussions for the real economy, and wage-labor bore the brunt of adjustments.

## IMF's Exchange-Rate-Based Disinflation Program and the 2001 Crisis

1998 turned out to be a crucial point in Turkey's recent macroeconomic history. By then, it was clear to the Turkish bourgeoisie and the state that the ongoing episode of *speculation-led patterns* of growth driven by hot money finances was on thin ice and was too risky. Maintained over conditions of almost hyperinflation at rates of 60–80%, and the ever deepening fiscal deficits of the government against the backdrop of GDI issuances carrying a real rate of interest exceeding 20%, it was clear that the Turkish macroeconomic structure was unstable and too risky. The public sector used to crowd out almost half of the private savings funds and the domestic economy turned into a bastion of financial speculation and arbitrage-led rent seeking.

In the meantime, the IMF itself was on the loss of severe credibility loss due to its "mis"-handling of the East Asian crisis that erupted in 1997. IMF's dogma on *austerity* at all expense, everywhere and under every condition, resulted in deepening of the 1997 crisis and meant severe deflation for the once-tigers of Asia. Thus, the IMF was in need of a "showcase" of successful stabilizer, and Turkey was a welcome agent to pursue an old idea about disinflation under an exchange-rate-based schedule, which had been pursued in Latin America and had failed. But this time, it was alleged, lessons were learned and Turkey's would be a totally new and indigenous strategy. The *Staff Monitoring Programme* (SMP) was initiated in 1998 to this end, and the IMF opened up a station in Ankara to follow the economy (in particular the government fiscal operations) more closely.

Thereby, a comprehensive disinflation program was enacted in July 1998 under the guidance of the IMF. The program administered under close supervision of the SMP aimed at improving the fiscal balances and reducing the long-lasting price inflation. However, the program could not have been put in full action due to the continued political uncertainty surrounding the general elections and two unfortunate earthquakes in 1999. As public expenditures continued to expand, fiscal balances deteriorated even further. Deficit-financing requirements exerted heavy pressures on the fragile domestic financial markets, giving rise to substantially high real interest rates. Finally, in December 1999, the government adopted another disinflation program, aiming at decreasing the inflation rate to single digits by the end of 2002. Aided by the supervision and technical support of the IMF, the new program relied on an *exchange-rate-based* disinflation program, coupled with monetary control through setting upper limits to the net domestic asset position of the Central Bank (CB). Accordingly, the CB committed itself to a policy of *no sterilization*, whereby changes in the monetary base would directly reflect changes in the net foreign assets of its balance sheet. The program further entailed a series of austerity measures on fiscal expenditures and set specific targets for the balance on the *primary budget*, that is, budget balance net of interest payments.

Main elements of this program is narrated extensively in the Turkish crisis literature. It was finally initiated in December 1999, by announcing a *Letter of Intent*. It was understood that it would cover a time horizon of three years, 2000 through the end of 2002. For the technical aspects of the program, the following paragraphs draw heavily on Yeldan (2002) and Ertuğrul and Yeldan (2003).

The program was based on three main components:

i. austerity in public expenditures subject to specific targets for non-interest fiscal surpluses;
ii. a pre-announced calendar for the rate of currency depreciation in line with the targeted rate of inflation; and,
iii. a monetary rule which subjected the liquidity generation mechanism to the net foreign asset position of the Central Bank (CB), thereby forcing the CB to act as a *semi-currency board*.

The program announced that the rate of currency depreciation would be set according to a pre-announced calendar, thereby fixing the *nominal values of an exchange rate basket* on *a daily basis* throughout the year. For this purpose, the CB declared an exchange rate basket consisting of 1 US$ + 0.77 Euro, and announced a daily calendar of depreciation rate which added up to a cumulative 20% by the end of 2000. The pre-announcement of exchange rate depreciation in accordance with such a *tablita* was regarded to be the backbone of the program in its attempt to break the inflationary inertia of three decades.

The idea of declaring an exchange rate basket and fixing its daily values throughout the year was not a new experiment, as indicated above. Similar programs were administered in Latin America in the 1980s under the name of *exchange rate-based disinflation*. The primary example was its implementation in Chile in 1981 through 1983. It generated a very high external deficit and collapsed with a series of onerous adjustments. Then, starting from 1991, it was also implemented in Argentina, under its *convertibility programme*. Argentina had initial success in bringing its inflation to an end, but after the second half of the 1990s, especially with Brazilian devaluation in 1998, it lost competitiveness very quickly due to its fixity of the exchange rate (at 1 US dollar exchanging for 1 Argentinian peso). The Argentinian economy collapsed along with Turkey in 2001.

What was allegedly unique in the Turkish program was the argument that it entailed *an exit strategy*. Accordingly, the exchange rate basket (the *daily tablita*) would be fixed only in the first 18 months of its initiation; and thereafter it would gradually be allowed to float within limits. The limits would be expanded at 6-month intervals to leave it to free float at the end of the stabilization plan horizon—31 December 2002. The details of this "exit strategy" is portrayed in Fig. 8.4.

As can be observed the exchange rate basket of "1$ + 0.77 Euro" was announced on a daily basis to generate a cumulative "depreciation" over 2000; and then would be granted partial floating within a band of 7.5% starting from June of 2001. This band would then be expanded at rates of additional 7.5% from end to end at every six months until 31 December 2002, after when the Lira would be under free float along with *an inflation targeting central bank* proper.

In order to sustain the *tablita* on exchange rate depreciation, the program further limited the CB's rule of monetary expansion only to *changes in its net foreign asset position* in its balance sheet. For this purpose, specific upper ceilings were set on the *net domestic assets* of the CB. More specifically, the CB's stock of net domestic assets was fixed at its December 1999 level. It was further announced that the CB would be allowed to change its net domestic asset position within a band of ±5% of the monetary base, to be revised at three-month intervals. To be able to

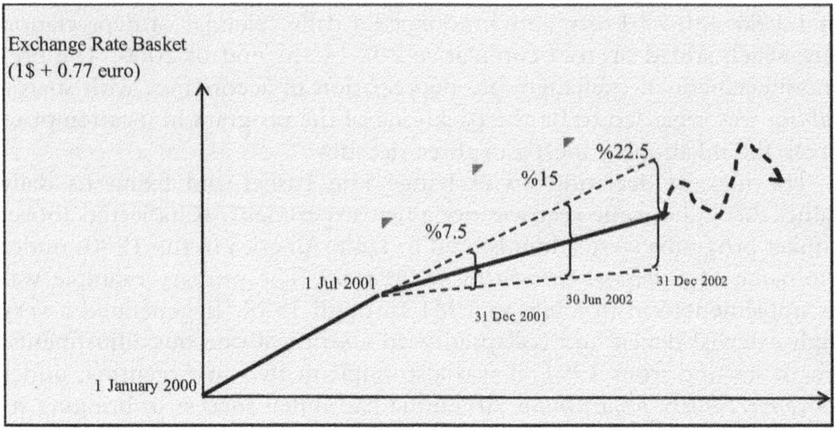


**Fig. 8.4** Path of the nominal exchange rate basket under the stabilization program, January 2000–December 2002 (*Data source* Central Bank of the Republic of Turkey)

meet the liquidity needs of the banking sector, the reserve requirement ratios were significantly lowered.

In order to evaluate the implications of this rule more clearly, one should observe that the CB balance sheet has the following operational identity:

$$Monetary\ Base = Net\ Foreign\ Assets + Net\ Domestic\ Assets$$

As a result of restrictions set on the upper ceiling of net domestic assets, the program limited monetary expansion only to increases in the stock of net foreign assets. This means that the CB would not be able to increase the stock of money supply by, for example, borrowing foreign exchange from the banking system or by using IMF's credit facility. Furthermore, since the CB was constrained in not to increase its domestic assets, this meant that it could not open any domestic credit neither to the public sector, nor to the private banks who were failing as a result of any liquidity shortage. The CB would be able to issue Turkish Lira and expand its monetary base only by purchasing foreign exchange from the banking sector in a manner where its foreign liabilities would not be increased.

Thus, according to this rule, the liquidity generation mechanism available to the CB practically meant a regime of *semi*-currency board in monetary operations. Within this mechanism monetary policy was restricted to the direction of foreign exchange flows, and as such, the most important element to sustain the liquidity needs of the economy depended upon the continuation of foreign credit available to the system.

These technical aspects of the program relied on the ***monetary approach to the balance of payments*** in its theoretical foundations. This approach was used by the IMF researchers in their country program modeling exercises for the determination of the liquidity generation mechanism and the resolution of the balance of payments equilibrium. This approach, which provides the underlying frame of reference in almost all IMF-style austerity programs, expects the real exchange rate to be in long-run equilibrium at its purchasing power parity level, and maintains that the domestic supply of money will be "endogenized" in a regime of open capital account. A simple portrayal of this theoretical apparatus is narrated in Fig. 8.5.

Accordingly, suppose that an initial equilibrium money supply is being generated in the money market at some "equilibrium" rate of interest, $R_0$. Suppose that (due to most probably attracted by the perfect foresight of the exchange rate values ahead, which eliminated all the depreciation risk) there is an inflow of foreign financial capital. Then the CB is not

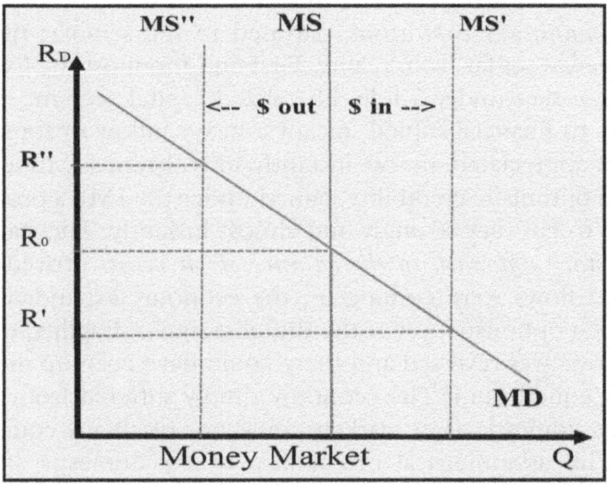


**Fig. 8.5** Theoretical expectations of the currency board operative

allowed to sterilize, and passes all this new inflow as monetary expansion. The Money supply shifts out to MS'. This means a reduction of the equilibrium interest rate to R'. If, on the other hand, there is an outflow of foreign capital, then the CB allows the money supply to shrink, the money supply shifts to the left MS'' to yield a higher rate of interest at R''.

Thus, it was expected that the liquidity available in the domestic economy would be managed directly by interest rate signals in *smoothly* operating financial markets: rising domestic interest rates would invite foreign inflows allowing for monetary expansion. Excess liquidity, in turn, would be signaled through lower rates of interest, letting foreign capital outflows to balance once again the equilibrium level of liquidity in the domestic money market. The market, through its free operations is expected to deliver an "optimal" interest rate domestically. This optimal interest rate was to be conditioned by the movement of the exchange rate basket under the daily scheme and would converge to the depreciation envisaged –20% for the first year. The theoretical expectation was that when both the exchange rate and the rate of interest would be falling in a controlled manner, this process would force the domestic inflation on prices to stabilize. After three years of experience, the program would end, given its *exit strategy*.

The Turkish bureaucracy was, in dramatic words, bewildered. These models of *imaginary capitalism*, narrated in the seminar rooms of the IMF, however, were far from reality. First and foremost, by fixing the rate of exchange basket under a fully liberalized capital account that granted full mobility to financial capital, meant a heavy inflow of foreign finance. Turkish Lira appreciated almost instantly in real terms. Monetary expansion and the optimistic credibility gained under the IMF's protégé led the interest rate to fall very strongly and almost instantly. The stability aspect of the *monetary approach to the balance of payments* proved to be only one-sided: as flows were coming in, the economy expanded and everything has been optimistic; yet at the slightest sign of fragility, the direction of foreign flows was reversed and there could have been no mechanism to reach a new equilibrium. The economy simply suffered from severe illiquidity, as the domestic asset markets could not reach any equilibrium and collapsed. This asymmetrical mechanism of the domestic asset markets was clearly the result of shallow and fragile nature of the asset markets, and the deregulated financial deepening.

The fall in the interest rate and the real appreciation of the Turkish Lira were welcomed vehemently. Consumption and investment expenditures, led by cheapening imports, exploded. Current-account deficit widened to an unprecedented 4.8% against the GDP, and there occurred a heavy short-term foreign indebtedness. Against all this, Ertuğrul and Yeldan (2003: 8) vividly comment that:

> Given these structural conditions, the program should have envisaged the destructive effects of such a possible liquidity squeeze on the interest rates and on the fiscal balance. The Central Bank was deprived of all of its traditional tools of austerity and crisis management and was left defenseless against possible "speculative attacks" and "sudden stops." Under these conditions, it is no surprise that the viability of the program would finally suffer when the "uneasy speculators" shift focus and decide to reverse their flows, leaving the incipient country illiquid and dried out.

It has to be underlined that the CB had, in fact, successfully administered its role as the "currency board," supplying domestic money in response to changes in its foreign-asset position. Figure 8.6 portrays the evolution of this mechanism during the first 10 months, just before the eruption of the first turbulence in late November 2000. The figure discloses the paths of the monetary base, open market operations (OMOs), net foreign assets (NFA), and net domestic assets (NDA) of the CB, as measured by the end-of-week observations, between January 7 and December 1, 2000. As seen in the figure, the CB successfully expanded its monetary base mostly due to the rise in foreign inflows over the course of the program.

Thus, the basic message that emerges from the data disclosed in Fig. 8.6 is clear: Turkish monetary authorities *successfully* implemented the monetary program within the given targets, conditioning the CB operations to net foreign inflows. In this sense, the outbreak of the November 2000 crisis and the ultimate collapse of the program in February 2001 cannot be attributed to any divergence from monetary targets. Quite the contrary, the culminating financial chaos can only be understood within the realm of the successful implementation of both the exchange rate (basket) depreciation targets and the liquidity generation mechanism as followed by the CB—mimicking a currency board.

In fact, the unavoidable appreciation of the domestic currency, accompanied by the explosion of foreign capital inflows, was already in progress,

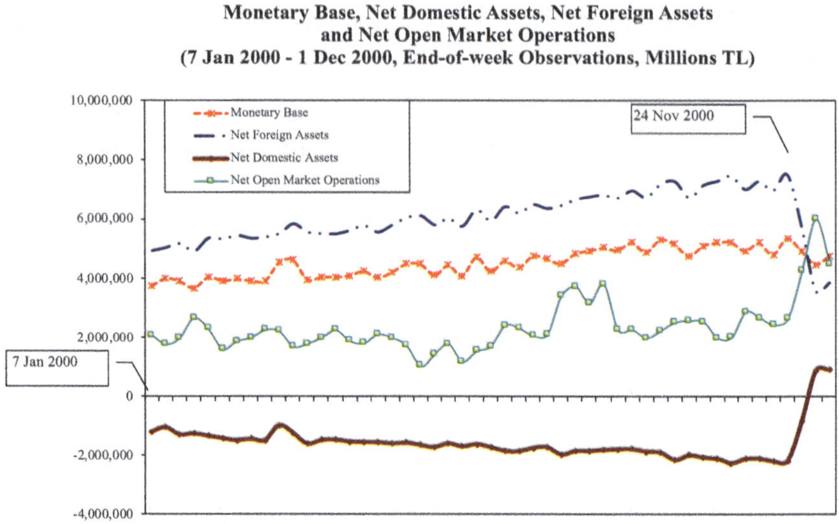


**Fig. 8.6** Monetary base, net domestic assets, net foreign assets and net open market operations, 7 January 2000–1 December 2000, end-of-week observations, million Turkish Liras (*Data source* Balance sheet reports of the Central Bank of the Republic of Turkey)

deepening the financial fragility of the domestic economy. A very strong upturn in domestic absorption (accompanied by the appreciation of the Turkish Lira) and the impact of the Customs Union with the EU were the two major reasons behind the rapid expansion of the current-account deficit that reached 9.5 billion US dollars by the end of 2000. This outcome was solely due to the deterioration of the trade balance.

Under these conditions, the economy suffered from yet another financial crisis in February of 2001. These events led to an acute liquidity crisis and the consequent demise of the disinflation program. Turkish Lira was forced to get off the "fixed anchor" and started to free float on 22 February. The exchange rate, as measured by TL/US$, depreciated by 47.7% in six weeks. The crisis conditions spread to the real economy with massive lay-offs and increased social unrest. Once again, the bust phase of the financial cycle struck the Turkish economy after an interval of only two years.

The reform saga of Turkey would continue with the continuation of the IMF directives, then to be pursued with the newly appointed Minister Mr. Kemal Derviş from the World Bank, along with the introduction of a "new" *Transition to Strong Economy Program* in the hasty rhetoric of "fifteen laws to be enacted in fifteen days." This program is examined and discussed in the next chapter of this volume.

## Concluding Comments

The 1990s were a period of "lost decade"—yet for whom? Clearly, the unregulated and under-supervised banking system was unleashed to gain "speculative rents," while the brunt of adjustments fell on the wage-labor. The rise of "financial rent" took a significant toll of the distribution of aggregate income. Financialization was carried out through the massive borrowing requirements of the public sector, which was strapped into a vicious cycle of "borrowing – high interest costs – re-borrowing." This cycle could sustain itself until the contagion of the Asian crisis and would lead to one of the most peculiar experiments in the history of monetary economics—the IMF-led exchange-rate-based disinflation program that was initiated in December 1999. In the words of Balkan and Yeldan (2002: 51):

> The post-1989 experience shows the serious problems confronting a developing economy that moves into full external and internal deregulation of its financial system under conditions of high inflation. The specter of capital flight became the dominant motive in policymaking and created unsustainable commitment to high real interest rates and expectations for cheap foreign exchange. Meanwhile links between the financial sector and the real sector have been severed. Instability in the rates of interest and foreign exchange created feedbacks which led the economy further into instability.

Turkey's post-1989 experience also shows how a "peripheral economy," trapped within conditionalities of *neoliberal restructuring*, lost instruments of an indigenous development strategy and was strangulated under the caprices of global finance capital, dictating a speculation-led growth with premature deindustrialization. This new form of conditionality meant the restructuring of traditional forms of *dependency*, based on an international division of labor pushing the underdeveloped world toward becoming producers of primary/agricultural goods and raw materials, and consumers of manufacturing durables under a regime of "embedded liberalism." This global division of labor had reached its limits in the 1970s, as technologies in the developed economies matured and industrial profits started to fall (given the unwarranted rise of the organic composition of capital).

"*End the financial repression*" was the battle cry of global capitalism. Financial flows were liberalized, new instruments of finance were created globally within, what Susan Strange termed, *casino capitalism*, and manufacturing industries moved off to the new sweatshops of the globe. An unstoppable race to the bottom was started as the underdeveloped nations were one by one stripped off their domestic savings and were pushed into an ever-expanding list by way of which globalization dictated them to privatize, liberalize, deregulate, and adopt flexible norms of labor employment.

As part of an ideological brainwash, the less-developed countries began to be termed as "new emerging markets" or "emerging economies," and concepts such as "development," "industrialization," "working classes" or "bourgeoisie" came to be replaced with a new jargon comprising terms like "austerity," "financialization" and "market players." The "new emerging markets" were, in turn, conditioned to a deflationary path where their macroeconomic policies were restricted to a balanced budget, entrenched fiscal expenditures, and a relatively contractionary monetary policy with an *ex ante* commitment to high real interest rates. While this new episode of *financial dependency* replaced the traditional forms of industrial/agrarian duality, dynamics of capitalism were in operation and the global economy was making headway onto the 2008–2009 crisis.

## Note

1. The *tablita*, meaning "little table," was the term coined to refer to the schedule of exchange rate fixity over the calendar year, given the exchange-rate based disinflation programs that were administered in Chile (1981–1983) and Argentina (1990–2001). The schedule gave a perfect foresight for the path of the *nominal* spot value of the market exchange rate and gave clear incentives for tradables to expand. The expectation was that, through "fixing" the market value of the rate of exchange, inertial dynamics of inflation would also be put under control.

## References

Adelman, I., & Yeldan, E. (2000). Is this the end of economic development? *Structural Change and Economic Dynamics, 11*, 95–109.

Akyuz, Y. (1990). Financial system and policies in Turkey in the 1980's. In Aricanli & Rodrik (Eds.), *The political economy of Turkey*. Macmillan.

Akyuz, Y. (2003). *The developing countries and world trade. Performance and prospects*. ZED Books.

Akyuz, Y., Flassback, H., & Kozul-Wright, R. (2008). Globalization, inequality and the labour market. In A. Kose, F. Senses, & E. Yeldan (Eds.), *Neoliberal globalization as new imperialism: Case studies on reconstruction of the periphery*. NOVA Science.

Balkan, E., & Yeldan, A. E. (2002). Peripheral development under financial liberalization: The Turkish experience. In Balkan, N. & Savran, S. (Eds.), *The ravages of neo-liberalism: Economy, society and gender in Turkey*. Nova Science Pub.

Balkan, E., & Yeldan, E. (1998). Financial liberalization in developing countries: The Turkish experience. In Medhora & Fanelli (Eds.), *Financial liberalization in developing countries*. Macmillan.

Boratav, K., & Yeldan, A. E. (2006). Turkey, 1980–2000: Financial liberalization, macroeconomic (in)-stability, and patterns of distribution. In L. Taylor (Ed.), *External liberalization in Asia, post-socialist Europe and Brazil* (Ch. 14, pp. 417–455). Oxford University Press.

Calvo, G., & Vegh, C. A. (1999). Inflation stabilization and BOP crises in developing countries. In J. Taylor & M. Woodford (Eds.), *Handbook of macroeconomics* (pp. 1531–1614). North Holland.

Diaz-Alejandro, C. F. (1985, February). Good-bye financial repression, hello financial crash. *Journal of Development Economics, 19*(1–2), 1–24.

Dornbsuch, R., Godfajn, I., & Valdés, R. (1995, June). Currency crises and collapses. *Brookings Papers on Economic Activity, 2*, 219–270.

Duménil, G., & Lévy, D. (2004). Neoliberal dynamics: A new phase? In K. van der Pijl, L. Assassi, & D. Wigan (Eds.), *Global regulation. Managing crises after the imperial turn*. Palgrave Macmillan.

Epstein, G. (Ed.). (2005). *Financialization and the global economy*. Edward Elgar Press.

Epstein, G., & Yeldan, E. (2008). Inflation targeting, employment creation and economic development: Assessing the impacts and policy alternatives. *International Review of Applied Economics, 22*(2), 131–144.

Ertuğrul, A. & Yeldan, A. E. (2003). On the structural weaknesses of the post-1999 Turkish disinflation program. In Z. Onis & B. Rubin (Eds.), *The Turkish economy in crisis* (pp. 53–66). Frank Cass.

Harvey, D. (1989). *The condition of postmodernity*. Blackwell Pub. https://doi.org/10.4135/9781446213742.n14.

Köse, A., Senses, F., & Yeldan, E. (2007). *Neoliberal globalization as new imperialism: Case studies on reconstruction of the periphery*. Nova Science Press.
Krippner. (2006). The financialization of the American economy. *Socio-Economic Review, 3*, 173–208.
McKinnon, R. (1973). *Money and capital in economic development*. Brookings Institution.
Orhangazi, Ö. (2008) *Financialization and the US economy*. Edward-Elgar Publications.
Shaw, E. S. (1973). *Financial deepening in economic development*. Oxford University Press.
Taylor, L. (1998). *Lax public sector, destabilizing private sector: Origins of capital market crises*. Center for Policy Analysis, New School for Social Research, Working Paper Series III No 6 July.
Yeldan, A. E. (1995, June). Surplus creation and extraction under structural adjustment: Turkey, 1980–1992. *Review of Radical Political Economics, 27*(2), 38–72.
Yeldan, A. E. (2001). *Küreselleşme Sürecinde Türkiye Ekonomisi: Bölüşüm. Birikim. Büyüme*. Iletişim.
Yeldan, A. E. (2002). On the IMF-directed disinflation program in Turkey: A program for stabilization and austerity or a recipe for impoverishment and financial chaos? In N. Balkan & S. Savran (Eds.), *The ravages of neo-liberalism: Economy, society and gender in Turkey*. Nova Science Pub.

CHAPTER 9

# From Domestic to Global Crisis: Turkey During the 2001–2009 Period

*Erol Taymaz and Ebru Voyvoda*

## Introduction

As elaborated in the previous chapter, Turkey's "lost decade," the 1990s, was marked by volatile growth, macroeconomic instability and political disorder. The subsequent decade, encompassing the post-2001 crisis adjustments, provided the Turkish economy with apparently momentous opportunities to achieve structural transformation for "catch-up." The recovery from the 2001 crisis, the severest downturn of the economy in the history of the country, was sharp and solid. High and chronic inflation was finally curbed thanks to the inflation-targeting regime adopted firmly by the central bank, whose "independence" was enacted after the

E. Taymaz (✉) · E. Voyvoda
Middle East Technical University (METU), Ankara, Turkey
e-mail: etaymaz@metu.edu.tr

E. Voyvoda
e-mail: voyvoda@metu.edu.tr



E. Özçelik and Y. Özdemir (eds.), *Political Economy of Development in Turkey*, The Political Economy of the Middle East,
https://doi.org/10.1007/978-981-16-7318-4_9

crisis. Evidently, "unsustainable" public debt, amassed during the 1990s, which had substantially constrained the macroeconomic policy space and hampered capital accumulation, was also reduced to manageable levels under strict fiscal austerity.

As an exemplar of the conventional postulate, according to which crises play crucial roles in re-structuring economic, political, and institutional orientations, the 2001 crisis undoubtedly transformed the policymaking environment in Turkey. On the political front, the crisis swept the parties that formed the coalition government since May 1999 below the 10% election threshold. Starting with the elections of November 2002, the "stable" governments formed by the Justice and Development Party (JDP, *Adalet ve Kalkınma Partisi*) were widely supported nationally and internationally, as it promised change for putting an end to the chaotic dynamics generated by the coalition governments of the 1990s. The post-crisis adjustment program of the coalition government, launched in May 2001, was designed by the heavy involvement of the World Bank and the International Monetary Fund (IMF). Besides, the support of the US to Turkey as a "strategic ally" in the Middle East in the aftermath of the 9/11 attacks, along with the anchor provided by the European Union (EU) for democratization, constituted the main pillars of international sponsorship to the JDP governments during the 2002–2009 period. The Copenhagen and Maastricht criteria of the EU were additionally instrumental in Turkey's implementation of policies that would lead to important yet impermanent transformations in the political-economic, institutional, legal and social spheres (Öniş & Şenses, 2007).

The post-2001 era of the Turkish economy has constituted the "second phase of neoliberal restructuring" in accordance with the key principles of the "Post-Washington Consensus." Ensuring "good governance" through autonomous market-regulating institutions (such as the ones in banking, finance and energy sectors), promoting consumer protection and succeeding in maintaining pro-competition policies through "politics-free" regulations were then acknowledged to be necessary for sustained and equitable growth. In juxtaposition to the policies of the original "Washington Consensus," which defied active involvement of the state in the economy, the Post-Washington Consensus recognized the state as a broader political-economic institution that should have assumed an important and complementary role to deliver appropriate regulations, along with social protection and welfare to some extent (Bakır & Öniş, 2010; Burki & Perry, 1998; Stiglitz, 2005; Öniş & Şenses, 2007).

In effect, Turkey's seemingly fully-fledged restructuring endeavor took place in an international environment where ample global liquidity was directed toward developing countries that offered relatively higher yields, especially for speculative financial capital. High real interest rates under the inflation-targeting monetary regime and large privatization programs were conducive to attracting both voluminous short-term capital inflows and significant levels of inward foreign direct investment (FDI) so as to support the dominantly domestic demand-led growth. Thus, it was rather easy for the JDP governments to receive also the support of various domestic actors, comprising not only export-oriented big corporations integrated with the global, and especially European production networks and the bureaucratic elites of the new regulatory agencies, but also small- and medium-sized enterprises and households that would benefit from the domestic credit boom fueling private investment and private consumption.

Yet, toward the end of the decade and in the aftermath of the 2008–2009 global financial crisis, it has become clear that, failing to fulfill the requirements of social, institutional, and economic transformations, Turkey's performance has turned out to be bleak in terms of re-structuring toward inclusive and sustained growth. In this chapter, we analyze the main characteristics of the re-structuring efforts in the post-2001 period, along with the "new" modes of integration of the Turkish economy to the global markets. In the next section, we present an overview of the global shifts that had profound effects on the developing economies. After that overview, we turn to the reflections of the global environment on Turkey's domestic restructuring and tensions of primary distribution. Next, main components of the macroeconomic and international environment are analyzed to frame the dynamics of economic growth in Turkey during this period. The last section concludes concisely.

## Global Economy at the Dawn of the New Millennium

### *The Global Background: The Bust Cycle of 1998–2001*

It seemed that the global economy, toward the turn of the millennium in 1999, had already left the hectic 1997/1998 conditions behind. The devastating impacts of the financial crises in East Asia (1997), Russia (1998) and Brazil (1999) seemed to have ended, along with the waning of repercussions on the rest of the developing economies (especially the ones integrated to Asian trade networks and those dependent on large inflows of foreign capital). Developing countries as a whole, but especially those in these regions showed strong recovery in output growth thanks to the revival of exports resulting from the solid manufacturing base (along with home-currency depreciation) in East Asia and the rising commodity prices in the case of Russia (UNCTAD, 2001).

The major stimulus to put the developing economies back on favorable growth tracks in this period came from the developed world, and dominantly from the US. The US economy, which recorded relatively stable output growth rates in the second half of the 1990s, also acted as a major source of demand for the exports of the recovering developing countries. Such a growth pattern was fed by several domestic and international factors, which then also caused the accumulated risks and the inevitable halt to gain global dimensions. The rise of the new high-tech sectors, especially bolstered via massive investments in information and communication technologies (ICT), provided spill-over effects to the rest of the US economy. Rising stock prices, mainly in these high-tech sectors, along with relatively low interest rates, provided the basis for increased private demand for investment and consumption. Flow of capital into the US economy in the aftermath of the severe financial crises in the developing countries, and the rising demand for US assets by the current-account surplus economies of recovering Asia and China led to the appreciation of the US Dollar and stimulated import demand. Soaring demand for US assets contributed massively to rising asset prices, and also increased capital gains and elevated private spending. Thus, the US economy was able to grow at the higher-than-potential rate of 3.9%, while the unemployment rate was reduced down to 4.0% in 1999 (Gordon, 2003; Kraay & Ventura, 2005).

Yet, such attributes of the growth pattern that caused the US economy to become the major source of global demand also led to the accumulation and expansion of severe imbalances and fragilities; not only for the US economy but also for the global economy as a whole, under the conditions of globalization and increased interdependencies via the intensification of "real" and "financial" networks (UNCTAD, 2000). The capital flows heading back to the US economy led to the appreciation of the US dollar, increasing import demand and widening the current account deficit (See Table 9.1). Such inflows also fed credit expansion and acceleration in asset prices, especially the bubble in the

**Table 9.1** GDP Growth Rate, Current Account Balance and the Real Effective Exchange Rate, 1999–2009

| | *1999* | *2000* | *2001* | *2002* | *2003* | *2004* | *2005* | *2006* | *2007* | *2008* | *2009* |
|---|---|---|---|---|---|---|---|---|---|---|---|
| **GDP growth (%, based on 2015 USD)** | | | | | | | | | | | |
| **WORLD** | *3.5* | *4.4* | *2.1* | *2.3* | *3.1* | *4.5* | *4.1* | *4.5* | *4.4* | *2.0* | *−1.3* |
| **Developing economies** | **3.7** | **5.6** | **3.2** | **4.3** | **5.6** | 7.7 | 7.1 | 7.9 | **8.3** | **5.6** | **3.3** |
| Africa | 2.7 | 3.7 | 4.2 | 5.4 | 5.3 | 5.9 | 6.2 | 5.9 | 6.1 | 6.1 | 3.8 |
| Latin America and the Caribbean | −0.1 | 3.5 | 0.5 | −0.4 | 2.0 | 6.3 | 4.7 | 5.6 | 5.8 | 4.0 | −2.2 |
| Asia | 3.6 | 5.6 | 3.0 | 4.2 | 5.4 | 6.7 | 6.3 | 6.9 | 7.5 | 4.4 | 2.6 |
| Eastern Asia | 3.7 | 5.5 | 3.5 | 4.4 | 5.1 | 6.0 | 6.2 | 7.0 | 8.1 | 4.6 | 2.9 |
| Transition economies | 5.4 | 9.2 | 5.9 | 5.2 | 7.4 | 7.8 | 6.8 | 8.6 | 8.8 | 5.4 | −6.1 |
| China | 7.7 | 8.5 | 8.3 | 9.1 | 10.0 | 10.1 | 11.4 | 12.7 | 14.2 | 9.7 | 9.4 |
| Turkey | −3.4 | 6.6 | −6.0 | 6.4 | 5.6 | 9.6 | 9.0 | 7.1 | 5.0 | 0.8 | −4.7 |
| **Developed economies** | **3.4** | **3.8** | **1.6** | **1.4** | **2.0** | **3.1** | **2.7** | **2.9** | **2.4** | **0.1** | **−3.4** |
| USA | 4.8 | 4.1 | 1.0 | 1.7 | 2.8 | 3.8 | 3.5 | 2.8 | 1.9 | −0.1 | −2.5 |
| EU-15 | 3.1 | 3.8 | 2.3 | 1.2 | 1.1 | 2.3 | 1.9 | 3.1 | 2.8 | 0.2 | −4.4 |
| **Current Account (billion USD)** | | | | | | | | | | | |
| **WORLD** | *−124.2* | *−160.0* | *−186.1* | *−138.5* | *−81.7* | *8.5* | *30.2* | *179.2* | *238.7* | *89.2* | *206.7* |
| **Developing economies** | **45.4** | **99.1** | **76.1** | **136.9** | **228.6** | **295.6** | **459.4** | **679.5** | **778.8** | **769.4** | **405.1** |
| Africa | −12.0 | 16.7 | 6.1 | 1.3 | 13.0 | 25.2 | 64.0 | 80.3 | 66.4 | 57.9 | −30.6 |
| Latin America and the Caribbean | −56.9 | −49.1 | −54.2 | −17.9 | 7.7 | 21.0 | 32.6 | 48.7 | 7.2 | −43.2 | −32.7 |
| Asia | 114.3 | 131.3 | 124.1 | 153.7 | 208.0 | 249.6 | 362.6 | 550.8 | 705.8 | 754.8 | 469.3 |
| Eastern Asia | 175.6 | 177.8 | 134.4 | 189.3 | 241.9 | 317.9 | 354.2 | 458.9 | 639.1 | 624.8 | 489.5 |
| Transition economies | 20.8 | 46.1 | 29.6 | 25.6 | 29.5 | 59.8 | 84.2 | 91.5 | 53.7 | 89.0 | 34.6 |
| China | 21.1 | 20.5 | 17.4 | 35.4 | 43.1 | 68.9 | 132.4 | 231.8 | 353.2 | 420.6 | 243.3 |

(continued)

**Table 9.1** (continued)

| | *1999* | *2000* | *2001* | *2002* | *2003* | *2004* | *2005* | *2006* | *2007* | *2008* | *2009* |
|---|---|---|---|---|---|---|---|---|---|---|---|
| Turkey | −0.9 | −9.9 | 3.8 | −0.6 | −7.6 | −14.2 | −21.0 | −31.2 | −36.9 | −39.4 | −11.4 |
| **Developed economies** | **−190.5** | **−305.2** | **−291.8** | **−301.0** | **−339.8** | **−346.9** | **−513.4** | **−591.9** | **−593.8** | **−769.2** | **−233.0** |
| USA | −286.6 | −401.9 | −394.1 | −456.1 | −522.3 | −635.9 | −749.2 | −816.6 | −736.6 | −696.5 | −379.7 |
| EU-15 | −2.6 | −67.1 | −19.7 | 24.0 | 21.7 | 87.5 | 37.6 | 30.9 | 3.3 | −119.0 | 43.8 |
| **Real Effective Exchange Rate (1999:100)** | | | | | | | | | | | |
| **WORLD** | | | | | | | | | | | |
| **Developing economies** | **100.0** | **105.0** | **104.3** | **101.9** | **94.4** | **93.6** | **99.3** | **104.5** | **108.2** | **111.0** | **106.6** |
| Africa | 100.0 | 104.2 | 99.1 | 92.4 | 94.4 | 100.7 | 107.1 | 112.0 | 112.4 | 116.0 | 108.5 |
| Latin America and the Caribbean | 100.0 | 108.0 | 110.2 | 103.9 | 95.0 | 96.4 | 106.0 | 112.3 | 116.5 | 121.5 | 114.3 |
| Asia | 100.0 | 103.8 | 102.9 | 102.5 | 95.1 | 92.9 | 96.4 | 100.5 | 103.8 | 105.4 | 102.7 |
| Eastern Asia | 100.0 | 102.3 | 101.5 | 100.4 | 93.6 | 90.1 | 90.8 | 91.2 | 91.3 | 89.9 | 91.2 |
| Transition economies | 100.0 | 104.6 | 107.8 | 106.5 | 106.2 | 121.3 | 140.4 | 162.5 | 175.8 | 194.9 | 165.7 |
| China | 100.0 | 103.2 | 109.4 | 110.2 | 108.2 | 109.0 | 110.7 | 114.5 | 121.5 | 135.6 | 141.5 |
| Turkey | 100.0 | 108.5 | 96.6 | 109.5 | 121.6 | 125.4 | 134.8 | 131.8 | 136.8 | 140.4 | 133.5 |
| **Developed economies** | **100.0** | **94.7** | **95.1** | **98.5** | **105.9** | **104.6** | **97.0** | **91.1** | **87.7** | **84.6** | **89.4** |
| USA | 100.0 | 101.5 | 106.9 | 107.7 | 96.3 | 94.9 | 102.4 | 89.0 | 84.0 | 80.2 | 86.5 |
| EU-15 | 100.0 | 88.9 | 89.0 | 94.4 | 105.8 | 108.0 | 101.5 | 98.5 | 99.6 | 96.1 | 96.4 |

*Source* UNCTADStat, https://unctadstat.unctad.org. *Note* An upward movement of the REER *represents* appreciation and a ***downward movement represents depreciation of the domestic currency*** high-tech sectors of the economy, thereby creating financial gains to boost private investment and consumption. Thus, while the US economy became the dominant source of global growth, it also spread the possible consequences of such imbalances to other developed[1] and developing economies.

With the purpose of cooling down the economy and containing the over-accumulated risks in the financial markets, the Federal Reserve (Fed), the central bank of the US, started to raise the interest rate in June 1999 and continued to do so until mid-2000. The pace of output growth reduced sharply, leading to the surfacing of the imbalances and the realization of accumulated risks. The ICT sector led the sharp fall in asset prices via the burst of the "dot.com" bubble.[2] Reversal of expectations; accelerated falls in consumer confidence, consumer wealth and private consumption spending; and the sharp decline in private investment were all indicators of significantly falling growth rates in the second half of 2000 and in 2001. The sluggish growth in the US economy unfolded rapidly to other developed and developing economies through real and financial channels. The exacerbated geopolitical uncertainties following the September 11 attacks in 2001 contributed further to the spread of the slowdown (UNCTAD, 2002).

### *The Dusk in the Making: The Boom Cycle of 2002–2007*

The beginning of the new millennium was, thus, marked by a slowdown of the global economy, mainly induced by global interdependencies, increased financial openness, expansion of credit markets, inflation of asset prices, and self-fulfilling expectations. Yet, both the dynamics leading to the slowdown in the center of the capitalist system and the subsequent policy responses would also pave the way for another "boom and bust" cycle that culminated in the "global financial crisis" of 2008–2009. Increased interdependencies during this period, through real and financial channels, produced and spread common shocks, adversely affecting the growth patterns, and restricted the policy space for the developing world as a whole. However, the Turkish economy during both the bust (1998–2001) and the boom (2002–2007) cycles stood out as one of the few countries in the periphery to exhibit additional structural vulnerabilities.

By the current- and capital-account liberalization moves throughout the 1980s, Turkey turned out to be one of the early adopters of the neoliberal policy framework. Yet, following the decade of external liberalization policies and integration with the global economy, deep boom and bust cycles of the 1990s clearly demonstrated the constraints of a "fully" open developing economy. With the suppression of the government's space in conducting independent monetary and exchange rate policies, the Turkish economy became substantially exposed to speculative short-term capital movements. Such cycles of "speculation-led" growth trapped the economy with high real interest rates and an overvalued domestic currency, leading eventually to serious balance-of-payments difficulties (Boratav, 2018; Cizre & Yeldan, 2005; Onaran, 2006). Along with the escalation of the public debt and government solvency issues, ever-increasing vulnerability to external shocks and contagion effects of international financial crises eventually surfaced in the crises of 1994, 1999 and 2001. Thus, large swings of capital movements from developing countries to the "center" in the 1998–2001 period and the "correction" of the global imbalances from 2001 onward created additional instability for the Turkish economy.[3]

Sharp devaluation of Turkish lira in 2001, associated with a sizeable flight of foreign capital, led to the severe contraction of the economy, escalating unemployment and soaring inflation rates. Yet, the post-crisis adjustment, introduced as "Turkey's Program for Transition to a Strong Economy" (TPTSE), relied mainly on attaining the "proper mix of stabilization measures" to reinvigorate the confidence and flow of international financial capital. The TPTSE entailed drastic cuts in public spending, monetary contraction and transition to a flexible exchange rate system, along with substantial reductions in public employment and wages (The next section elaborates on TPTSE in detail). Therefore, relatively high interest rates were instrumental not only in bringing the inflation rate down, but also in attracting a decent portion of the increased global liquidity during the 2002–2007 period. Turkish lira then started to appreciate, rendering Turkey one of the few developing countries to give sizable current account deficits (See Table 9.1). Thus, the high-growth period of 2002–2007 was dominantly financed by foreign-capital inflows. However, at a time of increased global liquidity and augmented global demand for (manufacturing) exports, Turkish economy was deprived of the much needed competitive exchange rate. Consequently, Turkey missed the opportunity to take steps to restructure its economy (and manufacturing industry in particular), whereas the burden of the subsequent adjustment toward a competitive real exchange rate mainly fell on the wage-earners through reductions in real wages (Orhangazi, 2019; Voyvoda, 2020).

The post-recovery process in the US involved the Fed's reduction of interest rates, tax cuts on the fiscal-policy front and increased military expenditures due to the wars in Afghanistan and Iraq. The lower interest rates also led to lower mortgage rates for households, causing the construction sector to grow rather rapidly. On the other hand, Europe recovered more slowly under the conditions of the "Stability and Growth Pact" and tight monetary policy. It was only in 2003 (and after a period of continuous appreciation of the Euro) that the European Central Bank (ECB) joined the policy of lowering interest rates. Yet, Europe and Japan, the other two centers of the developed world, mostly failed to accompany the US in increasing domestic demand enough to stimulate growth in the global economy. Such a holdback from the "other" developed regions was considered a "missed" opportunity to contain the accumulation of the global imbalances during the 2002–2007 period (UNCTAD, 2008). The US economy in the post-2001 period once again turned out to be the main source of global demand and growth. While monetary and fiscal policies, along with interest rate differentials, were instrumental in shaping the growth patterns of the developing countries, the exchange rate movements were closely concomitant with large flows of global liquidity.

Trying to avoid currency appreciations in the post-1997 period, Asian countries, particularly East Asian ones, were able to maintain competitive exchange rates (See Table 9.1), and became the new centers of "industrialization" and main exporters of manufactured goods to the US and the rest of the global economy. The increased demand by the manufacturing exporters for raw materials and primary commodities created a global setting characterized by rising trade volumes and stronger revenues for commodity and oil exporters. Trade and production networks especially in Asia brought about dynamism in global markets and accelerated global growth. The growth rate of developing countries as a whole hit the record high of 7.7% in 2004 and remained around 8.0% until 2008. Per-capita GDP in developing countries increased by almost 30.0% between 2003 and 2007 (UNCTAD, 2007).

As of 2007, the current account surplus of the developing economies increased to around 780 billion US dollars, with East Asia accounting for 82.0% and China alone for 45.4%. On the deficit side, the US alone recorded a negative 736.6 billion dollars (See Table 9.1). Such levels of global imbalances in the second half of the decade were indicative of the extent of accumulated risks and fragilities, which eventually led to the global financial crisis of 2008–2009.

Developed economies, and particularly the US, became major exporters of assets during the 2002–2007 period, as the foreign-exchange reserves accumulated through the current account surpluses of developing countries and oil exporters generated a large demand for financial assets in the "safe centers" of the world economy. Massive inflow of capital, leading to easy access to credit, asset price bubbles and opportunities for speculative activities and gains crafted a financial environment where private consumption continued to increase at relatively high rates in the US.

With the collapse of the sub-prime mortgage market, however, the fragility of the financial system was quickly exposed. Complexity of the financial institutions and markets, which shaded the risks and fragilities involved, also added to the collapse and the spread of the chaos, notably in the US, but also at the global level due to the vastly integrated international environment. The near-collapse of the financial sector in the US led to a major credit crunch, which affected the real economy through accelerated reductions in production activities and private consumption. The spread of the crisis to the developing economies worked through various channels, such as trade, foreign asset positions, capital outflows and overly-financialized markets for primary commodities (Eichengreen, 2010; Griffith-Jones & Ocampo, 2009; UNCTAD, 2009).

All in all, increased reliance on financialization and the financial system for correcting accumulated imbalances, once again, backfired so as to augment the risks and fragilities in the global economy. In the dust and heat of the global financial crisis, Turkey, along with several transition economies, recorded one of the severest downturns among developing countries in 2009.

## Conciliatory Politics for the Consolidation of Power

The precarious conditions of the post-2001 adjustment were revealed by unemployment rates soaring to 8.9% in 2001 and 10.8% in 2002 (from 7.0% in 2000). Inflation rate was as high as 53.0% in 2001, while the depreciation rate of Turkish lira against US dollar reached almost 100% from 2000 to 2001. Such conditions certainly called for an extensive response, which came under the close supervision of and a new

Stand-by Arrangement with the IMF. The components of IMF conditionality were reflected in the main policy document, the TPTSE, which was prepared and initiated by an economic team led by Kemal Derviş, a Vice President of the World Bank then. Mr. Derviş was invited as the Treasury Minister by Bülent Ecevit, the prime minister of the coalition government. In a nutshell, the TPTSE not only aimed to restore the severely wrecked macroeconomic balances; but to transform the institutions and the decision-making processes in the economy in line with the key principles of the Post-Washington Consensus. Therefore the TPTSE incorporated a whole set of issues concerning the banking sector, fiscal balances, agricultural policies, social security and privatization in order to revive the then-halted "structural reforms." (Atiyas, 2012; Bredenkamp et al., 2009). The main motivation of the TPTSE nevertheless rested on the reduction of public debt and fiscal dominance on the asset markets. The objective was to provide a signal of "confidence" to international financial investors and bring around the reversed capital flows to support economic recovery toward higher growth rates (BSB, 2001; Telli et al., 2008). In particular, the program aimed at reducing the non-interest expenditures of the public sector to achieve a primary-surplus target of 6.5% of GDP on the one hand, and steering the monetary policy toward "price stability" via "inflation targeting" on the other. The central bank was granted "independence" in April 2001 to work toward this sole mandate. Hence, the expectations were steered toward the foreign investors' presence to contribute substantially to the "sustained growth" path of the economy. Accordingly, the fiscal, monetary and structural policies (including privatization, social security reform, agricultural reform, banking and finance regulation) were designed to enhance credibility and reduce country risk perception in international markets.

In the first elections following the 2001 crisis, the JDP came into power. It was soon understood that the strong fiscal-austerity dimension of the TPTSE would deprive the economy of the much needed funds for social safety spending, while the adverse dynamics of "adjustment" would have devastating effects not only on wage-earners but also on all other vulnerable segments of society. Thus, the devastating repercussions of the 2001 crisis on all societal groups, along with the discontent on the crisis (mis-)management of the coalition government, underlined the economic foundations of the collapse of the coalition parties and the striking success of JDP in November 2002 elections (Öniş, 2004). Yet, the newly elected government remained loyal to the policy framework of the TPTSE, and renewed the relationship with the IMF via a new Stand-by Arrangement in 2005 (IMF, 2005).

Post-2001 global adjustment during this period also came about under the auspices of the "Cologne Summit" of G7/8 in June 1999 to "reshape" the global financial system toward a "new institutional financial architecture." Recurrent financial crises in developing countries during the 1990s (Mexico in 1994, East Asia in 1997, and Russia and Brazil in 1998–1999) brought about a new round of discussions questioning the efficacy of widespread adoption of "full liberalization" policies of the "Washington Consensus," which apparently fell short of supporting structural transformation for development. Instead, there was a call for a paradigm shift toward a "Post-Washington Consensus" that would re-define the role of the state and the state-market relations. Accentuating the importance of building a global financial system that would go beyond avoiding economic crises, the "new paradigm" should have involved "regulations" for establishing a well-functioning and transparent financial regime that would ensure macroeconomic strength and financial stability, whereby resources would be steered toward "productive activities" that would have long-term growth impacts (Gore, 2000; Stiglitz, 2005; Öniş & Şenses, 2005, 2009).

Consequently, economic policymaking, along with institutional and legal frameworks, and ultimately processes of political representation were all transformed in Turkey during the post-2001 period. The patronage of the IMF, the EU anchor (via the approval of the 1994-application for EU membership in 2004), and commitment to the principles of the Post-Washington Consensus helped Turkey to attract increasing shares of global financial liquidity, especially in the first half of the 2000s. All these factors paved the way for a favorable environment whereby the Turkish economy could grow at high rates that would be unattainable through domestic savings alone. And, as outlined above, the extraordinary benevolence of international financial markets under the rosy conditions of post-2001 global adjustment was also effective in the revival and acceleration of private capital inflows, allowing for a sharp resurgence of the economy. The growth rate of real GDP, following the deep collapse in 2001, jumped to 6.4% in 2002 and 9.8% in 2004. After almost four decades of high inflation, price stability was finally achieved by reducing the inflation rate to single-digit levels in 2005. Stringent commitment to the primary-surplus target in budget management brought the (net) public debt-to-GDP ratio down to 32.3% in 2006 Q4 from 64.3% in

2001 Q4 (Ministry of Treasury and Finance, Public Finance Statistics). Such an auspicious economic environment was also hailed politically, backing the rise of the JDP at the local elections in 2004 and the general elections in 2007.

However, despite rapid growth, lower rates of inflation and increased access to foreign capital; the Turkish economy not only failed to achieve structural transformation toward sustained growth, but also generated major economic and political vulnerabilities by relying on speculation-led growth under the whims prescribed by foreign actors. With respect to Turkey's political economy in this period, one can emphasize the typical attributes of a "reactive state" that accommodates itself to the heavy influence of international players and displays no significant autonomy to devise and implement sound policies for structural transformation (Öniş & Şenses, 2007). Hence, external actors were influential not only in restructuring the economy, but also in shaping the policymaking environment via their influence on the institutions of governance, the legal system, and the social and political order. Such dependence on international circles during this second period of neoliberal restructuring caused major economic deficiencies at the national level, such as the rather weak association of productivity gains with the meager trend of investment, employment and remuneration of labor.

Therefore, one of the most striking features of high economic growth in Turkey during the 2002–2007 period was the co-existence of high and persistent unemployment, warranting the term "jobless growth" (ILO, 1996). Despite the very rapid growth of the sectors of the economy, employment generation was sluggish and deficient, causing average annual unemployment rate to be 9.9% in the 2002–2007 period. The average annual growth rate of real GDP during the period was around 7.1%, while employment growth stood only around 1.3% (TurkStat National Accounts and LFS). Moreover, with the dissolution of agriculture and population moving from rural to urban areas, employment share of agriculture continued to decline from around 28.9% in 2002 down to 23.5% in 2007. In addition, with the proletarianization of especially small businesses, the share of wage-employment in total employment increased in this period. Yet, the share of wages in total income declined steadily. Hence, despite rising productivity that elevated output growth rates, real wages stayed stagnant, worsening the primary distribution against labor. Deterioration was observed not only in wage shares, but also in social rights and working conditions. Confronted with "flexible" labor markets and large-scale privatizations, wage-labor suffered from high degrees of informalization and dislocation (Bahçe & Köse, 2017; Ercan et al., 2010).

## A Missed Opportunity for Sustained Growth

Turkey transformed its economic-policy institutions and priorities as a response to the 2001 crisis. Thanks to strict adherence to the stabilization and structural adjustment programs, strengthening of the financial system and favorable external relations, the inflation rate, one of the main symptoms of instability, was reduced swiftly after decades of high and persistent inflation. The inflation rate (as measured by the implicit GDP deflator, the ratio between nominal and real GDP where real GDP is measured as chained volume series) was well above 50% throughout the 1990s, but it declined to one-digit levels from 2005 onward. Similarly, interest rates also declined rapidly in the same period. For example, the *real* interest rate on commercial loans dropped from around 25% in 2002 to 6.6% in 2007 (see Table 9.2)[4].

The economy responded rapidly to the propitious changes in domestic and foreign political climate. After a 5.8% decline in 2001, *real* GDP expanded by 7.2% per year on average in 6 years in a row so that it was 50.0% higher in 2007 than its level in 2001. The period of economic stability and growth, finally achieved after the "lost decade" of the 1990s, could provide an impetus to reposition Turkey within the international division of labor by serving as a stepping stone to a long-term and sustained growth path. Turkey's articulation with the world economy could be transformed effectively by structural changes in production and foreign trade. However, the policymakers preferred to rely on international financial flows and the expanding world economy to achieve short-term success, letting the "market" lead the economy toward a dependent and fragile structure. Indeed, the 2008–2009 crisis in the world economy exposed the high degree of dependence and fragility of the Turkish economy through two major channels: Sources of funds for growth, and the structure of production and trade, that is, the mode of articulation with the world economy.

**Table 9.2** Main Economic Indicators, 2000–2009

| | *GDP (billion USD)* | *GDP growth rate (%)* | *Inflation rate (%)* | *Real interest rate on commercial loans (%)* | *Current account balance/GDP (%)* | *FDI stock/GDP (%)* | *Gross external debt/GDP (%)* | *Construction and real estate/GDP (%)* |
|---|---|---|---|---|---|---|---|---|
| 2000 | 273.6 | 6.9 | 49.4 | | −2.6 | 6.9 | 43.3 | 13.7 |
| 2001 | 200.8 | −5.8 | 53.0 | | 4.5 | 9.3 | 56.6 | 13.1 |
| 2002 | 239.3 | 6.4 | 37.6 | 24.6 | 2.2 | 6.8 | 54.2 | 12.4 |
| 2003 | 314.7 | 5.8 | 23.3 | 27.2 | −0.2 | 9.7 | 45.8 | 12.5 |
| 2004 | 407.8 | 9.8 | 12.4 | 19.3 | −1.6 | 9.1 | 39.5 | 13.4 |
| 2005 | 504.9 | 9.0 | 7.1 | 10.0 | −2.4 | 13.8 | 33.8 | 14.0 |
| 2006 | 553.4 | 6.9 | 9.4 | 11.7 | −4.0 | 16.9 | 37.6 | 15.1 |
| 2007 | 678.8 | 5.0 | 6.2 | 6.6 | −4.1 | 22.4 | 36.8 | 16.3 |
| 2008 | 771.9 | 0.8 | 12.0 | 13.7 | −3.4 | 9.8 | 36.3 | 16.5 |
| 2009 | 647.4 | −4.8 | 5.4 | 8.1 | 0.0 | 21.3 | 41.5 | 16.0 |

*Source* Electronic Data Delivery System (EDDS) of the Central Bank of the Republic of Turkey. *Note* All data presented in the table are authors' own calculations by using the main indicators. GDP is measured at current US dollars, whereas GDP growth rate refers to the growth rate of real GDP (chained volume series)

### *Financing Growth and the Current Account Deficit*

During the 2001 crisis, the Turkish lira depreciated almost by 100% against the US dollar, and, as a result, the share of exports in GDP rose by almost 7 percentage points (to 27.2% in 2001), whereas the share of imports in GDP remained almost unchanged (22.7%). Consequently, an unprecedentedly high trade surplus was recorded (4.5% of GDP). Exports continued to increase rapidly after the crisis, albeit at a lower rate than that of GDP. Imports, however, exhibited a much faster growth partly because of the gradual appreciation of the Turkish lira until the 2009 crisis, but mostly because of the increasing dependence of the economy on imports. The trade deficit reached 4.0% of GDP in this process. The link between the trade deficit and economic growth has become even stronger after the 2009 crisis. Substantial trade deficits were run in almost all post-crisis quarters together with positive growth rates.

The trade deficit, or, to be more precise, the current account deficit caused mainly by the trade deficit, is financed by foreign capital generally in the form of FDI and borrowing. It should be noted that the size of the current account deficit is, by definition, equal to the (positive) difference between aggregate investment and aggregate savings. If a country runs a current account deficit, its investment exceeds domestic savings (by the size of the deficit), and it finances the difference by using foreigners' savings, that is to say, generally by FDI and foreign borrowing.

The FDI stock in Turkey increased from 19 to 152 billion USD from 2001 to 2007 and the services (financial and insurance activities, information and communication services, and wholesale trade) received two thirds of foreign investment. After a sharp decline in 2008, the stock of FDI has remained around 160 billion USD until 2020, that is to say, FDI did not play any significant role as an external source of finance after the 2009 crisis.

While FDI was not sufficient to finance the current account deficit, the Turkish economy continued to borrow during the 2002–2008 period. The gross external debt increased almost monotonically from the first quarter of 2002 until the third quarter of 2008 (from 114 to 292 billion USD). However, the rate of increase in external debt was lower than the GDP growth rate, thanks to the appreciation of the Turkish lira in the first half of the 2000s, and the external debt-to-GDP ratio declined from 57% in 2001 to 34% in 2005. This ratio tended to increase after 2005 because of the increasing dependence of the economy on external debt to finance the current account deficits (for a detailed analysis of growth-current account deficit-borrowing links, see the next chapter in this volume).

There was a change in the composition of the foreign debt stock as well. The private sector accounted for about one third of the gross external debt stock in 2002. Since the government encouraged borrowing by the private sector, the share of the private sector jumped to two thirds of the total debt stock in 2008. The private sector has become more sensitive to exchange rate fluctuations and reversals of foreign capital flows due to its increasing external debt stock, as revealed first during the 2009 crisis, and later in 2018–2019 crisis amid worsening foreign relations.

A rapidly growing economy provides ample opportunities for the reallocation of resources, for example, toward productive and innovative activities that can boost competitiveness to pave the way for a sustained growth path. In order to understand if the Turkish economy achieved the type of resource reallocation toward productive and innovative activities, we need to analyze the activities and sectors that benefited the most from economic growth during the post-2001 period.

As mentioned above, the Turkish lira depreciated by almost 100% in nominal terms in 2001, but appreciated slightly after 2003. Since the inflation rate in Turkey was still higher than its trade partners' average inflation rate, the domestic producer price-index-based real effective exchange rate (PPI-REER) increased considerably after the 2001 crisis. The Turkish lira appreciated in real terms by 22% from 2003 to 2008 (The consumer price-index-based REER appreciated even more, that is, by 33%). The real appreciation of the home currency favors imports at the expense of exports, and thus it was blamed for causing import-dependent growth. However, the competitiveness of exporters depends on unit-labor-cost-based real effective exchange rate (ULC-REER) because it captures the effects of changes in productivity and labor costs. The ULC-REER did not have any apparent upward trend, and fluctuated around the mean value in the same period, implying that the negative impact of the appreciation of the Turkish lira was compensated by declining unit labor costs in Turkey.

Although the exchange rate movements denominated in terms of unit labor cost did not have a particularly negative effect on exports, the appreciation of the Turkish lira in terms of producer (and consumer) prices favored non-tradable over tradable activities, for example, services over manufacturing. When the lira appreciated in real terms, tradable products tended to be cheaper relative to non-tradable goods because imports pushed down the prices of tradables. This process helped to control or even reduce inflation as long as the country could finance its current account deficits by foreign sources (FDI and borrowing). However, such a process also imposed disincentives on manufacturing activities that were essential for long-term sustained growth.

All in all, the Turkish economy turned out to be increasingly dependent on external sources to finance growth. In order to understand the transformation, if any, in the pattern of articulation to the world economy, we will now analyze how the structures of production and foreign trade have changed within the same process, that is, how the resources have been allocated among different activities.

### *Structural Change in Production and Foreign Trade*

The Turkish economy grew on average 7.2% in the 2002–2008 period, but, expectedly, the growth was uneven across sectors. By far, the growth champion was the construction sector that grew two times faster than the economy, mostly as a result of pro-construction policies adopted in the post-2001 period. The manufacturing industry performed somewhat better than the rest of the sectors (8.2%). The real estate services sector was at the other extreme with the lowest average annual growth rate of 1.4%. Agriculture was another main loser, so to speak (1.6%).

"Real output" in Turkey's national accounts is calculated as a chained volume series. Output of a sector in a given year is calculated in the preceding year prices, and linked to the previous year's output to get "real output" series that are "free" from price effects. The change in monetary value of a sector's output is equal to the multiplication of price changes and changes in real output. Therefore, one needs to analyze price changes at the sectoral level as well in order to fully understand the direction of structural change in the economy.

The average price level in the Turkish economy, as calculated by the implicit GDP deflator, increased by 11.6% per year from 2002 to 2008. The construction sector had a slightly higher increase (12.1%), whereas the real estate services sector had the highest increase in the same period (20.9%). Although the "real" volume of real estate services expanded rather slowly, its share in GDP increased significantly from 7.9% in 2002 to 10. 4% in 2009 thanks to rising "prices" (that is to say, the rising "rental value of dwellings"). The share of the construction sector in GDP also increased in the same period (from 4.5 to 6.8%) as a result of the rapid expansion of its "output." By the way, these two sectors were the only sectors that increased their share in GDP by more than one percentage-point in the post-2001 period.

The "successes" of construction and real estate services are directly related to the economic-policy preferences of the successive JDP governments. The JDP has prioritized investment in public infrastructure (especially highways) and housing since it first came into power in 2002. The Housing Development Administration of Turkey (*Toplu Konut İdaresi Başkanlığı, TOKİ*) was established in 1990[5], but its mandate was expanded and regulatory constraints on its activities were eased by the JDP during the early years of its government. TOKİ was instrumental in the construction of housing for the poor and urban infrastructure (schools, mosques, etc.), but, more importantly, it was also a useful tool for the appropriation of land rents in urban areas through "land development" and for-profit projects, along with redistribution of those rents through "clientelistic" networks (Özdemir, 2011). Although the JDP supported the neoliberal idea of reducing the state's role in the economy and privatized public companies *en masse*, TOKİ has become the main player in the construction industry. Moreover, the JDP actively supported the expansion of the (housing) construction sector through cheap credits extended by public banks. This policy has stimulated housing demand and raised prices in the real estate services sector.

In sum, the Turkish economy achieved rapid growth (above the long-run average) for six years after the 2001 crisis, but domestic savings were not sufficient to finance investment (including housing). The current account deficit had a tendency to increase over time, and it was financed by FDI and borrowing. During this process, the government prioritized the construction sector and channeled resources to support its growth. Thus, it was no coincidence that the correlation between the share of the construction-real estate sectors in GDP and the current account deficit was strong. Indeed, the current account deficit and the share of construction-real estate increased together after the 2001 crisis until the next one in 2009.

While the share of services in GDP increased during the period under consideration, the share of manufacturing continued to decline gradually, and hit bottom after the 2009 crisis (15.1% in 2010). The share of manufacturing in GDP bounced back to 19% in 2018 because the construction and real estate sectors could not keep their pace after the 2009 crisis. There was not any break in agriculture's long-term declining trend, and, eventually, the share of agriculture reached 6% in the late 2010s.

The position of a country within the international division of labor can be defined by the pattern of its foreign trade. Turkey was a typical developing country, specialized in the production of agricultural products that accounted for more than 60% of its exports in the early 1960s. Textile and clothing industries have been developed in the 1970s, and their share in exports exceed that of agricultural products in the mid-1980s. Thanks to the accumulation of industrial skills in metalworking, the machinery sector was able to increase its export share since the early 1990s. The motor vehicles industry, which also relies on metalworking technologies, gained momentum after the Customs Union agreement with the EU on 31 December 1995. The transformation in the pattern of foreign trade achieved by Turkey since the early 1960s (from agricultural products to textile and clothing, and to machinery and motor vehicles) was also observed in rapidly growing developing countries like South Korea, but it was much later and slower in Turkey (for a detailed analysis, see Taymaz & Voyvoda, 2012).

The pattern of foreign trade in Turkey has followed, to a large extent, its historical tendencies in the early 2000s. While the share of textile and clothing gradually declined, metals and metalworking industries increased their shares in total exports. During the 2002–2008 period, the fastest growing product categories were iron and steel (16.2 billion USD in 2008), motor vehicles (19.1 b), mineral fuels (8.3 b), precious metals and articles thereof (5.1 b), machinery and mechanical appliances (11.0 b), ships, boats and floating structures (2.8 b), iron or steel articles (6.2 b), and plastics and articles thereof (3.8 b). The combined share of these products in total exports increased from 30.4% in 2002 to 51.6% in 2008. (Product categories used here are defined at the 2-digit level of HS 1992 classification. "Products" may include the parts and components as well).

During the same period, apparel and clothing (15.6 billion USD in 2008), electrical machinery and sound recorders and television sets (8.4 b), textiles, made up articles (2.3 b), fruit and nuts (3.1 b), cotton (1.7 b), man-made staple fibres (1.1 b), man-made filaments (1.3 b), tobacco (0.9 b), and articles of leather (0.6 b) had the highest decline in export shares. These products' share in total exports dropped from 45.1% in 2002 to 24.8% in 2008.

As a result of the change in export structure, motor vehicles, iron and steel and machinery sectors have been the top 3 exported products in 2008, while the top 3 were apparel and clothing, motor vehicles, and electrical machinery, sound recorders and television sets in 2002. The list of the declining product groups include only textile and clothing and agricultural products with the notable exception of "electrical machinery and sound recorders and television sets."

"Electrical machinery and sound recorders and television sets" were an outlier among the declining export categories. The main exported product in this category was consumer electronics, and, more specifically, television sets. In contrast to motor vehicles, the consumer electronic industry did not attract any FDI in the 1990s. The industry increased its exports of cathode ray tube (CRT) color television receivers to the European countries in the second half of 1990s and the first half of 2000s, thanks to the provisional (1994) and definitive (1995 and 2002) antidumping duties on color television receivers originated in Turkey's main competitors, China, Malaysia, Korea, Thailand, and Singapore. Turkish consumer electronics producers benefited also from their geographical proximity to the European market that reduced the delivery time considerably. However, they lagged behind adopting the new LCD technology in their products, and lost their competitive advantage since the mid-2000s (for more detail, see Taymaz & Yılmaz, 2008).

Among the imported products, iron and steel (20.8 billion USD in 2008), mineral fuels (33.5 b) and motor vehicles (13 b) had the highest growth rate during the 2002–2008 period. While the imports of machinery (22.3 b), electrical machinery (13.4 b), and sound recorders and television sets (4.4 b) had the lowest growth rates in the same period.

Apparently, Turkey exports and imports iron and steel in large volumes, but a product-level analysis indicates that its exports and imports are rather different products. The bulk of "iron and steel" exports from Turkey are "iron or non-alloy steel; bars and rods" whereas imported iron and steel are "ferrous waste and scrap" and "iron or non-alloy steel; flat-rolled products," that is, inputs for iron and steel plants, and flat steel for motor vehicles and consumer durable goods. Turkey specializes in exporting certain types of products (mainly iron bars, used, for example, in construction), and imports a different product, sheet steel for its growing metalworking industries.

Turkey simultaneously exports and imports motor vehicles as well, but the pattern of specialization is quite different than the one observed in iron and steel. The motor vehicle industry attracted FDI in the early 1990s on the eve of Customs Union with the EU. The sector has been dominated by foreign firms, and production has been geared toward the European market. Production and exports of motor vehicles and components, especially light commercial vehicles, increased rapidly, and it has become one of the main exporter industries in the mid-2000s. Since the industry is well-integrated with the European production chains, imports of motor vehicles and components also increased almost at the same rate.

Finally, net export values (exports *minus* imports) show which sectors were competitive in the 2002–2008 period. In spite of structural change in foreign trade, apparel and clothing was by far the largest net exporter with 13.4 billion USD of net exports in 2008. It was followed by motor vehicles (6.1 b) and iron and steel (4.0 b).

We can drive three main results from the above-summarized analysis on structural change in foreign trade regarding the pattern of articulation with the world economy. First, there has been a gradual shift in the structure of foreign trade from labor-intensive products, like textile and clothing, toward medium-technology products, like machinery and motor vehicles, in the early 2000s. Although the accumulation of metalworking skills played an important role in making machinery and motor vehicles more competitive, the integration with the global production chains was decisive for motor vehicles. Foreign firms invested extensively in motor vehicles production in Turkey during the 1990s in order to export to the European countries. Exports of motor vehicles increased rapidly in the 2000s, but imports of motor vehicles (and parts and components) also increased almost at the same rate. Because of the dominant role of FDI, the development of the motor vehicles industry in Turkey has been dependent on the global strategies of the multinational companies.

Secondly, the shift toward medium-technology products has been quite slow, and necessitated intra-industry trade, that is, exports of medium-technology products have been accompanied by imports of similar/related products. Thus, labor-intensive products like textile and clothing was, and still is, the main foreign exchange earning sector in Turkey.

Finally, and most importantly, Turkey failed to shift its production and foreign trade structure toward electronics-based sectors that had, on average, higher value added per worker and grew faster than other sectors. Turkey was competitive only in the consumer electronics segment (CRT color television sets) in the late 1990s, but lost its competitiveness even in that segment after 2005 because domestic producers were not able to adopt the new LED technology. The share of "high-tech" products in exports has remained at negligible levels until 2020.

### *Sources of Growth and Productivity*

Turkish economy grew rather fast in the 2002–2008 period, but the construction and real estate services sectors were favored during the growth process. The share of manufacturing in GDP declined to some extent, but, more importantly, the structure of manufacturing and exports evolved gradually toward medium-technology industries (machinery and motor vehicles). Labor-intensive textile and clothing remained the most competitive sector, and "high-tech" products were almost nonexistent in exports. We can now analyze the sources of growth and productivity to shed light on the "quality" of growth.

Turkey experienced two economic crises in 1999 and 2001, and the capacity utilization rates (CURs) declined considerably in those years. Therefore, the economy could increase its output by simply increasing CURs without any investment. During the crisis in 2001, the CUR dropped to 70.9%, and it reached its "normal" level (around 80%) in just three years. In other words, the existence of underutilized production capacity helped to increase output rapidly in the first half of 2000s.

Real GDP increases if more inputs, capital and labor, are used. At the aggregate level, according to the Ministry of Development (formerly, State Planning Organization; now, Presidency of Strategy and Budget) data, employment declined by 0.3, 0.8, and 1.0% in 2001, 2002, and 2003 respectively, and increased on average 2% per year during the 2004–2008 period. During the whole period from 2002 to 2008, the average annual employment growth rate was 1.4%, slightly lower than population growth rate. Therefore, if the new employees had been endowed with the same level of capital as the current labor force, employment growth would have led to only a 1.4% annual increase in GDP.

However, labor productivity and output can also be increased by capital deepening, that is, by increasing the capital intensity of production. The share of investment in GDP can be used as an indicator for capital accumulation. Investment/GDP ratio was 23.7% in 1998, but it dropped sharply during the 2001 crisis (to 18.1%). Later on, the investment rate increased rapidly due to post-crisis economic stability and declining real interest rates, reaching its peak at 28.4% in 2006 (and then declining until the 2009 crisis). As discussed above, the share of the construction sector in GDP also increased in the same period, but it could explain only about one third of the increase in the investment share.

Real GDP can also be increased by technical change even if the quantities of labor and capital are constant. The increase in output with the same quantities of inputs is called "productivity growth," and there are a number of methods to measure the productivity growth rate. "Growth accounting" is one of the methods frequently used to measure "total factor productivity" (TFP). TFP calculations are based on a number of restrictive assumptions, and require information about capital and labor elasticities and quantities. As explained in note 4 at the end of this chapter, there are quite important data problems in estimating employment and output in Turkey for the period under consideration.

There are a few studies attempting to measure TFP growth at the aggregate and sectoral levels in Turkey for the period after 2000. Atiyas and Bakis (2014), in one of the most comprehensive studies on the topic, calculated TFP growth rates for the whole economy and main sectors (agriculture, industry and services) for the 1971–2011 period, and compared their results with those available in Penn World Tables (version 7.1). Their results suggest that the average annual TFP growth rate, when the "number of employees" is used for the labor variable, is 5.1% for the 2002–2006 period, which is substantially higher than the average rates in all previous periods (0.9% in 1971–1979, 1.4% in 1980–1989, and 0.6% in 1990–2001). The average TFP growth rate was 2.3% for the 2002–2011 period that includes the crisis year, 2009. When "total hours worked" is used instead of "number of employees" for the labor input, and when capacity-adjusted capital and schooling-adjusted labor inputs are taken into account, the average annual TFP growth rate is measured as 4.3% for the 2002–2006 period, that is to say, productivity growth explains almost two thirds of GDP growth in that period. However, these estimates for the 2002–2006 period seem to be too high as compared to earlier periods (see Altug et al., 2008 for a historical analysis).

A recent study on Turkey by the OECD (2021: 82) provides more reasonable estimates for TFP growth in the same period. According to this study, Turkey's average annual TFP growth rate was 1.5% in the 2002–2008 period. Moreover, the contributions of capital deepening, labor and CUR (defined here as the difference between actual and potential growth) were, on average, quite similar to that of TFP growth. Thus, each one of the four factors (TFP, capital deepening, employment growth and increase in CUR) explains around one quarter of GDP growth from 2002 to 2008. These results indicate that there was not a very remarkable increase in productivity growth in that period.

## Concluding Remarks

Turkey encountered a unique and favorable environment for rapid growth and structural transformation at the beginning of the third millennium. Economic and political stability was achieved after the devastating crisis in 2001. The EU membership seemed to be a real possibility. The overly-generous international liquidity provided funds for a sharp resurgence of the economy, and the economy bounced back rapidly. The period of stability and fast growth created conditions for transforming Turkey's role within the international division of labor.

However, the policymakers preferred to let the "market" to reallocate resources and regulate the economy in accordance with the neoliberal policy prescriptions, and did not design and implement any industrial policy that could transform the structure of production and foreign trade so as to underlie sustained growth. Instead, external resources were channeled to finance unproductive activities like housing and construction projects, and firms were encouraged to be competitive on the basis of low wages. Thus, the "market" determined the pace and direction of structural change. While the share of manufacturing in GDP declined, manufacturing itself gradually moved toward medium-technology industries like machinery and motor vehicles to serve the European markets. The motor vehicle industry, the "show case" of success, has been almost completely dominated by multinational firms. Because of the lack of a coherent policy and incentive structure, it turned out to be impossible to create an economic environment conducive for long-term investment (especially in the electronics-based sectors), which was necessary to achieve sustained growth. As a result, labor productivity, wages, skills of workers, investment in technological activities, and the share of high-tech exports have remained low, as compared to the European countries.

Turkey behaved as a "reactive state" during the period of 2001–2009, and has accommodated itself to "transnational power blocs," as exemplified by international organizations like IMF and the World Bank, and the Atlantic Alliance under the hegemony of the US, aiming at strengthening rather than changing its existing position within the international division of labor (Öniş & Senses, 2007; Taymaz & Voyvoda, 2015). In doing so, it has accumulated major economic and political vulnerabilities to maintain speculation-led growth under the whims of foreign finance. The world financial crisis in 2008 marked the end to this short period of high but unsustainable growth.

The early years of the third millennium, following the collapse of the economy in 2001, provided Turkey with a unique opportunity to challenge the path of dependent development. A proactive state could re-orient the economy toward a path of sustained and inclusive growth. However, the emerging "domestic political block" that included economically vulnerable "Anatolian capital" preferred to consolidate its power during this period by following conciliatory policies in line with the conditions imposed by the "transnational power blocs." As a result, the Turkish economy has continued to be dependent on the whim of foreign capital to grow, and its production structure remained dependent on European "value chains." It is thus no surprise that this short "window of opportunity," opened by the 2001 crisis which was caused by an IMF-designed experiment, was closed by the financial crisis in the "core" countries in 2008, without any long-run effect on the pace of economic growth and the pattern of dependence.

## Notes

1. See UNCTAD (2000) for a discussion of cross-border mergers and acquisitions by the EU and Japanese transnational corporations to capture gains from the rising tide of high-tech sectors in the US, along with their contributions to the spread of the financial bubble in technology stocks through the global economy.
2. Stimulated by readily available finance in a booming economy, especially in the form of venture capital, the rise of the "dot.com" e-commerce firms was a crucial component of the ICT investment boom in the second half of the 1990s in the US. The announcement of the Fed's policy to continue to raise interest rates in February 2000 led to concerns about the borrowing costs of the high-tech firms and to significant stock market volatility. With the onset of the realization of the speculative gains, the sharp reversal in investors' sentiment triggered what was then referred to as the "dot-com bubble" (Kraay & Ventura, 2005).
3. See Chapter 8 in this volume, as well as Akyüz and Boratav (2003), Yeldan (2002, 2006), Voyvoda and Yeldan (2005), and Boratav and

Yeldan (2006) for detailed analyses of the domestic and international factors leading to the turmoil of 1999–2001 in the Turkish economy.

4. Unless otherwise noted, all data presented in this section were downloaded from the Electronic Data Delivery System (EDDS) of the Central Bank of the Republic of Turkey in order to use, to the extent possible, consistent and up-to-date data (https://evds2.tcmb.gov.tr, accessed on February 12, 2021). The foreign trade data were obtained from CEPII (http://www.cepii.fr/, bilateral trade data, HS 1992 classification). The employment and capacity utilization data for the 2000–2009 period were from the Ministry of Development, Main Economic and Social Indicators 2014.

   There were a number of changes in the scope and methodology of data collection, which makes it challenging to make intertemporal comparisons. There were two main revisions in national-accounts statistics in Turkey since 2001. The first revision in 2008 moved the base year from 1987 to 1998, and introduced a number of modifications in methodology. As a result of this revision, GDP estimates increased substantially, for example, 2006 GDP rose by 31.6%. The second revision in 2016 adopted chain-linked series for volume indices (by reference year 2009) in addition to a number of other changes, and estimates based on the earlier methodology were revised upwards (for example, 2015 GDP rose by 19.7%). While the extent of upward shifts were lower for earlier years, growth rate estimates for recent years went up considerably (the growth rates for the 2012–2016 period were almost doubled).

   The Household Labor Force Statistics (LFS) provides (both formal and informal) employment data at aggregate and sectoral levels, and underlies a number of other statistics including the national accounts. The LFS has been conducted by the Turkish Statistical Institute (TurkStat) regularly since 1988, and there were three major changes in the survey methodology, in 2000, 2005, and 2015. Moreover, the TurkStat started to use the population data from the Address-based Population Registration System (APRS) in 2007, and re-estimated 2004–2007 LFS data on the basis of new APRS projections.

   The annual survey of manufacturing and services, collected by the TurkStat at the "plant" level, provided detailed sectoral level production and employment data until 2002. The TurkStat changed its survey methodology and coverage in 2002, and started to publish the data based only on administrative records in 2017. These changes in the coverage of the data and the data collection methodologies make it very difficult, if not impossible, to make intertemporal comparisons.

5. The Housing Development and Public Partnership Administration was established in 1984 but remained ineffective. In 1990, it was divided into two administrations as the Housing Development Administration (TOKİ) and the Public Partnership Administration.

## References


Akyüz, Y., & Boratav, K. (2003). The making of the Turkish financial crisis. *World Development, 31*(9), 1549–1566.

Altug, S., Filiztekin, A., & Pamuk, Ş. (2008). Sources of long-term economic growth for Turkey, 1880–2005. *European Review of Economic History, 12*(3), 393–430.

Atiyas, I. (2012). Economic institutions and institutional change in Turkey during the neoliberal era. *New Perspectives on Turkey, 47*, 57–81.

Atiyas, I., & Bakis, O. (2014). Aggregate and sectoral TFP growth in Turkey: A growth accounting exercise. *İktisat, İşletme Ve Finans, 29*(341), 9–36.

BSB (Bağımsız Sosyal Bilimciler). (2001). Güçlü ekonomiye geçiş programı üzerine değerlendirmeler. *Mülkiye, 25*(229), 11–60.

Bahçe, S., & Köse, A. (2017). Social classes and the neo-liberal poverty regime in Turkey, 2002–2011. *Journal of Contemporary Asia, 47*(4), 575–595.

Bakır, C., & Öniş, Z. (2010). The regulatory state and Turkish banking reforms in the age of post-Washington consensus. *Development and Change, 41*(1), 77–106.

Boratav, K. (2018). *Türkiye İktisat Tarihi*. İmge.

Boratav, K., & Yeldan, E. (2006). Turkey, 1980–2000: Financial liberalization, macroeconomic (in)-stability, and patterns of distribution". In L. Taylor (Ed.), *External Liberalization in Asia, Post-socialist Europe and Brazil* (pp. 417–455). Oxford University Press.

Bredenkamp, H., Josefsson M., Lindgren, C., & Serdengeçti, S. (2009). Turkey's renaissance: From banking crisis to economic revival. In E. Brau, & I. McDonald (Eds.), *Successes of the International Monetary Fund*. Palgrave Macmillan.

Burki, S. J., & Perry, G. E. (1998). *Beyond the Washington consensus: Institutions matter*. World Bank Latin American and Caribbean Studies, WB.

Cizre, Ü., & Yeldan, E. (2005). The Turkish encounter with neo-liberalism: Economics and politics in the 2000/2001 crises. *Review of International Political Economy, 12*(3), 387–408.
Eichengreen, B. (2010). Lessons of the crisis for emerging markets. *International Economics and Economic Policy, 7*, 49–62.
Ercan, H., Taymaz, E., & Yeldan, E. (2010). Crisis and Turkey: Impact analysis of crisis response measures. ILO.
Gordon, R. J. (2003). Hi-tech innovation and productivity growth: Does supply create its own demand?, NBER Working Papers 9437, National Bureau of Economic Research, Inc.
Gore, C. (2000). The rise and fall of the Washington Consensus as a paradigm for developing countries. *World Development, 28*(5), 789–804.
Griffith-Jones, S., & Ocampo, J. A. (2009). The financial crisis and its impact on developing countries. UNDP Poverty Reduction Discussion Paper PG/2009/001.
ILO. (1996). *World employment 1996/97*. National policies in a global context.
IMF. (2005). IMF Country Report No. 05/412. https://www.imf.org/external/pubs/ft/scr/2005/cr05412.pdf. Last accessed December 10 2020.
Kraay, A., & Ventura, J. (2005). The dot-com bubble, the Bush deficits, and the U.S. current account. In R. H. Clarida (Ed.), *G7 Current Account Imbalances: Sustainability and Adjustment*. NBER Books: University of Chicago Press.
OECD. (2021). *OECD Economic surveys: Turkey 2021*. OECD.
Onaran, Ö. (2006). Speculation-led growth and fragility in Turkey: Does EU make a difference or "can it happen again"? Department of Economics Working Paper Series, 93. Inst. für Volkswirtschaftstheorie und -politik, WU Vienna University of Economics and Business.
Orhangazi, Ö. (2019). 2000'li yıllarda yapısal dönüşüm ve emeğin durumu. *Çalışma Ve Toplum, 60*, 325–348.
Önis, Z. (2004). The political economy of Turkey's Justice and Development Party. Available at SSRN: https://ssrn.com/abstract=659463
Önis, Z., & Senses, F. (2005). Rethinking the emerging Post-Washington consensus. *Development and Change, 36*(2), 263–290.
Önis, Z., & Senses, F. (2007). Global dynamics, domestic coalitions and a reactive state: Major policy shifts in the post-war Turkish economic development. *METU Studies in Development, 34*(2), 217–250.
Önis, Z., & Senses, F. (2009). Turkish economy at a new stage of integration into the global economy – Towards a synthesis and the challenges ahead". In Z. Öniş, & F. Şenses (Eds.), *Turkey and the Global Economy: The New Phase of Neo-Liberal Restructuring and Integration in the Post-Crisis Era*. Routledge.
Özdemir, D. (2011). The role of the public sector in the provision of housing supply in Turkey, 1950–2009. *International Journal of Urban and Regional Research, 35*(6), 1099–1117.

Stiglitz, J. E. (2005). More instruments and broader goals: Moving toward the Post-Washington Consensus. In *Wider Perspectives on Global Development. Studies in Development Economics and Policy*. Palgrave Macmillan.

Taymaz, E., & Voyvoda, E. (2012). Marching to the beat of a late drummer: Turkey's experience of neoliberal industrialization since 1980. *New Perspectives on Turkey, 47*, 83–113.

Taymaz, E., & Voyvoda, E. (2015). 2023'e doğru sanayi, yapısal dönüşüm ve sanayi politikaları. *İktisat İşletme Ve Finans, 30*(350), 25–62.

Taymaz, E., & Yılmaz, K. (2008). *Integration with the Global Economy: The Case of Turkish Automobile and Consumer Electronics Industries*. Commission on Growth and Development Working Paper No. 37. World Bank.

Telli, Ç., Voyvoda, E., & Yeldan. E. (2008). Macroeconomics of twin-targeting in Turkey: Analytics of a financial CGE model. *International Review of Applied Economics, 22*(2).

UNCTAD. (2000). *Trade and development report: Global economic growth and imbalances*.

UNCTAD. (2001). *Trade and development report*.

UNCTAD. (2002). *Trade and development report*.

UNCTAD. (2007). *Trade and Development Report: Regional cooperation for development*.

UNCTAD. (2008). Trade and development report: Commodity prices, capital flows and the financing of investment.

UNCTAD. (2009). *Trade and development report: Responding to the global crisis: Climate change mitigation and development*.

Voyvoda, E. (2020). Ücretler, gelir dağılımı, eşitsizlik". In Sencer Ayata (Ed.), *Türkiye'de Yoksulluk ve Eşitsizlik Nedenler, Süreçler, Çözümler*, Sosyal Demokrasi Derneği.

Voyvoda, E., & Yeldan, E. (2005). IMF programmes, fiscal policy and growth: Investigation of macroeconomic alternatives in an OLG model of growth for Turkey. *Comparative Economic Studies, 47*(1), 41–79.

Yeldan, E. (2002). On the IMF-directed disinflation program in Turkey: A program for stabilization and austerity or a recipe for impoverishment and financial chaos? In N. Balkan & S. Savran (Eds.), *The Ravages of neo-liberalism: Economy, society and gender in Turkey* (pp. 132–156). Nova Science Pub.

Yeldan, E. (2006). Neoliberal global remedies: From speculative-led growth to IMF-led crisis in Turkey. *Review of Radical Political Economics, 38*(2), 193–213.

CHAPTER 10

# Neoliberal Framework and External Dependency Versus Political Priorities, 2009–2020

*Korkut Boratav and Özgür Orhangazi*

## Introduction

As discussed in the previous chapters, Turkey was among the early adopters of the neoliberal policy framework that has increasingly dominated the agenda of the world economy and its institutions. Rapid trade and financial liberalizations of the early 1980s were followed by the liberalization of capital movements in 1989. The 1990s witnessed boom-bust cycles of capital flows that generated episodes of economic growth, followed by sudden stops and outflows, resulting in financial

K. Boratav (✉)
Turkish Social Sciences Association, Ankara, Turkey
e-mail: korkut@boratav.com

Ö. Orhangazi
Kadir Has University, İstanbul, Turkey
e-mail: ozgur.orhangazi@khas.edu.tr



E. Özçelik and Y. Özdemir (eds.), *Political Economy of Development in Turkey*, The Political Economy of the Middle East,
https://doi.org/10.1007/978-981-16-7318-4_10

and economic crises. The poor design of the IMF-directed stabilization program implemented in 2000 led to another recurrence of such a cycle and resulted in a deep crisis in 2001. This crisis was followed by a series of structural and institutional reforms, still under the guidance of the IMF. The macroeconomic framework of the program reflected the global orthodoxy of Central Bank independence, inflation targeting, contractionary fiscal policy with primary budget surpluses and floating exchange rates. The program aimed to stabilize the economy through a mix of high interest rates and overvalued exchange rates. A widespread privatization program was accompanied by a series of deregulations aiming to diffuse "marketization" through all areas of socioeconomic life.

This extensive deregulation program, widespread privatizations, high interest rates, and an exchange rate policy allowing the Turkish lira to appreciate, coincided with an increase in global liquidity in the 2000s and resulted in accelerated foreign-capital inflows. While higher interest rates attracted short-term capital inflows, privatizations and deregulations in many sectors brought an increase in foreign direct investment. Adherence to the IMF's structural reform program further increased international finance capital's interest in Turkey. Capital inflows both supported economic growth and allowed the Central Bank to bring inflation down by keeping the Turkish lira overvalued. The Justice and Development Party (JDP) that came to power toward the end of 2002 continued to follow these policies to the letter. In fact, the JDP's adoption and implementation of the program were rewarded by the IMF in May 2005 with a new and exceptional credit line of 10 billion dollars, explicitly intended to provide "political capital" to the JDP for the 2007 elections (Boratav, 2018: 248; IMF, 2005: 75).

This pattern continued from 2002 to 2008, until the sudden stop of inflows and the decline in export revenues due to the global financial crisis sent the economy into a sharp recession. Yet, the quantitative easing (QE) policies of the US Federal Reserve System (Fed) and the European Central Bank (ECB) created an unprecedented expansion of liquidity in global financial markets, leading to renewed capital inflows to Turkey and similar economies (Akyüz, 2015). To take advantage of this increase in global liquidity, the Turkish government relaxed regulations that prevented non-financial firms with no export revenues from borrowing in foreign currency and the Central Bank initiated a reserve option mechanism allowing domestic banks to borrow from international banks at low interest rates and use them for credit expansion and for their required reserves.

While signs of fragilities began to surface starting in the mid-2010s, sudden capital outflows in 2018 led to a currency crisis followed by a recession into 2019. The renewal of capital inflows, albeit at relatively much lower levels, together with increased public spending and government's push for a credit expansion helped the economy recover slowly toward the end of 2019. Yet, the accumulated fragilities persisted, and Turkey was faced with the negative demand and supply shocks of the Covid-19 pandemic with a fragile economy trying to recover. Rapid capital outflows from the "developing and emerging economies," including Turkey worsened the situation and brought the economy that was already hit by the pandemic's negative economic shocks to the brink of a balance-of-payments crisis toward the end of 2020.

We start by depicting the global context in the next section and provide a brief overview of the period. After this overview, we first analyze the developments in external balances and then domestic macroeconomic dynamics in detail, before moving onto a discussion of the period from the 2018 currency crisis to the 2020 Covid-19 shock. In the last section, we provide concluding remarks on the political economy of Turkey in this period.

## Overview of the Period

The financial crisis that originated in the US subprime mortgage markets in 2008 spread quickly to the rest of the financial markets and the US economy, and from there to the rest of the world. Complicated derivative products were effective in the rapid spread of the crisis to the US and world financial system. The earlier signs of the crisis appeared in the subprime mortgage markets in 2007. In March 2008, the large US investment bank Bear Stearns declared bankruptcy and in July, the Federal Deposit Insurance Company had to take over IndyMac bank. The September of 2008 witnessed a series of bankruptcies of large banks and financial institutions, including the US-government-sponsored Fannie Mae and Freddie Mac that backed mortgage credits. As the financial markets froze, the fear of a systemic collapse led to a series of rescue operations organized by the US Treasury and the Fed, resulting in the largest bailout operation in history, despite the prevailing pro-market rhetoric. Especially after the collapse of the Lehman Brothers, the fear of a systemic collapse led the US Treasury and the Fed to intervene and organize the takeover of Merrill Lynch by the Bank of America. The insolvency of the American Insurance Group (AIG)—the insurer of the financial system required yet another massive bailout by the US government (Hein et al., 2015; Orhangazi, 2015; Wolfson & Epstein, 2013).

It was quickly realized that the US and the world economy were faced with the deepest crisis since 1929. The US Congress approved a Troubled Assets Relief Program (TARP) to be run by the US Treasury and assigned 760 billion dollars to that purpose. At the beginning of 2009, the new Obama administration enacted the American Recovery and Reinvestment Act (ARRA), which included various government spending items as well as tax incentives amounting to 800 billion dollars. On the other hand, the Fed, after decreasing the interest rate all the way down to near zero, began a QE program with the aim of purchasing troubled assets held by the banks to stabilize the financial system and to support economic growth by decreasing long-term interest rates in order to spur investment and consumption. The Fed's balance sheet shows that the total amount of QE from late 2008 to early 2014 reached around 3.5 trillion dollars. As the financial crisis spread to the rest of the world, central banks of the United Kingdom, Europe and Japan have also brought interest rates down and began implementing similar QE policies. The sum of total liquidity injected to the world financial markets is estimated to be somewhere between 10 and 15 trillion dollars (Caldentey, 2017).

This unprecedented expansion of global liquidity generated booms in financial asset prices of the advanced economies and started a new cycle of capital flows to "emerging economies" as finance capital sought higher yields as compared to the near-zero interest rates at the center. Furthermore, both banks and non-financial corporations in "emerging economies" began increasing their external borrowing to take advantage of the near-zero interest rates in the advanced economies. As Akyüz (2012, 2015) depicts in detail, this process resulted in furthering the financial integration of the "emerging economies" to the world economy and resulted in new forms of external vulnerabilities. The capital inflows led to currency appreciations, widening current account deficits, credit expansions and asset price inflation to varying degrees in these economies.

The sudden stop in capital inflows in 2009, together with declining exports due to the global economic slowdown sent the Turkish economy into a recession. Following 2009, similar to the 2003–2007 period, the 2010–2013 period witnessed large foreign-capital inflows, approaching to a total of 250 billion dollars in four years. In order to take advantage of the global liquidity and low interest rates, regulations were relaxed to allow non-financial firms with no export revenues to borrow in foreign currency. At the same time, the Central Bank began implementing a reserve option mechanism, allowing domestic banks to use foreign currency as part of their required reserves. Hence, the early 2010s witnessed an increase in the external debt of the private sector, both banks and non-financial corporations, as well as an increase in portfolio flows into the stock and bond markets.

Large volumes of capital inflows allowed the "success story" of the 2000s to continue into the early 2010s with high growth rates, especially as compared to most "emerging economies." In fact, by 2013, Turkey was being presented as an exemplary case by the World Bank: "Turkey's rapid economic and social progress holds many useful lessons for policy makers in other emerging markets and has been an inspiration to reformers, particularly in the Middle East and North Africa" (World Bank, 2013: 2).

However, a series of structural imbalances and financial fragilities were accumulating at the same time, complicated by their economic repercussions and incidence of political difficulties facing the JDP. Even in these years, wide current account deficits and unprecedented levels of private-sector external debt were accompanied by a domestic credit expansion, giving a "debt-led" character to growth and generating fragile balance sheets for non-financial firms. The government's almost exclusive focus on a construction-centered growth strategy together with the premature deindustrialization tendencies due to overvalued exchange rates for an extended period generated an unstable growth path, insufficient employment generation and persistent inequalities.

Fed's 2013 "tapering" announcement had a large impact on global financial markets and by the end of 2014 Fed stopped QE, announced its aim to "normalize" its balance sheet and began increasing the interest rates at the end of 2015. As Fig. 10.1 below shows, capital inflows to Turkey slowed down in this period, from 70.4 billion dollars in 2013 to 51 billion dollars in 2014, and 33 billion dollars in 2015.

As the global liquidity conditions have changed and foreign-capital inflows slowed down in the second half of the 2010s, both external and domestic fragilities together with the JDP's quest for electoral majority at all costs led the government to attempt keeping the rate of economic growth high via a low interest rate policy, which began to jeopardize both

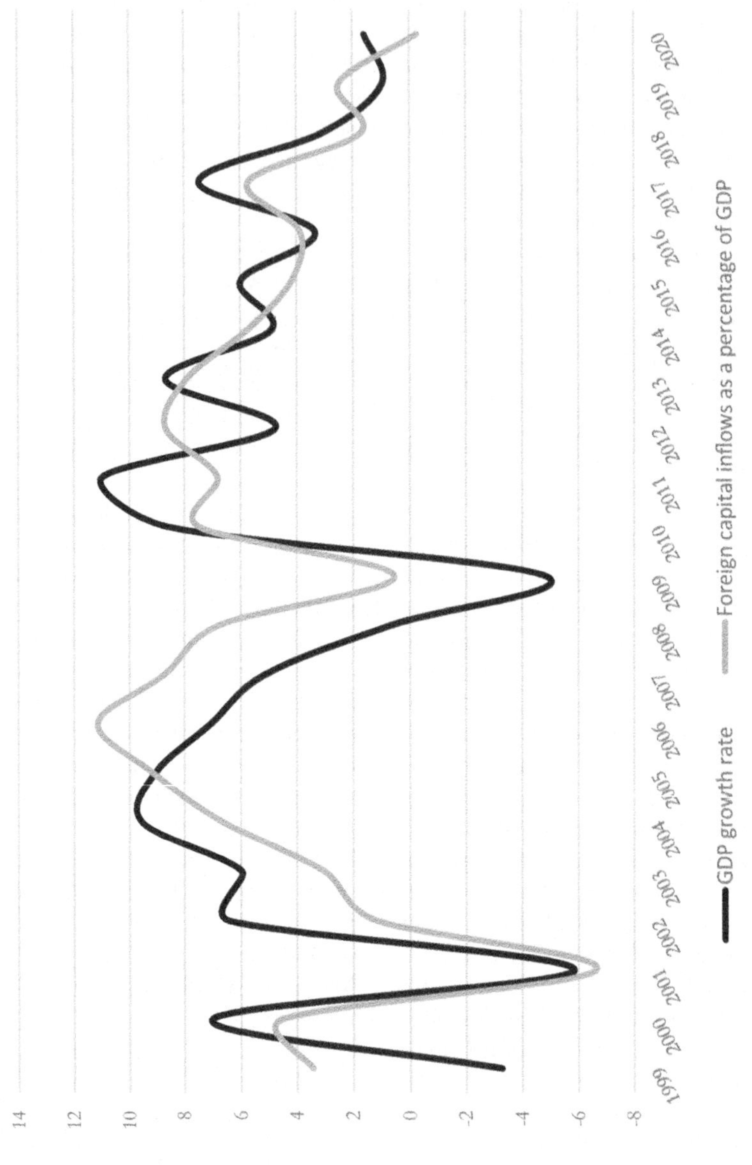


**Fig. 10.1** Foreign capital inflows (% of GDP) and GDP growth rate (%) (*Source* Authors' own calculations, using Balance of Payments and National Accounts data from the Electronic Data Delivery System of the Central Bank of the Republic of Turkey [https://evds2.tcmb.gov.tr/index.php]. Accessed on 1 March 2021)

the so-called independence of the central bank and its inflation targeting. In fact, President Erdoğan began to argue publicly that inflation itself was the consequence of high interest rates, despite briefings from the governor of the Central Bank, who emphasized that low interest rates would lead to currency depreciation and increased inflationary pressures via the pass-through effects (Başçı, 2015). In 2016, policy interest rates of the central bank were lowered and to ensure economic growth from 2017 onwards, the low interest rate policy was accompanied by various credit support mechanisms, such as the use of the Credit Guarantee Fund (*Kredi Garanti Fonu*), originally established to support small and medium-sized businesses. Credit expansion continued despite increasing debt-repayment problems in the non-financial sector.

The renewal of capital inflows in 2017, amounting to 48.8 billion dollars, helped growth in that year but also resulted in a widened current account deficit and historically high external debt levels. In the face of mounting vulnerabilities, sudden capital outflows triggered by a diplomatic spat between the US and Turkey led to a currency crisis in the summer of 2018 and sent the economy into a recession into 2019.

Economic slowdown together with liquidity problems in some of the financial markets in the US led the Fed to begin decreasing the interest rates again in the second half of 2019 and gave renewed impetus to global liquidity expansion. Turkey began receiving capital inflows again, although at lower levels. These inflows, together with increased public spending and government's push for a credit expansion helped the economy recover toward the end of 2019. Yet, the accumulated fragilities persisted and Turkey was faced with the negative demand and supply shocks of the Covid-19 pandemic with a fragile economy recovering from a recession. In short, as the government attempted to offset the adverse impact of capital-inflow slowdowns and reversals by an enforced credit expansion, it had to confront the external constraint twice, in 2018 and in 2020. In 2020, rapid capital outflows and persistent current account deficits resulted in a rapid depletion of Central Bank reserves and brought the economy to the brink of a balance-of-payments crisis. Following the sharp depreciation of the currency, the Central Bank governor and the Treasury Minister were replaced in November 2020 and the new economic team immediately began monetary tightening while promising austerity policies. This development helped stop capital outflows and started a new cycle of inflows by short-term financial investors, who wanted to take advantage of the high interest rates. Whether this return to orthodoxy will prevail or not is yet not clear.

## External Constraints

### *Dependence of Economic Growth on Capital Inflows*

Following the liberalization of capital movements in 1989,[1] the growth-recession cycles of the economy came to be driven mainly by foreign-capital flows and Turkey experienced four episodes of crisis within the next two decades (1994, 1998–1999, 2001, 2009). Before 1989, when capital flows were regulated and limited, the short-term growth dynamics of the economy were mainly determined by domestic factors. For example, a change in public spending (including investment), taxation or monetary policy would directly incorporate or impact the investment and consumption decisions, while the exchange rate policies would be formed in line with the needs of the export sector and/or import-competing industries. Changing domestic demand conditions would be the main determinant of trade and current account balances. The chronic trade deficit of Turkey would reveal itself through the following mechanism: *policy-linked or autonomous domestic demand expansion → growth → current account deficits → capital inflows.* An autonomous domestic demand expansion could begin from private investment due to "animal spirits" (in Keynesian parlance) or from an increase in real wages and salaries such as the one in 1989. After the liberalization of capital flows, the autonomy of domestic demand declined significantly as foreign-capital inflows started to become the main determinant of growth. The new mechanism became the following: *capital inflows → domestic demand expansion → growth → current account deficit.*

Figure 10.1 reflects the foregoing relationship between foreign-capital inflows and economic growth during, especially the first two decades of the twenty-first century. Indeed, this figure covers the main economic "success story" of the JDP. It should be kept in mind that the JDP came to power after the 1998–2002 period characterized by a declining GDP per capita. The following high-growth episode was due both to the "base effect" of the preceding five "lost years" and abundant capital inflows of the post-2002 era. The annual average growth rate of the economy in the 2002–2007 period was 7.3%. However, in the 2010–2015 period, the average growth was only 4.8%, despite continuing foreign-capital inflows, reflecting the decline of the potential growth rate of the economy in the 2010s.

The impact of capital inflows on domestic demand operate through various channels.[2] Capital inflows enable an expansion of liquidity, while inflows into stock and bond markets lead to asset price increases in these markets. Increases in demand through wealth effects or credit expansions are likely to follow. Banking sector's external borrowing can also be used to support domestic credit expansion and nonfinancial corporations' external borrowing stimulates domestic demand. A second type of dependency is observed when autonomous domestic demand expansion due to fiscal or monetary policy actions leads to a deterioration in the current account. In the Turkish case, this dependency was aggravated by the increased dependence of domestic production on imports, a point we will come back to shortly.

Inflows of foreign capital also allow the central bank to carry an expansionary monetary policy, while home-currency appreciation supports demand through the expectations channel. When capital inflows slow down, stop or are reversed, these processes also respond in the same way. However, the effects of inflows and outflows are not symmetrical. The positive demand effect coming from foreign-capital inflows gets smaller as the economy approaches full capacity. Expansionary fiscal policy, for example, during election periods, can still generate autonomous expansions in production. Or, in a similar vein, minimum wage increases such as the one in 2016 may lead to demand expansions. In such cases, when part of the demand increase is directed toward imports and leads to increases in the current account deficit, a corresponding increase in capital inflows is required to maintain economic growth. In the absence of capital inflows, a depletion of the central bank's foreign-currency reserves and/or depreciation of the home-currency would follow.

The second dependency indicator can be observed through the link between the growth rate and the current account deficit. Turkey historically suffered from chronic current account deficits. However, while these deficits constituted around 1 to 2% of the GDP before the 2000s, they have significantly widened in the 2000s and reached record levels in the early 2010s, as seen in Fig. 10.2. It was only in 2019, following the currency crisis of the preceding year, when the current account went into a surplus. But the current account moved, once again, into a deficit in 2020.

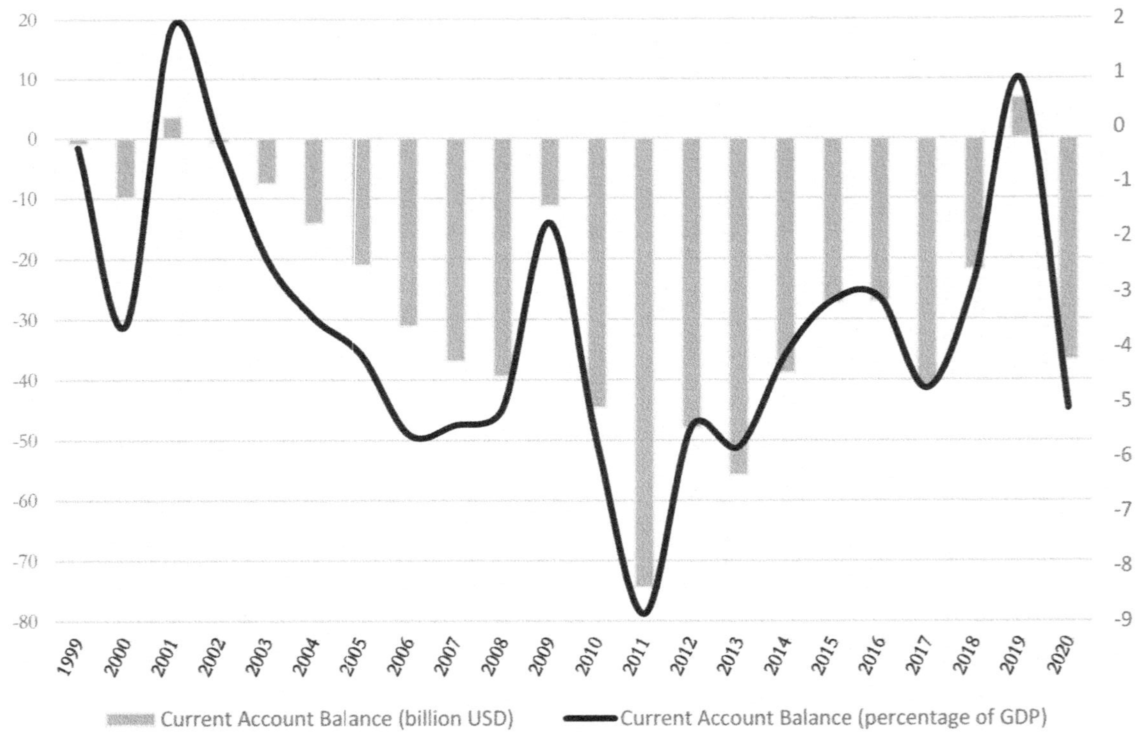


**Fig. 10.2** Current account balance in billion USD (bars, left axis) and as a percentage of GDP (line, right axis) (*Source* Authors' own calculations using Balance of Payments and National Accounts data from the Electronic Data Delivery System of the Central Bank of the Republic of Turkey [https://evds2.tcmb.gov.tr/index.php] Accessed on 1 March 2020)

In short, we observe two types of increasing dependency patterns during the 2010s. On the one hand, growth dynamics of the economy is directly determined by the decisions of international finance capital based primarily on global conditions. On the other hand, increases in domestic demand require additional external funding due to the rising import-dependency of the GDP in this period.

The persistence of current account deficits reflects the increased dependence of the economy on imports. According to the *Foreign Trade Statistics* of the Turkish Statistical Institute, in the 2010s, around 85% of the total imports were capital and intermediate goods. Calculations presented by Orhangazi and Yeldan (2021: Fig. 5) show that the Turkish Lira appreciated almost continuously in real terms from 2002 to 2011 and even though it started depreciating around 2013, it remained overvalued for much of the 2010s.[3] This long period of currency overvaluation led to increased dependence of production on imports, undermined export competitiveness in some industries and brought up worries about the premature deindustrialization of the economy. The results have been slow growth in industrial production and the declining share of this sector in the GDP (Bakır et al., 2017; Orhangazi, 2020; Rodrik, 2016).

Using input–output tables, Tek et al. (2017) show that import content of exports in manufacturing has increased from 27.2% in 2002 to 30.6% in 2012. A similar study by Yükseler (2019) finds that total import content of production in all sectors was 13.8% in 1985, 12.4% in 1998 and 18.9% in 2012. If one looks at the ratio of the imports in total value added for the same years, according to this study, the figures are 24.9%, 21.2% and 38.1%, respectively. Özmen (2015) and Karadam and Özmen (2015) also estimate an increase in the import-dependence of production. Karadam and Özmen (2015) show that Turkey is a net exporter in low-technology and a net importer in medium–high and high technology products.

The estimates presented by the OECD TIVA data-set show that Turkey's exports had an import content of 15.4% in 2005, which increased to 19.4% in 2011. From 2011 to 2016, parallel to global trends, this ratio went down to 16.5%, but was still higher than the 2005 level. The expanding sectors within Turkey's exports, such as motor vehicles, basic metals and electrical equipment, had the highest import content. Indeed, 29.1% of imported intermediate goods and services was used in the production of export goods. This ratio is below the OECD average of 45.5%, but shows an increase from the 2005 level of 25.2%. The leading industry in this aspect is motor vehicles with a ratio of 46.5%, indicating that this industry has become more integrated with the global value chains over time (Taymaz et al. 2011).

The depreciation of the exchange rate later in the 2010s was unable to trigger import substitution and export promotion. Therefore, current account deficits remained significantly higher than the pre-2000 period, both in dollar terms and as a percentage of the GDP. These observations suggest that import dependency of the economy has reached a level and a structural feature that cannot easily be reversed simply by short-run movements in relative prices. To better understand this crucial issue, further research is needed in terms of detailed and industry-specific studies. Reversing this structural deformation would require active industrial policies, together with a reevaluation of free-trade and capital-mobility.

We need to point out two other issues in terms of the external accounts. First, by the 2010s, current payments to international finance capital have become a large component of the current account deficit as the international investment position of the country worsened. Total payments to international financial capital[4] began increasing in the 2000s and were around 11–12 billion dollars per year in the early 2010s. By 2019, these payments approached 20 billion dollars. Second, this is also the period when domestic residents' capital outflows also increased significantly. Especially in the second half of the 2010s, such outflows surged at a remarkable pace. Between 2014 and 2019, resident capital outflows averaged to 15 billion dollars a year. In other words, foreign-capital inflows in the 2010s financed not only the trade deficit but also the current payments to international finance capital and resident outflows.

### *External Debt Accumulation*

Taking a closer look at the external debt position of the Turkish economy is crucial in understanding the dependence of the economy on capital flows. The ratio of external debt stock to GDP shows the weight of international finance capital on the domestic economy and its distribution across sectors and industries, its structure and its turnover rate all constitute potential fragilities, especially at times when global liquidity conditions change. For example, one of the transmission channels of the 2008–2009 global crisis to the Turkish economy has been through external debt repayments. In the thirteen-month crisis period, the credit flows to Turkey turned negative, amounting to 23 billion dollars due to the decline of the external debt turnover ratio. Between September 2008 and March 2009, net payment on the external debt amounted to 26.4 billion dollars (CBRT Balance of Payments Statistics).

An important component of capital inflows has started to become debt-generating flows, especially after 2009, when the interest rates in major advanced economies approached zero and global liquidity reached unprecedented levels due to the QE policies. Most of the external debt accumulation in the 1990s had resulted from public sector borrowing needs. Government budget deficits were seen as one of the main problems, and primary budget surpluses and widespread privatizations in the 2000s brought these deficits under control. Public debt-to-GDP ratios declined to "respectable" levels thereafter, as compared to most "emerging economies." On the other hand, external debt of the private sector, both banks and non-financial corporations, rapidly increased between 2010 and 2017 and reached record levels (Table 10.1). The increase in non-financial sector's external debt by around 50% was particularly significant. The relative decline of the external debt of the public sector came to an end after 2017 and as the financial sector has reduced its

**Table 10.1** External Debt

| | *Total external debt (billion USD)* | *Total external debt (percentage of GDP)* | *Short-term external debt (billion USD)* | *Public sector (billion USD)* | *Financial sector (billion USD)* | *Non-financial corporations (billion USD)* |
|---|---|---|---|---|---|---|
| 2010 | 291 | 37.5 | 77 | 89 | 89 | 102 |
| 2011 | 305 | 36.3 | 83 | 96 | 95 | 105 |
| 2012 | 342 | 38.8 | 102 | 106 | 116 | 112 |
| 2013 | 394 | 41.2 | 135 | 119 | 150 | 120 |
| 2014 | 407 | 43.3 | 137 | 121 | 164 | 119 |
| 2015 | 399 | 46.2 | 105 | 117 | 157 | 124 |
| 2016 | 408 | 46.9 | 101 | 123 | 149 | 134 |
| 2017 | 454 | 52.8 | 120 | 136 | 162 | 153 |
| 2018 | 443 | 56.9 | 117 | 140 | 139 | 158 |
| 2019 | 435 | 57.1 | 123 | 157 | 109 | 160 |
| 2020 | 435 | 60.7 | 134 | 166 | 102 | 146 |

*Source* Authors' own calculations using Balance of Payments and National Accounts data from the Electronic Data Delivery System of the Central Bank of the Republic of Turkey (https://evds2.tcmb.gov.tr/index.php). Accessed on: 1 March 2021. *Note* As of the time of writing this chapter, the latest external debt figure available for 2020 belongs to the end of Q3 in 2020. Public external debt figures do not include the external debt of the Central Bank external debt significantly, public external borrowing has picked up pace. The non-financial corporations, on the other hand, have begun reducing their external debt in 2020. This was a de-facto socialization of private debt carried out by the central bank, three state-owned commercial banks and, partly, the Treasury.

Total external debt as a percentage of GDP increased from 37.5% in 2010 to 60.7% by 2020 also, in part, due to the rapid depreciation of Turkish lira after 2017, leading to a significant shrinkage of the GDP in dollar terms. The short-term component of the external debt remained above 100 billion dollars throughout most of the period.

In short, during most of the 2010s, together with "hot money" inflows, debt-generating inflows started to become a more significant determinant of the domestic demand expansion. The rise of external debt also made the Turkish economy more sensitive to changes in global liquidity conditions as well as in global interest rates and exchange rates. New fragilities emerged as well, arising from the distribution of external debt among different sectors and also from the shifts in the turnover rate of the debt. The reversal of "hot money" inflows in 2020 coincided with the net debt repayments of both the banking and non-financial sectors, leading to a squeeze in available foreign currency and a rapid depletion of the foreign currency reserves of the central bank.

## Macroeconomic Dynamics

### *Domestic Credit Expansion and Increased Indebtedness*

When we turn to the domestic macroeconomic dynamics, one of the most striking observations for the 2010s is the unprecedented domestic credit expansion, along with increased indebtedness of both households and non-financial corporations as well as small- and medium-sized enterprises. Phases of high capital inflows supported domestic credit expansion through two channels. First, portfolio capital inflows led to an increase in financial asset prices and hence in the net worth that could be used as collateral. This process helped to decrease the observed leverage ratios. Throughout the same process, the rise of bond prices contributed to bringing domestic interest rates down. Second, banking sector supported part of this domestic credit expansion through borrowing from abroad. Clearly, these processes were not specific to Turkey. Credit and asset bubbles following the QE policies led to similar developments in other "emerging economies" (Akyüz, 2012, 2015).

Total credit to non-financial corporations (as a ratio of GDP) had begun increasing in 2005. This ratio was 17.8% in 2004 and quickly reached 40% in 2010 and 67% in 2016 when the pace started to slow down. Its peak value was observed as 68.6% in 2018, before coming down to 65.4% in 2019.[5] As we discuss below, the slowdown in credit expansion in the second half of the 2010s was met by the attempts of the government to initiate policies to support credit-led growth.

During the first years of the twenty-first century, credit to households was historically at very low levels in Turkey. In 2002, the credit extended to households as a ratio of GDP stood below 2%. The 2000s witnessed a rapid expansion of household debt, bringing this ratio to 16% in 2010. This increase continued for a couple more years and peaked in 2013 around 20% of the GDP. Credit flows to the households began declining in the following years and leveled around 15% by 2018. A significant portion of these credits was in the form of mortgage loans. As for the non-financial corporations, leading borrowers were in construction, real estate and energy sectors. As a result of the rapid expansion of credit, the debt service ratio, defined by the BIS as the ratio of interest payments to disposable income, increased from around 7% in 2010 to 15% in 2017 and 22% in 2018.

### *Construction-Centered Growth and Capital Accumulation*

The Turkish economy experienced a recession during the 2008–2009 global financial crisis with annual growth rates of the real GDP falling to 0.7% in 2008 and −4.8% in 2009. Thanks to renewed capital inflows the recovery from the recession was rapid with growth rates reaching to 8.6% in 2010 and then 11% in 2011. The growth performance was interrupted in 2016, partly due to the adverse economic impact of the failed coup attempt that year. However, a relatively strong growth rate prevailed during the 2010–2017 period, generating an annual average of 4.6%. Government-led credit expansion in 2017 pushed the growth rate to 7.5%. Yet, external constraints were reflected into foreign currency markets and starting with the last quarter of 2018, the economy moved into a recession for three quarters.

The share of investment in GDP oscillated between 24–30% during the 2010s, according to the *new* GDP series.[6] However, this investment figure can be misleading as another important development in this period has been the construction-oriented pattern of economic growth. From an expenditure point of view, the construction expenses constituted around 17% of the GDP in 2017, just before the 2018 currency crisis, rising from a low of 7.5% in 2004. When we exclude construction investments and look at rate of "gross fixed capital formation" (GFCF) only in machinery and equipment (excluding construction), we observe quite a weak performance, indeed. This GFCF-to-GDP ratio remained around 10% throughout the decade (Turkish Statistical Institute, National Accounts).

A deliberate policy of supporting the construction sector through rent generation and "clientelist incentivization"[7] emerged in the 2000s. The government went on a massive construction spree of building new public buildings, public universities, highways, subways, airports, hospitals and so on, mainly through public–private-partnership (PPP) contracts. As the primary budget surplus requirements limited the government's spending capacity, the Public Housing Authority (*Toplu Konut İdaresi, TOKİ*) was able to generate and realize urban rents allowing the government to finance large-scale infrastructure projects. The rents generated were transferred to business groups close to the government through the distribution of construction permits, "opaque" selection of projects and developers as well as the opening of public land to construction. The foreign-currency-based Treasury guarantees provided to the PPP projects served not only as another mechanism of rent generation but also as a channel of lavish transfers from the government budget to contractors in the medium run. A large number of changes made to the laws regarding public tenders and procurements gave way to widespread political favoritism (see, e.g., Gürakar, 2016). In addition, construction activities generated substantial employment and provided stimulus to the rest of the economy through increased demand for a large number of products from a variety of industries (Balaban, 2012; Çavuşoğlu & Strutz, 2014; Sönmez, 2015).

Two other factors supported construction growth. First, the decline in agricultural employment and migration toward cities increased the need for both housing and other types of structures (hotels, malls, hospital, schools and so on) as well as infrastructure. In addition, the 1999 earthquake had generated a further need for updating the housing stock.

Second, financial expansion and introduction of long-term housing loans increased demand. Price increases encouraged speculative demand as well. As discussed above, the growth of the construction sector accompanied the credit boom. In the second half of the 2000s, the construction and real estate companies also began borrowing from abroad. By 2018, external debt of these firms rose above 26 billion dollars from 1.5 billion dollars in 2006 (CBRT, 2018). The dependence of the construction-centered growth on credit expansion and external borrowing has proved fragile against shocks to the credit volume, interest rate or exchange rate. Mega-infrastructure projects, malls, ambitious housing projects financed through external credits were essentially oriented toward the domestic market. With the exception of the PPPs benefiting from government guarantees in foreign currency, these corporations had negligible foreign currency revenues. Dollar-based contracts to retailers merely transferred the currency risk.

### *Jobless Growth and Distribution Issues*

The 2000s and the 2010s witnessed increased proletarianization as the share of agricultural employment and small business ownership declined. The share of wage employment within total employment has secularly increased, with a brief pause during the global financial crisis of the 2008–2009, and approached 70% toward the end of the 2010s for the first time. However, the economy's capacity to generate employment did not keep up, leading to persistent high unemployment. The official rate of unemployment, which remained below 9% during the 1990s, stayed above 10% in the 2010s despite economic growth and exceeded 13% at the end of the decade. Most of the jobs generated in this period were in construction and services, while industrial and agricultural employment lagged (Orhangazi, 2019).

The broad unemployment indicator which includes discouraged workers hovered around 17% in the second half of the 2010s. One should keep in mind that the labor force participation rate (LFPR) was between 50–53% in this period, much lower than that of advanced economies, indicating a structural underdevelopment in the case of Turkey, which also limits the growth potential of the economy. This situation deteriorated further under Covid-19 pandemic conditions. By October 2020, the LFPR fell to 50% (from 53% a year ago), and the broad unemployment rate reached 27% (DİSK-AR, 2021).

A crude indicator of the wage share is the ratio of total employee compensation to the GDP. This ratio stood at 30% in 2010, slowly increased to peak around 36% in 2016 and remained around 33–34% for the rest of the decade. However, given that the ratio of wage employment to total employment reached historical heights in this decade, the increase in the wage share seems very small and partly reflects the fact that quite a large portion of the workers are employed at very low wage rates. According to the Turkish Statistical Institute's household income surveys, on average, around 40% of the workers receive a wage equal or very close to the minimum wage. While detailed and continuous series on wages are scarce in Turkey, various calculations and estimates show that the gap between productivity and wages widened in the 2000s and the 2010s (see, e.g., BSB, 2015; Orhangazi, 2019; Orhangazi & Yeldan, 2020).

On the other hand, in terms of the size distribution of income, persistent and widening inequalities have characterized the 2010s. For example, income share of the top one-percent has steadily increased after 2013, while that of the bottom fifty-percent declined (Orhangazi & Yeldan, 2020).

Boratav (2017) compares changes in per capita worker and farmer consumption with their per capita incomes between 2004 and 2013. It turns out that incomes of the two classes lagged behind GDP per capita, but total consumption of both classes rose at much faster rates. In per capita terms, annual average growth rates of GDP, total consumption, farmers' and workers' incomes are denoted by g(y), g(c), g(f), g(w), respectively. In both current and constant prices, the 2004–2013 movements can be summarized as follows: g(c) > g(Y) > g(f) > g(w). Rate of growth of investment lags behind consumption. Consumption-led growth is realized thanks to persistent and rising trade (current account) deficits. In per capita terms, earnings of farmers and workers lag behind GDP, but this deterioration of income shares is more than compensated by higher consumption levels.[8] Rising household indebtedness and higher social transfers from the central and local budgets are behind the improvement. The findings contribute to the explanation on the electoral support of JDP during this period, despite regressive changes in income distribution in class terms.

## 2018–2020: From the Currency Crisis to the Covid-19 Shock

Increased dominance of finance in the post-1980 world generated a series of financial crises as the financial integration of the "developing and emerging economies" increased. Sudden stops or sharp reversals in capital flows caused crises, for example, in Latin American economies in the 1980s and in East Asia in the 1990s. As discussed in the earlier chapters, Turkey experienced similar crises in the 1990s and the early 2000s. While the crises in the 1980s and 1990s remained limited to the periphery of the world economy, the 2008 crisis began in the US financial markets and spread to the European economies, threatening the very core of the system. The "developing and emerging economies" were also affected by the crisis, mostly due to a decline in their export earnings and a slowdown or a reversal in capital inflows. The unprecedented expansion of global liquidity following the 2008 crisis generated renewed capital inflows to these economies, including Turkey.

However, the Fed announced around mid-2013 that it would start tapering the QE purchases it began after the crisis. Taking this as a sign of changing global conditions, portfolio flows and bank credits to "emerging economies" declined or were reversed (IIF, 2017). As the Turkish lira began depreciating rapidly, the central bank had to intervene with an emergency meeting to increase the interest rates in early 2014. As it became apparent that the Fed was in no rush to decrease liquidity, the so-called taper tantrum soon faded away, and capital inflows to Turkey surged nearly to 50 billion dollars in 2017.

The post-2013 period displayed a central contradiction of the capital-inflow-dependent, debt-led, construction-centered growth model of the economy: low interest rates were crucial for the continuance of this growth pattern but the global conditions and capital mobility would ultimately force the central bank to concede sharp currency depreciations. In the second half of the 2010s, aiming to secure electoral support, the government chose to undermine the autonomy of the central bank to maintain credit expansion with full force in order to sustain economic growth. A major policy tool in this period was the use of the government-sponsored Credit Guarantee Fund, which was initially established to support small- and medium-sized businesses. The Fund was later used to support the rollover of large corporations' debt as well. However, growth supported by credit expansion also caused the current account deficits to persist, putting downward pressures on the Turkish lira and increasing the fragility of the economy (Orhangazi, 2020; Orhangazi & Yeldan, 2021).

Under these conditions, in 2018, a political rift between Turkey and the US triggered a sudden capital outflow, leading to a sharp depreciation of the Turkish lira and increased instability in the financial markets. The currency crisis rapidly evolved into an emergent debt crisis with a large number of firms applying for bankruptcy protection. Markets could only be calmed down by the central bank's sharp hike of the policy interest rates by 6.25 percentage points to 24% in September 2018. Starting in the last quarter of 2018, the economy went into a recession. Financial markets were subdued and resurgence of capital inflows in 2019 allowed some limited recovery and economic growth was around 0.9% for the whole year (Turkish Statistical Institute, National Accounts).

The outbreak of the Covid-19 pandemic imposed a shock on financial markets in March 2020. Emerging market securities suffered around 83 billion dollars in terms of outflows during March only, a much larger amount than that in a similar period during the 2008–2009 global financial crisis. Debt outflows were 31 billion dollars (IIF, 2020). The adverse shock spread immediately to Turkey. The negative economic impact of Covid-19 coupled with accelerating capital outflows, especially from the stock and bond markets, sent the economy into a sharp decline of 9.9% in GDP in the second quarter of 2020 (Turkish Statistical Institute, National Accounts), similar to most economies in the world. The policy response of the government in the third quarter of 2020 was another round of credit expansion, supported by the central bank's previous policy rate cuts from 12% in December 2019 to 8.25% in May 2020, which remained unchanged up till September, accompanied by further expansion of the public banks' credit volume. Meanwhile, the Covid-19 shock adversely affected exports, especially tourism revenues. These factors resulted in large current account deficits, that is, 36.7 billion dollars during 2020.

For most of the second and third quarters of 2020, the government tried the impossible. In an effort to prevent the Turkish lira from depreciating in a period of capital outflows and lowered interest rates, foreign currency reserves of the central bank were used extravagantly. It is estimated that the central bank burned through close to 100 billion dollars of foreign currency reserves in this process. This futile attempt to keep the value of the currency stable had to be given up in the fourth quarter as the *net* reserves of the central bank went into the negative territory. These inconsistent and erratic policies resulted in a depreciation of Turkish lira by 21% in real-effective terms from December 2019 up till October 2020 (according to the "real effective exchange rate" statistics of the BIS).

## Concluding Remarks

Taking a look at the Turkish economy under the JDP governments from 2002 to 2020, it is possible to make some general observations. First, the dependence of economic growth on the pace of foreign-capital inflows and the dependence of production on imports have increased while the external debt stock reached new heights. Second, economic growth increasingly took a debt-led character through continuous credit expansion, which at times was encouraged and supported directly by the government through public banks. Third, growth in this period was considerably construction-oriented, with limited contributions to increasing the pace of productive capital accumulation, raising the potential growth rate or reversing the "premature de-industrialization" tendency.

Adverse global liquidity conditions and hence the slowdown in capital inflows pushed the Turkish economy into a recession in the 2008–2009 period. Two further phases of economic contraction were encountered, first in late 2018 and in early 2019, and second, aggravated by the impact of the Covid-19, in the second quarter of 2020. In the last few years, the government has adopted a policy discourse that emphasized a "domestic and national development path" and blamed foreign speculators for the woes of the economy. Yet, this so-called domestic and national development path has remained a pretentious rhetoric, lacking any concrete policy reorientation so far. Attempts to support growth by suppressing domestic interest rates despite rapid capital outflows were self-defeating, ultimately resulting in a free fall of the Turkish lira. Given the degree of economic and financial integration of Turkey to the world economy, the official "domestic and national development path" discourse was, indeed, destined to fail. Sharp interest rate hikes in September 2018 and then in November 2020, both accompanied by changes in the economic management team, are a witness to this prominent failure. All in all, the demands of international financial capital ultimately prevailed.

It is important to keep in mind that the JDP has been in power uninterruptedly since November 2002. In its early years, it strictly followed the IMF program based on inflation targeting, primary budget surpluses and high interest rates, along with structural and institutional reforms and large-scale privatizations. Economic growth supported by high and partly speculative capital inflows accompanied this policy framework. After the 2008–2009 global financial crisis, QE policies and near-zero global interest rates helped domestic interest rates to decline in Turkey as well, supporting the credit expansion and the construction spree. This process paved the way for a surge in external debt stock and deteriorated the international investment position, leading to increasingly more fragile balance sheets of non-financial corporations. In the aftermath of the 2018 currency crisis, the government introduced a number of de facto and hesitant capital controls including limits on Turkish banks' currency swap operations in London as well as a tax on the purchase of foreign currency that was gradually increased. The 2009 deregulation that allowed non-financial corporations without foreign currency earnings to borrow in foreign currency was also reversed in 2018. However, such measures during the 2018–2020 period were not part of a well-designed program to deal with the crisis, but rather a patchwork of hesitant and sometimes incoherent measures.

Throughout all this long-term political-economic process; economic growth, credit expansion and clientelist rent-generating redistribution policies of the JDP governments have been critical to ensure electoral support. A special role was assigned to the construction sector as it enabled the government to support business groups close to itself and create *nouveau riches*, especially through lucrative public projects including the construction of roads, bridges, airports, hospitals and so on, as well as in mining and energy sectors. The small and medium-sized business groups close to the government benefited from both easy access to cheap credit and the persistence of "informalization" and "flexibility" in labor markets. De-unionization of the working class was a prominent feature of the JDP period. Privatization of public enterprises was practically completed, along with widespread privatizations of local and central government land. Substantial segments of public employment shifted to contractual status. Private provision and marketization of education and health expanded significantly. All in all, the state power was used to overcome the barriers in front of pro-capital dynamics, for both conventional surplus value production and accumulation by dispossession.

However, the inability to generate sufficient employment, relatively stagnant wages and persistent inequalities also necessitated social inclusion mechanisms. One way was to extensively use financial inclusion through expansion of credit to households. Under the JDP governments, the neoliberal marketization logic dominated the transformations in social security provision, health and pension systems as well as labor market regulations. In this regard, a series of social assistance programs were put in place, whereby various irregular transfers and benefits were carried out, in addition to the regular mechanisms of social policy. These transfers and benefits were extensively used as part of electoral politics as well. It is, however, important to note that these practices were not devised as collective rights based on the welfare-state framework of the earlier decades. In contradistinction, they relied predominantly on political discretion in favor of the electoral base.[9] One can also add the role played by faith-based charities, that is, Islamist associations linked to the government, which came to command large financial resources (Özden, 2014).

The preferred method of intervention during the Covid-19 crisis in 2020 was once again to push interest rates down and encourage growth through credit expansion. The share of additional spending on health, as well as direct and indirect transfers to stricken households from the central budget was meager, as compared to G20 countries. In Turkey, the main source used was the past accumulation of the Unemployment Insurance Fund.

All in all, neoliberal economic policies were accompanied by cronyism as well as populist and authoritarian politics, especially during the 2010s. JDP's Islamist and authoritarian orientation gradually prevailed over its pro-EU façade. 2013 was a turning point for the JDP as the Gezi uprising in İstanbul quickly spread to the rest of the country and threatened its hold on power. Authoritarianism began increasing following the Gezi protests and then intensified with the ending of the "peace process" between the JDP government and the Kurdish movement in 2015 just after the JDP failed to gain parliamentary majority in the June elections and pushed for renewed elections in November by refusing to form a coalition government. The renewal of the elections in November of the same year took place under conditions of widespread violence, which allowed the JDP to win the elections by attracting nationalist votes. The failed coup attempt in 2016 was followed by the JDP government's declaration of a "state of emergency" during which both those who were thought to be directly involved with the group behind the coup attempt and people affiliated with the left and/or Kurdish movements were severely persecuted.

The regime change toward an autocratic presidential system following the referendum in 2017 led to further integration of the JDP with the state apparatus and further alignment with crony businesses. This has been an episode during which the government has shifted to "quasi-fascist" methods of violent suppression at times, accompanied by a shallow rhetoric of nativism and nationalism in the face of economic turmoil. While the autonomy of the central bank and regulatory authorities disappeared almost completely, the JDP lost international credibility at the same time.

As Turkey moves into the next decade of the century, the neoliberal policy framework, that is, inflation targeting and fiscal austerity, seems to have returned with a revenge. If JDP's haphazard violations of the unwritten rules of the game observed during the past three years are repeated, "punishment" via a currency crisis triggered by unsustainable current account deficits will take place. Monitoring of conventional indicators (somewhat flexibly) will be carried out by credit-rating agencies and international banks. It should be noted that the IMF's anti-austerity revisions of its conventional economic doctrine documented during the October 2020 IMF/WB meeting are essentially addressed to advanced economies. Ongoing negotiations with a number of "vulnerable emerging and developing economies" show that conventional priorities continue to prevail there.[10]

Hence, any further credit-led support to the construction sector and sustaining the 5% growth target of the medium-term program are becoming increasingly more difficult. Constrained by its chronic external dependency, Turkey is probably locked within a potential growth rate of around 3% per annum in the medium term. This growth path cannot alleviate record levels of unemployment and widespread poverty prevailing in 2020.

JDP is facing a political impasse. It is confronting widespread dissatisfaction of popular classes—somewhat similar to the 2002 election when voters' reaction against the heavy austerity measures of the IMF program completely eliminated the coalition parties from the parliament. There is an additional complication: after so many years of widespread cronyism, corruption and mismanagement, the current leadership cannot afford to face the consequences of free elections. Further authoritarianism, repression and step by step moving into an Islamist-fascist regime appear as a possible option. At the time of writing this chapter, Turkey has been going through a structural economic crisis. It is yet early to predict the way the country will go through. Nonetheless, rising social discontent, sharpening contradictions within the ruling bloc and segments of capital can be expected.

## Notes

1. The liberalization of capital movements was essentially a response to the substantial increase in public sector wages and salaries that took place in 1989. A revived trade-union activism that year spilled into the public sector and the government had to concede wage and salary increases up to 142% in nominal terms. The liberalization of the financial account provided a mechanism for financing the consequent public sector deficit (Boratav 2018: 193).
2. See Akyüz (2012, 2015) for a detailed discussion of these mechanisms.
3. Bank for International Settlements' real effective exchange rate series show a similar pattern. See: https://www.bis.org/statistics/eer.htm
4. All data in this paragraph come from the balance-of-payments statistics provided by the Central Bank. The gross "investment income" outflows under the current account of the balance-of-payments statistics.
5. Credit data discussed here and in the next paragraph comes from BIS "Credit to the non-financial sector" statistics (https://www.bis.org/statistics/about_credit_stats.htm. Accessed on: December 19, 2020).
6. It should be noted that official methods of national accounts were changed by the Turkish Statistical Institute with the aim of bringing Turkish national accounts in line with the UN's SNA-2008 and EU's ESA-2010 frameworks. However, various aspects of the new GDP series were criticized by a wide range of economists. See, for example, Boratav et al. (2018). Before the revision investment-to-GDP ratio was around 20%.
7. Favoritism in public–private partnership *contracts*; arbitrary and numerous revisions of legislation and regulations *on government tenders* and revisions of *urban planning* by central and local governments in favor of particular contractors and of real estate owners were the three patterns of "clientelist intervention," all closely related to the construction sector. The third pattern affects urban real estate values immediately; but is neutral in terms of

income distribution in the short-run. Hence, "losers" in terms of wealth distribution can rarely emerge as an effective and oppositional pressure group.

8. GDP series before the 2016 revision is used.
9. For detailed investigations on these points, see, for example, Akça et al. (2014), Akçay (2018), Akçay and Güngen (2019), Buğra (2020), Yentürk (2018a; 2018b), Eder (2010), Powell and Yörük (2017), and Adaman et al. (2019).
10. For country examples, see Boratav (2020).

## References


Adaman, F., Arsel, M., & Akbulut, B. (2019). Neoliberal developmentalism, authoritarian populism, and extractivism in the countryside: The soma mining disaster in Turkey. *The Journal of Peasant Studies, 46*(3), 514–536.

Akça, İ, Bekmen, A., & Özden, B. A. (2014). *Turkey reframed: Constituting neoliberal hegemony*. Pluto Press.

Akçay, Ü. (2018). Neoliberal populism in Turkey and its crisis. IPE Berlin Working Paper No. 100/2018. Institute for International Political Economy.

Akçay, Ü., & Güngen, A. R. (2019). The making of Turkey's 2018–2019 economic crisis. IPE Berlin Working Paper No. 120/2019. Institute for International Political Economy.

Akyüz, Y. (2012). *The financial crisis and the global south: A development perspective*. Pluto Press.

Akyüz, Y. (2015). Internationalization of finance and changing vulnerabilities in emerging and developing economies. *South Center Research Papers* 2015/60.

Bağımsız Sosyal Bilimciler. (2015). *AKP'li Yıllarda Emeğin Durumu* (The State of Labor in the JDP years). Yordam.

Bakır, E., Özçelik, E., Özmen E., & Taşıran, A. C. (2017). Türkiye'de erken sanayisizleşme. In M. Koyuncu, H. Mıhcı, & A. E. Yeldan (Eds.), *Geçmişten Geleceğe Türkiye Ekonomisi*. İletişim.

Balaban, O. (2012). The negative effects of construction boom on urban planning and environment in Turkey: Unraveling the role of the public sector. *Habitat International, 36*, 26–35.

Başçı, E. (2015). Ekonomik Gelişmeler. https://www.tcmb.gov.tr/wps/wcm/connect/b2a7648f-6683-46e7-b033-f0dcf6b95565/TCMB_ErdemBasci_Cumhurbaskanlik.pdf?MOD=AJPERES. Accessed January 11 2020.

Boratav, K., Bulutay, T., Ege, Y., Türel, O., Türeli, R. A., & Uygur, E. (2018). Yeni Ulusal Gelir Serileri Üzerine Gözlem ve Değerlendirmeler. *Ekonomi TEK, 7*(2), 61–70.

Boratav, K. (2017). "Türkiye'de Sınıfsal Bölüşüm Göstergeleri, 2003–2014" (Class-based distribution indicators in Turkey, 2003–2014). In A. Makal, & A. Çelik (Eds.), *Zor Zamanlarda Emek* (*Labor in Difficult Times*), pp.7–36. İmge.

Boratav, K. (2018). *Türkiye İktisat Tarihi* (*Economic History of Turkey*). İmge.

Boratav, K. (2020). "Ekim 2020'de IMF'nin İki Yüzü" (Two faces of the IMF in October 2020) *Sol Haber*, October 23, 2020.

Buğra, A. (2020). Politics of social policy in a late industrializing country: The case of Turkey. *Development and Change, 51*(2), 442–462.

Caldentey, E. B. (2017). Quantitative Easing (QE), Changes in global liquidity, and financial instability. *International Journal of Political Economy, 46*(2–3), 91–112.

CBRT. (2018). Financial Stability Report 2018–1.

Çavuşoğlu, E., & Strutz, J. (2014). "We'll come and demolish your house!" The role of spatial (re)production in the neoliberal hegemonic politics of Turkey. In İ Akça, A. Bekmen, & B. A. Özden (Eds.), *Turkey reframed: Constituting neoliberal hegemony* (pp. 141–154). Pluto Press.

DİSK-AR. (2021). *İşsizlik ve İstihdamın Görünümü Raporu* (*Employment and unemployment outlook report*), January.

Eder, M. (2010). Retreating state? Political economy of welfare regime change in Turkey. *Middle East Law and Governance, 2*(2), 152–184.

Gürakar, E. Ç. (2016). *Politics of favoritism in public procurement in Turkey.* Palgrave.

Hein, E., Detzer, D., & Dodig, N. (2015). *The demise of finance-dominated capitalism: Explaining the financial and economic crises*. Edward Elgar.

Institute of International Finance. (2017). *Capital Flows to Emerging Markets,* June 5.

Institute of International Finance. (2020). *Global debt monitor: Sharp spike in debt ratios,* July 16.

IMF. (2005). IMF Country Report No. 05/412. https://www.imf.org/external/pubs/ft/scr/2005/cr05412.pdf. Last accessed December 10 2020.

Karadam, D. Y., & Özmen, E. (2015). Teknolojik Yetkinlik ve Türkiye Dış Ticareti. *Iktisat Isletme Ve Finans, 30*(357), 9–34.

Orhangazi, Ö., & Yeldan, E. (2021). Re-making of the Turkish crisis. *Development and change*, forthcoming.

Orhangazi, Ö. (2019). "2000'li yıllarda yapısal dönüşüm ve emeğin durumu" (Structural transformation in the 2000s and the state of labor). *Çalışma Ve Toplum, 60*, 325–348.

Orhangazi, Ö. (2020). *Türkiye Ekonomisinin Yapısı: Sorunlar, Kırılganlıklar, Kriz Dinamikleri* (*The structure of the Turkish economy: Problems, fragilities, and crisis dynamics*). İmge.

Orhangazi, Ö. (2015). Financial deregulation and the 2007–08 US financial crisis. In E. Hein, D. Detzer, & N. Dodig (Eds.), *The demise of finance-dominated capitalism: Explaining the financial and economic crises* (pp. 289–307). Edward Elgar.

Özden, B. A. (2014). The transformation of social welfare and politics in turkey: A successful convergence of neoliberalism and populism. In İ Akça, A. Bekmen, & B. A. Özden (Eds.), *Turkey reframed: Constituting neoliberal hegemony* (pp. 155–173). Pluto Press.

Özmen, E. (2015). Türkiye'de cari açıklar, dış ticaret ve finansal kırılganlıklar. *İşletme Ve Finans, 30*(351), 35–72.

Powell, M., & Yörük, E. (2017). 'Straddling two continents and beyond three worlds? The case of Turkey's welfare regime'. *New Perspectives on Turkey,* 57, 85–114.

Rodrik, D. (2016). Premature deindustrialization. *Journal of Economic Growth, 21,* 1–33.

Sönmez, M. (2015). AK Faşizmin İnşaat İskelesi [Construction Scaffold of JD Fascism]. NotaBene.

Taymaz, E., Voyvoda, E., & Yılmaz, K. (2011). Uluslararası Üretim Zincirlerinde Dönüşüm ve Türkiye'nin Konumu, TÜSİAD Yayın No: T/2011,12, 522.

Tek, E. Ö., Tümen, S., & Sevinç, O. (2017). "İthal Girdi Kullanımında Durum Tespiti ve Farklı Bakış Açıları" *Merkezin Güncesi, Uluslararası Ticaret*, TCMB, 29/12/2017.

Yentürk, N. (2018a). 'Türkiye'de Sosyal Koruma Harcamaları Kimi Koruyor?' ['Whom Does Social Protection Expenditure Protect in Turkey?']. In N. Yentürk (Ed.), *Sosyal Yardımlardan Güvenliğe Türkiye'nin Kamu Harcamaları 2006–2017* [*Turkey's Public Expenditures from Social Assistance to Security 2006–2017*], pp. 29–48. Bilgi Üniversitesi Yayınları.

Yentürk, N. (2018b). 'Yoksullara Yönelik Harcamalarda Ön Plana Çıkanlar' ['Major Expenditures Targeting the Poor']. In N. Yentürk (Ed.), *Sosyal Yardımlardan Güvenliğe Türkiye'nin Kamu Harcamaları 2006–2017* [*Turkey's Public Expenditures from Social Assistance to Security 2006–2017*], pp. 49–70. Bilgi Üniversitesi Yayınları.

Yükseler, Z. (2019). Türkiye Ekonomisinde Yapısal Değişim ve İthalat Bağımlılığı. *Mimeo.*

Wolfson, M., & Epstein, G. (2013). *The handbook of the political economy of financial crises.* Oxford University Press.

World Bank. (2013). *Turkey country report.*

CHAPTER 11

# Concluding Remarks

*Yonca Özdemir and Emre Özçelik*

The development story of Turkey was examined and explained in the chapters of this book, starting from the late Ottoman period until 2020. That story reveals that Turkey has developed to a certain degree and eventually has succeeded to become an upper-middle-income country. However, it has not been able to catch up with the advanced (high-income) countries, despite its eager historical efforts. It is even argued that Turkey recently suffers from the "middle-income trap" (Öniş, 2015; Öniş & Kutlay, 2013; and Öniş and Şenses's chapter in this book). Although Turkey is identified as an "emerging market," it has been

Y. Özdemir (✉)
Political Science and International Relations Program, Middle East Technical University, Northern Cyprus Campus, 99738 Kalkanlı, Güzelyurt, Mersin 10, Turkey
e-mail: yoncita@metu.edu.tr

E. Özçelik
Economics Program, Middle East Technical University, Northern Cyprus Campus, 99738 Kalkanlı, Güzelyurt, Mersin 10, Turkey
e-mail: ozemre@metu.edu.tr



E. Özçelik and Y. Özdemir (eds.), *Political Economy of Development in Turkey*, The Political Economy of the Middle East,
https://doi.org/10.1007/978-981-16-7318-4_11

undergoing serious political and economic difficulties, as of the writing of this text in 2021. In fact, Turkey has never had a smooth development process. It has obviously progressed, but its progress has been, more often than not, limited and precarious. When it comes to explaining why Turkey's development has not been more robust and sustained, chapters in this book indicate that Turkey, as a "semi-peripheral" economy, has generally suffered from both internal and external constraints associated with "dependent development."

This book was an attempt to link the domestic context of political-economic development in Turkey to the systemic evolution of global capitalism, with an eye to the country's mostly dependent position in the international division of labor. Each phase of global capitalist development and each crisis of the relevant phase were analyzed in the context of Turkey. In general, Turkey could not resist the dependency patterns of capitalist development, and mostly followed the global trends. The secular and cyclical fluctuations and shifts in the world capitalist system have regenerated or reinforced Turkey's dependency patterns over time, creating new domestic social tensions and political-economic problems. Throughout these successive phases, power blocs and development models were altered in Turkey, along with important changes in the interrelations among the state, the economy, and the society. Turkey has been similar to many other semi-peripheral countries insofar as it has passed through akin stages of capitalist development. Yet it also has had some unique historical characteristics.

In the introductory Chapter 1, we presented a concise theoretical and historical examination of the industrial origins and political-economic evolution of the capitalist world system in order to provide a general framework for the analyses of Turkey's development. As considered in the chapters of the book, Turkey, sometimes as a forerunner and sometimes as a laggard, has mostly proceeded through a "dependent" path of development, like other less-developed countries. However, Turkey's unique characteristics are noteworthy as well. First of all, it is essential to understand the late Ottoman period in order to grasp the *sui generis* origins of Turkey's dependent development. Unlike most of the less-developed countries, the Ottoman Empire was never officially colonized by the imperialist powers, but still got integrated, to a certain extent, into the world economy as a peripheral country through mainly free-trade agreements and financial coercion. The rise of Turkish nationalism in the early twentieth century, and then the establishment of the Republic of Turkey after its War of Independence, following the First World War, heightened the desire for economic independence. As a result, the young Republic tried to implement some national strategies to overcome its economic disadvantages and developmental weaknesses. In the absence of significant industries and lack of private capital, the state was naturally seen as the engine of economic development. In this regard, the *Kadro* movement of the first half of the 1930s was, especially an interesting case, which had early views analogous to some non-Marxist versions of critical approaches to dependent development. Members of the movement argued that only the state could resist the power of foreign capital, overcome the influence of local collaborators and devise a statist development strategy that would be in the best interests of the nation. They held the view that the struggle for "national independence" against imperialist powers was of upmost importance, and they seemed to believe in the possibility of a "classless society." Even though the intellectual activities of *Kadro* turned out to be short-lived, Turkey's developmental orientation during the 1930s, the Great Depression decade at the level of the world economy, resembled their views in some respects, especially in terms of prominent efforts to initiate statist industrialization and trade protectionism with an eye to the major goal of national economic independence.

As a matter of fact, by the early years of the Republic, there was not a real capitalist class in Turkey. As a highly agrarian economy of mostly small- and medium-sized farmers, bulk of Turkish society was poor but quite equal in the beginning. Nevertheless, it was well understood that capital accumulation and industrialization were vital for economic progress and independence. While Turkey tried to create an industrial bourgeoisie of its own, the dynamics of capitalism took their own course. As bourgeois classes emerged and grew with state support and got connected to global capitalism over the decades, an uneven course of development sprang up in Turkey. While there were many ups and downs throughout Turkey's capitalist development from the early twentieth century to the early twenty-first century, the country somewhat developed but became more unequal and remained dependent. Hence, today Turkey looks more similar to the ex-colonized countries of Latin America rather than Southern European countries in its proximate geography. Therefore, the case of Turkey suggests that global capitalism has a tendency to generate "convergence" in terms of "inequality" and "dependence" even among less-developed countries with very different historical backgrounds.

In Chapter 2, Seven Ağır explained and discussed the Ottoman roots of Turkey's economic dependency, covering the 1838–1908 period, which also coincides with the "first globalization era" at the level of the world economy. Unlike many peripheral regions, the Ottoman Empire was not directly colonized by the Europeans, but its sovereignty was curtailed indirectly through diplomatic pressures and economic treaties. While free trade led to "deindustrialization" during the first half of the nineteenth century, the second stage of peripheralization occurred during the second half of the nineteenth century through increased FDI and foreign borrowing. Increasing indebtedness resulted in the "bankruptcy" of the Ottoman Empire, which eventually led to the foreign control over its fiscal resources. Throughout the nineteenth century, the Ottoman elites also initiated some legal and institutional modernization reforms. All these reform efforts had serious economic, social and political implications. Increasing economic integration with the European powers had uneven effects for the Muslim and non-Muslim communities, benefiting the latter but worsening the opportunities for the Muslims. This process weakened artisans and small shopkeepers, while it helped enrich the non-Muslim commercial intermediaries, creditors and local powerbrokers whose interests were aligned with foreign merchants and investors. All this set of developments paved the way for the rise of Turkish nationalism, while the bureaucracy played a leading role as the actor with prominent stakes in a "nationalist" development agenda.

In Chapter 3, Zafer Toprak focused on the rise of economic nationalism between 1908 and 1929. Realizing the political and economic dependency of the Ottoman Empire, a group of modernist Ottoman elites, the Young Turks, rose to power as the Second Constitutional Era started in 1908. With a more nationalistic ideology, they tried to recover the political, social and economic status of the Muslim communities. Ottoman Empire's entrance into First World War on the side of Germany gave Young Turks the opportunity to also implement more "independent" economic policies. However, the Ottomans became one of the losers of the war with disastrous political and economic implications for the Empire. Eventually, the Nationalist Forces led by Mustafa Kemal Atatürk fought the Turkish War of Independence (1919–1922). After this war was won, a new and politically independent nation-state, the Republic of Turkey, was born out of the ashes of the Ottoman Empire in 1923. Once the Republic was established, war-worn Turkey endeavored to restore its economy, while trade policies had to be still implemented under quite "open economy" conditions as the country was obliged to keep the Ottoman tariff rates until 1929. In the 1920s, the government initiated the processes of state building, nation building, political institutionalization, cultural transformation, and socioeconomic change. Quite radical political and social reforms were pursued, along with some economic ones in agriculture, budget, and taxation, which were accompanied by the first phase of growth in modern industry and traditional manufacturing. The state was autonomous in its economic decisions, as a bourgeois class was almost non-existent. At the same time, however, the government was willing to create a national bourgeoisie as it was seen as an important factor of modernization. This can be called an effort to create a "bourgeoisie revolution from above," but a bourgeoisie created by the state support was inevitably state-dependent, that is, not an independent political force that could bring democracy. Hence, Turkey became a case that supports Gerschenkron's (1962) thesis, which was discussed in Chapter 1.

In the 1920s, the world could return to neither free-trade policies nor the pre-war classical gold standard, as the war and the ensuing peace treaties were accompanied and followed by the collapse of the international economy. Eventually, nationalistic trade policies deepened the economic difficulties, which culminated in the outbreak of a worldwide depression from 1929 onward. Like many less-developed countries, the Great Depression was a turning point for the economic development of Turkey. With the depression in the world, foreign trade collapsed (both exports and imports), foreign-borrowing possibilities became scarcer and costlier, unemployment rates soared, and bankruptcies proliferated. However, with the expiration of compulsory Ottoman tariffs rates in 1929, Turkey found the opportunity to implement more protectionist trade policies. Hence, in the dust and heat of the depression years in the world, Turkey intensified its economic independence efforts and recorded impressively high rates of growth and industrialization in the 1930s, which is generally known as the "statist-protectionist" period. In Chapter 4, M. Erdem Özgür and Eyüp Özveren examined this period and its sequel, from 1929 to 1947. As they explicated, with state planning and inward-oriented policies, significant industrial and infrastructural investments were undertaken during the 1930s with the purpose of creating an independent economic structure. The developing urban economy was the driving force, but farmers' contribution was also significant. By the late 1930s, Turkey became a producer of certain important consumption goods, which were previously imported. Agricultural sector also contributed to economic growth, but there was no change in social relations in the countryside. A tiny bourgeois class started to emerge in that period, and commercial and industrial sectors grew as well. Yet working classes were still concentrated in the state economic enterprises. In time, conflicts between statists and free-enterprisers began to arise among the government circles.

Although Turkey achieved rapid industrialization in the 1930s, this came to a halt with the Second World War. As a peripheral country, it was not easy for Turkey to break the dependency relations, which were established during the nineteenth century and continued until the Great Depression. With the outbreak of the Second World War, the Turkish economy started to suffer from increasing military expenditures, declining production, falling foreign trade, rising inflation, and war profiteering. The agricultural sector was hit the worst by the war and this, as well as the post-war international conjuncture, created completely different political dynamics in Turkey. The "statist" forces within the government weakened. The price controls implemented by the state, especially on foodstuff, led to black markets and speculation, which allowed some merchants to accumulate huge amounts of capital and wealth thanks to war profiteering.

After the Second World War, Turkey took its new position in the world dominated by the US. In Chapter 5, covering the 1947–1960 period, Yakup Kepenek elaborated how, after the war, Turkey shifted its economic policies and steadily entered the US sphere of influence under the conditions of emerging Cold War. By establishing close political and economic ties with the US, Turkey reverted to external dependence and agricultural specialization, along with the support of emergent private capital. This orientation was very much in line with the restructuring of global capitalism under US hegemony. Amid international and internal pressures, the government also started to democratize and made a transition to multi-party system on the eve of the period under consideration. A new party, Democrat Party (DP), supported by commercial capital and land owners, won the elections in 1950. Upon coming to power, the DP started to focus on the "comparative advantage" of Turkey, that is, agricultural production. Turkey also enjoyed "generous" financial and technical aid from the US at that time, which became a new form of dependency. A considerable portion of the financial aid was spent on importing tractors from the US, which significantly increased agricultural production and productivity in Turkey. Such policies favoring rural segments of society, which were neglected in the 1930s and the war years, pleased the landowning farmers, so they continued to support the DP. At the same time, this period saw many industrial startups, which grew into Turkey's largest private-sector corporations over time. These included urban capitalists that succeeded during the statist period and also the ones who accumulated capital in the agricultural sector and then migrated to cities.

The DP wanted to continuously support the agricultural sector, as farmers constituted its main vote base. It also sought to maintain high economic growth on a regular basis. Favorable global economic conditions of the early 1950s facilitated high growth rates in Turkey. Yet, when these conditions started to reverse, a foreign-exchange bottleneck emerged and foreign-borrowing requirement increased. The DP had no systematic economic planning and reacted to the new economic realities with ad hoc populist policies, which generated a high-inflation episode. The economic difficulties and vulnerabilities peaked in the second half of the 1950s and Turkey resorted to the IMF in 1958 for the first time in its history. Deterioration in economic conditions was accompanied by deterioration in democracy. The DP started to act increasingly in a more authoritarian way, escalating political tensions seriously. Having an economy based mainly on small producers, a high ratio of rural population (close to 70%), and a very weak civil society, Turkey was still not a mature capitalist country by the end of the 1950s. Only a certain section of Istanbul's industrial bourgeoisie was somewhat politically influential and they were not happy with the DP's ad hoc economic policies. As the DP insisted on engaging in authoritarian practices, concerns mounted over the difficulty of removing the DP from power through elections, as it had a fairly large vote base in rural Turkey. Eventually, the DP government was overthrown by a military coup in 1960, which was welcomed by, especially the urban segments of society.

As examined and discussed by Ümit Akçay and Oktar Türel in Chapter 6, the 1960 coup signaled the initiation of a new economic model, the ISI, which represented a different strategy for capitalist accumulation and a return to economic planning. With the new constitution of 1961, Turkey extended not only civil and political rights but also economic and social rights to its citizens, including the right to unionize and strike. Hence, workers in the industrial sector benefited from these changes, but these changes were introduced by the state itself in a top-down fashion, not as a result of workers' own organized struggle. Turkey still lacked a strong capitalist class at that time. However, during the ISI period, this class strengthened remarkably. Therefore, the ISI period can be considered a passage to a more advanced mode of capitalism, as Turkey made a transition from a capitalism of petty bourgeoisie to a higher level of capitalism with larger domestic corporations and more organized labor.

The economic policies of the 1960s emphasized industrialization, economic development and social justice. The pace of industrialization increased through public and private investments. Wages in the formal sectors increased along with industrial profits. Unlike some other countries implementing ISI, Turkey did not rely much on FDI during this period. However, relatively lower levels of FDI did not mean that the Turkish economy was becoming independent. For instance, Keyder (1987: 150–155) argued that Turkey's development during the ISI period was part of global capitalist development, and the Turkish economy was markedly connected to the world capitalist system. The economic policies included the protection of domestic industries by tariff and non-tariff barriers and the extension of the economic role of the government (especially through state-owned enterprises) with a focus on the domestic market. Although ISI was instrumental in Turkey's diversification of domestic production, most notably toward durable consumer goods (especially household appliances), its dependence on imports of intermediate and capital goods and foreign technology continued and even expanded.

Up until the 1970s, Turkey's large business groups supported the ISI strategy, as they were able to make huge profits in the protected domestic market, along with incentives provided by the state. However, as the global economic conditions deteriorated and their profit margins narrowed, they supported the 1971 military memorandum and intervention that curtailed some of the labor rights. Henceforth, difficulties arose in domestic capital accumulation under worsening global economic conditions triggered by the dissolution of the international monetary system and the First Oil Crisis in 1973. Labor unions became a heavier burden on capitalists under those circumstances. Despite increasing external imbalances, Turkey could continue with its ISI policies until the end of the 1970s thanks to the workers' remittances coming from Turkish migrant workers in Europe. The 1970s were also the years of extreme political instability in Turkey, as eleven government changes occurred between 1971 and 1980. There was also severe political violence between left-wing and right-wing factions. Delaying the crisis of ISI in Turkey turned out to be all the more difficult when the global economic conditions deteriorated further with the Second Oil Crisis in 1979. Confronted with a serious foreign-exchange bottleneck, Turkey's large current-account deficits were becoming more and more difficult to finance, as the country was unable to find external funds. The ISI model was brought to an end amid such a severe financial crisis. A neoliberal reform package, known generally as "24 January Decisions," was announced and started to be implemented in 1980. This reform package, which was supported by the IMF and OECD, was prominently anti-labor. It was not easy to implement it under democratic conditions. Hence, another military coup occurred on September 12, 1980, which is usually regarded as the harshest military takeover in the history of the country. The military regime that lasted for about three years proved to be instrumental in breaking the political deadlock and implementing the economic reforms by force.

24 January Decisions and the subsequent military coup signaled the beginning of the historically most crucial transformations in the Turkish economy, moving the country toward a market-based and export-led model, that is, neoliberalism. In fact, Turkey was one of the first developing countries to adopt the neoliberal policies, which were later also referred to as the "Washington Consensus" policies. These policies involved both stabilization measures and structural adjustment programs. This broad transformation from the state-led ISI to an export-oriented free-market model indicated a new mode of integration to the world economy, which required the reduction of domestic consumption, along with lower industrial wages and lower agricultural prices. This new model entailed important changes in Turkey's political-economic structure, as the developmentalist alliances of the ISI period were dismantled and new power blocs, such as rentier and exporting capitalists, emerged. The new 1982 constitution strictly limited civil and political rights, but especially the labor rights. The 1980s was the decade when a center-right alliance started to dominate Turkish politics (Waterbury, 1992). This alliance had a set of attitudes that favored private enterprise and reduction of state intervention in the economy. The "allies" and beneficiaries of this new export-led growth model were big holding companies and trading houses, the banking sector, upper strata of state bureaucracy, part of officer corps,

and some segments of urban middle classes, not to mention the support of the IMF, the World Bank, and international commercial banks.

In Chapter 7 by Ziya Öniş and Fikret Şenses, this radical shift in economic policy toward neoliberalism is elaborated through a review of gradual implementation of the first-generation neoliberal reforms. Trade and financial liberalization of the 1980s continued and deepened in the following decades and spread to most spheres of economic and social life, such as labor markets and agricultural, health and education sectors. Such a broad socioeconomic transformation had also important sociopolitical consequences. These policies were initially implemented by the military regime (1980–1983) and later under the Motherland Party (*ANAP*) governments (1983–1991). Turgut Özal, the architect of the 24 January Decisions, first served under the military government and then founded his own party ANAP, which came to power with the 1983 elections. The initial results of the neoliberal program were impressive, as export revenues increased significantly and the economy recovered from the turbulence of the late 1970s. Inflation was also somewhat curbed in the early years of the 1980s, but it later increased and became a major chronic problem for Turkey up until 2004. Exports increased with the devaluation of Turkish Lira and suppression of labor and wages within the context of the new export-led growth model. However, imports rose more than exports along with trade liberalization, and Turkey continued to run trade and current-account deficits. Özal's push to open up the capital account of balance of payments in 1989, despite the Central Bank's opposition, was a major turning point for the Turkish economy. Such financial liberalization before building up the necessary legal and institutional framework was considered "premature" and created an environment of rampant and long-term macroeconomic instability, as the Turkish economy was rendered highly vulnerable to financial shocks due to the volatile and speculative short-term capital flows. Corruption, rent-seeking, inequality, and structural poverty also increased in the first two decades of neoliberal transformation, similar to other developing countries implementing neoliberal policies.

In the 1980s, working classes and farmers were the main losers, while commercial bourgeoisie and rentiers benefited the most from neoliberal transformation. Despite the fact that Turkey returned to formal democracy in 1983, it could never become a fully fledged democracy under the 1982 constitution, which was endorsed by the military regime. Contrary to the claims of neoliberal ideology, "clientelism" and corruption continued and even intensified under neoliberalism.

Nevertheless, the losers of neoliberal policies could no longer be kept economically repressed under the "democratizing" political conditions of the late 1980s and early 1990s. Free political competition restarted in 1987. Under those conditions, Özal started to add a "populist" dimension to his neoliberalism, as his economic policies began to hit hard the lower and middle classes. As part of ANAP's electoral alliance was also hurt by neoliberal policies, they were provided with discretionary and compensatory public funds. With the labor strikes of 1989, wages were substantially increased. Eventually, in the 1991 elections, ANAP was removed from power, and a coalition government was formed by the two leading opposition parties.

Despite high hopes for equality, growth, and democracy, the 1990s turned out to be a "lost decade" for the Turkish economy, as analyzed by Erinç Yeldan in Chapter 8. It also witnessed unstable coalition-governments, paving the way for the rise of AKP in the early 2000s. Turkey maintained its neoliberal policies in this period, but no significant new reforms were introduced. Turkey was caught up in a vicious fiscal and financial circle due to its "premature" capital-account liberalization in 1989. The growing public expenditures were leading to high interest rates; high interest rates were attracting foreign-capital inflows, but they were causing the Turkish Lira to appreciate, leading to trade and current-account deficits. Hence, all macroeconomic balances went from bad to worse, while inflation rose to record high levels. All this was happening in a global context of financialization.

The "second generation" neoliberal reforms, which started to be implemented by many other developing countries such as Argentina and Brazil in the 1990s, were delayed in Turkey for political concerns up until the 2001 crisis. As explained by Yeldan, the 1990s in Turkey revealed the limits and the problems of financial liberalization relying on short-term capital inflows. This dependency on short-term foreign capital undermined the Turkish state's capability to design sound and credible economic policies that would promote long-term growth, economic development, and social justice. At the same time, global conditions for "emerging markets" deteriorated due to the 1997 Asian crisis, which later triggered the 1998 Russian and 1999 Brazilian crises. Sensing that the Turkish crisis was the next, in December 1999, the coalition government of the time agreed on a Stand-by Arrangement with the IMF, aiming to bring down inflation through an exchange-rate-based disinflation program, accompanied by the usual prescriptions of tight fiscal and monetary policies and structural reforms. In December 1999, Turkey was also granted the applicant status for EU membership; however, all the optimism faded away as the IMF program backfired and Turkey was hit first by a banking crisis in November 2000 and then by a very severe financial and economic crisis in February 2001.

In Chapter 9, Erol Taymaz and Ebru Voyvoda investigated the 2001–2009 period, when Turkey, as a "latecomer" among its peers, adopted the institutional "good governance" agenda comprising the "second-generation" neoliberal reforms within the context of Post-Washington Consensus. In the aftermath of the devastating crisis in 2001, the structural and institutional reforms that were delayed in the 1990s were finally initiated through an economic program designed and executed by an externally appointed economy minister, Kemal Derviş, who left his position as Vice President in the World Bank. The 2001 crisis was presumably the most devastating economic crisis in the history of the country, along with its drastic sociopolitical impacts. The Derviş reforms transformed the policymaking environment in Turkey, as the state's discretionary economic orientations were dismantled under the influence of the IMF, the World Bank, and the EU. Turkey could eventually stabilize its economy, but it did not suffice to prevent the complete defeat of the coalition parties in the 2002 general elections. AKP, which was founded just one year ago, won the elections with a significant parliamentary majority so as to put an end to the long-lasting episode of coalition governments. Behind AKP's electoral success was the immense loss of credibility on the part of the existing political parties due to the "lost decade" of the 1990s and the subsequent 2001 crisis.

The rise of AKP is linked to Turkey's entrance to a new phase of capitalist development after 2001, that is, the "second phase of neoliberalism." Thus, the crisis of the first phase of neoliberalism was resolved with a transition to its second phase. AKP continued with Derviş's reform package and even signed a new agreement with the IMF in 2005. Economic stabilization went hand in hand with the global economic boom, allowing Turkey to record high growth rates between 2002 and 2007. Economic growth helped AKP win the following elections and consolidate its political power.

Like everywhere else, this new phase of neoliberalism recognized the importance of rules-based decision-making processes and politically independent regulatory bodies. Along with the independence of the Central Bank, inflation was finally curbed remarkably. Reforms in the fiscal area resulted in significant reductions in budget deficit and public debt. New independent regulatory agencies were created, while privatization speeded up. All these domestic developments, accompanied by a financial-expansion episode at the global level, paved the way for unprecedentedly high FDI flows to Turkey. AKP's backbone was the small- and medium-sized enterprises, which highly benefited from these economic developments. These generally newer, smaller and provincial capitalists of mostly labor-intensive industries were among the founders and earnest supporters of AKP. Conservative and religious in outlook, they had not benefited from the state incentives during the ISI period, nor did they have very close relations with the state in the 1980s and 1990s, unlike the bigger and older corporations. As AKP came to power, these more provincial businessmen started to enjoy state benefits, especially through big public tenders that helped them to grow and start to rival the "senior" business circles represented by the Turkish Industry and Business Association (TÜSİAD). However, presumably, what was politically more beneficial for AKP were the new socioeconomic support programs covering the poorer sections of society, such as conditional cash programs, which increased the popularity of AKP, especially among the working-class people. In fact, this second phase of neoliberalism also emphasized social protection and welfare in the form of direct income supports and conditional cash transfers, which, however, were highly susceptible to political clientelism.

Helped with ample global liquidity of that time, for a while it seemed that Turkey was improving both on the economic and political fronts, as AKP also initiated some democratic reforms. However, as Taymaz and Voyvoda indicate in their chapter, this new political-economic orientation did not imply any significant shift in Turkey's dependent-development patterns. On the contrary, Turkey's current-account deficits not only persisted but also grew considerably, augmenting the need for and dependence on external finance through FDI and foreign borrowing. In fact, as the policymakers preferred to let the "market" to reallocate resources in accordance with the neoliberal paradigm and did not follow any well-designed industrial policy that could transform the structure of production and foreign trade, Turkey's dependency increased further and its economic growth could not be upgraded to a sustained path.

As a matter of fact, the optimism in the economy and politics started to gradually diminish once the effects of the 2008 global crisis kicked in. As liquidity in global markets shrank, FDI to Turkey decreased and the country started to rely more and more on short-term capital flows to maintain economic growth and finance current-account deficits. The growth rates started to exhibit higher volatility. Both before and after the global crisis, the years of higher growth rates were also the years of higher current-account deficits. This pattern indicated that Turkey's growth was based mainly on consumption and foreign debt, rather than on productive investment and employment-creating production. Thus, the Turkish economy became more dependent on foreign-capital inflows to sustain growth. In Chapter 10, Korkut Boratav and Özgür Orhangazi focused on this final and troublesome era of the Turkish economy characterized by severe financial instabilities along with increasing political authoritarianism. From 2009 to 2020, the accumulated vulnerabilities from the previous era persisted and deepened, while the crisis tendencies escalated. Eventually, starting from March 2020, Turkey's fragile economy was also faced with the adverse effects of the Covid-19 pandemic. Even before the pandemic, the Turkish economy's dependence on foreign-capital inflows and imports had increased, while the external debt stock had peaked. Under these worsening economic conditions, the popularity of AKP started to diminish while AKP and Recep Tayyip Erdoğan started to act in more authoritarian ways in both the political and economic domains. Since around 2010, civil and political rights have been increasingly curtailed, and political opposition has been repressed. Meanwhile, AKP has tried to maintain economic growth by relying on credit expansions. Hence, in roughly the last ten years, a "debt-led" economic growth has been further encouraged and supported by the government through an increasing role played by public banks. As Boratav and Orhangazi discussed, the Turkish economy has also faced a "premature deindustrialization" tendency as the prospects of productive capital accumulation worsened.

In the meanwhile, credit expansions and clientelist rent-generating redistribution policies of the AKP were somewhat conducive to sustaining its large electoral support. To be sure, AKP is not the first political party with clientelistic links to the electorate in Turkey, but it has created a more systematic and larger-scale clientelism due to its unprecedentedly long-lasting and high electoral performance and political dominance. Erdoğan's populist discourse has also been instrumental in consolidating his electoral support. Despite the fact that his supporters also started to suffer from worsening economic conditions, they continued to vote for AKP. In fact, the labor policies of AKP have been quite regressive, deteriorating the working conditions and structural power of labor. Indeed, the AKP era has also been the period of the most severe deunionization in Turkey. Yet the particularistic, Post-Washington-Consensus-inspired social policies of the AKP were quite effective in terms of dividing, co-opting, and pacifying the working classes and increasing overall clientelism in Turkey (Özdemir, 2020).

AKP's connections with the provincial small- and medium-sized bourgeoisie have also had crucial implications. The symbiotic relationships of these business groups with the AKP paved the way for a particular version of "crony capitalism" in Turkey. The economic resources at the disposal of AKP have allowed it to reward loyal businesses and punish the opponents. In return, the businesses nurtured by the AKP made investments in pro-government media, in-kind donations to the party, and pro-AKP charities and campaign contributions, supporting and prolonging the AKP hegemony. While AKP's political hegemony has grown, political tensions and societal polarizations have escalated. The 2013 Gezi protests, which started in Istanbul and spread throughout the country rapidly, were significant in terms of demonstrating the massive political discontent. In 2016, a coup attempt was averted by the government. Then, in 2017, through a slim majority in a referendum, the government replaced the parliamentary system with a Turkish version of presidential system, concentrating all the political power in the hands of President Erdoğan. In fact, the independence of regulatory agencies and the Central Bank began to be eroded from roughly 2010 onward; however, the presidential system carried the erosion to new heights. Erdoğan has constantly pressured the Central Bank to keep interest rates low, paving the way for the currency crises in 2018 and thereafter, leading to the enormous meltdown of foreign-exchange reserves held by the Central Bank. In the meantime, all economic and bureaucratic power shifted to the AKP loyalists. Concerns over nepotism have also mounted as Erdoğan appointed his son-in-law first as Minister of Energy and Natural Resources and then Minister of Treasury and Finance, who had to resign in late 2020 upon (presumably) the reserve-meltdown affair. Turkey has faced a complete politicization of its state institutions, weakened judiciary oversight and independence, and vanishing rule of law.

In sum, under a cross-class political coalition among the winners and losers of neoliberal globalization, AKP has led a conservative countermovement in Turkey (Güven, 2016). Although the 2019 local elections demonstrated the declining popularity of AKP, it remains to be seen whether a democratic change in the government is possible. As of the writing of this text in 2021, Turkey is in a deep political-economic crisis, but it is difficult to predict toward where the crisis will lead Turkey. Perhaps it is high time to remember Antonio Gramsci: "The crisis consists precisely in the fact that the old is dying and the new cannot be born; in this interregnum a great variety of morbid symptoms appear" (cited in Hoare & Smith, 1971).

All in all, this book as a whole suggests that Turkey is a captivating case to analyze the relationship between capitalism and democracy in a semi-peripheral context. It is one of the most prominent examples within the family of developing countries that failed to achieve sustained growth and development. Its dependency patterns have been historically instrumental in this failure. Having been unable to jump to the high-income country status, its failure in democracy is even more striking and discernible, but not surprising. After all, developing countries have particular structures and institutions that emanate from their national histories, which make it more difficult for progressive and pro-democracy classes to emerge and gain permanent strength. Turkey has been no exception in this regard. More recently, indeed, neoliberal globalization has made it all the more difficult to cultivate political-economic development due to its essentially pro-capital and anti-labor orientation. Consequently, despite the impossibility of predicting the future, we can at least suggest that the economic and political turmoil in Turkey is not likely to end in near future.

## References

Gerschenkron, A. (1962). *Economic Backwardness in Historical Perspective: A Book of Essays*. The Belknap Press of Harvard University Press.

Güven, A. B. (2016). Rethinking development space in emerging countries: Turkey's conservative countermovement. *Development and Change, 47*(5), 995–1024.

Hoare, Q., & Smith, G. N. (Eds.). (1971). *Selections from the prison notebooks of Antonio Gramsci*. ElecBook.

Keyder, Ç. (1987). *State and class in Turkey. A Study in Capitalist Development*. Verso.

Öniş, Z. (2015). Monopolising the Centre: The AKP and the Uncertain Path of Turkish Democracy. *The International Spectator, 50*(2), 22–41.

Öniş, Z., & Kutlay, M. (2013). Rising Powers in a Changing Global Order: The political economy of Turkey in the age of BRICS. *Third World Quarterly, 34*(8), 1409–1426.

Özdemir, Y. (2020). AKP's neoliberal populism and contradictions of new social policies in Turkey. *Contemporary Politics, 26*(3), 245–267.

Waterbury, J. (1992). Export-led growth and the center-right coalition in Turkey. *Comparative Politics, 24*(2), 127–145.

# Index





E. Özçelik and Y. Özdemir (eds.), *Political Economy of Development in Turkey*, The Political Economy of the Middle East,
https://doi.org/10.1007/978-981-16-7318-4

The manufacturer's authorised representative in the EU is Springer Nature Customer Service Centre GmbH, Europaplatz 3, 69115 Heidelberg, Germany. If you have any concerns regarding our products, please contact ProductSafety@springernature.com

Printed and bound by CPI Group (UK) Ltd, Croydon, CR0 4YY

30/09/2026

02225321-0012